The Forensic Accounting Deskbook

A PRACTICAL GUIDE TO FINANCIAL INVESTIGATION AND ANALYSIS FOR FAMILY LAWYERS

Miles Mason, Sr., JD, CPA

SECOND EDITION

The Forensic Accounting Deskbook

A PRACTICAL GUIDE TO FINANCIAL INVESTIGATION AND ANALYSIS FOR FAMILY LAWYERS

Miles Mason, Sr., JD, CPA

SECOND EDITION

AMERICAN BAR ASSOCIATION
Defending Liberty
Pursuing Justice

Cover design by Anthony Nuccio/ABA Publishing.

Printed in the United States of America.

23 22 21 5 4 3 2

Library of Congress Cataloging-in-Publication Data

Names: Mason, Miles, author.
Title: The forensic accounting deskbook : a practical guide to financial investigation and analysis for family lawyers / by Miles Mason, Sr.
Description: Second edition. | Chicago, Illinois : American Bar Association, [2019] | Includes bibliographical references and index.
Identifiers: LCCN 2018055635 (print) | LCCN 2018057144 (ebook) | ISBN 9781641053624 (epub) | ISBN 9781641053617 (print : alk. paper)
Subjects: LCSH: Forensic accounting—United States. | Evidence, Expert—United States. | Matrimonial actions—United States.
Classification: LCC KF8968.15 (ebook) | LCC KF8968.15 .M37 2019 (print) | DDC 363.25/6—dc23
LC record available at https://lccn.loc.gov/2018055635

THIS BOOK IS DEDICATED
to
my wife
Sharon Jones Mason
and to
my children
Anne, Miles, and Abigail

Contents

Appendices are available for download at http://ambar.org/Forensic2e

Foreword

For as long as I have known Miles Mason, he has been a thoughtful leader and practitioner in the domestic relations arena. I first got to know Miles over 18 years ago when we were traveling the Tennessee circuit together, lecturing from Knoxville to Nashville to Memphis. From that experience, as well as from observing him present several exceptional continuing legal education programs in Atlanta, I have come to understand that Miles is indeed one of the foremost authorities in the country on forensic accounting and business valuation in family law cases. Over the years, Miles has always been available to me and to others in our Atlanta, Georgia, firm to help with questions in this area, and we have benefited greatly from his advice. *The Forensic Accounting Deskbook* is the end result of over ten years of thought and energy that he has devoted to the subject, and it is wonderful that he has decided to share it with the rest of us.

Despite my having practiced family law for well over 20 years, as I read *The Forensic Accounting Deskbook*, I realized how inadequate my skills and knowledge are. From the beginning of the book all the way through to the very end, Miles makes it easy to understand the often-complex subject matter he discusses while at the same time making you aware of how much more there is to know. He then feeds it to you like spoon-feeding a baby. From the basic concepts and practical sample deposition questions to forensic accounting methodology and techniques, this book is a must-have for any practitioner of family law who handles cases involving contentious financial issues—and who doesn't?

While Miles is too humble to brag about himself or his family, I assure you there is much to brag about. Aside from his successful legal career and bar career, as well as being the leader and founder of his firm, Miles has an amazing family. His oldest daughter graduated from Savannah College of Art and Design here in Georgia, his son is a U.S.

Marine, his youngest daughter is in college developing her creative writing skills, and Sharon, his wife, is a joy.

I want to keep this foreword short since your attention span is better used in reading Miles's words, not mine. The importance of this book to the divorce practitioner, however, cannot be overstated. It is required reading for all members of our firm. While I have never enjoyed reading about tax issues and financial documents, *The Forensic Accounting Deskbook* was an easy read; it put me at ease, reassured me that much of what I do is correct, and educated me about other techniques, practices, and procedures that I need to improve upon. Thank you, Miles, for making me a better lawyer and for helping not only the readers of this book but also the general bar as a whole.

Randall M. Kessler
Atlanta divorce lawyer and Chair, American Bar Association, Family Law Section, 2011–12
Chair, Georgia Bar Family Law Section, 2011–12
Chair, Atlanta Bar Association, Family Law Section, 1996–97

Preface

I'm a family law attorney. That's what I do, and it's a great way to earn a living. But first I was an accountant. The inspiration for that initial career choice was my dad, who was a certified public accountant (CPA). He was smart, stern, well respected, and reserved about almost everything except Tennessee football. He was proud of me when I passed the CPA exam. Too soon thereafter, he passed away.

I was in law school at the time, pursuing what was destined to become my love and my vocation—the practice of family law. After getting my juris doctor and practicing for a few years, I began to realize how useful my background as a CPA was in the practice of family law. I began to see how family law, forensic accounting, and business valuation were intertwined. As a result, I began a journey to learn everything I could about the interaction among these three disciplines. And as I attended many national and regional accounting conferences and seminars, I felt closer to my dad. He had loved being a CPA, and I, in turn, loved learning how his chosen path in life added depth and dimension to mine.

During the journey, I listened to, met with, and co-presented with many of the nation's leading forensic accountants and business valuation experts. Experiencing the collegiality among these industry leaders has been a lucky break for me. Many have helped me with this book in different ways.

The Forensic Accounting Deskbook was written for both the experienced and the less experienced family law practitioner. For the more experienced, this book connects the dots and fills gaps among the interrelated topics of subpoena practice, accounting concepts, depositions, reports, methodology, financial statements, tax returns, and testimony. For the less experienced family law practitioner, this book provides a very basic introduction to core divorce concepts, such as asset identification, classification and valuation, income determination, and expenses. It provides a step-by-step explanation of very basic how-to mechanics and explores higher-level strategic concerns appropriate for high-asset and high-conflict cases. This book is intended to be useful to the solo practitioner, the partner in both the small and the large firm, the associate who needs a primer for her own edification, and the associate assigned to read the book for the benefit of the partner to whom she reports.

Forensic accounting is a majestic enterprise, very much worthy of the efforts of the smart, dedicated, and hard-working professionals who practice it. Those professionals help family lawyers win cases. In doing so, forensic accountants help clients keep money that might otherwise be taken from them by a difficult and confusing divorce process. If this book helps one lawyer work with one forensic accountant to prove one nefarious spouse is hiding, dissipating, or fraudulently conveying assets, all the work will have been worth it. Dad would be proud.

Miles Mason, Sr., JD, CPA

About the Author

Miles Mason, Sr., JD, CPA, is the founder of the Miles Mason Family Law Group, PLC, located in Memphis, Tennessee, and practices family law exclusively. Mr. Mason is married and has three children. He has authored two additional books, *The Tennessee Divorce Client's Handbook* and *Tennessee Parenting Plans and Child Support Worksheets*. Mr. Mason was named a Family Law Power Player by *Inside Memphis Business* magazine and honored as a Fellow of the Memphis Bar Foundation. In 2017 and 2018, Mr. Mason was selected as a Tennessee Super Lawyer. He is frequently asked by the media to comment on divorce for television news and local and national press including CNN, Forbes, and ABC. To learn more about Mr. Mason and his practice, visit MemphisDivorce.com.

Mr. Mason is an active member of the ABA Family Law Section. He has served on its CLE Committee and attended its Trial Advocacy Institute. He has also presented at several national conferences and written for the *Family Advocate*. For many years, he served as the Family Law Section's Liaison to the American Institute of Certified Public Accountants (AICPA). Mr. Mason is a past chair of the Tennessee Bar Association's Family Law Section. He has served as editor of the section's newsletter as well as on the editorial board of the *Tennessee Bar Journal*. Mr. Mason is a member of the AICPA's Forensic and Valuation Services section and the Tennessee Society of CPAs, and he has served on multiple planning committees for national and regional forensic accounting conferences.

Additionally, Mr. Mason has co-presented seminars with some of the nation's leading lawyers and business valuation experts including Randy Kessler, Tom Burrage, Shannon Pratt, Chris Mercer, Texas Supreme Court Chief Justice Linda Thomas, and Michael Kaplan. He has presented at national conferences including the ABA Family Law Section, the AICPA's Forensic and Valuation Services Conference, NACVA's Annual Consultants Conference and Forensic Accounting

Academy, Tennessee Bar Association, Tennessee Society of CPAs, and Mississippi Society of CPAs. Mr. Mason's favorite conference locations at which he has spoken include San Francisco; South Beach; Santa Fe; Stowe, Vermont; Bahamas; New York City; Boston; San Diego; Chicago; Dallas; and Las Vegas.

Mr. Mason is active in his community and, in 2017, was appointed by City of Memphis Mayor Jim Strickland to the Memphis and Shelby County Redevelopment Agency Board. The board is responsible for approving and administering tax incremental financing applications. Over the years, Mr. Mason has also been active on the boards of several nonprofit organizations. His nonprofit work includes serving as the vice chair of the National Conference of Christians and Jews (NCCJ), the Marguerite Piazza St. Jude Gala, and as president of the Christian Brothers High School (CBHS) Alumni Association. For his community service, Mr. Mason was inducted into the CBHS Hall of Fame. Mr. Mason received a BS in accounting from the University of Alabama (Roll Tide) and earned his JD from the Cecil C. Humphreys School of Law at the University of Memphis.

Acknowledgments

James J. Webb, for patient editing, encouragement, and friendship;
Sharon Jones Mason, for love and support;
Gail D. Baker, Esq., for all the positive energy when it was needed most;
Steven N. Peskind, Esq., for encouragement and advice;
Darrell D. Dorrell, CPA/ABV, MBA, ASA, CVA, CMA, DABFA, for contributions to the profession, this work, and freedom;
Michael G. Kaplan, CPA/ABV/CFF, CVA, MAFF, for contributions, patience, friendship, and mentoring;
W. Robert Vance, CPA, ABV, CFF, CVA, CFP, for countless contributions;
Kitty Jungkind, Esq.;
Z. Chris Mercer, ASA, and Barbara Price, for friendship, advice, and support;
Thomas F. Burrage, CPA/ABV, CVA, for contributions and advice;
Joe Epps, CPA/CFF/ABV, CFE, CVA, for editing, contributions, and review;
Gregory A. Gadawski, CPA/ABV, CVA, CFE, CIRA, for contributions;
Neil E. Aronov, PhD;
Odalys Z. Lara, CPA, CVA, CFFA, CFD;
Paul French, CPA/ABV, CVA, CFFA, BVAL;
Stacy Preston Collins, CPA/ABV, CFF;
D. Michael Costello, CPA/ABV, CFF, ASA, CFE;
Bruce Dubinsky, MST, CPA, CVA, CFE, CFFA, CFF;
Charles P. Rafferty, CPA, CFE, CVA, ABV, CFF;
Patrick B. Mason, Esq.;
Laura Valade, Esq.;
David Strauser, PhD;

Alan G. Crone, Esq., for encouragement to begin this journey;
R. Bruce Thompson, for friendship; and
Kathryn Owen, Kelly Nanney, Esq., Patrick Jones, and David Marshburn, Esq., for contributions, research assistance, editing, and support.

In Praise of *The Forensic Accounting Deskbook*

From reviews posted on Amazon:

"The Forensic Accounting Deskbook is exactly what its title suggests—the perfect deskbook. The minute I picked it up its contents were useful to my practice as a family law attorney. The tips, suggestions, and content were immediately useful and valuable. Within a week of reading the book I was using the information to cross-examine an opposing expert. The information in the book allowed me to cross-examine the expert with better questions and better background information, allowing my client to ultimately prevail. The book, while content heavy, is easy and fun to read. It is a book I recommend to all family law practitioners who have ever had, or ever will have, to deal with a financial matter in a divorce."

—Lori Nelson, Past Chair ABA Family Law Section

". . . excellent. It provides plenty of detailed information about the role of the forensic accountant in family law, without overwhelming the reader. It is 'chock' full of practical advice and background about forensic accountants. . . . A 'Must Add' for your practice library!"

—Kathleen Crouch

"The book is user-friendly, and it's intelligently written and thorough. . . . Even if you are a whiz at this stuff (I've met all of two or three attorneys that were), it would only trigger a deeper recognition of what to do next."

—T. W. Arnold

"The book is an outstanding guide to financial analysis and forensic accounting not only for attorneys, but also for accountants and fraud investigators. . . . The Forensic Accounting Deskbook closes with information on reports and testimony. Miles outlines a suggested format for reports, which is a useful checklist for any expert. More importantly, he details deposition and trial questions that should be used to establish the foundation for a forensic accounting expert's qualifications. The Appendix to the book includes several useful guides, including a deposition checklist for questioning an opposing forensic accountant. As with the rest of the book, this list of questions is incredibly thorough yet directed. I recommend The Forensic Accounting Deskbook to any attorney or expert witness working in the area of family law. There is something to be learned for everyone, and the numerous checklists, samples, and guides will be invaluable to your practice."

—Tracy

". . . the author brings to life for the reader what one might otherwise expect to be unexciting material by imparting throughout passion, humor, and shared anecdotes from both his primary profession as an accomplished family lawyer and his education, training, and experience as a Certified Public Accountant."

—masstennattymsw

"Although I myself am a 35+ year practitioner and course developer in this field, I was still able to learn invaluable tips and techniques from his book. You're never too old to learn and there's always someone that might have a better mouse trap. If you are a matrimonial attorney, especially one not dealing with complex business and financial matters on a regular basis, this book belongs on your shelf. It's malpractice not to have it, IMHO. And, if you are a CPA or similar investigator working in matrimonial litigation services, regardless of what stage you are in your career, this book belongs on your reference shelf."

—JDU

"Mr. Mason explained the subject matter very well and it kept me interested. I've read this book multiple times and I learn something new every time."

—Chelsea M.

Forensic Accounting Overview 1

The Goal Is to Dominate

Winning a football game 14–13 may be a satisfying result. Great football coaches say they plan not just to win but to dominate the competition 100–0. Great trial lawyers share that perspective. Winning a divorce trial begins with the process. The process begins at the first client meeting, where the successful lawyer begins to develop the themes and theories[1] of the case, which will later be woven into compelling opening arguments, effective direct examinations, and dominating cross-examinations. Even though most cases don't end in a trial, being prepared to win at trial 100–0 almost always creates the best environment for obtaining a favorable settlement. One of the tools you can

1. For an outstanding reference to themes, theories, and opening statements, see STEVEN N. PESKIND, THE FAMILY LAW TRIAL EVIDENCE HANDBOOK: RULES AND PROCEDURES FOR EFFECTIVE ADVOCACY (ABA 2013).

use in preparing that winning case—one often overlooked or underused by many family law attorneys—is the forensic accountant.

Whereas your client may direct you to "just protect" her, you know that protecting your client is the same as preparing to dominate at trial. It is not at all unusual for a client to say something like, "I have no idea what assets we have" or "I never saw any financial documents, and I can't get copies of anything," at which point you need to get to work. From obtaining all the documents you'll need in the case, determining red-flag facts and issues, and investigating potential problems to preparing for trial or drafting a proposed settlement agreement, a forensic accountant can make your job easier and enable you to be more thorough, which is critical.

In all divorces, there are four core financial components—assets, debts, income, and expenses. Forensic accountants can help with each of these components. In most divorces, your client will not be able to provide you with a discrete list of known assets, debts, income, and expenses that is completely and accurately reflected on the parties' financial statement and tax returns. Sometimes clients claim that their spouses are nefarious and are hiding assets or income, but clients often lack the documents and in-depth knowledge of the parties' assets required to prove those claims. A client's spouse may have secret accounts in unknown locations, there may be a business that pays way too many of the spouse's personal expenses, or the client may have heard the spouse refer through the years to a second set of books that is shown only to the IRS. In these situations, a forensic accountant can help organize the plan of attack, analyze documents, and look for the smoking gun that proves the nefarious spouse is lying.

At its best, the relationship between the family lawyer and the forensic accountant can become a very effective weapon in the advocacy arsenal. This is true even though the objective professional roles and ethical obligations of the two differ greatly. As a family lawyer, your role is to be a zealous advocate for your client. The forensic accountant, on the other hand, is an independent witness and can never be an advocate for your client. As an independent expert, the forensic accountant has no duty of loyalty to either you or your client. The forensic accountant may advocate only for his opinion or position and nothing else. From the perspective of the forensic accountant, the chips must fall where they may. The more you understand how the expert witness practices the craft of forensic accounting, the more you will understand how to use forensic accountants effectively and dominate the cases in which you're involved.

How a Forensic Accounting Divorce Engagement Case Can Go Very Well

Perhaps the best way to demonstrate the importance of a forensic accountant to a divorce involving complex financial issues is through a best-case scenario, taking a fictional divorce case through from the initial engagement by the client to the post-trial decision of whether to file an appeal.

Mrs. Smith hires you to represent her in divorcing her husband. You determine that the case needs a forensic accountant. Mrs. Smith agrees. You and she discuss a couple of options. You call a forensic accountant with whom you've developed a working relationship, and she confirms her availability and conducts a conflict check, which comes up negative. You verify the terms of engagement with the expert, making sure that Mrs. Smith understands and agrees to those terms, and finalize an agreement, thereby engaging your forensic expert during the earliest stage of the case.

Both you and Mrs. Smith immediately begin to notice the contributions of your expert. At your very first meeting as a team, your expert helps in planning the case. She helps develop a list of all the financial documents that will be needed. Her insight aids you in evaluating the various legal theories available in the case. She helps in assessing the strengths and weaknesses of the case. If she hadn't already, Mrs. Smith now begins to see the reason why the forensic accountant is on board and gains confidence in both you and her case.

After filing the petition for divorce, you begin discovery. Unfortunately, Mrs. Smith provides only a fraction of the documents you'll need in the case. As discovery progresses in waves, the documents and information you need begin to arrive in earnest. The forensic accountant begins to piece together the financial puzzle, a process that is part art and part science. She applies specific techniques and methodology and crunches the numbers. The resulting product of this effort is an easy-to-follow, clear, concise, and unassailable report.

The real power of the relationship among client, lawyer, and forensic accountant comes alive in the elegance of your expert's report. The report provides its intended audience, which includes Mr. Smith and opposing counsel, with a simple set of conclusions derived from many sources, including both people and financial records. The financial records include tax returns, financial statements, brokerage statements, loan applications, credit card statements, and personal financial information contained in computer files from various sources. When originally generated, each of these records had its independent reason for being. Loan applications normally present the financial information of a person or business in a favorable light and are thus rather expansive in describing assets. Tax returns, on the other hand, contain only reported income as interpreted under federal law. Often, for many reasons, the income on financial statements shown to banks significantly differs from that reported on tax returns to the IRS. Therefore, your expert's report accounts for all the available financial documentation.

You disclose your forensic accountant's report in discovery. The report is a simple tool engineered for successful advocacy of your expert's opinion. Your expert's curriculum vitae is attached, providing the foundation for admissibility of the testimony. The report details the sources of information and documents reviewed by your expert. It fully explains her methodology and techniques. Finally, the report summarizes the forensic accountant's conclusions, which are ready for the court to find as fact.

It is indeed possible that, upon review of the report, Mr. Smith and opposing counsel become willing to agree to a settlement favorable to Mrs. Smith. But they don't, and the case proceeds. You become a blacksmith, using the report as an anvil against which the case's financial arguments are forged and crafted. When deposed, your expert adheres to the report, explaining the techniques and methodology used and defending its conclusions. Opposing counsel is unable to mount a meaningful challenge to the report's premises, procedures, or conclusions. The opportunity again arises for a favorable settlement. But the case doesn't settle, and you begin to prepare for trial.

You complete the pre-trial document scramble. The forensic accountant's report is trial ready. The only remaining item of trial preparation is to draft the direct examination script of your expert. After completion of the initial draft of the script, you and your expert get together to thoroughly review it. Your expert suggests you use a couple of blowups from the report to aid in presentation. She suggests that certain key questions be added to help develop and explain her testimony, especially in anticipation of challenges by opposing counsel made during the deposition and in settlement negotiation. The final pre-trial preparation sessions are positive.

The case finally goes to trial. In your opening statement, you promise that you will prove the conclusions from your expert's report. You deliver this promise in classic Babe Ruth style, pointing to the left-center home run fence. The report and its conclusions are simple. Numbers don't lie. Courts trust certified public accountants (CPAs) because *people* trust CPAs. Your opening statement draws a circle of evidence, theme, and theory. The evidence and argument will complete the circle, resulting in a favorable ruling for Mrs. Smith.

During the presentation of your case, your direct examination of your expert takes the court on a step-by-step journey through her report. The forensic accountant serves as a respected, authoritative tour guide. The report acts as both a map and an itinerary. Her testimony highlights and educates the trier of fact on important documents, procedures employed, and resulting conclusions. The trier of fact knows where this road is leading and understands the journey because each step follows an easy-to-understand path. Questions flow from the lawyers and judge. Your expert's answers are presented in an informative, easy-to-understand manner and are more than just a recitation of a cold, impersonal series of formulas and numbers. The report comes alive in a fluid, simple, and elegant presentation.

On cross-examination, you can sit back and relax. Your expert witness is a confident and seasoned professional. She rarely needs your protection, which you offer through objections. She readily handles opposing counsel's tough and smart cross-examination questions. As in most trials, a few of the cross-examination questions have no answers. Your expert adroitly and calmly explains why the questions can't be answered. The cross-examination is a bust for opposing counsel.

In most divorces, both spouses' testimony can easily be attacked on bias. The court sees this for what it is. The spouses' decisions, choices, and lives are on trial. But the independent financial report of your expert supplements Mrs. Smith's testimony and dovetails nicely into the theme and theory of the case. Because Mrs. Smith's testimony is consistent with the expert's objective report, the trier of fact reaches a comfort level that her testimony can be trusted.

During the presentation of the rest of the case in chief, you mold the forensic accountant's conclusions to conform to your state's applicable statutory factors for alimony, property division, and child support.

While listening to the trial, the trier of fact must determine, decide, and render findings of fact and conclusions of law. While performing this task, the judge cross-checks the expert report over and over, like a nervous parent on a long family summer road trip, checking the trip itinerary again and again to make sure the family is squeezing in as much fun as possible while staying on schedule.

During closing, you once again hammer home the testimony of your forensic accountant. Because opposing counsel failed to mount a single serious challenge to the forensic accountant on cross, the expert's testimony provides the only set of incontrovertible facts presented by an unbiased witness. You confidently argue that the promises made during your opening statement have been fulfilled. The circle of evidence, theme, and theory of the case is complete.

When the judge announces the ruling, it proves to be very favorable to Mrs. Smith. The court's findings of fact and conclusions of law track your expert's conclusions almost word for word.

A week later, Mr. Smith and opposing counsel meet to discuss whether they intend to appeal the court's ruling. The technical record contains the victorious testimony. The court's ruling does not hinge on any technical legal issue but instead on the overall strength of the forensic accountant's presentation and credibility. Opposing counsel knows the appellate judges can also be swayed by the report's simple logic. Opposing counsel offers Mr. Smith little hope for success. At the end of that meeting, Mr. Smith decides to end it. There is no appeal. The case is won.

Forensic Accounting Defined

Now you've seen how a forensic accountant can add substantial value to a case, but what exactly is forensic accounting? Forensic accounting cannot be easily defined. Even CPAs struggle to explain what a forensic accountant does. The ABA's equivalent in the accounting profession is the American Institute of Certified Public Accountants (AICPA). CPAs are licensed through state boards of accountancy. Each state board of accountancy can create its own rules for licensing, but most rely heavily on the AICPA to set almost all important standards of practice and professionalism.

Forensic accounting has been described as "applying specialized knowledge and investigative skills to collect, analyze, and evaluate a financial situation, then communicate those findings in a courtroom, boardroom, or other venue."[2] Darrell Dorrell, a forensic accountant from Oregon, defines forensic accounting as "[t]he art and science of investigating people and money."[3]

Mr. Dorrell's definition is simple and makes sense. Without the people component, financial documents are merely numbers on a page. Tax returns describe a person's income and expenses resulting from the individual's life choices. Examples of those choices include selling stock, paying interest on a mortgage, and contributing to charities. Personal financial statements express net worth, income, and expenses. Those choices can include housing, cars, household help, and dining out. Also, individuals save money for emergencies, retirement, and college. Failing to save money also tells a story. As Dave Ramsey says on his radio show, "Children do what feels good. Adults make a plan and stick to it." Financial information tells the story of individual choice like no other. One cannot understand numbers on a page without also understanding the people whose decisions and actions they represent.

From a lawyer's perspective, the relationship between people and money needs to be admissible into evidence. Yes, a client can testify regarding assets, debts, income, and expenses. A client can also testify about classification and valuation of assets. But the art of creating relevant testimony from reviewing thousands of transactions, interpreting meaning, and drawing conclusions requires expertise. The client doesn't have the expertise and is biased. Furthermore, the lawyer can't testify. The lawyer must argue from facts and opinions in evidence. Plus, only expert witnesses can rely on hearsay. For credible, meaningful, and unbiased testimony, no one beats a forensic accountant.

Services Forensic Accountants Provide

Forensic accountants work in many areas of law other than family law and divorce, including damages calculation, mergers and acquisitions, fraud, criminal fraud, bankruptcy, personal injury, and wrongful death. For every aspect of law involving money, there is usually some expert

---

2. Robert Harris and Stephen Winters, *The Accountant's CSI: A Forensic Credential for CPAs*, originally appeared in Florida CPA Today and was reprinted at https://www.idcpa.org/, the website of the Idaho Society of CPAs.

3. Darrell D. Dorrell & Gregory A. Gadawski, Financial Forensics Body of Knowledge 486 (Wiley 2012). Every forensic accountant should have this book in his or her reference library. Family lawyers researching technical forensic accounting concerns should refer to it as well. The authors are two of the leading forensic accountants and valuation experts in the nation.

somewhere with the needed specific professional experience. Most forensic accountants will agree that family law is a great way to build a practice and can be very lucrative. Many enjoy it. Others will tell you they dread family law and it is only a means to pay the bills until other forensic work comes along. More than a few forensic accountants refuse to handle family law cases altogether because of the venom and ugliness often involved.

Forensic accounting is interrelated with business valuation. Many CPAs who value businesses are also forensic accountants. The AICPA lumps the two groups together in its Forensic Valuation Services Section. This book, however, ignores business valuation for the most part because the ABA publishes a great book on the topic, *The Lawyer's Business Valuation Handbook*.[4] Nationally, regionally, and locally, there is intense competition for high-end business valuation engagements. Business valuation engagements don't grow on trees. The top valuation experts earn well in excess of a million dollars a year.

The scope of services forensic accountants provide in family law is limited only by the complexity of the estate and the imagination of the client/lawyer/accountant team. Some of the more common tasks include the following:

1. **Marital balance sheet creation and analysis.** In all divorces, family lawyers must identify, classify, and value assets and liabilities. Also, the tax basis of each asset can be very important to the overall proposed division of the estate. The process of reviewing the documents provided by the client and obtained in discovery can be either simple or exhausting. Simple assets include bank accounts and publicly traded stock. Complex assets include pensions, stock options, and business ownership. Each asset and debt demands its own specific information for settlement or trial. Assembling this information early in a case can be a very useful tool in depositions, settlement negotiations, and trial preparation and presentation. Without a detailed marital balance sheet listing all assets and debts, how

4. SHANNON PRATT, THE LAWYER'S BUSINESS VALUATION HANDBOOK: UNDERSTANDING FINANCIAL STATEMENTS, APPRAISAL REPORTS, AND EXPERT TESTIMONY (ABA 2000). A second edition of this book, co-authored by Alina V. Niculita, was published in 2010. The edition used for reference in the writing of this book, however, was the 2000 edition, which is the edition referred to in all future citations herein.

is a lawyer going to analyze the proposed distribution percentage of the net marital estate?

a. **Asset identification.** Thorough divorce practice requires knowing and listing all assets and debts when drafting settlements. Is there a suspicion of hidden or overlooked assets? If so, the forensic accountant can help plan strategies for needed investigation. Does the tax return reflect interest income from an omitted bank certificate of deposit? Is there a capital gain from a mutual fund located within an undisclosed brokerage account? Every family lawyer's recurring nightmare is omitting an important asset from settlement paperwork.

b. **Asset classification.** The process of determining which assets are marital property (or community property) and which are separate property can be among the most challenging aspects of divorce work. What assets existed at the time of the marriage? What were the assets' values at the time of the marriage? Were there any inheritances or gifts? Was there transmutation? Are there tracing concerns or opportunities to defend commingling claims?[5] In many cases, the classification of appreciation of separate property can comprise the largest and most involved calculation in a case. Classification of appreciation of separate property can be described as the Forensic Accountant's Full Employment Act.

c. **Asset valuation.** Valuation is rarely as simple a problem as it seems at first glance. Expert assistance may be required to value accrued pension benefits and employee benefits including deferred compensation and stock options. Pensions and stock options require external information in order to calculate their value as of the date of their acquisition and as of the distribution date (separation or divorce). In fact, many pensions list values in statements to employees, but unless the asset is a 401(k), rarely will this calculation accurately reflect the asset's true value for divorce purposes. To properly value a whole-life insurance policy, the policy itself, declaration page, and tables must be

5. Experienced forensic accountants recommend engagement letters stating that the forensic accountant's work must be performed under the direction of counsel, not the client, to avoid the appearance of advocacy with complex tracing exercises.

reviewed to determine its cash surrender value, beneficiary, and owner. Finally, spouses often list quite different values on financial statements than those listed in discovery. This difference in value can make or break a case.

d. **Built-in capital gains. Structuring settlements for the best tax results can be very important to clients with wealth.** Never forget about an asset's tax basis. Tax basis is not simple and can be easily overlooked. A capital gain is the difference between the sales price (realization) less its tax basis. For some assets, rules for determining tax basis can be very complex. Stock and mutual fund basis calculation is fairly simple—their cost. In the divorce context, consequences can be disastrous if a party ignores built-in capital gains. For example, if one party receives a stock account worth $100,000 in exchange for another asset also worth $100,000, the spouse who ignores tax basis can be at a serious disadvantage. If the tax basis is materially different and the asset received must be sold shortly after the divorce to pay for college or debt caused by the divorce itself, the $100,000 is no longer $100,000 and may be worth significantly less. Forensic accountants can provide very important tax advice regarding this issue.

2. **Income determination.** Income is the most important factor for determining child support and alimony. Who earns what? Is the income reported to the IRS complete? Are the books cooked? Were there any cash transactions? Is there income that is not taxable but that is relevant for support? Can the CPA calculate imputed income from the spouse's monthly spending? Does a spouse's loan application contain admissions of a much greater income than reported in the case? On a W-2, what are the differences in the calculation among boxes 1, 3, and 5? Forensic accountants know their stuff.

3. **Lifestyle analysis.** For those states with alimony, many states' laws provide for considering the historical spending of the parties to determine the reasonable need of the supported spouse. Other states also consider the projected future active earnings from employment and passive earnings from investments, including projected investment asset appreciation. A lifestyle

analysis can be a powerful tool to present arguments in favor of or in opposition to larger alimony awards.

4. **Dissipation and fraudulent conveyances.** While every state may have subtle differences in its case law, questionable transactions should be identified, investigated, and analyzed. Wasteful spending in one marriage may be considered routine historical-lifestyle spending in another. Also, transfers to related parties can be fraudulent. Any transfer without consideration must be by gift, loan, or theft. No other options exist. All have relevance and significance in a divorce.

5. **Credibility and admissibility.** Proving the opposing spouse lied in discovery about assets, debts, income, or expenses can be very important. Proving that the claimant materially understated assets or underreported income can result in a powerful shift in relative negotiating strength. The larger the omission or misstatement, the more benefit may be obtained. Expert testimony may be required to admit into evidence analysis of the documents that help prove the lie. Plus, under the right circumstances, a forensic accountant's affidavit in support of a critically timed motion can help break up logjams in negotiations.

6. **Defending against the questionable opposing expert.** All in all, most experts are very serious about independence. This is especially true with forensic accountants. But there are several very derogatory slang terms used to describe those special few expert witnesses who are willing to accept pay in exchange for specific testimony. If you practice family law long enough, you will run across such an expert. Accountants can contrive ratios, formulae, and analyses that are intentionally dishonest. Usually, those experts see this type of testimony as a game. Unfortunately, this game can have a devastating impact on your client unless you mount a competent challenge to this tactic. For example, manipulation of a coverture factor in a pension calculation can result in a $100,000 swing in an estate in favor of the manipulating party. Defense requires an expert.

7. **Litigation support.** This is a catch-all phrase describing engagement planning and assistance in all phases of the case, including analyzing discovery, consulting on tax issues in settlement,

advising regarding additional needed investigation, preparing for deposition, developing trial strategy, and more. The only limit is the creativity of the lawyer and CPA. For example, a forensic accountant can review tax returns produced by the opposing party and advise the lawyer regarding supplemental schedules and documentation that should have accompanied the return filed with the IRS but that have not been produced in discovery.[6]

Forensic Accountant Certifications

A forensic accountant may possess many kinds of certifications. Described in the following are the most common credentials available. Not every expert has a perfect background for every engagement. Forensic accountants may possess many different subspecialties, including bankruptcy, computer forensics, damages, fraud prevention and detection, valuation, and, of course, family law. It is easy to imagine a CPA being very experienced in one area and not in another. Finding a weakness in your forensic accountant's experience, education, or application of a particular skill can be devastating if exposed at the wrong time. As a starting point, family lawyers should possess a basic understanding of the forensic accounting universe and know the credentials described in the following when engaging, utilizing, deposing, and ultimately cross-examining forensic accountants.

CPA. Almost all forensic accountants are certified public accountants. Some exceptions apply, such as the certified fraud examiner (CFE) and certified financial planner (CFP), which are discussed next. Like a law license, a CPA license is issued by the state. To obtain a CPA license, an accountant must meet very strict requirements for education and experience and pass a very, very difficult exam. CPAs dominate the

6. Cindy MacAulay, CPA/CFF, CVA, CDFA, a Director and forensic accountant with Dixon Hughes Goodman LLP, has spent many years providing various levels of litigation support to family lawyers in South Carolina and Tennessee. "All CPAs are expected to keep up with and understand impact of tax law changes. As a forensic accountant, I help family lawyers craft solutions to take advantage of, and avoid losing out on, child tax credit related opportunities. The 2018 tax law changes have been no exception." See "Sample Litigation Support Report" at Appendix E, written by Cindy to help a family lawyer negotiate a divorce settlement regarding the Child Tax Credit under federal income tax law in 2018 and moving forward.

field of forensic accounting, so much so that for the purposes of this book, it is assumed that all forensic accountants described herein are CPAs and possess the knowledge typically gained in practice as a CPA.

The CPA universe is dominated by standards and ethics set by the AICPA. Professional standards and ethics are discussed more in Chapter 10. States' governing bodies are most often called boards of accountancy. Individual state boards set licensing requirements in their respective jurisdictions but normally adopt most AICPA standards. All forensic accountants should be able to easily recount the prerequisites completed to obtain their particular CPA license. Prerequisites for becoming a CPA are an excellent topic for voir dire, establishing the foundation for the expert's qualifications, competence, and credibility. This is usually not summarized on the expert's curriculum vitae.

A majority of states have adopted a requirement of 150 hours of education to qualify for sitting for the CPA exam. For most, this means a master's degree in accounting is required to become a CPA. Some states allow graduate students to take the CPA exam during their final semester. States also have specific work experience requirements. Most require at least two years in public accounting or a longer period of time in private practice.

Then there is the CPA examination itself. It is tough. The CPA exam is the stuff of accounting industry legend. Only a small percentage of applicants pass it on the first try. Many never pass the exam. There are four parts to the exam, and each part is four hours long. Each part has a pass rate of less than 50 percent. All four parts must be passed within an 18-month period, or the parts that have been passed are forfeited and must be passed again. A minimum score of 75 is required on each part. As a comparison, the bar exam pass rate is generally between 70 and 80 percent in most states. Several areas of law, including basic business, contract, trust, and estate law, are addressed in one of the parts of the CPA exam.

There is no dishonor taking several tries to pass the exam. Typical experience requirements can delay obtaining the designation for up to two or more years anyway. For example, in a state that requires two years of public accounting (working for a traditional CPA firm in either an audit or a tax department), there may be a five-year experience requirement if working in a corporate setting. Successfully completing the CPA exam is almost always a CPA's first really important professional accomplishment. It is, and should be, an issue of personal pride.

Once CPA certification is obtained, maintaining it requires a significant number of continuing professional education (CPE) hours. Many states require as many as 80 hours every two years with very specific requirements by category. In many ways, the CPE required of CPAs is similar to the continuing legal education requirement for attorneys (and equally loved as well).

CFF. In 2008, the AICPA created the certified in financial forensics (CFF) designation. Current requirements may be viewed on the AICPA's website. In general, the successful applicant must be a CPA in good standing and have a minimum of 1,000 hours of experience in forensic accounting over a five-year period preceding the application for CFF designation. A certain number of continuing professional development CPD hours in forensic accounting is also required. The AICPA initiated an exam component in 2010. Specific relevant CPE is required for maintaining the designation. Again, for voir dire, consider asking the forensic accountant specific details about the expert's application requirements at the time the certification was obtained.

According to Barbara Andrews, the director of forensic services with AICPA, a CPA obtaining the CFF credential ensures that he or she has an "extensive knowledge of complex financial issues across a broad range of specialty areas including bankruptcy, insolvency and reorganization; forensic data analysis; economic damages calculations; family law services; fraud prevention, detection and response; financial statement misrepresentation; and stakeholder disputes." She also added, "It identifies those forensic accounting professionals who have certified their expertise to provide reliable forensic accounting services. The requirement for continuing education guarantees an ongoing high level of competency and knowledge."[7]

Many CPAs with the CFF certification also bear the designation of accredited in business valuation (ABV). Many forensic accountants' entry into forensic accounting was to supplement their business valuation practices, or vice versa. The typical credentials following a business valuation and forensic accounting expert's name will appear as follows: "John Smith, CPA/ABV/CFF." While there are no official posted statistics, there are over 5,000 credentialed CFFs in the United States. By sheer numbers, the CFF is arguably the dominant credential for forensic accountants.

7. Quote from personal correspondence with author.

MAFF. The National Association of Certified Valuators and Analysts (NACVA) created the master analyst in financial forensics (MAFF) credential.[8] To obtain the MAFF, you must be a member of NACVA, attend a course, and pass an exam. According to the NACVA website, "Achieve the Master Analyst in Financial Forensics® (MAFF®) certification and make the statement that when it comes to financial litigation, you are the 'Master' of the field."[9]

NACVA's members are almost exclusively CPAs who are forensic accountants and/or business valuation experts. NACVA certifies several credentials, including the well-known business valuation credential certified valuation analyst. NACVA presents training programs relevant to forensic accounting and business valuation through its Consultants' Training Institute, which is held throughout the year across the country. One of the courses it presents is its Matrimonial Litigation workshop, which is a five-day course for accountants looking to break into the family law field and sharpen existing skills.[10]

Forensic accountants who want to practice at a high level (and family lawyers who want an edge in cross-examining them) should consider attending two very important programs offered through the NACVA. First, take Darrell Dorrell's Forensic Accounting Academy, which delivers "the most all-inclusive training in forensic accounting available to date."[11] Then, take Michael Kaplan's Expert Witness Bootcamp.[12]

CFE. The certified fraud examiner is a credential created by the Association of Certified Fraud Examiners (ACFE). The ACFE was originally founded by former law enforcement officers, and its members

8. The MAFF replaced the prior certified forensic financial analyst credential offered by the NACVA.

9. https://www.nacva.com/maff.

10. The author attended NACVA's matrimonial litigation workshop and can recommend this for entry-level forensic accountants and family lawyers who want to sharpen their financial skills.

11. For more information, see https://www.nacva.com/faa. Mr. Dorrell is one of the nation's most respected thought leaders in the field. The author attended this program and cites Mr. Dorrell as a leading authority on methodology. For more discussion, see Chapter 6, generally.

12. For more information, see https://www.nacva.com/expertwitnessbootcamp. The author attended this program and highly recommends it to both CPAs and divorce lawyers of all skill levels. Michael Kaplan also teaches another program privately, the Court Room Bootcamp (see http://www.courtroombootcamp.com/).

commonly also include CPAs and private investigators. Fraud investigation is a large industry and a very important part of the forensic accounting universe. The skill sets possessed by professionals with this credential can be very helpful in divorces as well. A CFE is as good as any professional in helping to uncover hidden assets and fraudulent transfers. Some CFEs also have the expertise needed for the admissibility of testimony regarding electronic evidence and computer files. To obtain this designation, a candidate must meet minimum education requirements, pass an exam, and submit recommendations from professionals in the field.

Cr.FA. The American College of Forensic Examiners Institute certifies the certified forensic accountant (Cr.FA). To be eligible, an applicant must be a CPA in good standing and pass an examination. There is no experience requirement.

CFP. Certified financial planner is a designation most often obtained by investment advisors and insurance and company benefits salespeople. Many CFPs claim to have experience and expertise in divorce planning, taxes, and personal budgeting. Although it is not very common compared to CPAs, some CFPs will testify in divorce cases from time to time. Their CFP skills can be helpful in creating and testifying about a lifestyle analysis. In addition, a CFP can usually perform an estimated pension calculation.

CDFA. The certified divorce financial analyst (CDFA) certification is an effort by financial advisors to market themselves to divorcing parties. Most CDFAs seek referrals to divorcing spouses in need of financial advisors. Some want to testify. For clients who are uncomfortable with financial aspects of divorce (and personal finance), family lawyers should consider recommending those clients engage a CDFA to help explain terms and concepts and to help advise them regarding settlements with marital estates comprised of complex financial investments and retirement assets including pensions, annuities, and stock options.

There are even more credentials than these. In considering a possible forensic accountant, you must always think in terms of planning the voir dire. What minimum education, training, experience, examination completion, and/or professional recommendations were required by the expert's certificating organization? One hopes it wasn't just filling out a form, paying a fee, and submitting two cereal box tops.

Meeting and Engaging CPAs 2

How CPAs Become Forensic Accountants

Many certified public accountants (CPAs) begin their careers with traditional public accounting firms, spending several years in tax, audit, or consulting departments. In larger accounting firms, tax, audit, and consulting departments are distinct, with very little cross-training. In smaller accounting firms, accountants work in a combination of different engagements throughout the year, usually including compilation work and a grinding tax season. Compilation work is assisting small business clients with their general accounting needs and with cost accounting and financial statement preparation. Other accountants begin working in private accounting or industry and are employed by businesses in a variety of general accounting roles. A young accountant early in his career will almost always report directly to another CPA. Some obtain the required experience in a combination of public and private accounting.

Transitioning to forensic accounting is not challenging from a technical competence standpoint. Even though there is much to learn, almost all CPAs with a few years of experience have obtained the basic skill sets to perform the work. Many forensic accountants will jokingly admit that they sought out forensic accounting because the traditional accounting career was just a grind to them. Many enjoy the sporting and sparring of a deposition and look forward to the intellectual and professional challenge of staying calm under the pressure. As with family law, there are no two days just alike in a forensic accounting practice. The clients, lawyers, and issues are always unique. As one might expect, this difference attracts a different breed of personality to the forensic accounting universe.

While building their forensic accounting practices, most CPAs will maintain their tax or audit practices until they are ready to make the leap and go full time as a forensic accountant and/or business valuation expert. Business valuation and forensic accounting often go hand in hand, although the universes are distinctly separate in many ways. One important difference is that the business valuation universe is much larger than just CPAs. Several organizations credential business valuation experts, but almost all forensic accountants are CPAs.

Over time, a forensic accountant develops relationships with a core group of lawyers. A healthy forensic accounting practice usually results from as little as 20 or so leading litigators calling upon the forensic accountant for engagements. As with a family law practice, growing a practice means making more money by leveraging assignments worked by other CPAs and staff. Marketing professional services is one of the typical accountant's least favorite activities. Not many do it well. Successful forensic accountants socialize with lawyers at local, state, and American Bar Association meetings; speak at conferences; and present continuing legal education programs. Forensic accountants also often send out direct mail, invite lawyers to lunches, e-mail newsletters, and advertise.

Shopping Forensic Accountants before One Is Needed

The first step in hiring a forensic accountant should begin well in advance of getting a client who needs one. Every divorce lawyer should know as many forensic accountants as possible. Finding two or three from whom to choose for a specific engagement can be very challenging depending on the speed needed for the engagement and the locality. In many areas of the United States, forensic accountants can be scarce. In others, there can be many from whom to choose. Advance work is critical.

Unfortunately, some of the very best forensic accountants in the country don't even have websites. Most forensic accountants do not market their services effectively to attorneys—the very folks they should want to call them. Many rely primarily on word of mouth. Forensic accountants seem to believe all family lawyers stand around the courthouse discussing them. That may be true of some lawyers, but it is definitely not true of the majority. Whereas the most experienced forensic accountants have already established relationships with many of their area's usual suspects in the divorce bar, most are glad to meet new lawyers, regardless of their experience and size of practice.

To start the process of meeting forensic accountants, make a list of several forensic accountants to call. First, hit the Internet. In many states, CPAs are organized into societies (like state bar associations) and have websites with "Find a CPA" search capabilities. Search in your area. The National Association of Certified Valuators and Analysts' website, www.NACVA.com, has a directory listing members, many of whom are leading forensic accountants in their area.[1] Finally, type "forensic accountant" and the name of your area into your favorite search engine. Go to the result pages and print them out. As with lawyers, though, expect some forensic accountants to move between firms from time to time. Remember also that it is common for website information to be outdated.

When looking at CPA lists, you will notice that some CPAs will indicate that they practice in the area of matrimonial or family law as a subspecialty. Others will not. Some of the most experienced and expensive forensic accountants will not accept family law cases for a variety of reasons. But never trust the Internet. The information could be years old or just mistyped. Still, write down all the names you find. Follow the links provided to their websites, and print out the accountants' curricula vitae (CVs) and/or professional biographical information.

Visit as many websites as you can. Keep in mind that even the best forensic accountants can have poorly designed websites. Do not count a forensic accountant out because the person's website failed to provide

1. For forensic accountants working in family law, search "Specialty: Litigation—Divorce."

the needed information. Begin a notebook (or subfolder in your computer) of potential forensic accountants.

Now it is time to work the phones. Call the forensic accountants you've found and ask them to share the following information:

1. **Their CV or a professional biography.** At a minimum, a CV should list an expert's education, training, certifications, work experience, prior testifying experience at deposition and trial, publications, and seminar presentations. Also, an experienced expert's CV should comply with Federal Rule of Civil Procedure 26(a)(2)(B) and/or your particular state's equivalent, if any. Many CVs contain more information.
2. **The financial terms of a typical divorce engagement, including initial retainer and hourly rates.** Some will have higher rates for depositions and/or court appearances.
3. **Their preferred types of engagements and the types of engagements they will not accept.** This can often be unpredictable.
4. **References from other lawyers.** Call the lawyers listed. Ask three questions: (1) Would that lawyer hire the accountant again? (2) Were the work and report completed in a timely fashion? (3) Does the expert have any weird quirks? In these types of calls, many lawyers will be honest but may not answer questions not asked.
5. **Their marketing material, including brochures and any articles written by or about the accountants that are relevant to family law.**

The decision of whether to hire a particular CPA is very important. Usually, the more affluent family law clients will need forensic accountants, and more importantly, the more affluent family law clients will expect you to know the best forensic accountants from which to choose. Consider calling at least three forensic accountants and asking to meet each for lunch. Even though you may not have an immediate case in mind, you should not worry that you are wasting the forensic accountant's time. All litigators, regardless of their experience, will eventually have a case requiring the services of a forensic accountant, and the forensic accountant knows that. Forensic accountants understand that great engagements don't come around every day for any lawyer. But when that case comes, it might be big.

Offer to travel to each of their offices and leave for lunch from there. Check out the offices. Some will have a very corporate feel. Others will have a very Spartan feel. Look at their family photos, items revealing community involvement, and mementos. Lawyers should always trust their instincts when analyzing such information.

At lunch, you should pay attention to whether the rapport is natural. Does the forensic accountant tend to interrupt or talk over you? Is the rhythm of the conversation comfortable? Do the topics of conversation evolve fluidly? Smooth conversation at lunch between you and the expert will likely transfer into the courtroom. You should also actively listen to the forensic accountant's war stories. In listening to those stories, you can gauge the expert's ability to briefly explain a complex series of facts and events in context—an important skill needed for direct examination. In general, experienced forensic accountants consider themselves as not having "typical, boring CPA personalities." Most really aren't that boring, but some are incredibly so. A lunch with a person possessing a "typical, boring CPA personality" can be long and painful. Surviving those lunches requires patience and skill.

Most experienced forensic accountants will be very kind and appreciative of a phone call from a new lawyer. Lawyers are the very best potential referral source. Oddly enough, if you are a young or inexperienced attorney, an experienced forensic accountant may enjoy the lunch even more. The younger the lawyer, the longer the relationship can last. And for good or bad, experienced forensic accountants love to teach lawyers a thing or two when it comes to litigation. In working with less-experienced counsel, forensic accountants have a greater opportunity to add value to a case.

Counterintuitively, the most important objective of the lunch is not necessarily to find the best forensic accountants with whom to work but instead to avoid the major disasters. Luckily, most forensic accountants will number among some of the very best expert witnesses with whom you will ever work. Only a very few forensic accountants are train wrecks. Some are merely insufferably boring, whereas others are arrogant, intolerable, and rude. If the forensic accountant is not enjoyable at a casual business networking lunch, working with him on a stressful piece of litigation will be a nightmare.

When you get a case for which you determine a forensic accountant is needed, you will almost always need to finalize the expert choice quickly. That need for speed can often result in a hasty decision. You absolutely should not wait to find an expert until the immediate need arises. Coordinating lunch schedules with each expert candidate at the time the need arises can be very difficult or impossible. Do the lunches well in advance. Take the time. Make the next piece of litigation easier. You never know, but the forensic accountant may even refer a case to you in the meantime.

Selling Your Client on a Forensic Accountant

Once a client decides that she has need for or wants a forensic accountant, it is time to have "the talk" with that client. These conversations rarely go as smoothly as they should. Early in a case, most family law clients are skittish and cost conscious. How a lawyer recommends the engagement of a forensic accountant can be just as important as the objective reasons provided. For this conversation, simple is usually better. Keep in mind the perceived need of the client. Focus on whether the client is worried about hidden assets, income determination for the self-employed, or maximizing or defending an alimony claim. From there, you can point out other important services the forensic accountant can provide. Explain the following benefits of retaining a forensic accountant:

1. **Forensic accountants can save the client money** by charging less per hour and by taking less time to review and analyze documents in discovery than you would. Their hourly rates and those of their staff professionals are often lower than lawyers' rates. They can likely do the job more quickly. Forensic accountants know what they're doing. Many have prepared thousands of tax returns and reviewed thousands of financial statements over a career. Lawyers rarely prepare their own tax returns or financial statements.
2. **Forensic accountants can testify.** Lawyers can't. For example, if you discover evidence of an important hidden asset described on a tax return, you might not be able to get that information admitted into evidence without an expert to explain the relevance of that information.

3. **Forensic accountants can rely on hearsay because they are expert witnesses.** Fact witnesses can't. Almost all financial records are chock full of hearsay.
4. **A forensic accountant can be presented as an unbiased witness.** Even though he is ultimately engaged by the client, the forensic accountant's testimony cannot be bought. Applicable ethical restrictions demand independence. In the courtroom, the independence of a forensic accountant can be a powerful advocacy tool.
5. **Forensic accountants can smell problems.** Through years of education, training, and experience, forensic accountants develop judgment. This professional judgment allows them to analyze and discover important relationships among numbers on a page. They use the term "smell test" to describe this process. Certain financial information makes sense when it appears in conjunction with other information, and some information does not. For example, forensic accountants can analyze trends from tax returns by spreading numbers from multiple corporate tax returns. Red flags are raised when gross profits decline as gross revenues increase over multiple periods. When presented with a reason, a forensic accountant will generally have a good idea whether the explanation is credible or contrived for the divorce.
6. **Forensic accountants can shift the balance of perceived relative negotiating power.** As every case progresses, a party may feel that one or the other is winning. Engaging a forensic accountant sends a message to the other spouse that the details will not be overlooked. This simple strategic message often helps settle cases. If not, the issuance of the expert's report itself often frightens litigants to the settlement table. In a Sun Tzu sense, being prepared for war can prevent it from ever having to be fought.

As the forensic accountant selection process begins, you should also try to obtain as many basic documents as possible and have them in your office as soon as possible. Those basic documents include tax returns, financial statements, and brokerage and retirement asset account statements. Credit card and bank account statements fall into this category as well. As soon as you've chosen the forensic accountant, the more documents you have in hand in the beginning, the more accurate the expert's initial review will be. This sounds obvious and simple, but if time is of the essence, and it often is, the more information the forensic accountant has early on, the less likely it is your litigation team will be spinning its wheels in the discovery process.

Engaging a Forensic Accountant When You Have a Specific Client and Case

Once the client accepts your recommendation to engage a forensic accountant, it is time to begin the selection and engagement process. You should select two or three forensic accountants for initial consideration and contact each of the candidates in writing and ask for a conflict check. You should avoid the temptation to call a proposed expert and discuss the type of work needed. If the expert has already been contacted by opposing counsel or by the opposing party, the expert may not remember the call. He may only remember the name of the lawyer who called and a few of the basic facts. You might well get far into a discussion of your client's perception of the facts of the case before the expert realizes there is a conflict. Plus, if the forensic accountant is part of a larger accounting firm, he will need to check with the rest of the firm regarding potential conflicts. The risk of a conflict of interest[2] is directly proportional to the size of an accounting firm's tax, audit, and consulting practice. The more clients the firm has (especially individual and business tax clients), the more likely the firm will have a conflict. Send each prospective forensic accountant the following information:

1. Your client's name and address,
2. The opposing spouse's name,
3. The legal names of any businesses owned by either party,
4. Any DBAs (doing business as),

2. The most common situation occurs when a couple's tax CPA becomes an expert for one or both parties. Is a waiver of conflict of interest required? Can the CPA's waiver work? Very few state CPA societies will have an ethics-type opinion on this issue. But, it may be important in inquire. Experienced CPAs believe that this conflict of interest, serving the interest of one client over another, should not be waivable.

5. The name of opposing counsel, and
6. The case style, if the case has been filed.

If you have not already contacted the forensic accountant for the information described in the section titled "Shopping Forensic Accountants before One Is Needed," or if you have not received current biographical and practice information within the last year, you should request that information again. You should ask an assistant to follow up with the forensic accountant to confirm receipt of the request. Speed always matters. As with high school prom dates, the first person to talk with the preferred forensic accountant will likely get the date.

Early on, you should also consider researching any businesses owned by one or both parties. As a result, you will sound more intelligent and prepared when talking with your client and the forensic accountant. You can check out the business's website, research it through Google, search the local business journal's website, search industry journals, and search the county register's office and/or property deeds recording office. The register's office and/or property deeds recording office may record liens, judgments, and Uniform Commercial Code-1, which provide notice to the world of business loans secured by personal property. Learning something like the business's banker or other credit provider can be important information later because you will know where to send a subpoena, if needed. In addition, if there is a loan, there is almost always an accompanying financial statement. You might also consider talking to a few knowledgeable business acquaintances—such as stockbrokers, financial advisors, insurance salespersons, bankers, and transactional lawyers—about the business in question. It is amazing what information you can find on the street.

Once the forensic accountant has completed the conflict check, and only if that check has revealed no conflicts, call the prospective forensic accountant to discuss the case. An experienced forensic accountant can lead the conversation. An inexperienced forensic accountant may want you to take charge.

Why might you consider hiring a relatively inexperienced forensic accountant? Budget or availability frequently affects the decision. Most forensic accountants have more than enough education, training, and experience to handle most family law engagements. Doing the work itself is usually not the hard part. Effectively communicating the work performed and the opinion reached is the challenge. A relatively inexperienced forensic accountant might well be able to produce the needed work within the constraint of a tighter budget. Also, some of the more experienced forensic accountants may be too busy with current engagements to devote the energy and time required when you need it.

If you have obtained all the information described here, you need to have a face-to-face meeting with your client prior to choosing the forensic accountant. The decision is too important not to be handled intentionally and cautiously. Clients normally want every major litigation decision handled with their expected degree of precision and attention to detail. The selection of a forensic accountant can be a major decision. In the best-case scenario, the forensic accountant will be a very important and helpful addition to the litigation team. At that meeting with the client, you should determine if the client wants to personally meet with the forensic accountant candidates. Some will. Some will not. Most will rely on your advice. When in doubt, unless time is a serious constraint, recommend the client meet with each candidate personally.

Consider sending the client each accountant's CV, typical engagement terms, website address, and marketing material for review in advance of the meeting. Prior to the meeting, advise the client about the basics of hiring expert witnesses, including retainers, payment terms, and ranges of costs. You should explain that estimating the cost of issuing a report is always very difficult early in the case. The cost of depositions depends on the opposing counsel, not the client. Also, the client may decide she wants the expert to be involved in settlement negotiations and/or mediation. Finally, advise that the cost of a trial is never predictable.

Although there is no hard rule on this, consider holding the client/CPA interviews at your office. Schedule the meetings for specific time periods, either half an hour or an hour. That will usually be enough. Do not waste the forensic accountant's or your time prior to final selection. These meetings always seem to drag on too long. Once the forensic accountant is chosen, there is plenty of time to get started on the case.

If you are very comfortable with a particular forensic accountant (having worked on several cases together) and the client is experienced in business, you may suggest the client meet the forensic accountant at the forensic accountant's office without you. This will save the client your hourly rate, and the forensic accountant will know what to do. Remind all clients, however, that anything told to a testifying expert witness is not confidential, is not subject to any privilege, and is discoverable. The meeting will be productive.

Before any meeting, you should coach the client a bit on the most important attributes of a forensic accountant. The client should be looking for the best fit. If the engagement is anticipated to be a high-conflict case, the forensic accountant's professionalism, reputation, and overall technical competence will be paramount. Can the accountant, or any expert witness for that matter, answer questions in sentences of ten words or less? You can direct the client to request the following:

- Describe your education, training, and experience.
- Why are you a forensic accountant?
- Explain why your credentials are the best for my case.
- What are your most important strengths and weaknesses?
- Other than technical skill, what makes you different from other forensic accountants?
- What articles/books have you written? Are any relevant to my case?
- What are the organizations and committees in which you are a member? What conferences do you regularly attend? Is that important to you? Why or why not? Have you presented seminars on forensic accounting at any of these conferences? Are any of those presentations relevant to my case?
- How many times have you testified in deposition or in court? In cases similar to mine?
- If a business is involved, what experience do you have working with similar businesses?
- How many times have you been hired by opposing counsel's clients?
- Do you currently work for any of opposing counsel's clients?
- Are you friends with opposing counsel?
- Have you ever socialized with opposing counsel?
- If requested to do so, are you comfortable completing a report by a deadline?

The actual answers are not always as important as the way they are answered. The forensic accountant should not be offended by any of the questions listed above. Advise the client that, just as with lawyers, there is rarely a perfect match between client and forensic accountant. Correspondingly, a very important consideration is choosing the expert with whom the client is most comfortable. Comfort matters not in terms of whom the client would most like to chat with at a cocktail party but in terms of competence and experience. When things get hot, the client and team will need someone in their foxhole who knows how to handle tough situations and get tough jobs done.

Vetting Your Expert

Before you work with a new financial expert, ask for references from other attorneys. No reputable expert will balk at this. Seasoned vets will respect the request. Follow up. Call the attorneys. This same effort should be expended when researching an opposing financial expert witness.

Here are a few tips from Finding and Researching Experts and Their Testimony,[3] a whitepaper:

- Read the potential expert's CV. Is there anything in there that's a bit vague or confusing? That's a bad sign. If an expert witness can't draft a solid CV, how is she going to write a clear and cogent report?
- The expert's full name should also be provided. Look for the middle initial. If the name is too vague to result in a meaningful search result, consider whether that might be intentional. Be aware that potentially a large percentage of expert witness CVs contain falsified information.
- Visit Internet Archive's Wayback Machine function at https://archive.org/web/ to investigate an expert's prior year's CV if it was ever posted. What has changed? Has anything important been deleted?
- Check disciplinary records for all licensure- and certification-issuing entities of which the expert may be a member.
- Call attorneys who have opposed the witness. Do they have any old depositions available that they can share with you?
- Check YouTube for presentations, marketing, and testimonies related to your potential expert.

---

3. *Finding and Researching Experts and Their Testimony* by Jim Robinson, David Dilenschneider, Myles Levin & Nathan Aaron Rosen is a very thorough resource. The third edition, published Nov. 2014, is available online at https://www.lexisnexis.com/documents/pdf/20150520075233_large.pdf.

Resources for Researching Expert Witnesses and *Daubert* Challenges

The Daubert Tracker[4] is a searchable Internet resource that tracks cases going back to 1993. It claims to be updated daily. The Daubert Tracker is an aggregation of all reported and numerous unreported "gatekeeping" decisions from multiple jurisdictions collected into a unified and integrated database. This service is free as a benefit to American Institute of Certified Public Accountants Forensic and Valuation Services section members. One of the Daubert Tracker's key functions is cross-referencing expert witness testimony and results of challenges to admission as an expert with the overall results in the case.

The author found the Daubert Tracker to be a helpful and easy-to-use resource for researching forensic accountant expert witness testimony in legal decisions. It is searchable by different types of cases, including family law. Many of the legal decisions discussed in this work were discovered using this tool.

The Expert Witness Profile[5] is another resource for accessing background reports on expert witnesses. Organized by name, each profile summary includes information about an expert's testimonial history, challenge (*Daubert/Frye*) history, disciplinary history, licensing and certifications (including verification), educational background (including verification), professional background, associations and memberships, personal information, publications, and more.

Testifying or Consulting Expert?

Once the decision to hire a particular forensic accountant is made, one of the first decisions you'll face is whether the expert will be a testifying expert or a consulting expert. The expert you are hiring will most likely be a testifying expert. Designating an expert as a testifying expert means he must be disclosed to the other side. There may be mandatory disclosures under Rule 26 (see Federal Rule of Civil Procedure 26(a)(2)(B) and/or your state's equivalent). Everything the expert sees, reads, hears, and thinks is at risk as discoverable through discovery,

4. https://www.dauberttracker.com/index.cfm. The author expresses gratitude to Myles Levin for his explanation of the tool and its benefits.

5. https://expertwitnessprofiler.com/home.

depositions, and trial testimony. If there is a confidential fact or theory that must stay confidential, carefully consider whether to share it with a testifying expert. If the information is relevant to the testimony, it may need to be disclosed. The client must be advised of this, too. Clients tend to tell everyone on the team everything, so if something must remain confidential, caution your client about discussing it with the expert. Even though most opposing counsel won't dig for extraneous facts in discovery and deposition, you must nevertheless plan on receiving such questions from opposing counsel.

Consulting experts are extremely valuable for an important strategic reason. As most states' rules require disclosure of all witnesses broadly with respect to potential trial witnesses only, this is the legal basis for not disclosing consulting experts. Consulting experts, by definition, are not going to testify at trial. The information shared with them may be kept confidential through nondisclosure. If a potential expert is engaged in a consulting role only and the expert forms an opinion that is contrary to the client's position in the case, the opinion may be kept confidential and cannot be used against the client at trial.[6] If the same expert were initially engaged and disclosed as a testifying expert and that expert formed an opinion that was contrary to the client's case, the opinion would have to be disclosed on cross-examination and could

---

6. Generally, the facts known or opinions held by a consulting expert are not subject to discovery. Federal Rule of Civil Procedure 26(b)(4)(D), however, provides one exception for nonwitness consulting experts who have been retained or specially employed in anticipation of litigation or in preparation for trial. Under the exception, a consulting expert is subject to discovery upon a showing of exceptional circumstances for which it is impracticable to obtain the sought-after information by other means. For instance, a party may obtain the opinion of a nontestifying consulting expert where it is impossible to obtain the opinion from another expert. *See Braun v. Lorillard, Inc.*, 84 F.3d 230, 236 (7th Cir. 1996); *Spearman Indus. v. St. Paul Fire & Marine Ins. Co.*, 128 F. Supp. 2d 1148, 1152 (N.D. Ill. 2001); and *Delcastor, Inc. v. Vail Associates, Inc.*, 108 F.R.D. 405, 408–09 (D. Colo. 1985). The impossibility may arise due to the unavailability of other experts or the destruction of the condition at issue. A party may also obtain the opinion of a nontestifying consulting expert where replicating the sought-after information is too costly or where there is a substantial need for the information. *See Bank Brussels Lambert v. Chase Manhattan Bank,* 175 F.R.D. 34, 44–45 (S.D.N.Y. 1997); *Lilley v. Dow Chemical Co. (In re Agent Orange Product Liability Litigation),* 105 F.R.D. 577, 581 (E.D.N.Y. 1985); and *Crockett v. Virginia Folding Box Co.,* 61 F.R.D. 312, 320 (E.D. Va. 1974).

not be suppressed. Forensic accountants will testify honestly. It's what they do.

How should a competent and careful lawyer maneuver through this situation? The straightforward answer is to engage all forensic accountants as consulting experts first and learn their opinions in advance. Then later, determine whether to convert the consulting expert into a testifying expert. These gymnastics involve carefully crafting engagement letters and documentation of what documents were reviewed when, but in most cases, it does not add a material amount to the overall cost of the case.

If it makes a lot of sense to engage a forensic accountant first as a consulting expert and then wait until learning the expert's opinion before converting the expert to the testifying role and making a disclosure, why don't lawyers do this every time? There are at least two reasons. First, most divorce cases don't usually have "smoking guns" that will never be discoverable. For example, if a cheating husband is going to produce business credit card statements with approximately $15,000 spent on his girlfriend, there is no need to have an expert who can be secretive about that expense. For your forensic accountant, the secret girlfriend problem will involve only analyzing the information and adding up the disputed dissipation. In most cases, there is usually no special need for confidentiality regarding your forensic accountant and the documents shared with him.

The second reason most lawyers don't worry with the hassle of engaging an expert first as a consulting witness is that courts can disallow an expert's testimony for failure to timely disclose the witness. Lawyers should avoid the temptation to sandbag opposing counsel with an expert witness disclosure, waiting to disclose that expert until shortly before trial. At some point during her career, the lawyer who routinely utilizes this tactic will wait too long to make the disclosure and face a motion to exclude an expert witness for failure to timely disclose his existence. If the opposing lawyer wins the motion, the losing lawyer must explain this avoidable problem to the client. The conversation will be professionally embarrassing and painful. The client may have paid several thousands of dollars to a forensic accountant who cannot testify because of sandbagging.

Only rarely in most divorce cases is there a reason to hide the engagement of a forensic accountant at any stage in the case. Divorce counsel should recognize the pitfalls of trying to get cute with nondisclosure and learn how to exploit the opportunity if opposing counsel is using this tactic. If opposing counsel has converted a consulting expert to a testifying expert, it might be a red flag to dig a bit into what else the forensic accountant knows about a case beyond the numbers.

Reading, Understanding, and Explaining the Engagement Agreement

You should take the time to critically read all the terms of an expert witness's engagement letter. See Burrage & Johnson CPAs, LLC, Agreement for Expert Consulting Services, in Appendix A. It is often tempting to skip this task, thinking that the client is hiring the expert, not you. This is a mistake. Experts talk to one another at conventions and conferences and share ideas. Occasionally, a few of those ideas are not beneficial to lawyers or their clients. For example, some engagement agreements require a certain length of time after the engagement begins before depositions and trial dates may be set. Some forensic accountants are also tax professionals and won't agree to work at all in March or April. You might think that these boilerplate provisions won't be applied to your client's case. In litigation, however, things often get bumpy. Plan on it.

Certainly, a client never wants an expert witness mad at the lawyer or client. Payment and progress billing terms, minimum time and scheduling requirements, and pre-deposition and pre-trial retainer replenishments are just some of the hot-button contract issues about which forensic accountants may be very picky. Once the engagement agreement is signed and the expert is disclosed, the stronger relative negotiating position you have enjoyed in the relationship changes. The expert can always say "no" to a report deadline, deposition date, or trial date, regardless of the agreement. If a rift develops among a client, a lawyer, and an expert witness, the lawyer will be blamed for not pointing out, paying attention to, or otherwise navigating around the problematic expert witness contract terms.

Also, too many expert witnesses simply use a form they obtained from a form book or another forensic accountant and do not even understand all the contract terms contained therein. In these, and many other situations, if you request removal of an offending contract provision, many forensic accountants will simply remove the provision. Lawyers and clients should ask questions. Even experienced forensic accountants may have some fine points that need clearing up in their engagement agreements. Finally, know what part, if any, of the retainer is nonrefundable, and insist on that amount being disclosed in the agreement and brought to the attention of the client.

Advice to Lawyers When Hiring a Forensic Accountant

Michael Kaplan is a forensic accountant and business valuation expert.[7] In a teleconference presentation in 2009 to the ABA Family Law Section, he co-presented "Ten Ways That Attorneys Kill Their Own Experts."[8] The first two ways he discussed were very simple. First, lawyers too often hire the forensic accountant at the eleventh hour. Second, lawyers fail to establish realistic budgets.

Waiting until the eleventh hour is what lawyers do. Clients want to settle first and keep costs at a minimum, and lawyers want clients to be happy. Forensic accountants, as with all experts, cost money. You must be up front with your clients. If the case will crater without an expert and waiting until the very last minute may mean the client will risk not having an expert, then advise the client in writing to hire an expert. Explain to clients that all experts hate being called in at the last minute. If you are sincere and patient, most clients will understand the need for hiring the expert early in the engagement. A few clients, however, never will.

Lawyers often also fall into a pothole of establishing unrealistic budgets. The reason is simple and understandable. No one can predict with certainty the course and outcome of litigation. There is almost always one more document that you need. (Hence the name of the famous law school movie *The Paper Chase*.) Forensic accountants compare documents and look for what is missing or out of place. For example, looking at a tax return might give the expert the idea to cross-check an asset that does not appear on a particular brokerage account summary. What if there is a brokerage account that was not disclosed? Before accusing

7. Michael G. Kaplan, CPA, CVA, MAFF, of Los Angeles, California, is one of the nation's leading forensic accountants, instructors, and speakers. To learn more about Michael and his practice, visit www.Expert-Forensics.com.

8. Co-presented with Carlton R. Marcyan, JD, CPA, CFP, partner, Schiller DuCanto and Fleck, LLP, Chicago, Illinois.

the opposing party or opposing counsel of hiding the account, a conscientious lawyer should really review the several banker's boxes full of documents already produced to make sure. This effort may ultimately result in an excellent litigation advantage to the client; however, all this time and effort adds cost—unexpected cost. It adds up.

The best way to avoid jamming up the expert about his bill with the client is to have a very serious meeting early on with the entire litigation team and talk honestly about budgets. If the budget is lean, you must discuss this fact and make resulting strategic choices early. Don't fight every battle. If the budget is not lean and the stakes are high, the forensic accountant still must explain the scope of the work. Thousands of pages of information may be reviewed. Assistants may be performing data entry for days. The analysis may involve reviewing many years of records, including financial statements, tax returns, business financial statements, and computer databases with hundreds of thousands of entries. If the budget is not discussed and it gets out of hand in the mind of the client, there will be severe problems. These severe problems can be avoided by talking about them at the very beginning, as well as intermittently throughout the case.

The Game Is On—Getting the Documents as Soon as Possible

Family law litigation is a professional service. In many ways, litigation is like running a restaurant. In restaurants, servers take care of more than one table. Lawyers serve more than one client. Each time a server approaches her section, the server needs to check all the tables on that trip. If not, the server will constantly be jumping back and forth from the kitchen fulfilling only one need at a time. Efficient servers grab ketchup for table one, replace the sweet tea with unsweetened tea for table two, check on the entrees that are running late for table three, and run the tab for table four—all in one trip. Failing to do so will put the server in the weeds very quickly.

You need to try to consolidate discovery trips as often as possible. First, assemble all the client's documents as soon as possible and issue discovery. When discovery first arrives, review it in a timely manner. Determine what is missing and what the client can obtain without significant cost or hassle—and obtain those documents. Can any documents be obtained informally? If so, try to save resources. Consider simply asking your opposing counsel if your client's forensic accountant may visit the opposing spouse's business, interview management directly, and request documents. If not, must subpoenas be issued? Must you depose key financial witnesses? The easiest way for you to add tremendous expense and length of time to a divorce is to find yourself in wave after wave of uncoordinated discovery "trips to the kitchen."

Case Example: Experience Can Matter More Than Credentials

What happens if a spouse's financial expert is not a CPA and the opposing spouse challenges admission of the witness as an expert? A proposed expert having an accounting degree, being an enrolled agent with the IRS, and having appropriate experience can all go a long way in the eyes of the court. Credentials as a CPA are not always required.

The husband and wife in this California divorce case[9] had been married for 20 years before their 1995 separation. During the marriage, the husband was self-employed with a number of businesses. The wife was a stay-at-home mother for much of the marriage but had begun working as a teacher a few years before the separation.

The wife filed for divorce a month after the parties' separation. A year later she filed for Chapter 7 bankruptcy. When the bankruptcy trustee began liquidating community property, the husband filed a Chapter 11 petition. The two bankruptcy trustees eventually settled the case with the

9. *In re* Marriage of Rippey, No. A096767 (Cal. Ct. App. Feb. 20, 2003).

husband purchasing the wife's interest in the community property. After some follow-up litigation in the bankruptcy court, the case was eventually resolved. After trial in the state court, the wife was awarded $3,000 per month in spousal support for six years, along with attorney's fees of $25,000. Some outstanding property issues were also addressed.

A key issue at trial was the husband's income, since his most recent five years of tax returns showed extreme variations. The husband testified that during 1994, the family had a net loss of $167,000, with 1989 showing an adjusted gross income of over $270,000. However, there was testimony that the husband had access to profits from his winery business that were not reported on his personal taxes. The tax returns for this business were not prepared until after the separation and were never presented into evidence. The husband testified that many of the family's expenses were paid for with loans from friends and family members, although there was little or no documentation of these loans. The husband's bankruptcy filing indicated that these loans totaled $870,000. The husband claimed an income of only $2,665 per month but expenses of over $9,000 per month. He also claimed that his businesses were losing money.

The wife retained expert witness Linda Goldberg to testify as to the amount of funds available to the husband. The husband objected to this testimony on the grounds that Goldberg lacked adequate qualifications. The trial court admitted the testimony, and the husband appealed the admission of this testimony.

Goldberg had reviewed the husband's personal and corporate check registers and compiled a report showing the funds available to him for 1997 through 1999. She concluded that the funds available to him in each of those years were as high as $450,000. That amount, however, did not include personal expenses paid on behalf of the husband. When Goldberg included those amounts, she concluded that the funds available to the husband were approximately $450,000, $962,000, and $660,000 for each of the three years. In determining these figures, Goldberg had reviewed hundreds of pages and then summarized the information for each year. She testified that she had taken a very conservative approach and that her ultimate conclusion probably far understated the husband's true income.

The husband's attorney extensively cross-examined Goldberg and raised questions about the accuracy of her methodology. In particular, the witness was asked questions about possible cases of double counting.

On appeal, the husband argued that Goldberg's testimony should have been excluded because she was not a CPA. He pointed to a California statute that the practice of public accountancy included certification of reports or audits to be filed in court.

The appeals court rejected this contention, pointing out that trial courts have considerable latitude in weighing experts' qualifications. It went on to hold that a CPA license was not necessary since Goldberg's testimony did not amount to an "audit" or "examination" of the accounts within the meaning of the statute, in that she did not purport to verify the accuracy of the books. Since her testimony merely categorized the funds, the appeals court held that this did not amount to public accountancy for which a license was required. It went on to note that she appeared to be well qualified since she had a degree in accountancy, conducted a tax preparation and accounting business, had previous experience as an expert witness, and was an IRS enrolled agent. The appeals court noted that to practice before the IRS as an enrolled agent, one must pass an examination showing competence in tax matters and maintain competency through continuing education.

The husband also argued on appeal that the expert never attempted to meet with the husband to ascertain the source of funds. The appeals court noted that the documents examined were the husband's own books and records and that he had made no claim that they were inaccurate. The appeals court also pointed out that the husband was free to prepare his own interpretation of the same records, but he had not taken this step. It did note that the husband had the opportunity to cross-examine the expert and had done so at length. Therefore, the court of appeals held that the husband's objections went merely to the weight of the evidence and had been properly resolved by the trial court.

After concluding that Goldberg's testimony was properly admitted, the appeals court went on to examine the factors underlying the award of spousal support. It concluded that the award was amply supported by the evidence.

After addressing the other issues in the appeal, the court of appeals made a modification to a division of the wife's pension but otherwise affirmed the superior court's judgment.

Case Example: Income Determination Can Be Simple

Forensic accounting evidence does not need to be complicated to be effective. This is a perfect example of using simple financial analysis of deposits to prove a party's income.

The mother and father in this Louisiana child support income determination case[10] were married in Venezuela in 1995 and had two children. In 2001, they divorced in Venezuela, and the Venezuelan court awarded the mother primary physical custody and the father open visitation. The father was also ordered to pay child support. Both of the parents and the children later moved to the United States. The mother was living in Louisiana and the father in Texas when the father petitioned the Louisiana court for a specific visitation schedule. This was granted in 2009.

In 2012, a hearing was held on the wife's petition to modify custody and visitation. The trial court ruled on that matter in 2013, and the father was ordered to pay $2,365

10. De La Cruz Nezat v. Guzman, No. 2014 CU 0358 (La. Ct. App. Mar. 17, 2015).

per month in child support, retroactive to 2009, plus private school and medical expenses. The father then appealed to the Louisiana Court of Appeals.

The father argued that the trial court had erred in determining his income and that the record showed that he earned only $50,000 per year. The trial court had relied upon the testimony of the wife's expert, accountant Charles Theriot, who testified that records indicated the father's actual income was about $18,000 per month.

Theriot had analyzed the father's bank account statements and reviewed all deposits and withdrawals over a 19-month period. During that time, over $500,000 had been deposited, of which about $157,000 were transfers from one account to another. An additional approximate $20,000 was income from the father's current wife.

According to Theriot's analysis, this left about $345,000, more than $18,000 per month, which Theriot identified as the father's income. While Theriot was able to identify the source of many deposits, others were unidentified.

The father attempted to explain some of the unidentified deposits based upon how the banking system worked in Venezuela. He testified that he moved money for clients and that some of the funds shown in his accounts were interbank transfers of funds that did not belong to him.

But the appeals court noted that the lower court apparently had not believed these explanations. The trial court had noted that the father had previously earned $70,000 per year. Ultimately, the court set the father's income at $15,767 per month. The court relied on the average salary over a 52-month period as well as money that the father had received from his mother. After reviewing the evidence, the appeals court held that this figure was supported by the record, especially considering that the trial court had assessed the credibility of witnesses. It therefore unanimously affirmed the income determination. Since other portions of the lower court's order had been either affirmed or reversed (producing a dissenting opinion with respect to one issue), the appeals court remanded the case for further proceedings.

Case Example: Classic Income Determination

It may seem appropriate to simply average three years of income when attempting income determination cases that deal with varying annual incomes. However, forensic accountants should not neglect other relevant factors that can play a role in the determination.

The husband and wife in this New Jersey divorce case[11] were married in 2005 and had two children before their 2010 separation and divorce. At the time of the marriage, the wife, an attorney, worked for a New Jersey firm and had a salary of $102,000 per year. She was later hired by a New York firm, where she made a salary of $175,000 per year. However, she was laid off just before the birth of the couple's first child. The parties agreed that she would stay home to raise the children and possibly work part time. At the time of the parties' separation, she was working about 26 hours per week, earning $67.50 per hour. For a time, she was employed full time again, with a salary

11. Elrom v. Elrom, 439 N.J. Super. 424, 110 A.3d 69 (App. Div. 2015).

of about $80,000 per year, but lost that job prior to trial. She asked the court to impute her income at that amount.

The husband was a software engineer, technical writer, and web developer. Prior to trial, he earned a base salary of $120,000 per year, with a potential to earn up to $295,000 per year. He also owned a company that did consulting and sponsored an annual trade show.

The wife claimed that the husband hadn't been forthcoming with discovery regarding his income. She testified that the husband had income from clients "on the side" and royalties from a book. She discovered that he had recently started a company in Nevada. He had also withdrawn money from a business account and transferred it to an account in Andorra. The husband stipulated that the account in Andorra held almost $68,000.

The wife's expert witness was Larry Frankel, CPA, CFF, a forensic accountant. To calculate the husband's income, he examined the funds that had been deposited into the parties' bank accounts. He calculated that the husband's company had deposited over $900,000 for a three-year period. He concluded that the husband's profit, exclusive of taxes, was 70–80 percent of this amount. He reached this conclusion by assuming 20–30 percent for overhead.[12]

The husband offered the expert testimony of Gary Young, whose vocational evaluations addressed the likely earnings of the parties. He set the husband's likely earnings at $120,000 per year as a software engineer and technical writer. He based this on the husband's resume and a telephone interview, although he did not consider the husband's earning capacity as a consultant.

Although he did not interview her, Young testified that the wife's earning possibilities ranged between $108,000 and $178,000 per year. He conceded that he did not factor in parenting responsibilities.

The husband also offered the testimony of information technology recruiter Jonathan Klopchin. He pegged the husband's earning potential at between $100,000 and $165,000 per year, with some possibility of exceeding $200,000 per year.

The husband argued that Frankel's analysis of the bank deposits was flawed since some of the deposits had been rental receipts and

---

12. There was apparently no basis for this assumption provided in the opinion. Apparently, the husband never contested it at trial or on appeal. So, can one assume the amount favored the husband as compared to the account percentage?

funds that had been withdrawn and later redeposited. Although his 2010 income had been $252,000, he asserted that he no longer had some of the consulting fees and that another client had just terminated his services.

To compute support, the trial court had to set the income for each party. For the wife, it imputed income of about $80,000 per year, which was the salary she had earned at her last full-time job.

After considering the husband's previous earnings, the trial court declined his request to impute income of only $120,000 per year. Instead, the trial court used the approach of the wife's expert and imputed income based upon gross receipts, discounted by 20 percent to account for expenses. It found that the gross receipts for the most recent three-year period ranged between $257,000 in 2011 and $321,000 in 2010. The court imputed income based upon this three-year average.

The husband appealed. Among his arguments, he claimed that his imputed income was too high and the wife's was too low.

The husband first argued that imputed income is appropriate only in cases of intentional unemployment or underemployment, but the appeals court disagreed. Imputation of income can be appropriate in other cases, including cases where a party has failed to provide adequate financial information or cases where a party has control over earnings.

Here, the trial court found that the defendant had historically received earnings from a variety of sources, such as employment, consulting, and royalties. Frankel had reviewed the business deposits, and the trial judge had been in the best position to weigh credibility in light of claims that some of these income sources had dried up.

The trial court had called the husband's claims "borderline preposterous" in light of documented past earnings and noted that the vocational expert had completely ignored consulting and royalty income. Based upon its review of the evidence, the appeals court concluded that the trial court's findings were supported by the evidence. Looking at a three-year average of earnings was an acceptable approach.

The husband, who had appeared pro se at trial, also argued that the trial court should have appointed an expert to determine his earning capacity. But the appeals court pointed out that even though this might be proper in some cases, it was not required. The husband had failed to reveal all the relevant facts to even his own experts, which resulted in a distorted analysis. The evidence of the wife's expert, Frankel, was more than adequate to support the lower court's findings.

The income imputed to the wife was appropriate. Even though she had previously held higher-paying positions, it was proper for the lower court to consider that she had been dismissed from her previous position and also had parenting responsibilities. The husband also raised issues regarding child support and property division. The appeals court vacated a portion of the support award but otherwise affirmed the lower court's judgment.

Accounting for Lawyers 3

This chapter describes the basics of accounting and financial reporting, highlighting typical document flow. Understanding important key accounting concepts assists attorneys in communication with a business's accountant or with a forensic accountant. The more a lawyer knows about the relationship among business owners, management, certified public accountants (CPAs), chief financial officers, financial statements, internal reports, general ledgers, and tax returns, the more effective she can be in advancing the interests of her clients.

Some business owners are very close to their accountants. Some share hobbies, like traveling together on golf junkets or to watch The Masters golf tournament in Augusta, Georgia. Others maintain distance and independence. Because clients put food on accountants' tables, accountants will always feel a tension between remaining independent and pleasing their clients, regardless of ethical requirements. CPAs are human beings. When a client divorces, a few CPAs may even help to actively conceal financial statements, documents, money, and other truths about the client's finances or business. Even though only a small fraction of CPAs may ever engage in deceptive conduct, lawyers must develop a counterstrategy to deal with those CPAs who do attempt to deceive.

The material in this chapter is admittedly dry, but it is important. The concepts described form the conceptual framework needed to craft effective deposition, direct-examination, and cross-examination questions. Like law, accounting does not always lend itself to a linear progression. The concepts and terms presented herein are highlights from only several semesters of basic accounting courses. The goal of this chapter is to provide an overview of accounting concepts in the context of issues a family lawyer will most likely face when working with a forensic accountant or business valuation expert.

Key accounting terms used herein appear in boldface when they are first introduced. Before worrying too much about obtaining a complete understanding of each term, feel free to rely on your forensic accountant to put any term's meaning into context for your particular case. Also, there are many references herein to a "target." In the context of this book, the target of a lawyer and forensic accountant is, collectively, the opposing party/business owner and related closely held entities. For example, if one of the divorcing spouses is a business owner, the owner and business are collectively the target of the lawyer and forensic accountant working for the non–business owner's spouse. Or if a divorcing party is an important salesperson, the employer might help assist the salesperson by deferring income (i.e., sales commissions) until after the divorce. In this situation, the salesperson and the business he or she works for may also be collectively referred to as the target.

Accounting Basics

An **accounting information system** tells the business owner(s) and others about the financial position of the subject business. It begins with many, many transactions and ends in financial statements, tax returns, and/or audit opinions. In retail department stores, for example, businesses purchase inventory, make sales, and receive payments. In addition, stores pay the salespersons' base pay, their commissions, the rent, and for advertising. As described in more detail later, the store records the transactions in various ledgers, eventually resulting in a posting to a general ledger. The general ledger collects all transactions and forms the basis for assembling the information from various accounts to become financial statements. As part of that process, the numbers are used to complete sales tax, income tax, and other corporate tax returns.

Complying with today's record-keeping and financial reporting requirements can be very expensive, even for profitable businesses. Often, less profitable and smaller businesses have innocent reasons for not having adequate accounting systems. Forensic accountants know what record-keeping systems are appropriate for various-sized companies. CPAs have a great feel for not only what information should exist but also what will likely not exist given the size and profitability of a particular enterprise.

Cynics believe financial statements are merely window dressing that tells the users what business owners want them to believe. In general, this chapter explains and illustrates the functions businesses should perform with respect to accounting systems. The process of identifying, collecting, measuring, and communicating financial data is rarely simple. Not all businesses follow sound accounting practices. Many small businesses legitimately seek to cut corners to save costs.

Accounting information is used by internal users (ownership and management) and external users. If the ownership and management of a subject business are separate, you should not assume they are either independent or acting in concert. With any business, it can be very difficult to ever possess an accurate picture of the true interpersonal relationship that might exist between the two. The true natures of these relationships are rarely written down in a "smoking gun" memo.

In general, external users do not have direct knowledge of the true financial picture or what management sees in its own reports. Again, cynics may say external users never have any knowledge except for what management wants the picture to show. CPAs worry about foreseeable users. In general, foreseeable external users include the following:

1. Investors,
2. Potential investors,
3. Financial analysts,
4. Creditors (banks),
5. Vendors,
6. Customers,
7. Trade associations,

8. Stock exchanges,
9. Financial press,
10. Taxation authorities (IRS and state), and
11. Regulatory authorities (state and federal).

For external users to better rely on this information, the accounting profession creates its own set of theoretical principles and practical applications. **Generally accepted accounting principles (GAAP)** are a collection of accounting concepts and principles designed to ensure that financial statements are reliable, relevant, and as standardized as possible.

Know that accountants' ethics state that their first responsibility is to serve the public. The public includes nonclients. CPAs know that investors and creditors are the most likely foreseeable readers of the financial statements and other disclosures they prepare, certify, and issue. What makes financial statements audited by independent accounting firms so important is that CPAs as a group have tremendous professional integrity and a sincere fear of professional sanction for impropriety.

If there is a conflict between a duty of loyalty to the public and to a client, the CPA must side with the public. Independence is the first and foremost watchword. While the profession has had its difficult moments, there is no group with more credibility, integrity, and independence. As a lawyer developing a strategy in your case, you should assume that a CPA will comply with subpoenas and answer deposition questions truthfully. At the same time, you must be prepared to critically examine the responses provided and, eventually, to cross-examine the CPA on the stand.

Accountants who engage in **management accounting** generate **internal management reports,** often based on **cost accounting principles.** The reporting of financial information to be used by internal users need not conform to GAAP for several reasons:

1. The reporting is confidential.
2. External users will not rely on the reporting.
3. Relevant information may need to be comparable or meaningful for financial analyses comparing time periods only within the same company (e.g., for the purposes of computing sales bonuses), not between companies.

4. Management accounting reports are rarely reviewed by external CPAs.
5. There are many methods from which to choose when it comes to cost accounting and, therefore, internal reports are the easiest to manipulate.

Because of the ease of manipulating internal reports, if the target's management accountants voluntarily produce internally generated reports, forensic accountants should be very skeptical in relying upon them.

Financial statements and accompanying notes report the economic impact of completed business transactions. "Financial statements" is a term that can be used by different people to mean different things. To CPAs, it means the balance sheet, income statement, and, if prepared, the statement of cash flow. Smaller businesses may not create a statement of cash flow. Also, financial statements can include a statement of retained earnings. An example of a set of financial statements for a small business is offered in Appendix B. Notes and the accountant's report are not included.

The **balance sheet** reports a business's assets, liabilities, and owners' equity on a specific date. Think of this report as a static picture of the business at a particular instant in time, usually as of December 31. Sometimes, this is called the **statement of financial position.**

Other types of financial statements report operations over a period of time. The **income statement** reports revenues, gains, expenses, losses, and net income. This can also be called the **statement of income. The statement of retained earnings** reports changes in accumulated earnings. Finally, the **statement of cash flow** breaks down changes in cash during the period. The statement of cash flow provides information about inflow and outflow of cash, as well as an explanation for the cause of the inflow and outflow. By analyzing historical cash flow, users can make projections about future flow. Cash flow is broken into three main categories and miscellaneous subsections:

1. **Cash flow from operations.** Operations describe the primary purpose of the business. For a mature company, operations must generate significant cash or there will not be a business for long.
2. **Cash flow from investing activities.** Investing activities describe the sale or acquisition of operation facilities (plant, property, and equipment) and the sale or purchase of investments.

3. **Cash flow from financing activities.** Financing activities describe borrowing or ownership sales used to obtain cash for the business.

The single greatest advantage for a lawyer evaluating a target's business is that at least one of the end users will likely need to see a healthy business. For example, a bank providing a credit facility (loan, line of credit, letter of credit, etc.) will likely loan more money or charge a lower interest rate the better the financial position of the business. But some crafty targets understand this and can intelligently understate valuation of assets and personal net worth years in advance of a divorce to the minimum point of profitability needed for the credit facility. To the nonowner spouse, the risk of this strategy is greater if the target has a personal relationship with the lending entity's credit officer or does not need his entire net worth listed to qualify for needed credit. Also, the lawyer for the nonowner spouse must worry more if the target is well educated, has a master's degree in business administration with a concentration in finance, or is an investment banker.

Sophisticated business owners also meet one another at industry conferences. They brag and share successful asset protection strategies. Some cynics may say that "asset protection" is a phrase describing legally shielding assets from greedy future ex-spouses and/or potential creditors. Targets can also have experienced estate planning counsel and loyal tax advisors who have special interests in serving the target's long-term financial needs, regardless of the stated objectives.

Public Filing of Financial Statements

Before a company may issue new securities or sell securities across state lines pursuant to the Securities Act of 1933, it must prepare and publish a prospectus. A great deal of information must be provided, including the central focus of the prospectus—audited financial statements. Following the sale of securities, and as a matter of public record, there must be a filing of 10-K reports, which are audited financial statements, and 10-Q reports, which are unaudited quarterly statements.

For most publicly traded companies (large and small), these may be found on the Internet, often in an "investor relations" section of a company's website. For targets who are owners and/or key members of the management of publicly traded entities, be sure to read 10-Ks, 10-Qs, and related notes for updated information as the case progresses, especially if stock options are a major asset. Notes are discussed in more detail later. You will be surprised how much important information may be learned from notes to audited financial statements.

Accrual and Cash Basis

Most financial statements are prepared on the **accrual basis.** The accrual (or deferral) of a transaction helps match revenue and expenses to a given period of time. This "matching principle" helps provide readers with more reliable information. Under the accrual basis, transactions are recorded in the period in which the event occurs rather than when cash actually transfers. This recording (also called realization) creates a more reliable image of the operations during a given period. Although the goal is to match expenses with revenue, another goal is for the accounting methods to be consistently applied, also allowing for financial statements to be comparable across various time periods.

Cash-basis accounting involves recording transactions based only on the timing of actual cash payments and receipts. Most professional services businesses, such as law firms, are cash basis for income tax purposes. For example, when a law firm makes a copier lease payment, the payment is recorded as an expense in the period in which the check is issued, regardless of the month to which the payment related. If the firm were on an accrual basis, the invoice for a copier lease expense related to December operations might be paid late the following January. In that case, the expense would be recorded in December but also shown as a liability (payable) on the December 31 balance sheet. Keep in mind that firms can legitimately have two sets of books. A firm can keep a set of books for tax purposes (cash basis) and another set of books for management review (accrual basis).

On the revenue side, for accrual-basis financial statements, revenue is recorded only when there is a completion of the earnings process and collection is reasonably certain. For example, an accrual-basis law firm may record revenue billed to an insurance defense client when it is billed, rather than when it is later collected, because the effort generating the revenue occurred during the recording period and because collection is reasonably certain. For most family law firms, lawyers will normally record the revenue only when it is collected, for both financial statements and tax returns.

In accounting, there are always some close judgment calls. Generally accepted accounting principles require consideration of the principles first when making these judgment calls. For example, when deciding to accrue or defer a particular transaction, accountants are directed to be conservative. When in doubt, accountants should record or "book" expenses and defer recording revenue. This results in the least favorable result for the subject business. The conservative principle can work against the team investigating the target's accounting system because a target may want to depress results of operations shown on financial statements during periods of marital discord. In this case, being legitimately conservative may also help the target for divorce purposes. Forensic accountants know how this works and can devise methods to test for judgment calls that are overly aggressive when deferring revenue.

When preparing federal income tax returns, almost all businesses begin with the financial statements and make adjustments to them. In order to report the least amount of income, claim the most expenses legally allowed, and help clients legitimately save on taxes, honest and hardworking tax CPAs help businesses make these adjustments. Some adjustments are simple. If revenue received in the current tax year can be reported in a future year, it will be. Other adjustments may require judgment calls. For those judgment calls, the IRS may require evidence to substantiate adjustments appearing on the returns. Often, tax CPAs prepare complex calculations to justify these adjustments. These complex calculations may appear on supplemental schedules and may be attached to the filed returns. But many supporting schedules are not required to be filed with the return. If a tax CPA prepares such a supporting schedule but does not attach it to the return, the schedule will be stored in the tax CPA's client's file for safekeeping in the event the return is ever audited. In fact, the client may never be provided with a copy of the schedule or even know it exists.

As an example, increasing bad-debt expense is a favorite tactic of accrual-basis business owners. Determining what percentage of receivables is collectible entails a judgment call. Take the hypothetical company XYZ, Inc., for instance. Over the last five years, the estimated percentage of bad debt to ending-year accounts receivable averaged 4.5 percent. The tax returns for each of the previous five years reflected that constant percentage. In preparing the current tax return (the owner's divorcing year), the tax accountant for XYZ, increased the estimated bad-debt expense to 7.0 percent. To justify that increase to the IRS, the target's tax CPA charted the pattern, showing that, although there had been a 4.5 percent average over the most recent five-year period, the two most recent years' bad-debt expense had increased to 4.9 percent and 5.6 percent. The rest of the increase was based on the projected economic downturn. Increasing bad-debt expense reduces net income. That reduced net income obviously helps in the divorce—ultimately causing a reduced negotiated child support and alimony obligation. For tax and divorce purposes, targets can obtain a two-for-one benefit.

By making a dozen or so relatively minor judgment-call adjustments, say 2 percent of gross revenue here and 4 percent there, before you know it, real money is disappearing like magic from the divorcing-year income of XYZ's owner. The client's forensic accountant must be able to challenge some or all of the adjustments. To do that, he will need to review the tax returns, all supporting schedules (not just those filed with the tax return), all financial statements used to generate the returns, and possibly even the detailed general ledger. The company's general ledger will contain the detailed building blocks for the financial statements and tax returns. From there, the forensic accountant may be able to form an opinion helpful to the case.

They Call It "Accounting" Because of the Accounts

Financial transactions and economic-events information are recorded in accounts. Accounts describe specific assets, debts, revenues, and expenses, as well as any changes to them.

The following permanent accounts appear on the balance sheet:

1. Assets,
2. Liabilities, and
3. Owners' equity (general term).

The following temporary accounts appear on an income statement:

1. Revenues,
2. Expenses, and
3. Gains or losses.

The ending account balances for permanent accounts appear as beginning balances for the next year's accounting period. Temporary accounts are closed out at the end of a reporting period, and their balances begin at zero in the next period.

The **accounting equation** is assets = liabilities + owners' equity or assets – liabilities = owners' equity. All accounting is based upon a **double-entry system.** This system is the forensic accountant's best friend because out-of-balance books show their secrets. If an undergraduate accounting student really understands double-entry accounting, he will get an "A" in the first year. Although not terribly complex, this singular concept has turned many accounting major wannabes into marketing majors. The double-entry system records the following:

1. The change in a resource and
2. The source or reason for the change.

For example, when a law firm receives a $1,000 payment for legal services, this is recorded as

1. An increase in cash (of $1,000) and
2. An increase in revenue (of $1,000).

An important reason for the double-entry system is to make sure that the accounting equation remains in balance.

Journal entries are the tools by which accountants code information into the accounts. As discussed, GAAP provides the overarching theory behind journal entries. Transactions posted in accounts are the bricks with which financial statements are built—one at a time. **Debits** and **credits** help give organization to this austere but symmetrical symphony. These are accounting terms that the forensic accountant may use. In abstract, you may never need to know the distinction. If necessary, the forensic accountant can explain what you will need to know in the context of the particular problem at hand. **Adjusting journal entries (AJEs)** is the method of recording accruals and deferrals because they are not completed transactions.

Debits and credits are recorded for the balance sheet and income statement accounts. For example, an increase in assets (debits on the balance sheet) can occur in conjunction with an increase in liabilities (credits on the balance sheet). When a business purchases a vehicle with debt, the debit is recorded and the asset account increases. Also, the liability account is credited because the business owes the bank. The dollar amounts of the debit and credit entries equal. In another example, when an employee is paid cash, the payroll expense is recorded with a debit. Correspondingly, the cash account (an asset) is credited, reflecting the reduction in cash in the bank. Again, the amounts of the credited and debited transactions equal.

When transactions are transferred from journals to ledgers, they are posted. Posting may also alter some of the computerized data from a chronological format to account classification in the applicable ledger. There are two different types of ledgers. The **general ledger** is the collection of all transactions in all accounts. Your forensic accountant will almost always want complete access to this. The general ledger is grouped into accounts in a standardized order, from permanent accounts through temporary accounts. Each account is also numbered and categorized for reporting organization. **Subsidiary ledgers** are information-assembly stations. For example, specific customers may have separate subsidiary ledgers, but the sales recorded from all customers will appear in the general ledger collectively in a specific account. General ledger accounts are used to compile financial statements.

Divorce lawyers should know what general ledgers look like and what they can mean to forensic accountants. Every family lawyer's firm that compiles financial statements has general ledgers; they just aren't always printed out for the owner's review. Experienced forensic accountants can review the target's general ledger and perform a general review for entries that don't "smell right." Forensic accountants might review the general ledger to look for the following:

1. Nonroutine transactions with higher-than-normal dollar amounts,
2. Unnecessarily complicated transactions,
3. Adjusting entries clearing out account balances on unusual dates,
4. Owners' equity transactions,
5. Loans to and from the business and owners, and
6. "Usual suspects" expense accounts (e.g., travel, meals, marketing, and conferences).

Every accounting system is different. Some basic functions, however, are routine. The monthly or annual accounting routine can be comprised of the following:

1. Transactions and events occur.
2. Transactions are journalized.
3. Transactions are posted from the journal to the general ledger.
4. An unadjusted trial balance is prepared.
5. Adjusting journal entries (AJEs—accruals and deferrals) are made.
6. An adjusted trial balance is prepared.
7. Financial statements are prepared.
8. Closing entries are journalized to prepare for the next period.
9. After closing, a trial balance is created.
10. Reverse-adjusting journal entries are made.

In the context of the period end-closing, AJEs affect transactions that apply to more than one accounting period. Normally, most AJEs are routine and are made the same way (and reversed the same way, too) every period. AJEs come in two flavors: deferrals and accruals. **Deferrals** adjust cash before expense and revenue recording. For example, at the end of the year, if a law firm prepays its January rent in December, the accountant may reduce the rent expense and show the prepayment as an asset. Then in January, the rent expense is increased and the prepaid rent asset is removed. This deferral is made so that the law firm shows 12 months of rent payments on its financial statements rather than 13 months. The rent expense is accurately recorded on the financial statements.[1] The deferral is that portion of the expense that applies to another time period.

Accruals account for cash flows that occur after the current period. Accrual adjustments are made because cash is to be received in another period, but all or part of the payment applies to efforts completed in the current period. An example is payroll that is payable to the staff owed at year's end but that won't be paid until the next year. Yet another example is interest revenue accrued but not received. The amount due

1. This example can also illustrate an important difference between financial-statement preparation and tax returns. If the law firm is a cash-basis taxpayer, that firm may claim a deduction of 13 months of rent payments in a single tax year. The following year, or prior year, if only 11 months' payments were made, the firm may deduct only 11 payments, even though there were 12 months in the year.

at the period's end will be shown as interest receivable. Examples of other adjusting journal entries include

1. Estimations of bad-debt expense,
2. Recognition of inventory losses due to theft or spoliation,
3. Accounting errors, and
4. Cost-of-goods-sold adjustments.

"Extraordinary items" is an accounting term of art describing a gain or loss. If material, the transaction or event should be reported in the notes to financial statements. Know that, for an item to be extraordinary, it must be both unusual and infrequent. GAAP takes into account the need for financial statements to be comparable among periods. Whether a financial statement is prepared for an investor or a lender, CPAs anticipate that financial analysts will be critically plying their trade. An extraordinary item prevents periods from being comparable. For example, if an earthquake damaged a company's plant and repairs required a shutdown of operations for six weeks, the financial result will be devastating for that year, even if all other aspects of that year's results were outstanding. In theory, because earthquakes are unusual and infrequent, financial analysts may "back out" those expenses to predict future profits from operations.

What is **"material"**? "Materiality" may be the most vaguely defined term in accounting. Roughly translated, if an error or contingent event is, in the judgment of the CPA, material, then it must be reported. For example, if the potential loss of a lawsuit can adversely affect the business, it should be recorded as a contingent liability and/or reported in the notes to audited financials. In another context, if an accounting error does not materially misstate the earnings of the business, the error may not need to be corrected. Divorce lawyers should understand that materiality is subjective. The forensic accountant knows to keep a close eye on all noted transactions and errors not deemed material.

Intangible assets and **intellectual property** are asset descriptions or categories that can appear on balance sheets. Intellectual property includes patents, trademarks, copyrights, and trade secrets. Intangible assets include all types of intellectual property and goodwill. Also, know that intangible assets often exist and still do not appear on a financial statement because GAAP says not to record them.

Intangible assets are strange animals in the accounting world. Accountants struggle to handle them correctly. In today's information age, intangible assets, including intellectual property, can comprise the target's most important assets. In fact, some of the most valuable assets of a target's business may not appear on its balance sheet simply because there may not be a reliable method of valuing it. In general, accounting principles require an arm's-length transaction to establish the value of an asset. And unless the intangible asset has been purchased, GAAP may not allow it to be recorded.

Discovering the existence and importance of intellectual property can be exceptionally challenging, and a failure to identify the true value of these very real business assets could make a huge difference in the overall outcome of a divorce. For example, take a business that recently developed a patent. The expense for developing the patent appeared in the company's expenses over a four-year period. But that patent may not appear on the balance sheet as an asset, even though the business expects the patent to generate hundreds of thousands of dollars of revenue annually. If the assets are valuable enough, consider hiring a specialized appraiser just for the intellectual property.

Professional judgment plays an important role in evaluating and recording many transactions. For example, if a target's business pays $1,000,000 for another business appraised at $750,000, should the asset be recorded at $1,000,000 or at $750,000 on the balance sheet? The target's accountant may list the difference of $250,000 as goodwill. Another factor in the accounting decision may revolve around maximizing tax benefits. When evaluating questionable transactions recorded in various financial records, the forensic accountant may have to perform some investigation or research to determine how a transaction should have been recorded in comparison to how it was recorded.

If you are not knowledgeable about business in general, you should try to learn. Every business has at least one **driver.** "Driver" is a general business term, not an accounting term, describing what brings business in the door. For Coca-Cola, advertising increases sales. For new cars, recommendations from existing owners are key. Law firms have rainmakers. A target may have strategic advantages that include intellectual property or some trade secret. Figure it out. To learn about business, *Inc.* magazine and *The Wall Street Journal* are good places to start. Talk business with business owners. Also, learn about stocks and related financial analyses. Watch wacky stock-picking TV shows. Learning the language of business is always helpful.

In general, many assets are subject to **depreciation**[2] because they will not last forever. An asset is depreciated or "written off," reducing its value as an asset over a period of time determined as its "useful life," often three or five years. Depending on the type of asset, it is depreciated (or, for natural resources, depleted) by utilization of one of many different methods. Some methods are very complicated. Making sure the right method is used is part of a CPA's job.[3] For example, oil and gas reserves are treated differently than computers. And most assets have very specific depreciation rules for tax return purposes. Changing depreciation methods in a divorcing year may be a giant red flag because that change may greatly depress claimed net income. **"Amortization"** is a very similar concept, but it is a term more often used to describe reduction in intangible assets, such as goodwill (discussed later), and reduction of debt by regular payments of interest and principal sufficient to pay off a loan.

"Capitalizing" cash outlay can involve purchasing something and, instead of showing the cash paid out as an expense, recording it as an asset. Unless the asset is liquid, it will likely be **depreciated** over time. A very basic example may be the cash purchase of a delivery truck. For tax purposes, the truck must be recorded as an asset and depreciated over a period of years. That depreciation in future years results in a deduction in those future years, even though the cash was expended only in the year in which the asset was purchased.

---

2. Your state's child support guidelines and case law may allow exclusion of depreciation as an expense for purposes of income determination. This means that depreciation may be added back to determine income. Review those rules (and case law interpreting them) with your client's forensic accountant and ask for input. Explaining your client's argument in negotiations and/or court may require the assistance of an expert.

3. Depreciation is not designed to accurately reflect any particular asset's fair market value. It is an accounting concept to assist with a conservative presentation of financial statements. An asset that is "fully depreciated," shown on financial statements as having no value, may have value and might be sold for substantial sums of money. While businesses use one depreciation method for a particular asset for tax return preparation, another method for the same asset may legitimately be used for financial statements. Also, smaller businesses may, to reduce the need for adjusting entries, choose to account for depreciation on their financial statements the same way they do for tax purposes.

Compare this to leased assets. For certain types of leased assets, depending on accounting rules or federal income tax law, the accounting for the asset may require it be capitalized, shown as an asset, and depreciated over time, even though the asset is owned by another company. Depending on the specific structure of the lease, this may be referred to as a **"capital lease."** Many businesses may lease assets instead of purchasing them outright to take advantage of very specific tax rules that allow deducting cash outlay in the period in which the cash expense is actually paid, reducing tax liability.

Examples of transactions in which a cash outlay can result in a capitalized intangible asset include purchasing a patent or copyright, making a business acquisition, and incurring associated legal fees. Also, legal fees to protect the value of an intellectual property right may be capitalized under certain circumstances to comply with the matching principle required by GAAP. Expenses generally not capitalized include research and development and marketing expenses.

Depending on the amount, of course, the accounting judgment call of whether to capitalize expenses incurred for an asset may have a huge impact on a target's income statement. For tax purposes, the Internal Revenue Code has very strict rules and interpretations relating to these transactions. In situations in which a business capitalizes assets purchased, the Internal Revenue Code may require that the company defer associated expenses over a period of time, often resulting in a greater tax liability for the year the cash was actually expended compared to the liability owed if the company were allowed to deduct the entire amount of the cash outlay in the year the money was paid. All companies should legitimately want to deduct as much expense as soon as legally allowed in order to reduce tax liability. But for financial statement purposes, capitalizing outlay, and not showing the cash outlay as an expense, improves the results of operations. Remember, even though both financial statements and tax returns are often provided to lenders, the ability to show greater profits results in greater borrowing ability and lower interest rates. But in a divorcing year, the target may want to depress earnings on both the financial statements and tax returns, getting that "two-for-one" benefit—lowered tax liability and reduced claimed income available for support.

It is also important to know that an accounting department may legitimately generate multiple sets of books for a company. Even if the business owner's spouse says that the business owner mentioned having "three sets of books" prior to the divorce, having three sets may not be inappropriate. For example, many companies may have one set to show the public and lenders, a second set for tax purposes, and a third set for management analysis using an alternative cost accounting method. As long as the public, including investors and banks, are not shown the financial statements compiled using the alternative cost accounting method, there may be no improprieties in having three sets of books.

What may make the forensic accountant's or business valuation expert's ears perk up, however, is learning about the existence of a fourth or fifth set of books. For example, if the business compiles one set of books for the banks, another for the IRS, a third for management to analyze, and a fourth to show investors,[4] did the accounting department also engineer a fifth set of books specifically to be produced in discovery for the divorce? That would be a dangerous game to play. The primary reason why forensic accountants often spend a great deal of time comparing financial statement information provided to them is to catch this ploy. If the financial records produced in discovery differ from those provided to the IRS, the failure to correctly capitalize assets could stick out like a sore thumb. If you can prove that the business owner "cooked the books" for divorce purposes, you can destroy that business owner's credibility. That is because this sort of accounting manipulation will usually result in much less income being declared than was actually earned.

Deferred charges result from the prepayment of long-term expenses to be incurred in the future. Again, the reason for the deferral is to report the economic event in the appropriate period. Deferred charges are allocated over more than one year, and prepaid expenses are generally expended within one year.

In a business context, **liquidity** refers to the ability of a business to operate and pay its debts. Banks and other financial institutions offering credit facilities to businesses are very concerned with liquidity. Lawyers can benefit from understanding some basic concepts credit officers and business valuators often consider when analyzing financial information. The forensic accountant can certainly take the lead

4. In general, investors should be presented with the same set of financial statements shown to the rest of the public and to financial institutions lending money to the business.

with these issues. In an economic sense, there are two forms of capital: equity and debt.

Many businesses with smart concepts fail because they are inadequately capitalized. Often, business owners count on future profits to capitalize business ventures, failing to understand that capitalizing with profits is expensive because it requires using post-tax dollars. So to create $75,000 of capital, before paying any profits to the owner, as much as $100,000 in profits may be required. This can create problems if the owner wants to eat and pay a mortgage at the same time. Because of this problem, many business owners turn to debt for capital. Debt, however, creates its own set of problems. Every business experiences some downward business cycles. In an economic downturn, exhausting available credit for capital needs can be deadly.

Current liabilities are debts expected to be paid within one year. **Current assets** are generally liquid assets, including assets that can be converted to cash within a relatively short period of time, and include prepaid assets. **Working capital** is the difference between current assets and current liabilities. Current assets divided by current liabilities is defined as the **working capital ratio.** These figures help measure businesses' ability to pay bills and keep going.

Audits, Reviews, and Compilations

If financial statements are issued with the assistance of a CPA, the assistance provided must be characterized as a

1. Compilation,
2. Review, or
3. Audit.

Compilations involve a CPA firm assisting in compiling financial statements in conformity with GAAP, but that is all. The CPA firm does not check the work and does not certify to the accuracy of the financial statements in any way.

Audits are the thing. In a sense, audits are the CPA's seal of approval. The physical result of an audit is the CPA's opinion letter. Financial statements are always the representation of management, and when CPAs audit them, they are not checking to detect fraud. Audits do tell those who rely on the financial statements that they can be fairly certain that the accounting methods are correct and internal controls are adequate. Lawyers must understand that, if management wants to commit fraud, an audit may not catch it. Accounting malpractice cases result from end users, stockholders, or lenders suing the CPA who "signed off" on the audited financial statements when the accounting firm should not have done so.

Reviews are not nearly as common as audits and compilations. Reviews generally involve CPAs performing some specific testing for a specific end user. The specific testing can also be called **agreed-upon procedures.** In any event, if a review is being performed for the target's business, the forensic accountant should be able to help the lawyer understand why. Reviews involve less work than audits, although both serve an attestation function. Compilations require very little effort on the part of the CPA compared to audits and reviews.

Audits can be the divorce lawyer's mother lode of information. No business wants annual audits because they are time consuming and expensive. Audits are completed because someone or something important requires them, such as

1. Ownership not involved in management (e.g., stockholders),
2. A credit facility, and
3. Securities regulations for publicly traded companies.

When financial statements are audited, an **audit opinion** is issued. The opinion letter is just a few paragraphs. Considerable time and money are spent for this letter to declare that the financial statements are presented fairly in accordance with GAAP.

Audited financial statements will almost always include required **disclosure notes** (also called **notes** or **disclosures**). These provide summarized explanations of important financial situations and nonfinancial considerations. Often, auditors draft the notes for the business. Examples include

1. Significant accounting policies and changes therein,
2. Pension plan details,
3. Maturity dates for debts and receivables,
4. Credit facility requirements and restrictions,
5. Effects of major future events, and
6. Contingent liabilities (pending lawsuits).

Notes relate only to items that are material to the overall financial picture. For example, Disney is not going to be required to disclose a detected fraud scheme that resulted in a $100,000 loss because Disney's annual revenue is close to $55 billion. The loss is not material. The notes help give readers a complete economic picture of a company's financial affairs. Notes can refer to any of the schedules in the financial statements. Some notes may not refer to any particular financial figure. For example, a contingent liability (pending lawsuit) may be described and disclosed but indicate that no liability amount has been determined. If the chances of the opposing party prevailing are remote, the contingent liability amount may not be listed.

The very first (or last) page of an audited set of financial statements is the **auditor's report** (or **accountants' report** or **independent accountants' report**). The opinion letter has three sections:

1. Introductory paragraph,
2. Scope paragraph, and
3. Opinion paragraph.

Financial statements are the representation of management's accounting. The audit report is an opinion about the financial statements, specifically whether the auditors agree with the accounting methods used by management. There are four possible types of letters:

1. Unqualified opinion (nicknamed "clean" opinion),
2. Qualified opinion,
3. Adverse opinion, and
4. Disclaimer of opinion.

The family lawyer need only understand that clean opinions are what a target needs and usually gets. If the auditor requires adjustments to the financial statements for a clean opinion to be issued, management usually makes them. With some audits, management may make all suggested changes. If any opinion was issued other than clean (unqualified), the forensic accountant will know to be on alert.

Changes in accounting firms handling an audit can be a red flag. The most common reason for the change in firms is cost. Back in the day though, companies rarely saw changes in auditors because management wanted the relationship's longevity to demonstrate stability.

In today's post-Enron world, however, failure to change auditors can be an unspoken tip that management and the auditors are too chummy. Another reason for a change in auditors could be that the previous auditor issued an opinion other than an unqualified opinion or required changes to the financial statements that angered management.

Forensic accountants know all of this. Always look to CPAs for help when planning difficult cross-examination of other CPAs. They know what answers sound right and what answers are gobbledygook. The difference between winning and losing a trial may be as simple as understanding when one piece of a puzzle does not fit with another. Almost any time a scheme or scam is caught, it's usually because one small piece to the puzzle didn't fit or some question went unanswered when the answer should have been simple.

Case Example: Income Determination the Hard Way

Family lawyers and forensic accountants must always be prepared to do their best with the documents and information presented to them. In the case discussed below, a business owner failed to provide adequate and accurate financial records but still proceeded to complain that the outcome of the case was not in his favor. The failure to produce accurate financial records may be used against the nonproducing party in court. How expenditures can be used to prove income and business valuation is discussed in detail below.

The mother and father in this California divorce case[5] were married in 1987 and had three children together when the mother filed a petition for dissolution in 1998. The next year, the parties agreed that the father would pay monthly family support of $3,158. This support would terminate upon the mother's remarriage. The court reserved all other issues, and the mother continued to reside in the family home, which was owned by the father's parents. In

5. *In re* Fry, No. B179920 (Cal. Ct. App. Sep. 20, 2006).

2000, the mother remarried and moved into a home with her new husband. In 2003, the court modified the order to require monthly child support of $1,856 from the father.

The primary asset in question was the business operated by the father, a waste disposal business. The mother asked that the business be valued as of the date of separation.

The wife's expert witness was Mark Kohn, CPA, who specialized in forensic accounting. Kohn testified that he had requested financial documents relating to the business, including accounts receivable, aging reports, bank statements, canceled checks, invoices, customer lists, tax returns, and general ledgers. He testified that he received partial information for the period from 1998 to 2000 but that the records were insufficient to allow him to make an informed opinion as to the value of the business in 2003.

His analysis of bank records indicated that the business may have been grossing between $3.5 and $4 million per year between 1999 and 2000. However, the tax returns showed that the net or taxable income was less than $30,000 per year.

The father testified that despite his best efforts, he was unable to keep the business going when it lost its lease in 2003. He testified that the primary assets were 50–60 disposal bins, and he had transferred these to another entity to pay a business debt. The entity in question actually belonged to his father.

Even before the business shut down, the father testified that there had been a significant downturn in business. He testified that even though he didn't know the exact figures, the revenues kept going down while expenses kept going up. No tax returns were prepared after 1999, and the father offered no documents to confirm these statements.

The father did concede that most of his personal living expenses were paid from the company's checking account.

The employee who handled bill paying between 2001 and 2003 testified that she kept account records on a computer but never ran a report or provided financial reports to any accountant. She testified that she didn't necessarily keep a copy of paid bills and that bank statements were kept in a desk drawer but not organized. She did remember paying personal expenses such as private school tuition and the mortgage payment. She also testified that the bank account was usually negative and that there were more bills than money each month. However, she had no documents to support that statement.

After hearing the evidence, the trial court first ruled that the valuation of the business would be as of the date of the separation in 1998. It noted that the business value was based mostly on the father's efforts and that there had been a willful refusal to deliver the necessary documents to establish the value at the time of trial.

At the trial, on the valuation issue, Kohn testified that he had not received sufficient reliable financial records to calculate the value in the usual manner. Instead, he based his opinion of the company's income and value upon the couple's expenditures. Based upon lifestyle and expense information provided by the mother, he concluded that the couple lived like those earning $500,000 per year but reduced that figure to $375,000 in his calculations.

He then subtracted $100,000 as a reasonable salary for the father and subtracted an additional $41,000 representing return on equity to arrive at $234,000. He multiplied this number by three to come up with $700,000 as the value of the goodwill of the business. He arrived at a similar value for the goodwill by starting with a monthly gross income of $173,000, assuming disposal fees of 37.5 percent and using a multiplier of 6.5.

After calculating the value of the goodwill, Kohn added in the value of assets obtained from the tax returns and subtracted documented debt. He thus arrived at a total value of the business of $1.113 million. He did not subtract debt allegedly owed to the father's father, since he found nothing to authenticate it as a valid debt.

The father called his own expert witness, appraiser Ben Eubanks. However, the trial court struck this testimony on the grounds that Eubanks lacked the necessary training, education, and experience.

The trial court adopted Kohn's valuation and held that the business was worth $1.113 million. The trial court noted that some doubts were raised during cross-examination, but, due to the father's evasiveness and dishonesty, all doubts would be resolved against him.

Because the $1.113 million business and other assets had been attributed to the father, he was ordered to make an equalizing payment of over $463,000 to the mother. The father was also ordered to pay child support and private school tuition. He then appealed to the California Court of Appeals.

The father first argued that the lower court had erred in setting the value of the business as of the date of separation, but the appeals court agreed with the lower court that the "bad bookkeeping" necessitated this date for the valuation. It noted that this is true even if the bad bookkeeping is not intentional. Instead, the controlling factor is that a party should not be allowed to benefit from confusion for which he or she is responsible.

The appeals court agreed that the inability to set the value as of the time of trial was unquestionably due to the father's failure to produce organized and coherent records, and it did not matter whether the failure was deliberate or due to sloppiness. The appeals court held that this constituted sufficient cause to set the value as of the earlier date.

The father than attacked Kohn's opinion on the grounds that the methodology was "spurious." He argued that a better result could have been obtained by researching the market to determine what such businesses sold for based upon the ownership of trucks and dumpster bins.

But none of the witnesses in the case—including those favorable to the father—had suggested this method of valuation. The father's father, who was also in the disposal business, suggested one multiplier on long-term accounts and another multiplier for short-term accounts. Kohn had used this method in addition to his original calculation and had come up with a similar result.

The appeals court also pointed out that even though the father pointed to a number of potential discrepancies in Kohn's calculation, he did not follow up with specific arguments as to how these affected the final calculation. The appeals court concluded that the few potential mistakes did not change the outcome.

The father also criticized Kohn's testimony in that it had relied upon the couple's lifestyle, such as their ownership of a yacht. The appeals court agreed that financial documents would have been a better method. However, those documents were simply unavailable because they had not been maintained, and there were no backup documents. The use of the lifestyle evidence was further supported by the father's admission that most family expenses were paid out of the company account. Thus, it was reasonable to establish that income by looking at the amount of those expenditures. The appeals court reiterated that since the father had made a traditional valuation impossible by failure to keep or produce business records, he could not complain that the expert had to use an alternative method.

While the appeals court did go on to reverse the child support calculation, it affirmed all other orders, including the property distribution.

Case Example: Importance of Hiring Your Own Expert

If a forensic accountant's testimony is adverse to your client, as a family lawyer you should consider advising the client to engage another expert witness to challenge that adverse testimony. This applies even if the forensic accountant is court appointed or joint appointed.

The father and mother in this California child support case[6] were married in 1998 and had two sons. They were divorced in 2003 and resolved many of the property issues at that time. However, they continued to reside together until 2011, when the mother moved out. The father went to court in 2012 to request a formal custody order. At that time, he also requested child support based on his claim that the mother earned significantly more than he did. He was originally granted child support, but eventually the mother countered with bank statements showing that the father had deposited over $150,000 in 2011, despite an income tax return showing a gross income under $40,000.

---

6. *In re* Marriage of Moon and Ma, No. A148336 (Cal. Ct. App. Apr. 25, 2018). This case is unpublished and may be cited or relied upon in California only in certain very limited circumstances.

The mother requested that the court appoint a forensic accountant to sort out the discrepancy.

After resolving some other issues in the case, the court appointed forensic accountant Leslie Dawson, CPA, to analyze the father's earning history. Approximately eight months later, Dawson provided the court and the attorneys with a report summarizing her findings. She concluded that the father's annual income in 2012 was over $96,000, as opposed to the $24,000 he had claimed. She computed his average annual income at $108,000. The father also received money from friends and family, and when those sums were included, the 2012 income was almost $118,000, making his average annual income over $130,000. Based upon this information, the father stopped receiving child support, and a trial was held on the remaining issues in the case, including whether the father would be required to pay child support himself.

At trial, Dawson testified consistently with her prior report. She had uncovered four sources of income. Income from his job as an insurance broker had been reported on the tax returns. However, Dawson also uncovered rental income for a duplex, income from car sales, and payments from friends and family. Dawson noted that during 2012, the father had sold 28 cars and none of this income had been reported on tax returns.

The father offered little in the way of rebuttal testimony. Some of his friends testified that the payments from them had been loans. One of the friends testified that the father was a car "hobbyist" who had bought and sold "cool" cars for the past 25 years.

After addressing some of the remaining property issues, the trial court ordered child support based upon Dawson's findings. The father was ordered to pay $1,089 per month in child support, plus arrearages. He was also ordered to pay back the child support that had been paid to him. The father then appealed.

On the child support issue, the father argued on appeal that the expert witness's findings were unreliable since she relied upon income information from 2011 and 2012, even though the hearing was held in 2015. He called the reports "historical data" and argued that it was improper to use this information to determine his current income. He argued that the lower court should instead have used the income and expense declaration that he filed, which showed a much lower monthly income.

The appeals court first pointed out that the 2015 income declaration was very similar to the one he had submitted in 2012 and that the forensic accountant had shown that the earlier declaration significantly understated his income. The appeals court agreed with the lower court that this supported an inference that the 2015 declaration contained similar deficiencies. It also noted that evidence supported the conclusion that the car sales, rental income, and transfers from family and friends were continuing. The father's arguments went only to the weight of the evidence and did not render Dawson's conclusions insufficient.

The father also argued on appeal that the lower court had erred in appointing the forensic accountant in the first place. He claimed prejudice because Dawson was characterized as a court-appointed expert but "functioned as an expert witness for" the mother. He argued that the court "was giving [him] the direction that he could not obtain his own expert witness." The appeals court quickly rejected this argument. The relevant court rule allowed the appointment of an expert witness. The expert's report was available for more than a year before trial, and "[n]othing prevented [the father] from obtaining his own expert to rebut her testimony."

Case Example: S Corporation Problems

A child support modification case from Maryland[7] exposed problems inherent in determining a parent's income as minority owner of a subchapter S corporation.[8]

The trial court's judgment was reviewed by the court on the mother's motion for reconsideration. The court vacated the judgment and remanded for further proceedings, namely, to determine the father's actual income and the mother's request for an award of attorney's fees.

In analyzing the wife's appeal, the court focused on whether the trial court erred or abused its discretion by disregarding or minimizing the father's small business income, relying heavily on the forensic accountant's testimony.

The couple's 1995 child support agreement had the father paying 75 percent of the two children's daycare

7. Walker v. Grow, 170 Md. App. 255, 907 A.2d 255, 2006 Md. App. LEXIS 78.

8. Subchapter S corporations are often referred to as S corps. For more information, see www.IRS.org and instructions for the 1120S form.

costs plus $925 per month. When the children were 12 and 14 years old, their mother petitioned for increased monthly support because the children's needs and the father's income had increased, resulting in a material change of circumstance.

The mother, as residential parent, was a county attorney in the Pro Se Project. The father was chief operating officer and 30 percent minority shareholder of Aliron Int'l, Inc. (Aliron). On his 2003 federal income tax return, the father's taxable income was $277,175. However, his financial statement for support calculations stated gross monthly wages of $12,360.25 (or $148,323 per year). Aliron paid for his and his children's health insurance, his cell phone, and costs of overseas business trips.

Gabrielle Kaufman, CPA, testified as a forensic accounting expert and also testified regarding her personal knowledge as tax preparer for both the husband and Aliron. She described the nuances of Aliron as a subchapter S corporation and its tax impact on the husband. Under tense questioning from the judge, Kaufman verified the accuracy of the husband's financial disclosure despite the apparent disconnect from adjusted gross income (AGI) on his 2003 tax return.

In this "above guidelines" child support analysis, the trial court determined the father's monthly income to be $12,442 and mother's to be $4,165 for a total combined adjusted actual income of $16,607 per month.

The court criticized, but did not overrule, the trial court's method of extrapolating from the statutory schedule in resetting the father's monthly payments at $1,609. So long as neither arbitrary nor based upon incorrect legal principles, child support orders are within the sound discretion of the trial court when parents' adjusted actual income exceeds the $10,000 per month scheduled maximum in the guidelines.

In computing the father's actual income, the mother contended the trial court erred in not including pass-through corporate income. Actual income is income from any source, including income from a closely held corporation.

Kaufman explained how the husband's tax returns as an Aliron shareholder did not provide his correct and actual income. The "whole purpose of being an S Corporation is to avoid double taxation." Essentially, the corporation pays no tax at the corporate level. Instead, its earnings pass through to the shareholders who must report profits and losses on their state and federal income tax returns.

The CPA testified how federal returns do not reflect shareholders' actual income. The husband did not "technically receive" the income reported on his returns. First, as minority shareholder he had no right to force a distribution. Second, Aliron had to retain cash to fund its ordinary and necessary business expenses—operations, payroll, and bills.

Illustrating her point, Kaufman provided a 1040 tax return without pass-through income retained by Aliron and also the husband's actual shareholder Schedule K-1 (2003). From the K-1, Kaufman subtracted

- Ordinary income or loss from trade or business activities;
- Rental real estate, royalties, partnerships, S corporations, trusts, and the like;
- Investment income;
- Tax-exempt interest income;
- Charitable contributions;
- Section 179 expense deduction; and
- Property distributions, including cash.

Subchapter S corporations may pay estimated tax payments directly to the IRS on the shareholder's behalf. In that situation, the owner is not taking home that money for purposes of child support's parental income determination. Kaufman testified that most distributions were related to quarterly estimated tax payments made on profits from the current year's income and, possibly, from some business investments. She calculated the father's actual annual income to be $149,359, done within a reasonable degree of accuracy. The trial judge had Kaufman repeat her calculations on the stand, which she did. She started with an AGI of $272,835 from the husband's actual 2003 tax return and made subtractions using the judge's calculator, arriving at $149,359.

Ultimately the trial court found the husband's income to be slightly less than Kaufman calculated. The support award was based on his actual income of $12,442 per month or $149,304 per year.

The court held the trial court did not err in admitting Kaufman as an expert witness to assist the court in understanding the evidence or determining a fact at issue in the case. Kaufman was qualified as a CPA and an "expert on tax planning and consulting for closely held corporations."

Nor did the trial court err in relying on Kaufman's calculation despite her unfamiliarity with Maryland's statutory definition of actual income for child support calculations. Forensic accountants who testify do not necessarily need to be experts in family law legal concepts in order testify as to an expert opinion. The forensic accountant always has his or her hands full when testifying regarding complex analysis and reconciling among family law legal concepts, individual and corporate income tax law, and general accounting principles. Noting the trial court's authority to "believe or disbelieve, accredit or discredit" any part of an expert's testimony, the court would not second-guess the weight accorded the evidence.

The court held that "distributions from an S corporation that are used to fund necessary business related investments are not required to be included in the computation of the parent's actual income." The trial court may consider whether subchapter S income on the parent's tax return was actually received or was pass-through income unavailable to pay child support.

As a rule in Maryland, like many other states, a parent's pass-through income should not be included unless he or she is using the corporate form as a shield to manipulate income and avoid child support. The trial court considered pass-through income and distributions as "ordinary and necessary [business] expenses required to produce income and not income available to the parent." There was no attempt by the father to use the subchapter S entity to avoid paying child support. The trial court did not err or abuse its discretion in determining the father did not actually receive money retained by Aliron or distributed to him so he could pay his personal tax liability on Aliron's earnings or business investments (including the Aliron office building).

The court remanded the case for examination of the father's other income sources, review of certain child-related expenses, and to determine whether the wife should be awarded her attorney's fees.

4 The Hunt for Hidden Assets—Red Flags, Schemes, Scams, Lies, and Damn Lies

Many books and articles have been written for lawyers and forensic accountants about searching for hidden assets in divorce. Experienced forensic accountants know what to look for and where to look for them. This chapter is crafted to help lawyers obtain needed documentation, to explain why certain documents are essential, to demonstrate how to listen for red flags from clients, to make it easier to interface with the accountant working the case, to aid in explaining the work to the client, and to enable lawyers to understand the role of the forensic accountant's report.

At their most basic, like any other type of lie, financial lies come in two forms: commission and omission. Financial statements can be false because of both types of lies. A very simple lie of commission is lying on an interrogatory concerning the balance of an investment account. Lies of omission constitute nondisclosure. An example of nondisclosure is a failure to disclose that a brokerage account exists. Nondisclosure can be the most challenging type of lie to explain to courts. Without a brokerage account statement, how do you prove the account exists? Understanding lies and their overall importance in divorce cannot be separated from an understanding of human nature. Evidence comes from documents. Many documents come from discovery. Without discovery, there may be no evidence. What comes first, the chicken or the egg? It may well be the documents.

In divorce, some bad actors refuse to provide even basic discovery, such as credit card statements and cell phone records. In a motion to compel, a judge may ask you why certain documents are needed. Your opposing counsel might claim the document search is a fishing expedition or is otherwise unduly burdensome. The judge may then go one step further, asking whether there is evidence of wrongdoing or an affair. This is human nature—curiosity. At its most basic, where will the evidence of adultery or dissipation most likely be found? In credit card statements and cell phone statements. Then it's up to you to be a strong and relentless advocate for your client.

The Continuum of Lies

Some targets lie. For the purposes of this book, business owners and their businesses are collectively referred to as targets. The two cannot be separated because of the control owners have over their businesses. The target is capable of coordination. Is deferring income recognition hiding assets? What about inappropriate expenses? What if the IRS does not object to deduction of travel and entertainment expenses paid by the target at a conference? What if the target's girlfriend is an employee? The forensic accountant's investigation must take into account all of these aspects. One of the first steps to putting the investigation into context is understanding that there is a continuum of lies. Some lies are worse than others. If the liar is caught, some lies come with harsher penalties than others. You need to ask your client early on this important series of questions: Is the target bold enough to

- Lie on company expense reimbursement forms?
- Manipulate company books?
- Conspire with a low-level employee to alter company books?
- Lie on state sales tax returns?
- Create dummy vendors and pay expenses from the company to the dummy?

- Enlist co-owners' help to secrete nontaxable income in cash?
- Form offshore legal entities to hold siphoned cash?
- Conspire with the company's inside certified public accountant (CPA)?
- Conspire with the company's "independent" CPA?
- Lie on financial statements to banks providing credit facilities (*overstating* income and net worth)?
- Lie on financial statements to banks providing credit facilities (*understating* income and net worth)?
- Lie on written discovery under oath?
- Lie on tax returns (with or without help from a tax preparer)?
- Lie at deposition while looking in the eye of opposing counsel?
- Lie at trial in front of a judge?

Some lawyers may have a hard time understanding that targets perceive certain lies as more dangerous than others. For example, some targets believe that failing to report cash receipts (understating income) on a federal income tax return is much more egregious than claiming exaggerated personal meal deductions and entertainment expenses. Some may say IRS agents expect some fudging on "business" dinners. That's why they are only partially deductible. But if the cash receipts are not recorded and the amount is meaningful, the agent may consider initiating criminal prosecution.

One serious dividing line for targets is the deposition. Will the target lie in deposition? Some won't. The involvement of their spouse's forensic accountant may keep the target honest. If the forensic accountant has been through the general ledger and examined canceled checks and invoices, that may be enough to keep the target honest. That is why it can be beneficial to disclose the expert's existence as soon as possible. For other cases, a target's honesty may depend on the reputation of the forensic accountant. If word gets back to the target that the CPA is very talented, the target may throw in the towel, admit the manipulation, and salvage what credibility remains.

Some targets will continue to lie even when caught. If the manipulation is not detected prior to the deposition, you can bet the farm the target will lie. The target may even be emboldened to lie. In those circumstances, the mere act of getting the target on the record and under oath creates a benchmark to work against. One concept resonates with clients: "Even though your spouse may lie, we are going to ask him the right questions under oath and make him commit perjury to do it." Proving the perjury may be a tremendous challenge. But if the lie is ever proven, there will likely be hell to pay.

In the Disney movie and theme park ride *Pirates of the Caribbean*, a nefarious voice calls out, "Dead men tell no tales." From the first audit classes in college, accountants are taught to think like thieves. Audit courses cover both simple and complicated theft schemes. Seminars and books continue training in fraud detection after one becomes a CPA. Most CPAs will tell lawyers that, if given the right documents and enough time, almost all fraud schemes can be detected. At its most basic, if revenue received by a business is recorded in an accounting system, pulling cash out leaves a paper trail—somehow, somewhere. Some trails are easier to discover than others. If the revenue received is never recorded in the first place, however, all the investigative methods and techniques in the world won't catch it on the company books. This is because the recording was never there in the first place. Some situations create hints. These hints suggest problems. They are called red flags. A really, really smart scheme tells no tales and leaves no red flags. But thankfully, such schemes are rare.

Red Flags

Family lawyers must be able to spot red flags. Some red flags may be known by clients but misunderstood. By its very definition, a red flag should be the basis for reasonable concern and suggest the need for investigation. Unfortunately, red flags are often imbedded in very emotional facts. Some clients know their spouses are greedy and usually know when they're lying about something. Others only suspect the lies.

To be effective, divorce lawyers and CPAs need to be students of fraud. Movies can be important teachers. Watch *The Sting*, *The Grifters*, *House of Games*, or *Ocean's Eleven.* As you will learn from these movies, all successful fraud and theft schemes share the following common elements:

1. They play on the victim's greed.
2. They involve a diversion.
3. They rely on one or more deceptions.
4. They deflate the victim.

The victim is often in on some aspect of the fraud, hoping to receive a serious profit in return for little effort or risk. The diversion and deception can be either elaborate or simple—it doesn't matter. Some call this the difference between the "long" and "short" con. But for fraud schemes to have real elegance, there must be deflation. The victim truly believes the money is gone and is unrecoverable.

In the Academy Award–winning *The Sting*, the victim, mobster Doyle Lonnegan, left $500,000 in cash at a gambling hall while attempting to escape suspicion for the murder of Robert Redford's character. The murder never actually happened. Doyle believed he was in on a horse-racing gambling fix. He believed he couldn't lose the bet. Fortunately for the perpetrators of the fraud, leaving the cash behind meant leaving it in their hands. The victim simply walked away from a lot of money. Doyle believed that, if he made an inquiry to the police about the missing money, he would be required to explain his presence at an illegal gambling facility at the exact time a person died.

In divorce actions, simple plots involve handing cash or transferring ownership of valuable assets to buddies, siblings, or parents to hold for the divorcing party until sometime after the final decree. Well-thought-out scams usually come with deceptive cover stories, financial statement manipulation, and lying under oath. Better cover stories involve failing businesses, gambling addictions, and other personal failures. The more believable the story is that the money is gone, the more likely the victim will give up looking for it.

For example, if the target's business owns a vacant building, the target may complain that the property taxes are long overdue and the building is worth less than the cost of paying them. Prior to the divorce filing, the target brags that the business sold the building to a stupid investor in exchange for the investor getting "stuck" with having to pay the overdue taxes. While the business may be rid of the purported albatross, the business and marital estate is purportedly saved thousands of dollars. The reality is quite different. The taxes were never behind, and the purchaser was the target's nefarious financial advisor and personal friend. The transfer was recorded, but the handshake deal will result in the stockbroker and target splitting the profits from its sale a year or so after the divorce.

Divorce victims mirror fraud victims. Fraud victims are often too embarrassed to report the crime. Spouses married to persons lying, cheating, and stealing in the divorce become demoralized. The target counts on the victim's will breaking down. Victims blame themselves and want to settle for less than a reasonable settlement. Your role as psychologist comes into focus here. When you know that proving the fraud is likely just around the corner, counseling your client becomes essential. Issuing one more subpoena, arguing another motion to compel, or simply taking a key deposition can turn the tide. In divorce, though, optimism is often a commodity in short supply.

To detect schemes using financial statement manipulation, timing is important. Benchmarks are key. At one point in time, the target was not scamming, the marriage was solid, and generating income was a good thing. Finding that benchmark point in time helps the CPA figure out ways to "triangulate" what is truth and what is deception. Red flags describe noticeable changes in the financial *status quo*. Somewhere between the cause and effect, the red flag sticks out. The following is a list of red flags, offered to give you a flavor of what your legal team should be listening for when talking with a client. Pre-filing red flags include the following situations:

- The spouse maintains complete control of bank account information and online passwords.
- The spouse is secretive about financial affairs.
- The spouse has a P.O. box or private mail drop box that receives account statements and bills.
- The spouse has meaningful unreimbursed business account expenses.
- The spouse has deleted one or more personal financial programs, such as Quicken or QuickBooks.
- A computer containing important financial records has mysteriously crashed, and the spouse has removed the hard drive for a data retrieval attempt, never to be seen again.
- The spouse begins to engage in cash transactions for larger purchases.
- The spouse stockpiles or stores cash.
- Business tax returns cannot be reconciled with financial records.
- The spouse is pushy when obtaining signatures on important documents, like tax returns and deeds—"I need to get this to our accountant *today*."
- There is an execution of mutual durable power of attorneys for "estate planning" purposes.

- The spouse uses a fly-by-night tax accountant, not a CPA.
- The spouse brags about his bartering ability.
- The spouse and the business switch accountants just before filing for divorce.
- The spouse goes on out-of-town business junkets with his befriended, slippery financial advisor.
- There are elaborate trusts, possibly including "generation skipping" trusts.
- SIDS (Sudden Income Deficit Syndrome)—"My business is failing"—crops up.
- The spouse suffers an income decrease without a corresponding reduction of expenses.
- The spouse makes unusual purchases of flashy items, such as a car and jewelry.
- Marital and/or business investments have suffered a dramatic decrease in value.
- The spouse is making outrageous allegations against your client.
- The spouse is always busy and hard to contact.
- The spouse exhibits a raging anger when not in complete control.
- The spouse has multiple cell phones or numbers over a relatively short period of time.
- The spouse makes frequent trips to countries with relaxed banking laws.
- The spouse exhibits childish greed and claims of entitlement.
- The spouse makes unusual purchases of toys or art that could be sold later.
- The spouse has recently been drawing on large amounts of debt.
- The spouse is involved in drug abuse.
- The spouse is involved in more frequent gambling than usual and is placing money "on account" with casinos.
- The spouse has multiple business or personal bank accounts without obvious reasons for having that many.
- The spouse has undertaken a new business venture with distant partners and is vague on the details.
- The spouse is bragging about the ease with which personal expenses are run through his business.

- The spouse's personal debt has been improperly paid by the spouse's business and fudged in financial records.
- The spouse's business causes a reduction in cash based on management decisions.

Post-filing litigation tactics include the following ploys:

- The spouse accuses your client's attorney (you) of "just running up the bill."
- The spouse badmouths your client's forensic accountant as incompetent and/or wasteful.
- The spouse refuses to produce obviously relevant documents, such as bank statements, credit card statements, financial statements, and investment account statements.
- The spouse claims that basic financial documents do not exist, or even worse, never existed.
- The spouse initiates scorched-earth tactics to frustrate discovery.
- The spouse's business refuses or fails to produce basic financial records—such as the general ledger, the cash receipts journals, or inventory records—that can be used to substantiate management claims of poor financial performance.
- The spouse and/or the spouse's business promises discovery but never produces.
- The spouse continues to claim that his business is failing.

Severity of Lies

Not all lies are equal. Some lies are more important than others. To borrow some baseball analogies, an example of a home run lie might be an interrogatory answer denying infidelity combined with finding in the car glove compartment of the spouse a jewelry store receipt for a Rolex Lady-Datejust (with diamond dial and bezel, of course), complete with a Christmas card including a sexually graphic thank-you note that predates the interrogatory answer. An example of an uncovered lie that is a double is the good old business credit card statement with the Victoria's Secret charge. Finally, an example of a single lie might be a business owner deducting personal meals and entertainment expenses through the business. Single lies are illegal, unethical, and dishonest. But, unfortunately, judges hear a lot worse every day and are not moved by them. For small single lies, there are two keys. First, proving any lie with a document, especially a document signed by the target, is more powerful than any other proof. And second, if you string enough single lies together with a meaningful amount of dissipation, your client can achieve the same credibility destruction as with a home run lie.

Financial Lies Come in Many Flavors

Targets usually have very specific and predictable objectives. In committing fraud in a divorce, the target's goals are to

1. Hide, understate, or undervalue certain assets;
2. Overstate debts;
3. Report lower-than-actual revenue; and/or
4. Report higher-than-actual expenses.

Some tactics are predictable. As with any scheme, there are, from the perspective of the target, various advantages and disadvantages. Predictable strategies include the following:

- Hoarding unrecorded cash

  Advantage: Removing cash (currency) lacks a paper trail, and offshore bank accounts are relatively easy (from a legal standpoint) to open.

  Disadvantage: Laundering over $100,000 in currency can be time consuming and will likely require travel. Depending on the circumstances, this tactic could involve the very serious criminal acts of money laundering, violation of cash transfer reporting requirements, federal income tax fraud, and perjury.
- Secreting already-recorded cash receipts

  Advantage: This can be completed as part of a complex accounting scheme, which may be too complicated or expensive to discover.

  Disadvantage: Once cash is recorded, its absence or transfer is discoverable.
- Understating revenue

  Advantage: The target has lots of options from which to choose. Some are simple and easy. Deferring revenue by manipulating the timing of revenue or accounts receivable may not constitute tax fraud.

Disadvantage: Depending on the business owner's sophistication, this can require a fairly predictable co-conspirator. If the co-conspirator is placed under oath, the scheme could result in perjury charges for the target.

- Excessive bonuses or perks

    Advantage: This is easy for the boss to pull off.

    Disadvantage: Bonuses and travel and entertainment expense accounts are the first places accountants look in investigations. Excessive bonuses will stick out if the target is claiming a disastrous year. Regarding excessive perks, the IRS requires particular supporting documentation for travel, entertainment, meals, company car, fringe benefits, and credit card receipts. The failure to maintain that documentation is another red flag and could easily result in the target's loss of credibility.

- Payment to fictitious vendors and employees

    Advantage: This can be hard to detect.

    Disadvantage: If the nonbusiness-owner spouse has a "Deep Throat" or snitch inside the business, the forensic accountant or business valuation expert might know exactly where to look. The scheme may require a co-conspirator (controller, payroll clerk, or accounts payable clerk) to assist with the criminal tax fraud. Plus, the fictitious employee rarely actually shows up to work. Fictitious vendors can be more of a challenge. Some forensic accountants may have software that performs statistical analyses to help spotlight suspicious transactions.

- Overstating debts or making a creative bad-debts expense adjustment

    Advantage: The manipulation will be camouflaged among many other transactions. This can be an effective method of hiding money in plain sight. Cash need not be moved to accomplish this.

    Disadvantage: If a forensic accountant performs a comparative financial analysis and the manipulated amount is meaningful, these noncash adjustments should stand out. Plus, there may be no backup documentation for these adjustments.

- Overstating accruals

    Advantage: It is very easy to overstate the amount owed to a vendor. For example, recording three months of a copier lease payable in December rather than one month.

Disadvantage: If a forensic accountant compares payables to supporting documents, the misstatement is easy to catch. Like many manipulations, for it to be successful, the target may create its own fictitious paper trail. It takes creativity, determination, and discipline to manufacture supporting documents.

- Nondisclosure of tangible assets

  Advantage: This is a simple shell game. The target pays money for assets and expenses them instead of showing them as assets.

  Disadvantage: The existence of tangible assets can be observed. Capital leases may involve monthly payments for assets, leaving a paper trail.

- Inventory "errors" that depress net income

  Advantage: Delaying the recording of certain inventory transactions, making pricing errors, and miscounting inventory can easily manipulate the cost of goods sold, resulting in artificially depressed profits.

  Disadvantage: Forensic accountants can compare to previous financial periods. Spikes (or valleys) in inventory as a percentage of gross revenue compared to benchmark years can illuminate this problem. Plus, if the divorce drags on and covers an additional period, the errors may reverse themselves out, causing more income in the subsequent period.

- Nondisclosure of intangible assets (intellectual property or trade secrets)

  Advantage: This is very clean. Due to the difficulty in valuation, generally accepted accounting principles may require that intangible assets not appear on books or tax records until sold.

  Disadvantage: Valuable intangible assets or intellectual property may be disclosed in company marketing brochures (e.g., bragging about a newly developed process), in newspaper articles, or on bank loan applications.

- Manipulation of retained earnings and capital, which could be the company holding more cash than was its practice before the divorce and not paying excess profits to owners or strange, one-time equity account transfers involving debt or cash

Advantage: The owner has actual authority to control and manipulate distribution to and from capital accounts.

Disadvantage: Depending on the circumstances, transactions with equity can be fairly transparent to forensic accountants. For example, a forensic accountant reviews 2008 and 2009 operations, and in both years the company had around the same amount of profit. On December 31, 2008, cash reserves were $300,000. On December 31, 2009, cash reserves were $600,000. Given that profit was about the same, no major investment decisions were made, and no capital outlay was required, the divorce itself becomes the obvious reason for the cash accumulation, resulting in lowered "wages" to the owner.

- Creation and maintenance of trusts

  Advantage: Assets in a trust can have income. The income tax can be paid by the trust, and its income will not flow into the beneficiary's personal income tax return. Trusts can exist for years, lying undetected by the other spouse.

  Disadvantage: Most standard interrogatories ask about the existence of trusts. Usually, the target's regular CPA will prepare the tax returns. If the target fails to list the trust in an interrogatory answer and the client discovers the trust through a subpoena to the CPA, the scheme can be detected.

"What Is Best in Life?"

In *Conan the Barbarian,* as they sit around a roaring campfire, the Wu Master asks Conan, played by Arnold Schwarzenegger, "Conan, what is best in life?" Conan replies, "To crush your enemies. To see them driven before you. And to hear the lamentation of their women." In the courtroom, catching the target in a lie made under oath is good. Catching the target in a lie with an obvious intent to lie is great. But ultimately, the best in life is for the trier of fact to crush the business-owner spouse in a ruling. Trial courts can vindicate the nonbusiness-owner spouse by doing the following:

- Granting the nonbusiness-owner spouse substantially more than 50 percent of the assets,
- Valuing the assets in favor of the nonbusiness-owner's valuation expert, and/or

- For alimony or child support, declaring the target's income much closer to the target's real income rather than the target's purported income.

More on Bad Debt Manipulation

To understand **bad debt expense** manipulation, you must understand business. Businesses sell goods and services. Customers should pay. Some don't. When customers don't pay, certain accounts receivable adjustments can be made to reflect the nonpayment after income has been realized. But how does an accountant know when a customer will not pay? In accrual-basis accounting, businesses record revenue when the goods or services are provided and invoices are issued. In many accrual accounting businesses, collection is fairly predictable. Recording the revenue when sales are made is not a big deal.

As an example, consider family law firms. Most family law firms are cash-basis taxpayers. The reason is simple. Lawyers want to pay taxes only on revenue actually received. Who would want to pay taxes based on a receivable that may never be collected? This is different from many companies that sell products to customers who eventually pay their bills. It's just the timing of the payment that creates the accounting issue.

Those companies selling goods and services with accrual-basis accounting can usually estimate a certain percentage of uncollectible revenue and write it off. This estimation is based on collection results from prior years. This write-off or write-down reduces accounts receivable and reduces income by increasing an account called bad debt expense. This happens even though no one knows precisely which debt will not be collected. This practice helps prevent the overstatement of profits, which is a very legitimate accounting goal, even outside a divorcing year. The business's revenue stays the same, but the bad debt expense increases. By increasing the amount of bad debt expense (which is an estimate anyway), the target effectively reduces personal income in the divorcing year through the exercise of accounting judgment.

When testing for bad debt expense manipulation, forensic accountants can perform a multi-period analysis. Before the CPA performs the analysis, a forensic accountant may ask questions similar to the following:

1. What is the pattern of write-offs? Over a period of several years, analyze the amount compared to gross revenue.

2. Which items were referred to a collection agent or collection attorney?
3. Were all items referred to a collection agent or attorney made in the ordinary course of business?
4. Trace particular accounts written off. After the receivable was written off, was it ever collected? Was it received in cash? Was it received off the books? Or was it paid to an intermediary?
5. Does the target continue selling to the business responsible for the bad debt?
6. What is the industry standard practice for recording and writing off bad debt?
7. Is the timing of write-offs suspicious in relation to the divorce timing?

When calculating bad debt as a percentage of gross revenues over a multiyear period, the forensic accountant is looking for a big jump in bad debt expense in the divorcing year. For example, consider the following chart:

Year:	2007	2008	2009
Sales:	$550,000	$600,000	$650,000
Bad Debt Expense:	$11,000	$15,000	$42,500
Percentage:	2%	2.5%	6.5%

If the divorce was filed in late 2008, there was probably no manipulation at that time. If the business is on a calendar year, the entries for adjusting bad debt are likely made from January to March. The forensic accountant can and will ask questions. The target's accountant may have plausible answers. In the end, the detail follow-up may tell the tale. If there was one really bad account from one particular business, check out that business. In prior years, was there a collection issue? Did the debtor company go out of business? Is that business owner a friend of the target? Was there a lawsuit filed?

More Details on Other Schemes

Businesses that sell goods compile inventory. Most either purchase or manufacture goods or do a combination of both. The plan is to sell those goods for significantly more than they cost to manufacture, assemble, ship, and sell. The difference between the sales price and cost is gross margin. Raw materials are purchased and processed, and certain labor costs may be added. During this process and before the goods are ready for sale, the asset is described as "work in progress." At the end of the process, the goods become inventory ready to be sold. Raw material, work in progress, and inventory are all assets. When inventory is sold, revenue is generated. But the cost of that revenue generation must be deducted. **Cost of goods sold** is calculated and subtracted from revenue to calculate gross profit.

Cost of goods sold can be the largest expense of many companies. How that cost is determined significantly affects profit calculation. Accounting majors take an entire undergraduate course about cost accounting. There are many ways to account for inventory and its relationship to revenue. Two of the most basic are first in, first out (FIFO) and last in, first out (LIFO). In FIFO, the cost of the first item purchased is the cost of the first item sold. If the most recent inventory purchases are much more expensive than the first purchases, profit in the current period will be higher than in the later period when the more expensive goods are sold, if they are sold at the same price.

Changing cost accounting methods in a divorcing year is an easy way to manipulate earnings. If the accounting change resulted in a sharp decrease in profits, catching the change may not be difficult. But proving that a target intentionally depressed income this way can be challenging. The target may be able to produce an accounting witness who claims the change in the inventory cost accounting method will benefit the business in the long run. If that is the case, however, the owner may be indirectly presenting evidence of a better financial future instead of the usual doom-and-gloom characterization of the business in divorcing years. That can turn into a good thing for the nonowner spouse.

For almost all retail endeavors or resellers, inventory management is a very important aspect of doing business. Liquor stores and bars are good examples. To prevent and catch employee theft, inventory must be taken every week or month. Taking inventory means compiling a list of every type of liquor, wine, and beer sold. One or more members of management who are not regular sellers of that inventory must take that list of inventory and personally physically count the number of bottles and kegs on the shelves. Those numbers are entered into the computer and compared to what the inventory management system says should be in inventory on that date at that minute. The computer often notes significant variances for management to investigate. Taking inventory is tedious, time consuming, and mind numbing. Businesses that don't take inventory regularly may be robbed blind by employees who know there is no way to be caught stealing unless inventory is regularly taken. In a divorcing year, a business owner can manipulate the physical inventory (the personal count) and significantly reduce profits for that period.

A **cash receipts journal** is the accounting platform for voluminous transactions, usually sales. In general, it will record amounts collected, dates, customers, and some types of infrequent transactions. Manipulating cash is easiest *if* transactions are never recorded. For example, a restaurant owner finds it much easier to get away with taking cash from the cash drawer without recording the sales in the register than if the sales are recorded and then cash is removed. Each register creates a tape for the end of the day. If the sales were recorded, the day's tape would not match the deposit. Once cash transactions are recorded, however, the challenge is to remove the cash without anyone noticing. Almost all owners can circumvent their own internal controls designed to prevent theft from them because it is theft *by* them.

There are many other ways for owners to remove cash, some smart and some dumb. Because of the nature of double-entry accounting systems, if someone else oversees reconciling two pieces of information, an honest accountant or supervisor will catch the person stealing. If the person stealing also signs the reconciling person's paycheck, there is no one to whom to report the theft. Smart targets with an accounting degree or master of business administration may rely on their financial expertise to pull it off. Also, look for interpersonal or familial ties between the target and the person in charge of recording cash transactions. Does the cash receipts journal total match the bank deposits total? Do the bank deposit totals match the cash account totals in the general ledger? Do sales receipts match cash deposits? Do cash deposits match sales recorded in the general ledger? Forensic accountants know this stuff.

An **accounts receivable journal** is a record of the amounts customers owe and the amounts reduced when invoices are paid. At the end of each month, the various columns are posted to the general ledger, affecting cash, accounts receivable, and revenue. A crafty bookkeeper may enhance her personal earnings by pulling cash payments and sharing them with the owner. But what will the bookkeeper do to the books to keep them accurate for actual customers? The customers will want to know the correct amounts owed if they call in to check their balances. The bookkeeper will either record cash accurately, resulting in receivables being out of balance, or keep a second set of books. Forensic accountants know this, too.

Adjustments

"Adjustments" is a general term describing what forensic accountants do to help triers of fact determine a true value or a true income. In a business valuation context, experts "normalize" earnings by making adjustments to the income statement. "Normalization of earnings" means determining the true income of the business under normal circumstances with a neutral owner who does not run extraneous and personal expenses through the business. For example, a business valuation expert may add back a girlfriend's salary to the company's stated income. If the business earned $400,000 during the year but the owner paid his girlfriend (who never once appeared in the office) $35,000, the normalized earnings are $435,000. Some normalization adjustments may not be corrections of nefarious behavior. If the spouse of the business owner is also on the payroll but does not work, that expense may be added back as well.

Normalizing earnings is essentially the same process for income determination issues in divorce as it is in business valuation. For both business valuations and income determination work, the starting point is the stated earnings of a business. The earnings are taken most commonly from the income statement or a tax return.

Forensic accountants can compare the business's tax return and financial statements, looking for differences. These differences are called "reconciling items." From the beginning figure of stated income, the forensic accountant might suggest a few adjustments to compute the owner's real business income. Examples of adjustments are as follows:

1. **Target's salary.** Compare the salary of the target to reasonable compensation for similar positions within the industry. If it is too high, the business may fail. If it is too low, the business may have excess earnings.
2. **Salary for the target's relatives.** Who is on the payroll? What do they do? Oh, really?

3. **Automobiles.** Deducting certain automobile costs (purchase, lease, maintenance, and fuel or mileage) is very common, regardless of divorce. A deduction of the cost of a target's daughter's car while she is in college should be added back into net income.
4. **Life insurance.** Who is insured? It is not unusual to see employees insured who are not regularly at the office.
5. **Conventions.** Compare length of stay to actual conference time. For Las Vegas conventions, analyze credit card statements, ATM receipts, and so on. Would a neutral business owner let the current owners (if they were employees) stay at the Bellagio at $450 per night to attend a simple trade conference held at the Las Vegas Convention Center?
6. **Recent real estate transactions/changes.** For larger business transactions, look for related party transactions. For example, prior to the divorce, the business leased new warehouse space at a much higher cost. What if the building is owned by the target's brother, best friend, or golf buddy? After the divorce, the related party can settle up with the target.
7. **Depreciated items.** Many state child support laws disallow depreciation as a deduction for business owners. Check the rules.

Every forensic accounting engagement involves analyzing a complex series of facts and a dizzying volume of transactions. Forensic accountants understand schemes well. Their education, accounting experience, and training set them on a path to be experts. Applying their techniques and methodologies begins with receiving information from you and your client. The more helpful information provided earlier in the engagement, the less likely the accountant will spin his wheels looking for the wrong thing. It is your job to coordinate the information flow.

Experts do not always understand the litigation process well. You must never assume the forensic accountant has what he needs. You must not overestimate your client's understanding of what the team needs to do to admit into evidence relevant testimony. Understanding the relationship among the schemes, the work needed to detect the schemes, accounting terms, and legal processes helps set the stage for you, the family lawyer, to analyze reports and negotiate favorable settlements. If the case won't settle, you are tasked with taking surgical depositions, directing effortless examination of the client's expert, and crushing opposing witnesses to expose the target as a big fat liar.

Managing Forensic Accounting Investigation Costs

Unlimited divorce war chests are unusual. What if the fraud does not exist or is undetectable? What if the target directs opposing counsel to engage in scorched-earth discovery wars? Good luck. The reason targets engage in scorched-earth discovery tactics is because those tactics can work. Clients can run out of cash, get frustrated because the bills get too high, and settle for much less than what is equitable.

To clients, the plan is the thing. It is a belief. For some clients, the plan is doing what the lawyer says to reach a settlement. To lawyers, the plan is getting the forensic accountant to issue a report that frightens the target into settling. For forensic accountants, the plan is making the lawyer and client happy, getting paid for all their hard work, and getting hired again in the future. One trouble with "the plan" is that it can change without your knowing it. Clients forget the plan. Their goals may change. The money to fund the plan may run out. The forensic accountant may lose optimism in finding what is sought, whatever it is. All of this can change, spoil, and rot like a dead squirrel in the attic. You may not know exactly what animal has died or where the corpse may be exactly, but the smell can be enough.

This aspect of family law may be the hardest part of your job. It can also be the easiest to mismanage. Your client has certain expectations—high or low. The forensic accountant is always going to do his best. And you are there in the middle, like an orchestra conductor. This Bermuda Triangle has no simple answers, no cure-alls, and no shortcuts. There is only one weapon at your disposal here—honesty.

You must talk to your client. Sometimes this is unpleasant. Lawyers like to win. Lawyers are like carpenters, measuring twice and cutting once. When handling divorces with forensic accounting engagements, lawyers may feel like they are not cutting enough. Clients want to understand the plan. They need to understand the plan. But often, clients don't have a law license or a CPA license and may never have understood the plan in the first place. Nevertheless, lawyers must explain that the work is important and that, if the right lies are uncovered, there may be a settlement on the horizon. These are words of hope and optimism. Again, in divorce, optimism can be a commodity in short supply—just like money. Lawyers must be honest about budgets and reality.

Then there is the forensic accountant. The CPA could be working away, drilling into the financial statements and not billing as he goes—what's known as "progress billing"—but instead waiting to bill until the report is complete. The next thing you see is a bill for forensic accounting services as large, or larger, than your own current outstanding balance due. You must communicate with the forensic accountant. Seek progress billing. Even if the forensic accountant resists, push for progress billing, and share that with your client.

You must be honest with everyone. Tell your client to obtain and maintain a divorce-fee war chest. Advise your client that divorces in general, and forensic accountant discovery and business valuation in particular, are almost always more expensive than originally expected. Meet with your client and the forensic accountant regularly. Listen to your client. Listen to the forensic accountant. Remind everyone of the plan. Have your client's goals changed? Has the forensic accountant's advice changed? Given the economic realities of the situation, does it sound like the plan will work? If the CPA's engagement objectives begin looking like they are too expensive, change them. In forensic accounting terms, it is called redefining the scope of the engagement. List the stated objectives and goals. Prioritize. Be realistic. Confer with your client and the accountant and start cutting specific tasks and objectives. Failing to have the tough conversations will get lawyers in trouble every time. Redefining objectives in advance is always much easier than accepting failure later. When finishing a status conference, schedule the next one. Put tough advice to your client in writing. Remember that helping clients make tough choices is a large part of your job description.

Case Example: Proof of Disappeared Funds Shifts Burden of Proof

A family lawyer who represents a client accused of wasting or dissipating funds should strongly advise his or her client to engage a clever, experienced forensic accountant to come up with a credible and compelling explanation of how the funds were actually not wasted or dissipated. If this is not done, courts may find dissipation even without direct evidence of intentional conduct.

The husband and wife in this Texas divorce case[1] were married in 1968. They were both retired when the husband left the marital residence in 2013. At this time, the wife was disabled and unable to care for herself or travel outside of the home. The wife filed for divorce in 2014. The husband appeared pro se at trial.

While the divorce was pending, the husband lived for a time with his new girlfriend. He provided few details as to his spending during that time, other than that it was for "regular expenses I had to do to live." He also testified that

1. Matter of Marriage of Walzel and Walzel, No. 14-16-00637-CV (Tex. Ct. App. Jan. 30, 2018).

the couple had purchased a lot in Belize in 2010 and that he had established a bank account in Belize. He admitted that he had sent money to that account unrelated to payments for the property.

He also admitted that he had made over $700,000 in withdrawals from a retirement account as well as additional withdrawals from other accounts. He was vague as to how this money was spent, other than that it was "used to live a better life and that's where it all went."

The wife retained as her expert witness Beverly Ryan, CPA, who attempted to trace approximately $800,000 in retirement distributions and withdrawals that had begun in 2005. Ryan reviewed tax documents, bank statements, and real estate documents.

The expert believed that the records in her possession were deficient, and she asked to meet with the husband to fill in the gaps. The husband, however, refused to meet with her or provide additional documents. Ultimately, Ryan testified that she was unable to account for almost $750,000 of distributions and withdrawals. She noted that there had been over $40,000 in cash withdrawals, mostly through ATM machines.

The trial court assigned most of the remaining assets to the wife and included a finding that the husband had wasted community assets in the amount of approximately $800,000. The husband appealed.

Spouses have a fiduciary duty to the other, the violation of which constitutes a fraud upon the community. Waste is one type of fraud that occurs when a spouse wrongfully depletes the marital estate without the other spouse's knowledge or consent. There is also a presumption of waste when one spouse disposes of the other spouse's interest in community property without his or her knowledge or consent. Expenditures for the benefit of a paramour establish waste. Once the complaining spouse has met the burden of proof to show that the transfers took place, the burden of proof is placed on the disposing spouse to show the fairness of the transfer.

The husband argued on appeal that Ryan's testimony failed to satisfy the wife's burden of production since the expert allegedly made certain assumptions in arriving at her conclusion. In particular, the husband argued that it was improper for the expert to assume that he was the only one who had access to the funds and had directed the withdrawals.

However, the appeals court quickly dispensed with this argument. It first noted that the husband had admitted to making withdrawals of

$703,000. He had also admitted to transferring money to the account in Belize and to spending money while living with his girlfriend. Furthermore, other witnesses had testified that the wife was disabled and unable to leave the house. The husband had apparently testified that she was indeed able to leave the house, but the appeals court noted that this boiled down to a credibility determination. The husband's credibility was lacking, a determination that was reinforced by the fact that he had attempted to establish himself as the wife's guardian.

The appeals court held that the evidence supported a finding that the husband had disposed of assets without the wife's knowledge, thus giving rise to a presumption that he had committed waste. As such, evidence of specific transfers of funds was unnecessary. Unaccounted-for funds that were in the control of the spouse can be found to be dissipated.

Since the wife had established the transfer of funds, the burden of proof then shifted to the husband to show his fairness in the use of these funds. The husband had not met this burden. The only evidence showed that an undisclosed amount was sent to Belize and another undisclosed amount was spent on behalf of the girlfriend. The husband had not even testified in his own case in chief, and his cross-examination of the wife and other witnesses had not established the fairness of the transactions. For these reasons, the court of appeals affirmed the lower court's judgment.

Case Example: Stock Option Fraud

In 2011, the Washington Supreme Court affirmed the valuation determination of employment stock options in divorce.[2] The trial court relied almost exclusively on the wife's forensic accountant's valuation method and calculation. This case involved competing expert witness testimony regarding a proper damages award following a spouse's fraudulent exercise of stock options.

The couple married in 1987 and separated in 2004. In the divorce, their stipulated agreement divided 15,000 PACCAR stock options along with various other community assets. The husband began receiving annual stock options in April 1999 as employment compensation from PACCAR. Nontransferable, the options remained in his possession.

Each option had a set price and 10-year expiration date between April 27, 2009, and January 15, 2013. The agreement gave each spouse the right to choose when to exercise his or her PACCAR stock options. At the wife's

2. Farmer v. Farmer, 2011 Wash. LEXIS 670, 172 Wn. 2d 616, 259 P.3d 256 (2011).

direction, the husband was to duly exercise the stock options representing her share. That is not what happened.

After reaching a stipulated agreement but before entry of the decree, the husband fraudulently exercised all the community options, immediately sold the stock, and netted himself $444,664.63 after taxes and expenses ($491,000 gross). The wife discovered the fraud when a $491,000 deposit ran through the husband's bank account. The trial court granted her request for relief from the decree and awarded damages. The husband lied. He subsequently tried to "finesse" the wife into exercising options to hide his fraud. And he was held in contempt for refusing to produce documents relating to the stock sale. Enigmatic as to why he did it, the husband did not benefit from his fraudulent exercise of the community stock options.

The trial court used the framework of conversion and tort damages in awarding an amount sufficient to make the wife whole again. Assessed damages were based upon the present value of the stock options as calculated by her forensic accountant, Ronald Nelson, CPA. The resulting award substantially exceeded what was realized from the sale of the wife's share, although it was held to be neither a windfall nor punitive. The case was affirmed with three supreme court justices dissenting.

Noting the abundance of reasonable valuation methods, the majority opinion looked to the three main stock-option valuation methods used in divorce: Present value, retained jurisdiction, and deferred distribution, with the latter two approaches being wait-and-see valuation solutions.

Using the present value method, Nelson calculated $617,553 in damages because of the husband's wrongful exercise of the wife's stock options. Nelson analyzed PACCAR stock performance over the previous 10 years and arrived at a 20.235 percent annual rate of return. He made two key assumptions: the options would be held until the day before expiration, and the rate of return would remain constant.

Although the husband's declaration challenged the wife's valuation as "inappropriate and unreasonable," he failed to offer a competing analysis of future value. The trial court reaffirmed its $617,553 stock option valuation, having relied on Nelson's opinion because his was the only expert opinion provided. The trial court agreed to discount Nelson's valuation to present value.

Both spouses presented expert testimony on what the discount rate should be. Nelson proposed a 6 percent discount rate. The husband's forensic accounting expert, Steven J. Kessler, proposed a 15–20 percent discount rate. Kessler disputed Nelson's original valuation, but it was too little, too late. Because valuation was already decided, the portion of Kessler's declaration disputing Nelson's valuation was stricken as untimely. On review, the court noted how "it was not until the [trial] court called for further information on the correct present-value calculation that [husband] submitted an expert opinion challenging Nelson's calculation." The trial court adopted Nelson's 6 percent discount rate, awarding the wife $487,325 in damages. The intermediary court affirmed, holding no abuse of discretion in awarding damages to compensate the wife for her loss. Given the "trial court's broad equitable authority to divide assets," the measure of damages properly put the wife "in as good a position as she would have been" had the husband not acted in bad faith. The husband again appealed.

Reviewing the trial court's measure of damages, the court rejected the husband's argument for a "single, categorical rule for measuring the value of stock options when the stock price increases after conversion."[3] Applying tort damages on a theory of fraudulent conversion to make the wife whole again was not an abuse of discretion, and nor was the ultimate remedy an abuse of discretion.

In tort, there are seven generally accepted measures of damages for conversion of stock. Each involves taking a value snapshot

- At time of conversion;
- At the highest value from time of conversion to a reasonable period after;
- At the highest value from conversion to a reasonable period after the owner has notice of conversion;
- At the highest value from when the owner has notice of conversion to a reasonable period after;
- The higher value at conversion and highest value from notice of conversion to a reasonable period after;
- The highest value at conversion until the lawsuit is filed; and
- The highest value from conversion until trial, verdict, or judgment.

3. *See In re* Marriage of Langham, 153 Wn. 2d 553, 106 P.3d 212 (2005).

There is no universal method of calculating damages. Emphasizing a tradition of significant deference to the trial court, the court upheld the present value measure of damages as one of many accepted approaches.

By inference, the husband contended Nelson's calculations were unduly speculative. The trial court was held to have properly exercised its discretion in calculating damages using the present value method. Weighing Nelson's declaration against the husband's opposing assertions, the trial court found Nelson to be more credible and accurate, properly basing its damages award on that expert's calculations.

The dissent argued otherwise. Instead, the *Brougham* valuation rule was controlling because "complete umbrella protection by being awarded the highest possible valuation of the property from the time of its taking to the entry of judgment or its return" unfairly benefits the victim.[4] The wife in the instant case should not suffer a loss from her husband's wrongful conversion, but "neither should she be granted the windfall of blanket protection against the market risk." The dissent required valuation at a reasonable time after the sale, explaining how the inherent nature of a stock option is in benefiting the holder with "a reduced risk of loss and a greater likelihood of profit."

The dissent rejected Nelson's assumption the wife would have exercised her options at expiration without supporting evidence. The trial court could not have relied on competent evidence of the wife's intent to exercise her options because no evidence of such intent is reflected on the record. By contrast, the record supported an assumption the wife might have sold her options sooner. She testified how it took her a while to "adjust to [her] current income level," as divorce forced her "to make huge adjustments and changes in lifestyle and spending habits." An award based upon valuation at option expiration was "speculation and conjecture."

The $487,325 judgment against the husband more than doubled what he received on the wife's half of the PACCAR options. Had the trial court applied *Brougham*, the damages award would have been $237,450. The *Brougham* rule's measure of damages was "the highest value of the property wrongfully and knowingly converted between the time of conversion and a reasonable time after the victim learns of such conversion." Without credible evidence on remand of the wife's intent to hold her options until expiration, damages should be calculated

4. Brougham v. Swarva, 34 Wn. App. 68, 661 P.2d 138 (1983).

based upon "the highest value of her stock options between the date she discovered [husband's] wrongful conversion and a reasonable period of time thereafter."

The court held the damages were not punitive because the valuation method was supported by expert testimony. The dissent viewed the award as punitive in effect, if not deliberately so. Basically, the dissenting judge said the damages award was way too high. Putting that in forensic accounting terms, the damages award failed the so-called sanity test.

For purposes of discussion only, let us assume the dissenting judge is correct on all points listed in his opinion. The family lawyer must always keep in mind that a particular forensic accountant can flat-out beat his or her opposing expert and win. Once that happens, appellate courts may have little motivation to overturn the decision. There are two reasons for this. First, the appellate judges may not understand the complex financial concepts involved. Second, the standard of review applied simply will not allow for reworking a trial court decision that was a choice between two expert witnesses' testimony.

Discovery—Documents, Details, and Transactions

5

Document review is the lifeblood of forensic accounting. Obtaining the right documents in a timely fashion is often the single most important task the family lawyer can perform to help the team win. With the necessary documents, forensic accountants have a chance at finding important needles within stacks of needles. Without all the necessary documents, the entire exercise may be a waste of time. The important "smoking gun" document may have been withheld.

Tracing financial transactions from one account's monthly statement to another account's monthly statement can be like following a trail of bread crumbs. The transactions are the crumbs. The account statements are the trail. Removing one monthly statement can remove both the crumbs and the trail. A single missing brokerage statement could be the very statement the opposing spouse does not want you to see.

The Impact of One Missing Statement

If the ending balance of a brokerage account statement from a particular month, say January, matches the beginning balance for March, it is not necessarily true that there was no meaningful financial activity during the intervening month for which no record has been produced—February. No can really know what happened during February by looking at the March statement. The same could be said for a single missing page from the February statement. Any particular amount, say $60,000, could have been deposited and the exact amount withdrawn. The nonproducing spouse's claim that the statement was misplaced and there was no activity must be treated like any other red flag.

If the brokerage account balance was reduced by $45,000 during the month of the missing statement, the reason might be simple and important. For example, the payment of $45,000 could be a transfer to a local jeweler for a girlfriend's engagement ring—a clear case of dissipation. Uncovering these crumbs requires discipline and patience. Poring over statements to make sure that everything has been provided in discovery is tedious. But uncovering the particular transaction the nefarious spouse wants hidden can be a devastating blow to that spouse's credibility, materially altering the relative negotiating positions of the parties.

Always obtain documents quickly. Discovery, unlike fine wine, never ages well. If a key document has not been produced and you have not figured that out, the nonproducing spouse gains more confidence and boldness as time passes. In a pinch for time, you can always ask the forensic accountant to help review discovery for thoroughness. This is an important, although boring, aspect of what forensic accountants call "litigation support." If needed, call the forensic accountant for help. Do not let an opposing party breathe a sigh of relief rolling into mediation knowing that you have overlooked a missing document that has not been produced. That single missing document may be the most important one of all.

Time Frame for Valuation and Analysis

All family lawyers understand that identifying assets and debts at the date of distribution (either of separation or of divorce) is important. What is the next step? Depending on state law, know what dates are important, asset by asset. Yes, all marital (and community property) assets need to be valued as of the date of distribution (separation or divorce). But the law of most states analyzes classification issues (marital versus separate property or community versus separate property) with balances and values as of the date of marriage or date of acquisition, if later than marriage. Very early in the case, determine what the key dates are for classification and valuation concerns. Share those dates with your client and team. Timelines help with this. Also, definitely share those important dates and their relevance with your forensic accountant.

Formal versus Informal Requests

Sure, informal agreements to exchange financial information and documents can help save clients money. But what happens when an opposing party "forgets" to disclose a brokerage account containing several hundred thousands of dollars of transactions? If the nondisclosing party failed to disclose an asset as part of an interrogatory answer signed under oath, the court could find the nondisclosing spouse committed perjury or fraud. From that finding, the court will have a factual basis on which to grant relief. Without that finding, the court may deny your request for relief, such as a request to vacate a particular ruling, which you make once you've discovered the undisclosed asset. In California, if one party fails to disclose a particular asset, the court can, upon a finding of oppression, fraud, or malice, award 100 percent of the undisclosed asset to the other party, even after final judgment.[1]

---

1. *See* Cal. Fam. Code §§ 721 (regarding fiduciary relationship applying to community property transactions), 1100(e) (duty "to make full disclosure to the other spouse of all material facts and information regarding the existence, characterization, and valuation of all assets in which the community has or may have an interest"), 1101(h) ("Remedies for the breach of the fiduciary duty by one spouse, as set forth in Sections 721 and 1100, when the breach falls within the ambit of Section 3294 of the Civil Code shall include, but not be limited to, an award to the other spouse of 100 percent, or an amount equal to 100 percent, of any asset undisclosed or transferred in breach of the fiduciary duty."), 2100(c) (requiring that "a full and accurate disclosure of all assets and liabilities in which one or both parties have or may have an interest must be made in the early stages of a proceeding for dissolution of marriage or legal separation of the parties, regardless of the characterization as community or separate, together with a disclosure of all

If a settlement is reached in a divorce case in which one party fails to disclose an asset, the defrauded spouse can file an action to "unsettle" the case. The court making the determination will almost surely first determine whether discovery was completed. Some courts may find that the complaining spouse waived discovery by not requiring that it be completed. If so, the court may refuse to vacate the order approving the settlement. You absolutely must know your state's law on nondisclosure and what role, if any, formal discovery plays in that determination.

Fraud will almost always be sufficient cause for overturning a settlement agreement. Proving in court the defrauded spouse relied upon an asset disclosure in an interrogatory answer should not be difficult. A spouse relying upon an informal response, not under oath, however, may not have the same opportunity. The rules of civil procedure exist for a reason. Take advantage of them whenever possible.

Some clients will either ignore advice to require formal discovery or insist on preparing a settlement before litigation is initiated. When representing the less-propertied spouse, as a fallback position, insist that the more-propertied spouse execute a detailed financial affidavit listing all assets, debts, income, and expenses. Make sure that the affidavit states that the affiant understands and consents to the affidavit being used to prove that full disclosure took place; that the other spouse is relying upon the information; and that the document accurately reflects the assets, debts, income, and expenses of the disclosing party. A financial affidavit is better than nothing.

Finally, always, always, always pay attention to what terms are expressed in the settlement agreement regarding disclosure and reliance on disclosure. As a practical matter, all settlement agreements should state whether there was full disclosure and whether that disclosure was relied upon. Some clauses may specifically state that full disclosure was

---

income and expenses of the parties," and also requiring updates of material changes to same), and 2556 (giving the court continuing jurisdiction over community estate assets and liabilities not previously adjudicated in the proceeding); CAL. CIV. PROC. CODE § 3294(a) (providing punitive damages "[i]n an action for the breach of an obligation not arising from contract, where it is proven by clear and convincing evidence that the defendant has been guilty of oppression, fraud, or malice"). For an example of the application of these statutes, see *In re Marriage of Rossi*, 108 Cal. Rptr. 2d 270, 90 Cal. App. 4th 34 (Cal. App. 2001) (court awarded to innocent spouse 100 percent of lottery winnings hidden by guilty spouse).

waived. Still other settlement agreements may affirmatively state, in one part of the agreement, that there was full disclosure and reliance and then contradict that statement in another provision. Careful representation requires paying attention to what may appear to be boilerplate language and making sure that the settlement agreement accurately reflects the roles that disclosure and reliance played in that particular case.

Interrogatories and Requests for Production of Documents

All attorneys handling divorce cases should assemble a standard set of forms for both interrogatories and requests for production of documents. Then, as required, these forms should be tailored for specific situations, including divorce, post-divorce child support actions, and post-divorce child support matters for self-employed obligors. Creating (or borrowing) a great set of standard interrogatories is an important, but often boring, task. Almost all experienced family lawyers have really sweated over their forms and are comfortable with them.

Consider assembling two sets of discovery interrogatories: one for documents where the opposing party is an employee of a company owned by a third party and another for documents where the opposing party is self-employed.

Lawyers understand that there are basic documents that must be reviewed in every case. Your forensic accountant can help with ideas for categories of necessary documents in particular cases. For most divorce cases, the CPA will want the following:

1. Personal tax returns, plus W-2s, 1099s, and K-1s;
2. Personal financial statements;
3. Loan documents including, but not limited to, applications for loans and personal financial statements issued to the credit facility;
4. Insurance policies, declaration pages, and current statements;
5. Bank statements and canceled checks;
6. Brokerage account statements, canceled checks, and the name of the investment advisor;
7. Retirement account summaries and statements (IRA, 401(k), and pension);

8. Copies of personal bookkeeping software, such as Quicken or QuickBooks, and reports;
9. Trust agreements and account statements;
10. Expense account reimbursement forms and schedules;
11. Credit card statements (business and personal);
12. Cell phone records (business and personal);
13. Ownership documentation and the legal description of all real estate owned and all securitized debt associated therewith;
14. Lawsuit documents;
15. Appraisal documents;
16. Gift and loan documentation to and from the spouse and third parties;
17. Sources and amounts of any income not reflected on tax returns; and
18. Existence and location of safety deposit boxes.

For most divorce cases in which your opposing party is self-employed or a business owner, the CPA may want the following:[2]

1. Federal and state business tax returns and supporting schedules and worksheets;
2. K-1s, 1099s, and W-2s issued to the owner and related parties;
3. All contracts between the business and its owners, including employment and loans;
4. All business-organizing documents, including but not limited to corporate charters, minutes, stock transfer logs, partnership agreements, membership agreements and buy-sell agreements;[3]

---

2. For a more detailed list of documents needed for business valuation, see SHANNON PRATT & ALINA V. NICULITA, THE LAWYER'S BUSINESS VALUATION HANDBOOK (2nd ed. ABA 2010) Exhibit 27-2 at pp. 472–73.

3. Buy-sell agreements can be far more important legal and business documents than most business owners and family lawyers believe. If triggered, a buy-sell agreement will determine the return an owner might receive (or not receive) for a life's work. The author strongly recommends purchasing Z. CHRISTOPHER MERCER, BUY-SELL AGREEMENTS FOR CLOSELY HELD AND FAMILY BUSINESS OWNERS (Peabody Publishing 2010), available on Amazon.

all operating agreements, including but not limited to all ownership records; and recordings showing all directors, officers, stockholders, partners, and members and their respective percentages of ownership;

5. Financial statements;
6. General ledgers;
7. Appointment books or professional calendars;
8. Access to accounting software;
9. All business loan documentation including, but not limited to, personal financial statements from owners with personal guarantees, loan applications, and all other loan submission documentation provided to the credit facility;
10. Bank statements and canceled checks for all accounts;
11. Employment manuals and benefits summaries;
12. Pension plans, profit-sharing plans, or other retirement plan documents and all current benefits statements and summaries;
13. Expense reimbursement policies and summaries for owner;
14. Documentation of all real estate owned, securitized debt associated thereto, and associated contracts, such as leases;
15. Billing from CPAs and business attorneys;
16. Documents from lawsuits involving the company and/or the spouse in his or her capacity as owner, partner, officer, and so on; and
17. Appraisal documents.

Beyond these basic documents, there are always specific additional documents you'll need, depending on the type of business owned by the opposing party. For example, if the opposing party is a personal injury lawyer, your forensic accountant may want to review a schedule of all cases listing costs advanced and work in progress. For dentists, their equipment can be important. For doctors, do their medical records themselves have value? Do they own part of an MRI or CT scan? Construction company owners may have contracts where they are paid based on the progress of the project. Many forensic accountants already know what is important or can figure it out quickly. One of the many benefits of having a forensic accountant on board with the team early is being able to tailor discovery early in the case rather than supplementing the pleadings later in the case. Seeking additional documents is part of family law, but to the extent it can be reduced, you will save your client time and money.

To finalize your own set of interrogatories, an excellent starting point is the guidelines in Illinois Supreme Court Rule 213 (amended in 2017).[4] They are simple and thorough. Next, hit your local law library for various form books. Or ask a couple of experienced lawyers you respect if you can have a copy of their discovery forms. If you are uncomfortable asking other lawyers in your area, attend the ABA Family Law Section's conferences. Often, lawyers from other cities are more comfortable sharing their forms with lawyers outside their jurisdiction. Finally, determine if attorneys file discovery in your local jurisdiction. If so, go to the courthouse and look up some divorce cases handled by local attorneys you respect. Pull the jackets and copy the discovery issued. Ultimately, you should make your discovery your own, constantly upgrading your discovery forms as you see the need for specific discovery requests that you do not currently have in your forms.

By many jurisdictions' local rules, interrogatories are limited to 30 or so (including subparts) unless a separate motion is filed requesting the issuance of more. This is an overlooked opportunity for the family lawyer, as they can often issue more. If additional questions require court approval, family lawyers should consider filing the motion asking permission to issue more than 30. Most judges agree that the effective and efficient use of interrogatories can help keep expenses down, possibly reducing the overall cost of the case by allowing for shorter party depositions on the otherwise tedious financial aspects. Granted, depositions provide a greater opportunity for follow-up questions, but obtaining basic information earlier in the case through interrogatories can be strategically important.

Written Discovery or Depositions?

In a typical case, should a family lawyer get as much financial information as possible through written discovery or save important topics for deposition? With written discovery—interrogatories and requests for production of documents—you must assume opposing counsel will

4. *See* http://www.illinoiscourts.gov/SupremeCourt/Rules/Amend/2017/122917.pdf.

review her client's responses. Instead of getting from an opposing party answers and responses that have been filtered through opposing counsel, many lawyers want to put the party on the spot at the deposition, hoping to get some answers the deponent wishes she had not given. Is it important that the answers be spontaneous?

For example, in a custody case, a major bone of contention is proving which parent has been the primary caregiver. Some litigants can't answer the question, "How much does a gallon of milk cost?" The same parent might struggle with the question, "What is Tommy's current shoe size?" Obviously, if the question were posed in interrogatories, the parent would have time to work up the answer.

However, for many financial questions, such as expenses, most answers at deposition will not have to be precise and correct at the time. Many answers can be amended or corrected later. For example, consider the question, "What is your monthly car payment?" If the deponent answers $450, but the real answer is $523.75, the deponent can usually correct this later. Yes, there could be some damage to credibility, but few judges require litigants to have a perfect memory. Also, some nervousness in a deposition or trial can be excusable. Furthermore, the answers to some questions, especially those questions regarding precise financial details, can be predicted: "I don't know. Given some time, I could look up my check register and determine that answer for you."

Some lawyers have the opinion that spontaneous answers provide the deponent with a greater opportunity to lie or make mistakes. Capitalizing on those lies or mistakes can result in negotiating leverage. Other lawyers weigh as a more important factor the possible increased speed of settlement. Because most cases settle and many settlement proposals are drafted well in advance of depositions, some family lawyers want to get as much financial information as quickly as possible. Ultimately, the decision whether to seek particular financial information in written discovery or at deposition is a strategic one. This decision is best made by you, your client, and your forensic accountant discussing it as a team.

The Search for the Holy Grail and the Discovery Catch-22

Highly compensated employees and business owners often want to buy what they cannot otherwise afford with current available savings. This means borrowing. Borrowing means loan applications. Loan applications require the borrower to provide personal financial statements and affirmatively declare his personal net worth and annual or monthly income. The greater the net worth and income claimed, the greater the amount of credit, and possibly the lower the interest rate charged. This is true for both business and personal loans. Many targets,[5] even when borrowing money for their business, can be held personally liable for any representations made in applying for the loan. Many loan applications cite on their face that the financial statements and information contained therein are subject to criminal charges of perjury. In addition, state law may contain specific criminal statutes making lying on a loan application a crime.

One important category of financial documents is tax returns. Targets pay tax CPAs a great deal of money to assist with tax advice. A tax CPA's advice always involves reporting the lowest legally allowable amount of income in the period and showing the greatest amount of expenses allowable. For these reasons, targets are often very eager to disclose tax returns. Loan applications, however, often present a target's financial condition in the best possible light. Targets are usually not as excited about the prospect of disclosing loan applications and their supporting documentation.

When you are representing the nonbusiness-owner spouse (also sometimes referred to as the "out-spouse"), the Holy Grail of discovery is the personal financial statement. In a Tennessee case, *Powell v. Powell*,[6] Mr. Powell contested his wife's expert valuation of his interest in a check-cashing business. Mrs. Powell's expert, a CPA and certified valuation analyst, valued the business at $2,290,000. Mr. Powell's expert, his CPA, valued his business at $385,482. Prior to the divorce, Mr. Powell had sought loans from various financial institutions and had valued his own business on his financial statements at $3,370,000. The trial court considered Mr. Powell's valuation of his interest in the business made on those financial statements and accepted the wife's expert opinion. The court of appeals upheld the trial court, noting that the valuation provided on the financial statements was an admission

5. As discussed in Chapter 3, in the context of this book, the "target" of a lawyer and forensic accountant is, collectively, the opposing party/business owner and related closely held entities.
6. 124 S.W.3d 100 (Tenn. Ct. App. 2003).

against interest properly considered by the trial court. According to the court of appeals, "the financial statements provided by Mr. Powell [were] evidence which more strongly supported the valuation placed on the business by Mrs. Powell's expert, as opposed to that of Mr. Powell's expert."[7]

When you are representing the nonbusiness-owner spouse, interrogatories should always ask the target spouse to list all loan applications, and requests for production of documents should include the request to produce them. When the target fails to list loan applications, either for business or personal loans, this can be very important for impeachment purposes. Judges understand lying by omission.

How do you investigate whether a spouse has completed a loan application that was not disclosed in discovery? There are a few common ways:

1. Is interest expense reported on a business financial statement or tax return? If so, there is some sort of financing involved, and there may be a loan. Most business loans require personal guarantees, annual renewal, and submission of personal financial statements, including net worth and income declaration.
2. Was there a refinancing of a mortgage loan? If so, the mortgage company keeps the loan application. Search local real estate transaction recordings. In many states, this is the county register's office. All loans secured by real estate should be recorded. Consider issuing a subpoena to the mortgagor. See Example 5-3.
3. Search the register's office for loans or other credit facilities secured by real estate, inventory, or other assets. Securitized loans are often documented there. Once they are found, issue the financing company a subpoena seeking loan applications and financial statements of the more-propertied spouse associated therewith.
4. Guess. Most targets have a favorite bank. Targets usually bank personally with the financial institution loaning the business money. Send the family banker a subpoena requesting the

---

7. *Id.* at 106.

financial statements submitted with any loan applications by the spouse or business.

If your client suspects a loan application exists, and maybe even knows a particular financial institution has made a loan, should you wait for the written discovery to come back to see if the loan will be disclosed or send the subpoena immediately? This is an important strategic decision. If the subpoena is issued prior to receiving written discovery, the target may disclose the loan application. If the subpoena is sent to the wrong financial institution, the target may be emboldened to intentionally omit the information. Or if the subpoena is issued to the right place, the target may answer the interrogatory truthfully but fail to provide the loan application, citing the subpoena itself and thereby seeking to avoid production. By answering the interrogatory truthfully but failing to provide the loan application, the target may be waiting to see the subpoena results. For whatever reason, if the subpoena results fail to produce the needed loan application, the target may then claim no application was made. If one arises later, the target may claim to have failed to keep a copy of the loan application or claim that the paperwork had been lost or misfiled. In any event, this is a common Catch-22 for lawyers handling divorce cases.

Like many issues in divorce, this Catch-22 presents a judgment call that you, your client, and your forensic accountant should make together as a team. This is where experience comes into play. Subpoenas cost money and take time. Waiting to receive written discovery saves money, but time is lost. Often, time is the greater enemy. In other cases, cost is the greater enemy. Patience must be weighed against procrastination. There is never an absolutely correct solution to this problem.

Subpoenas

If bacon is the duct tape of the restaurant industry because everything tastes better with bacon, subpoenas are the duct tape of family law. When the opposing party won't give up documents in a discovery, attorneys can issue subpoenas. In divorces, there is a fairly small group of likely subpoena recipients—generally, those third parties, such as banks that have issued loans to the target, that are likely to possess any of the financial documentation needed by your forensic accountant (see the list of usual subpoena targets in this chapter). Talented family lawyers (and their paralegals) are experts at utilizing subpoenas *duces tecum* with production in lieu of appearance. Check your jurisdiction's rules. If your rules provide for production of documents in lieu of appearance, definitely add this tool to your arsenal. Know your jurisdiction's procedural and evidence rules with respect to authenticating the documents received. If the procedural rules are followed, the documents produced can be introduced directly into evidence. This can save money and help compress time if the opposing party is dragging his feet.

Because the subpoena recipient may not be familiar with subpoenas and their procedure, or may merely be unfamiliar with subpoenas that allow for production in lieu of appearance, consider two additional touches. First, include a friendly letter from you, the issuing lawyer, informing the recipient of the requirements of the subpoena and that the custodian of records can call you (or your paralegal) with any questions. Second, place a notice on the face of the subpoena and the exhibit explaining how it can work. Here is an example:

> *Pursuant to [your state] Rules of Civil Procedure [cite the rule], in lieu of appearance, the Custodian of Records may provide the documents listed on Exhibit "A" by the date of appearance specified in this Subpoena, provided that the Custodian of Records provides an Affidavit swearing under oath that the documents produced are authentic to the best of the Custodian of Records' knowledge, information and belief, and further, that said Affidavit states whether or not all documents listed on this Exhibit have been produced.*

Note that, for some unknown reason, some recipients (and opposing counsel) do not always understand the whole "in lieu of appearance" thing and think there must be an in-person appearance at an actual deposition. Read your jurisdiction's subpoena issuance rules carefully and handcraft a written protocol for your paralegals to follow for trial subpoenas, deposition subpoenas, and especially subpoenas *duces tecum* with production in lieu of appearance. Sometimes a simple follow-up phone call can make the difference between compliance and frustrating noncompliance.

Many subpoena recipients may also require payment in advance for research and copying costs. When discussing these costs with your client, be sure to explain the following:

1. The value of obtaining information and documents directly from third-party sources;
2. The potential benefit of finding the smoking gun information or document to settlement leverage;
3. The cost of discovery motions to compel at the lawyer's hourly rate; and
4. The potential benefits of obtaining the documents more quickly than through compelling documents.

If the estimated copying cost is reasonable, consider paying it. If the estimated copying costs are too high, see if you can obtain scanned documents in portable document format (PDF). Also, determine if some part of the subpoena request can be eliminated to save cost. If the research and copying cost is still unreasonable, make sure you understand your state's law. There may be some limitations listed in statutes. If a bill for subpoena compliance is issued after production, determine if it is reasonable. If you don't know, call experienced lawyers in your jurisdiction and ask around. If the amount requested is unreasonable, consider offering to pay a reasonable amount and negotiate the cost like anything else.

Family lawyers must also create subpoena exhibits for their forms files. Subpoena exhibits are attached to subpoenas and list the documents to be produced. Create thorough lists of documents typically needed from each category of recipient. Before issuing the subpoena in a particular case, be sure to tailor it. Handcrafting requests can help reduce the risk of motions to quash and of objections claiming the document list is overly broad and unduly burdensome.

Family lawyers often need to issue subpoenas to the following:

- The employer of the opposing party—see Example 5-1;
- The "employer" of the self-employed opposing party—see Example 5-2;
- The mortgage company, for loan applications—see Example 5-3;
- Brokerage firms and financial advisors—see Example 5-4;
- CPAs—see Example 5-5;
- Banks—see Example 5-6; and
- Credit card issuers—see Example 5-7.

Example 5-1
Employer of Opposing Party

To: Custodian of Records
Acme Funeral Homes, LLC

Deliver any and all employment records, memoranda, supplements, and updates for ***Michael Smith*** (hereinafter "Employee"), Social Security Number with last four (4) digits ***#XXXX***, date of birth ***XX/XX/XX***, ***for January 1, 2017 to current date***, including but not limited to:

1. Employee's entire personal file, including, but not limited to, employment records to present date;
2. Documentation regarding employee work schedule, including an explanation of whether Employee is working full-time, whether Employee could be working additional time, how much additional time Employee could be working and what steps Employee must take to work additional time;
3. The vacation time applicable to Employee, including a description of how much time Employee has already taken and the date for same;
4. Application for employment including resume;
5. Summary payroll records showing total hours worked, gross pay, and deductions for years listed above and current year-to-date including but not limited to W-2s or 1099s;
6. Employment agreements or contracts;
7. Commendation and disciplinary records;
8. Performance evaluations or job performance ratings;
9. Documentation of pay increases or decreases;
10. Detailed descriptions of compensation formulas including but not limited to base pay, commissions, stock options, and/or bonuses;
11. Copies of minutes from any Board of Directors or Members meetings discussing compensation for Employee;
12. Documentation of termination if Employee is no longer employed;

13. Notice of separation if Employee is no longer employed;
14. Documentation, notes, or memoranda Employee prepared and requested to be included within Employee's personnel records;
15. Documentation of actual cost to Employee of health insurance, dental insurance and/or vision insurance for Employee only;
16. Documentation of actual cost to Employee of health insurance, dental insurance and/or vision insurance for Employee and family members' coverage;
17. For each pension, profit-sharing, savings, stock option, employee stock purchase plan, or other employee benefit plan, employee welfare plan, employee pension plan of any type sponsored you as employer, whether full-time or part-time, and whether ERISA plan, military pension, or federal, state, or local pension or retirement plan, or any other type of employee benefit or retirement plan whatsoever, produce for each such plan:
    a. All annual benefits statements for Employee;
    b. The summary plan description;
    c. The plan's QDRO procedures;
    d. Any booklets, pamphlets, information sheets, or other written materials distributed by the plan or the plan sponsor to employees or participants generally concerning rights to receive plan benefits, types and forms of benefits payable, options, and elections available under any plan;
    e. Any other documents concerning Employee's rights to receive plan benefits, types and forms of benefits payable, options, and elections available under any plan;
    f. Any correspondence or e-mail correspondence generated internally or with Employee, Employee's previous employer, and any plan administrators concerning any Employee elections of types of benefits, beneficiary designations or modifications, investment options and alternatives, this court proceeding, or any other topic or matter regarding Employee.

Example 5-2
Employer—Opposing Party Self-Employed

To: Custodian of Records
Smith Plumbing Co.

Any and all documents showing the following ***for the years 2017 to current***:

1. Owners, ownership interests, and percentage of ownership of Smith Plumbing Co., whether prepared formally or informally, including but not limited to the following: corporate charter, minutes of shareholder's meetings, minutes of board of directors meetings, contracts, stock certificates issued, bylaws, and minutes of organizational meetings.
2. All federal income tax returns and supporting schedules filed on behalf of and for Smith Plumbing Co., including but not limited to Form 1120.
3. All W-2s, 1099s, K-1s, or other applicable Internal Revenue Service forms showing compensation or profit sharing from Smith Plumbing Co. to Bradley W. Smith.
4. Copies of all professional or business licenses issued by the state of Tennessee in the name of Bradley W. Smith, whether or not issued on behalf of Smith Plumbing Co.
5. Copies of the last two federal quarterly tax payment schedules filed by Smith Plumbing Co.
6. Summaries of any and all compensation or profit sharing paid to Bradley W. Smith by Smith Plumbing Co.
7. Copies of any documentation of any company application package or company loan documentation for any loan made to Bradley W. Smith from Smith Plumbing Co.
8. Copies of any and all employment agreements, ownership agreements, or any other contracts between Bradley W. Smith and Smith Plumbing Co.
9. Copies of any documentation of fringe benefits or expenses reimbursed and paid by Smith Plumbing Co. on behalf of or for Bradley W. Smith, including but not limited to the following: company car, meals and entertainment, health insurance, retirement benefits, 401(k), Keogh, and stock option plans.

Example 5-3
Mortgage—Loan Application

To: Custodian of Records
Mortgages R Us

Deliver any and all mortgage loan application documentation, including but not limited to loan application forms completed, financial statements, proof of income, federal income tax returns, asset listings, and/or other supporting schedules or documents provided to Mortgages R Us for loan number 123 by Bradley W. Smith and Sheri B. Smith, Husband and Wife, for the purchase and/or refinancing of 5945 Fulmer Way Lane, Knoxville, Tennessee, on or about December 10, 2018.

Example 5-4
Brokerage Firms and Financial Advisors

To: Custodian of Records
Acme Brokerage Firm

Deliver the following records and documents pertaining to Timothy Smith, Social Security number 123-04-1891, ***for years 2017 to the current date***:

1. List any and all accounts titled in the above-listed person's name, individually or jointly, including personal, corporate, or business accounts, open at any time during the above-stated time period;
2. List any and all accounts from which the above-listed person could withdraw funds at any time during the above-stated time period;
3. All account papers, including but not limited to new account forms, client agreements, signatory authority cards, and forms associated with opening and maintaining accounts;
4. Annual or "year end" statements, quarterly statements, monthly statements, copies of canceled checks, deposit slips, and deposit items;
5. Transaction listings of all checks written and wire transfers showing payee and payor or transferee and transferor;
6. All authorizations for specific transactions;

7. All loan applications and margin account applications, including but not limited to forms completed, personal or business financial statements, net worth statements, proof of income, federal and state income tax returns, and asset listings provided to you in any and all applications, whether or not approved;
8. Print computerized records maintained but not regularly printed showing internal "master pages" or summaries of account designations and settings and provide applicable code keys explaining listing designations; and
9. All account cancellations and related supporting documentation.

Example 5-5
CPAs for Business Owner and Business

Definitions and Time Limitations Applicable to This Subpoena Only:

"Client" is defined as Defendant/Plaintiff (List name), in addition to legal entities that Defendant/Plaintiff (List name) owns in part or in whole and/or for which Defendant/Plaintiff (List name) is a beneficiary, trustee, or member of a board of directors or management.

"CPA" is defined inclusively as the witness to which this subpoena is addressed, the firm of the subpoena recipient, and the individual CPA responsive to Client's accounting, tax, or consulting needs. "CPA" also includes records from Client's previous CPA firm(s), whether or not held, stored, or otherwise available at either firm's office(s).

Time Limitation. For tax preparation work, the seven (7) most recent tax returns. For all other engagements, the five (5) most recent completed years, calendar or fiscal, and current year-to-date work performed, including work in progress.

Deliver any and all records of Client, including but not limited to the following:

1. Financial statements and opinions generated (whether compilation, review, or audit) and reports from other consulting engagements (formal or informal), including work papers, confirmation documentation, and supporting documentation, whether prepared by CPA or Client, for each.

2. Tax returns (federal, state, and local), supporting schedules (whether or not attached to return and whether prepared by CPA or Client), attachments, notes, work sheets, work papers, and amended returns.
3. Budgets, forecasts, financial analyses, appraisals, buy/sell agreements, deferred compensation agreements, shareholder or partnership agreements, financial projections, narratives, proposed and final offering memoranda, legal opinions, and bond indentures, whether prepared by Client, CPA, or any third party.
4. Legal documentation with respect to Client's status as owner of legal entities, including but not limited to minutes, articles of incorporation, trust documentation, and LLC and partnership operating agreements.
5. Employment agreements possessed by CPA, including Client, to which Client is a party.
6. Correspondence with Internal Revenue Service and state or local taxation agencies relating to or on behalf of Client.
7. Documentation concerning related-party transactions.
8. Billing records (summary and detail) from CPA to Client and from Client to CPA, if any.
9. Engagement letters between CPA and Client.
10. Correspondence and email between CPA and Client.
11. Correspondence and email between CPA and any financial institution, bank, or lender transacting business with Client.
12. CPA's internal document retention policy.
13. Insurance policies and declaration pages of CPA, showing insureds, beneficiaries, face amounts, and cash surrender values.
14. List names and addresses of all associations, partnerships, corporations, enterprises, trusts, limited liability companies, sole proprietorships, or other entities in which Client has or has had an interest or claim or has claimed any interest, including management or board of directorships, the nature of Client's

interest, the amount of or percentage of Client's interest, and documentation recording or describing any valuation of the entities' or Client's interest.

15. Offers to buy or sell any interests described in this Exhibit.
16. Documents relating to any business or personal transactions between CPA and Client, including but not limited to leases, contracts, promissory notes, mortgages, loans, gifts, and financial transfers, whether or not for consideration.
17. List dates, times, locations, attendees, and purposes of all personal and business trips on which CPA and Client accompanied each other.

Example 5-6
Banks

Deliver the following records and documents pertaining to Timothy A. Smith, Social Security number 123-456-7890, ***from January 1, 2017, to date***:

1. For any and all accounts with Bank of America; including but not limited to personal accounts, corporate or business accounts, and any accounts from which he is authorized to draw funds; all bank statements, copies of canceled checks, deposit slips, deposit items; and
2. Any and all loan application documentation, including but not limited to loan and credit application forms completed, financial statements, proof of income, federal income tax returns and asset listings, provided to Bank of America in application for any loan, whether or not approved.

The requirements of T.C.A. Section 45-10-106 have been met.

Many states have specific requirements and limitations for subpoenas issued to banks. Include the procedures and requirements in your firm's operations manual. Every time you issue subpoenas to banks, make sure your staff follows the procedures to the letter. Some custodians of records may not tell you when or why there was a refusal to comply with the subpoena. If the failure to comply was based on a simple legal requirement, it can be embarrassing.

Example 5-7
Credit Card Issuers

Pertaining to any and all accounts in the name of Josiah D. Smith, Social Security number 123-456-7890, ***from June 30, 2017 through the current date***, deliver the following records and documents:

1. Any and all account information and documentation, including but not limited to monthly statements for personal, corporate or business accounts, or for any accounts from which the account holder is authorized to draw funds;
2. Any and all account application documentation, including but not limited to loan application forms completed, financial statements, proof of income, federal income tax returns and asset listings for prospective or actual accounts; and
3. Copies of any and all internal memoranda, notes, or audio recordings documenting the application made, by whom, and if such application was made over the phone.

Depositions

Depositions are often the first time clients see their lawyer work. Some clients expect this occasion to be caustic and confrontational. It certainly can be. But many experienced lawyers believe the best way to get information from a deponent is to be nice, gently involving the deponent in friendly and informal conversation. Prepare your client accordingly.

Depositions are important. For third-party witnesses, consider including with the subpoena another list of documents for the witness to produce. Compare the documents produced to the documents produced through other discovery. Maybe there will be an alteration that results in exposing a lie, possibly even under oath.

If there is a suspected co-conspirator, consider deposing her. Make the co-conspirator commit perjury to assist the target. Some co-conspirators won't want to lie under oath. The presence of the court reporter recording everything said is a powerful tool for honesty. Even if the co-conspirator initially agreed to help fudge up some recording of certain financial transactions for the divorce, lying at a deposition is a completely different situation. You never know. Issuing a deposition subpoena to a key third-party witness has resulted in many favorable divorce settlements.

If the witness also happens to be financially savvy, say the target's controller, strongly consider asking the forensic accountant to attend to assist with follow-up questions. Keep in mind, though, that everything you say to your forensic accountant may be discoverable if that expert is going to testify. If your client's forensic accountant is only a consulting expert, then what is said to the expert can be kept confidential. If the budget allows, you may want to have two experts.

Supplementation

Know your state's rules on discovery supplementation. If the rules require a special request for supplementation, consider filing a notice of request for supplementation every four to six months. As many divorce cases tend to drag on much longer than they should, be vigilant about supplementation requests early enough before trial so that, if the opposing party fails to supplement, there is enough time to file a motion to compel its production. Or if there is a scheduling order, include pre-trial supplementation deadlines. As always, advise your client to be prepared to produce what is requested and explain why pre-trial supplementation is vitally important. A single gap in monthly account statements is important for the same reason the final discovery production must include all relevant monthly statements.

Discovery and Research about Opposing Experts

Typical expert witness interrogatories require disclosure of the name, address, and telephone contact numbers of each expert witness who will offer any testimony. The interrogatory will also request the subject matter on which the expert witness is expected to testify, the conclusions and/or opinions of the expert witness, and the basis therefore. A document request should also include the expert's qualifications, curriculum vitae, and report, if any. In addition, know if your state's rules track Federal Rule of Civil Procedure 26(a)(2)(b), which has specific expert disclosure requirements. If so, don't be shy in sending opposing counsel a request for compliance with the rule.

As soon as you know the name of any opposing expert, begin with some basic research. First, ask your expert about the opposing expert. What are the expert's reputation, strengths, and weaknesses? Next, find the expert's website. What does the expert claim to do for a living? Is the expert's curriculum vitae (CV) available online? Has the expert ever written any articles relevant to the issues in your case? If so, print them out. Read them. Does anything stick out as unusual? Know that in high-asset, high-conflict cases, a tremendous amount of resources and energy may go into the investigation and neutralization of expert witnesses.

Does the CV list the lawyers representing the prior clients for whom the expert worked? If not, ask which cases, if any, in which the expert testified on behalf of clients represented by current counsel for the opposing party. Can the expert's former clients' opposing attorneys be found to call for background intelligence? What certifications does the expert hold? Do the certifying organizations list public discipline online? If the case justifies the resources, consider a civil case check for judgments against the expert and maybe a quick background check. Also, check for the expert's name appearing in appellate opinions as an expert. Print them and read them. You never know. You may get lucky and find something very helpful.

Obtaining Tax Documents Directly from the IRS

If you represent the non-income-generating spouse, your client may not have prepared or been in possession of copies of the tax returns. Particularly nefarious targets may produce tax returns purportedly signed by both parties and submitted to the IRS that, in fact, were not the completed forms actually submitted. To confirm directly with the IRS what was submitted, you have two primary options.

To obtain copies of actual tax returns, go to the IRS website (www.IRS.gov). Print and read the instructions for Form 4506. Once submitted, it can take several weeks to get results. To simply confirm that copies of the tax return the client possesses were actually filed or the documents obtained in discovery were actually submitted, use Form 4506T to request a transcript. The transcript is the raw-number inputs into the IRS system from various line entries. All family lawyers (and paralegals working for family lawyers) should have these forms in their files. Submitting either IRS form does not take much time. The lead time on the information return is the issue. Even if you only confirm that the tax returns in your possession are the ones actually filed, that fact alone can be helpful by eliminating that aspect of possible fraud.

Tax returns are important. Certainly, proving income is the primary objective. But tax returns also list important other sources of income—assets. For example, if interest income is reported, that will be recorded by the entity paying the interest on a 1099-INT form submitted directly to the IRS and the taxpayer. Dividend income is reported on 1099-DIV. Interest and dividend income are reported to the IRS on Schedule B. Reviewing tax returns is discussed in more detail in Chapter 7.

Tax returns are also important because of their upper-tier status on the hierarchy of the continuum of lies. If the nonowner spouse can prove in court that the target knowingly lied on a tax return, the target's credibility will suffer. Depending on the gravity of the lie, the trial court may determine that, because the target has lied on tax returns to the IRS, the target is also able, capable, and apt to lie to the court.

Researching Public Records and Assets

Researching public records via the Internet has never been easier. There are several simple places one can and should research regularly. Search all parties' names and known names of businesses and d/b/as (doing-business-as names). Consider using the following resources:

- Tax assessor's office—lists real property;
- Register of deeds office—lists real property transfers, liens, trust deeds, mortgages, and UCC-1s;
- Secretary of state's office—lists business, some owner information, and registered agents for service of process;
- Local newspaper and business journals—contain articles featuring business owners and their businesses;
- Civil and criminal courts (federal and state)—often business owners may be sued individually and in their capacity as business owners; and
- Bankruptcy courts—bankruptcy filings list assets and creditors.

Even experienced family lawyers can find documents and not understand their importance in relation to other aspects of the case. Examples include corporate formation records, minutes, financing statements, UCC-1s, and durable powers of attorney. Any one document may make sense to the family lawyer, but often these documents comprise only part of the story. Developing professional relationships with corporate lawyers, trust and estate lawyers, and real estate lawyers can be very helpful. Call them up. Subject to any ethical restrictions concerning confidentiality, show them what you have and talk through the typical document execution associated with the transactions evidenced by the documents. Going the extra mile to understand the documents you currently have could result in your issuing exactly the right subpoena to exactly the right entity, resulting in discovery of a smoking gun document.

Production Memos, Deficiency Memos, Gap Charts, and Bates-Stamping

Receiving discovery is important. In the middle of the examination of a witness in court, proving what discovery documents were or were not exchanged can be just as important. For example, at trial, one lawyer is cross-examining a party on the witness stand. Seeking to impeach the witness with a document, the questioning lawyer hands the document to the other lawyer just prior to submitting it to the witness. But the other lawyer objects to the use of the document on the grounds that it had not been produced in discovery. The questioning lawyer states the document was produced. What is the judge to do? The judge will not want to spend time elongating a divorce trial over a dispute between two lawyers claiming a document was or was not produced in discovery. There may have been thousands of pages of documents exchanged. Judges do not want to decide credibility between two lawyers. Nevertheless, assuming the document is significant, the issue is important. At that moment, the argument over production or nonproduction matters a great deal. Being right and winning the argument may be two different things.

Unless there is documentation listing specific documents produced and corresponding numbers of pages, there is no way to effectively argue production disputes in the courtroom. Industrial-sized discovery cases usually require that lawyers determine if the documents should be Bates-stamped. Whether to Bates-stamp discovery in a family law matter is a question of judgment—weighing cost relative to benefit. Physically stamping documents is not the hard part. You can find copiers or copy services to stamp documents with reference letters and numbers. Indexing the documents page by page and document by document, however, can be tedious beyond description.

Bates-stamping documents in a family law matter is always tricky because of the way clients perceive preparation. If you Bates-stamp from the beginning of the case and the case settles, the cost is sunk and appears wasted. If you wait until the settlement negotiations fail to begin the Bates-stamping process, the task itself could be overwhelming as other time commitment pressures mount. On the other hand, if you complete the Bates-stamping project, the case is tried, and no discovery production dispute occurs at trial, the client may still claim the Bates-stamping was overkill because there was no dispute. Obviously, preventing the dispute was the result. In any event, even if it's patiently explained in advance, clients don't always see the benefit in lawyers being prepared.

For a good discussion of Bates-stamping, see the first chapter of *The Divorce Trial Manual*.[8] At trial, if the contested document is Bates-stamped, checking the index of documents cross-referenced by number should be relatively simple. If the case's budget does not call for a Bates-stamping protocol, consider creating your own discovery production memorandum procedure. Discovery production memoranda can be a less-expensive organizational tool used to memorialize documents produced and documents received in discovery. Once discovery is exchanged, the attorney preparing the memorandum can share it with opposing counsel. The enclosure letter should also request opposing counsel review the list to determine whether the memorandum is accurate and complete. Upon review, if there are any inaccuracies, the reviewing lawyer should notify in writing the lawyer who prepared the memorandum. In the absence of a dispute, the producing counsel can claim to have prepared an accurate memorandum the court can rely upon.

Example 5-8 is a portion of a discovery production memorandum.

8. Lynne Z. Gold-Bikin & Stephen Kolodny, The Divorce Trial Manual, Chapter 1, pp. 8–9 (ABA 2003).

Example 5-8
CONFIDENTIAL INTERNAL MEMORANDUM

To: Attorney
From: Paralegal
Date: November 11, 2018
Subject: Picard v. Picard
Document Production Index Memo
Documents Produced by Wife on November 10, 2018

This memorandum describes documents produced by Wife on November 10, 2018. The documents were hand-delivered by Wife's counsel's paralegal on November 10, 2018. The documents were in scanned (PDF) format on a compact disc and were Bates-stamped. The documents were reviewed by Paralegal on November 10, 2018. The following documents were received:

1. Statements dated 1/1/16 to 10/1/18 for Fleet Bank Checking Account with account number ending in #5864 in the names of J. L. Picard and Beverly C. Picard. (Bates-stamped 00001–00088)
2. Statements dated 1/1/16 to 10/1/18 for Excelsior Brokerage Account with account number ending in #3946 in the names of J. L. Picard and Beverly C. Picard. (Bates-stamped 00089–00132)
3. Statements dated 1/1/16 to 10/1/18 for Excelsior Roth IRA Account with account number ending in #5736 in the name of Beverly C. Picard. (Bates-stamped 00133–00176)
4. 2017 annual statement for Khitomer Life Insurance Policy with policy number ending in #9578 in the name of Beverly C. Picard, insured J. L. Picard. (Bates-stamped 00177)
5. Monthly statement dated 10/1/17 for Enterprise mortgage loan with loan number ending in #2184 in the names of J. L. Picard and Beverly C. Picard. (Bates-stamped 00178)
6. Statements dated 1/1/16 to 10/1/18 for The Doctors' Visa with account number ending in #9372 in the name of Beverly C. Picard. (Bates-stamped 000179–000198)

Discovery deficiency memoranda list documents that have not been produced but should have been. These can be very helpful in conjunction with motions to compel. It is generally a good idea to send opposing counsel the memorandum, in the form of a letter, to give her an opportunity to correct the deficiencies before you are forced to file your motion to compel. The discovery deficiency memorandum can then simply be attached as an exhibit to the motion to compel. You should also update the memorandum as the case progresses. Example 5-9 is a portion of a discovery deficiency memorandum.

Example 5-9
CONFIDENTIAL INTERNAL MEMORANDUM

To: Attorney
From: Paralegal
Date: November 11, 2018
Subject: Picard v. Picard
Discovery Deficiencies Memo

Deficiencies with Respect to Answers to Interrogatories

Interrogatory No. 9. For this request for a list of all marital property, including type of property, basis for claim that it is marital, cost of acquisition, and present value, Wife failed to provide an itemized list of furniture, furnishings, art, and appliances in the marital residence and the present value of each item. Husband no longer resides in the marital residence and therefore is unable to compile this list.

Interrogatory No. 10. For this request for information regarding business interests, including nature of interest, percentage of interest, and estimated value of interest, Wife failed to provide her estimated value of her medical practice and the percentage of her interest.

Deficiencies with Respect to Requests for Production of Documents

Document Request No. 2. For this request for documents reflecting the income, expenses, assets, or liabilities for any business interest, Wife failed to produce partnership income tax returns, balance sheets, profit and loss statements, income statements, or other documents reflecting the income, expenses, assets, or liabilities of her medical practice.

Document Request No. 6. For this request for general ledgers, payroll ledgers, and depreciation schedules for any business interest, Wife failed to produce any documents responsive to this request for her medical practice.

Document Request No. 8. For this request for evidence of ownership or control of a business interest, Wife failed to produce the partnership agreement for her medical practice.

Discovery gap charts list documents produced and not produced, account by account, monthly statement by monthly statement. The gap chart can also be color coded to show when each statement was received. It can be a very powerful tool because it helps organize documents and can be blown up either as demonstrative evidence or as a visual aid in the court room. See Example 5-10.

Example 5-10
Discovery Gap Chart

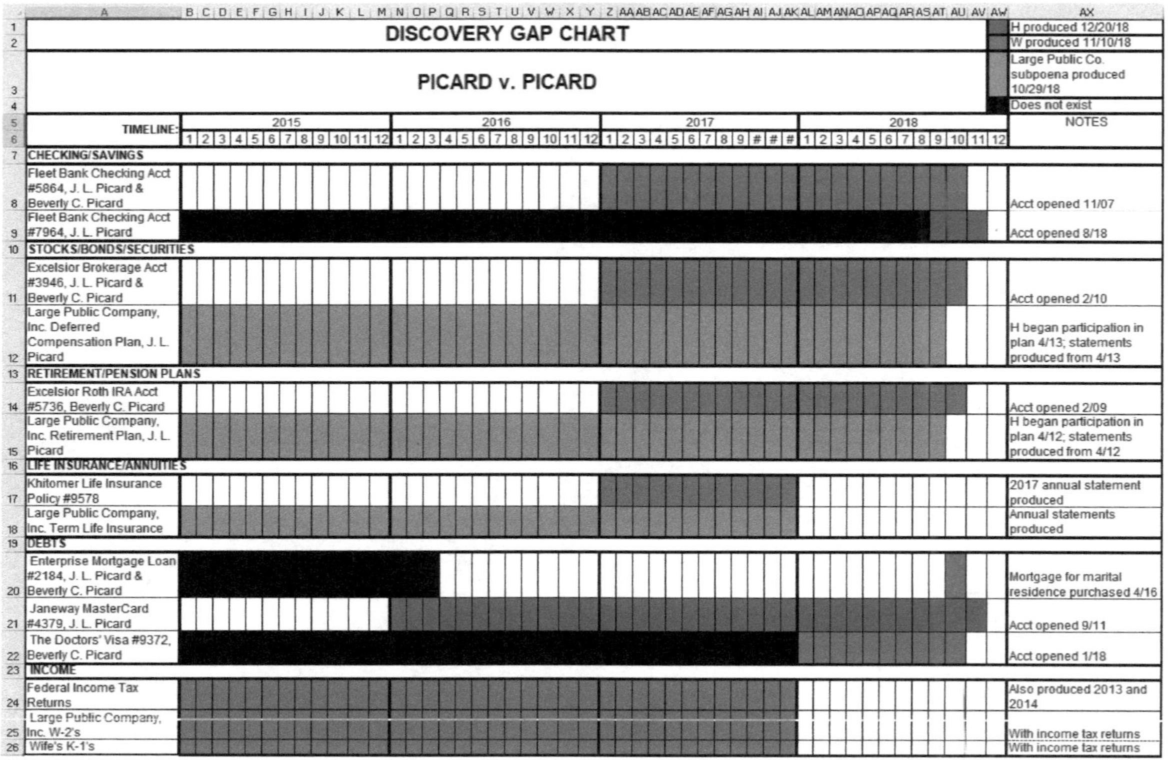

Case Example: Litigation Support with Discovery Gone Wrong

Reviewing discovery production and tracking discovery deficiencies are both excellent uses of forensic accountants aiding in litigation. However, in the case described below, overly relying on accountants cost the attorney in question a discovery sanction of $50,000. If a family lawyer hires forensic accountants to outsource certain litigation support functions, it is still the lawyer's responsibility to ensure that the accountants know what they are doing and double check their work. As much as family lawyers may try, certain aspects of high-conflict cases cannot be totally outsourced.

The husband and wife in this Illinois divorce case[9] were married in 1985. The husband was successful as a trader and investor and had amassed substantial wealth for the family, with the marital estate eventually growing to over $21 million. The couple had four children, and the wife was a stay-at-home mom. At the time of their

9. *In re* Marriage of LaRocque, 2018 Ill. App. 2d 160973 (Ill. Ct. App. May 31, 2018).

2014 divorce, one of the children had passed away and the others were emancipated. The status of the couple's wealth was one of the hotly contested issues in the Du Page County trial court.

In the mid-2000s, the husband had retained an attorney to create a comprehensive family estate plan. As a result, over the years, a number of irrevocable trusts were formed. The wife signed documents regarding those trusts but later denied knowing the details of the estate planning process. As a result of these trusts, the children would ultimately reap substantial estate tax benefits. However, the wife later alleged that these trusts really constituted the husband's "divorce planning."

Prior to trial, the husband moved for summary judgment and argued that all of the trusts had been transferred irrevocably and therefore were not part of the marital estate. This motion was supported by affidavits and exhibits comprising thousands of pages.

The evidence included affidavits by estate planning attorneys Michael Hartz and Jonathan Graber, who testified that the primary objective of both spouses was to provide an orderly distribution of their property with minimal estate taxes for their children upon their deaths.

The wife countered that she had only signed the documents because of misrepresentations on the part of the husband. She also argued that many of the transfers had taken place after the marriage had irretrievably broken down.

The wife supported her argument with an affidavit by her expert witness on the subject of accounting, Tom Levato. Levato's affidavit focused on alleged deficiencies in discovery documents produced by the husband. The affidavit also claimed that some pertinent documents were missing.

The trial court granted the husband's motion for summary judgment. It held that the trusts were separate legal entities, and therefore neither party had an interest in them. For the purpose of the divorce, the trusts were neither part of the marital estate nor the nonmarital assets of the parties. The trial court had noted that the wife's failure to read documents before signing did not constitute a defense and that none of the trustees had violated any fiduciary duties. It did point out, however, that the wife was free to argue at trial that the husband had committed fraud or dissipation.

The litigation was extremely contentious and included motions for sanctions against the wife's attorney. In the summary judgment motion, the wife had argued that some of the discovery requests had not been complied with. One of the wife's attorneys finally admitted that the requested documents had, in fact, been received but that the accountant they retained had forgotten to inventory them.

The trial took two phases. Since the wife claimed that the husband had engaged in divorce planning after the marriage had broken down, the first issue was to determine the date at which the marriage began its irretrievable breakdown.

This first phase of the trial focused upon the death of the couple's eldest son. His health had taken a turn for the worse in 2010, and he died in 2014. The wife claimed that the 2010 date corresponded with the beginning of the end of the marriage and argued that transfers after that date should be closely scrutinized. However, the trial court noted that even though both parties had consulted with divorce lawyers in the years following their son's illness, the couple continued to live together until 2014 and even took a vacation to Mexico together that year.

The husband denied divorce planning, claiming that he didn't believe that the relationship was in trouble until it began becoming volatile a few months after the couple returned from Mexico.

After hearing the evidence, the trial court agreed with the husband and set the date of irretrievable breakdown in early 2014, after the parties returned from their Mexico vacation.

With this issue decided, the second phase of the trial commenced. Much of this phase focused on the wife's claims that the husband had dissipated assets. The trial court agreed with the husband that there had been no dissipation and that all of the trusts had been created and funded for proper purposes. It specifically noted that estate planning for the benefit of children did not amount to intentionally diminishing the marital estate. It valued the estate at just over $21 million and ordered this amount to be split equally between the two spouses. The trial court also awarded the wife $30,000 per month in alimony. In addition, it ordered the wife's attorney to pay $50,000 to the husband as sanctions for the earlier claims that discovery had been incomplete. Both the wife and the attorney then appealed to the Illinois Court of Appeals, which first addressed the summary judgment motion. It agreed with the lower court that the husband had established that the transfers to the trusts were appropriate.

The appeals court noted that, even though an accountant had been involved in the document review process, the wife had never produced any expert testimony as to the critical issue of the trusts' legitimacy.

Similarly, it agreed with the lower court that the wife's failure to read documents before signing them was not a defense.

The appeals court then turned to the wife's arguments that the husband had been guilty of depletion or dissipation of the marital estate. After a careful analysis of the evidence, it again agreed that the lower court's rulings had been proper.

The court then turned to the separate appeal by attorney Howard Rosenfeld. The attorney argued that the lower court had abused its discretion in granting a $50,000 judgment against him personally as sanctions for his position during the summary judgment motion. On this point, the husband argued that the opposition to the motion contained "numerous misstatements of the law and the evidence." He pointed out that the wife had retained a trust expert but that no affidavit from this expert had been offered.

The wife and her attorney, on the other hand, argued that they had over 4,000 pages of exhibits to go through and that they were under no obligation to "just go along" with the husband's agenda.

The husband also argued that the wife's attorney had made many requests for irrelevant documents. He argued that the most egregious conduct was the wife's contention that he had failed to produce certain documents. The husband's attorney had responded to these allegations and even cited the relevant Bates numbers for the allegedly missing documents. The wife and her attorney later admitted this mistake but insisted that there had been "no desire to waste the court's time."

The lower court had agreed that the wife had the right to investigate her claims, but the trial judge had been forced to spend an entire afternoon trying to figure out which documents had not been produced. At that hearing, the husband's attorney had insisted that the documents had been produced and even reiterated the Bates numbers. Even then, attorney Rosenfeld stuck to his position that documents were missing, telling the judge that the accountants reviewing the documents had told him they were missing.

The judge was apparently not pleased and pointed out to the attorney that his reliance on the accountants would not shield him from liability if the husband's attorney demonstrated that he had, indeed, produced the documents. After being satisfied that the documents had been produced, the court entered judgment of $50,000 against attorney Rosenfeld for unnecessarily increasing the costs of the litigation.

The court of appeals held that these sanctions were appropriate. It pointed out that the attorney had made serious allegations of misconduct and that those allegations were not supported by the evidence. In addition to the claims of missing documents, the appeals court focused on the wife's allegations, such as the claim that the estate planning "read like a manual for manipulating the marital estate." The appeals court, after reviewing the evidence, concluded that there was no evidence of any scheme and that some of her allegations defied common sense.

On the issue of the allegedly missing documents, the appeals court was not charitable. It noted that attorney Rosenfeld discounted the matter as a "mere mix-up" by the accountant. But the appeals court reminded him that the correct way to resolve such a mix-up would be to work with the opposing counsel to "resolve the dispute in a professional manner" instead of doubling down on the claim that the documents had never been received. This, according to the appeals court, not only wasted the time of the court and the opposing attorney but also "contributed to the toxic dynamic."

The appeals court concluded by noting that the sanctions were not just for making a mistake but also for the way that mistake was handled. For these reasons, the court of appeals found that there had been no abuse of discretion and that the sanctions should be affirmed.

6 Methodologies, Investigation, and Techniques

Family lawyers commonly ask forensic accountants questions similar to the following:

- Did Mary hide assets?
- Can we prove Terry commingled his inherited money and marital investment account?
- How do we prove that Betty's proposed property division, if invested wisely, will take care of her for life?
- How do we compare Joe's property settlement proposal to Lilly's most recent proposal?
- What is the value of Missy's pension to the marital estate?

When these types of questions are posed, certified public accountants (CPAs) usually take over and, in return, ask a bunch of follow-up questions. Some questions may be in "CPA speak." If so, you and your client must patiently listen before answering. During this initial stage, if the forensic accountant is not familiar with the basics of family law, you are responsible for educating him. If the engagement includes issues such as commingling, dissipation, or pension calculation, the legal analysis can get quite involved. If the accountant is familiar with the law, you will usually only have to review the report to confirm that you both are on the same page.

While this dialogue takes place, the forensic accountant is linking concepts. In forensic accounting terms, the CPA is "scoping"—determining what information sources are needed, usually financial documents, and what techniques may need to be applied.

Every forensic accountant engagement involves methodology, investigation, and techniques. Family law engagements are no different. Some CPAs may never think in those terms, however, even when employing them. In one sense, labeling these processes can be overkill. But there is one very important reason to label these processes—preparing to defend against a *Daubert* challenge.[1]

Understanding methodologies, investigation, and techniques is very important when challenging reports, deposing opposing experts, and planning trial questions. Some experts have a difficult time explaining why they did what they did—they just did it. Lawyers should try to understand why forensic accountants do what they do before they challenge what was actually done. When an expert cannot explain the process, you can exploit that inability. Challenging the tasks performed then becomes much easier than challenging how the tasks were completed and how the conclusions were drawn.

This chapter explains concepts forensic accountants consider before doing what they do. From the very first meeting to gather information to completing a high-level ratio analysis, the forensic accountant travels a road. Some roads are simple, and others are complex. Even when roads have been traveled efficiently and accurately, the forensic accountant still must be able to explain why particular paths were chosen. If the forensic accountant cannot do that, the result can be embarrassing.

Methodology describes the process by which the engagement progresses. It is the game plan. Like lawyers, forensic accountants develop game plans independently, based on professional judgment. Professional judgment is a function of education, training, and experience. Just like lawyers and litigation strategy, no two forensic accountants will perform the same set of tasks on any given case. But all CPAs must

1. *Daubert* challenges are discussed in more detail in Chapter 11.

follow certain ethical and professional mandates for all engagements. CPAs must do the following:

1. Exercise due professional care,
2. Accept only engagements they can handle with professional competence,
3. Maintain independence and objectivity,
4. Avoid conflicts of interest,
5. Rely upon sufficient relevant data,
6. Plan all engagements, and
7. Adequately supervise staff.[2]

Even if a CPA says he does not follow a formal methodology, you can be sure that there is an informal one. Whether it was haphazard or formally planned, the CPA began the engagement, did some work, and concluded with an opinion. As a family lawyer, you should understand methodology for several reasons:

1. Reports and direct examinations can be structured by methodology.
2. Deposition questions can be designed to uncover and dissect poorly conceived methodology.
3. *Daubert* challenges can be mounted around the methodology used or lack thereof.
4. Cross-examination can be deadly if the CPA cannot adequately describe the methodology utilized.

All methodology includes defining the scope of the engagement. Examining the definition of the engagement can expose potential professional conflicts, conflicts that, if undiscovered or not remedied, can lead to devastating results. For example, a conflict can relate to competence. You or your client may want the CPA to step beyond the forensic accountant's education, training, and experience to testify on a subject in which he may not be competent. Inexperienced CPAs often don't want to say "no" to an attorney because they are afraid that the attorney will use another expert witness for all future engagements. If the expert

2. See Chapter 10's discussion of the AICPA's *Code of Professional Conduct*.

does not have experience in a certain area and undertakes the engagement anyway, there are specific steps he must take to ensure that the engagement is completed with due professional care. As part of that process, the expert should be prepared to describe in detail the efforts undertaken to become competent in the new area. If not, the opposing expert can effectively criticize the expert's decision to undertake the assignment.

How does an expert witness, such as a forensic accountant, get caught in this conflict? The answer is fairly simple. Take a hypothetical case. Mr. Corleone is divorcing Mrs. Corleone. On advice of counsel, Mrs. Corleone hires a forensic accountant, Mr. Brasi, CPA, to search for hidden assets, add up dissipation, and provide litigation support. In response, Mr. Corleone hires Mr. Hagen, CPA, to defend. Mr. Hagen is Mr. Corleone's business CPA. During the case, Mr. Brasi also opines about the value of appreciation of separate property. In response, Mr. Corleone's lawyer determines he needs a report in opposition. Mr. Corleone's lawyer leans on Mr. Hagen to testify, and Mr. Hagen sheepishly agrees. He forms an opinion on the valuation of certain appreciated property. Unfortunately for Mr. Corleone, Mr. Hagen has no education, training, or experience in valuing assets. During cross-examination, that lack of competence is exposed. The judge agrees with Mrs. Corleone's attorney that Mr. Hagen is not competent to testify on valuation issues. At trial, Mr. Hagen is allowed to testify on all issues except valuation because he cannot be admitted as an expert on that issue. Mr. Hagen should have stood firm and refused to testify on valuation issues, even upon the insistence of Mr. Corleone's attorney. If asked under oath in future engagements, Mr. Hagen will now have to say that he has been proffered as an expert witness on valuation and has been rejected as such by a court.

Methodologies and Scoping

In terms of defining itself, forensic accounting is still a developing profession. CPAs are not required to possess any particular credentials in order to be accepted as a testifying expert. Even though there are certification tests for certain bodies of knowledge, such as the certified in financial forensics and master analyst in financial forensics credentials, there is no official body of knowledge a CPA must possess to be a forensic accountant. Regardless, the professional competence required of forensic accountants is a serious matter. Even though there is no overarching theory that encompasses all forensic accounting, some critics have argued that there should be. One attempt at creating an overarching methodology is the Forensic Accounting/Investigation Methodology©, or FA/IM© for short. FA/IM© has been developed by Darrell D. Dorrell, CPA, ABV, MBA, CVA, ASA, CMA, DABFA, CFF. He is one of the nation's leading authors, lecturers, and nationally recognized speakers on forensic accounting. FA/IM© seeks to define a comprehensive and structured format appropriate for all types of engagements, including divorce litigation.

FA/IM© is structured by a "Process Map," which is organized into four phases and thirteen stages. See Example 6-1. Don't worry. This chapter describes only its highlights. Not all stages necessarily apply to every forensic accounting engagement. Nevertheless, it is helpful for family lawyers to grasp the overall framework to better comprehend what is done, what can be done, and why.

Example 6-1
FA/IM© Process Map

1. **Foundational Phase.** In the Foundational Phase, forensic accountants define the engagement and assemble and prepare baseline data that will support and drive the investigation.
   a. **Assignment Development.** Assignment development shapes the context and the framework of the engagement. Whether presented by a client, a civil lawyer, a criminal investigator, a prosecutor, or a defense attorney, assignment development is, at its most basic, the communication to the forensic accountant describing what the accountant is expected to do. In a divorce matter, the assignment may be as simple as reviewing the discovery, helping to determine the existence or nonexistence of undisclosed assets, and identifying suspicious transactions. Initially, the forensic accountant may be engaged for a simple determination of whether any red flags exist. If they do, then the lawyer and client may rely on the accountant to suggest recommended work and propose a projected budget.
   b. **Scoping.** Scoping defines the forensic accountant's responsibilities and the depth of document review and analysis to be

Example 6-1
FA/IM© Process Map

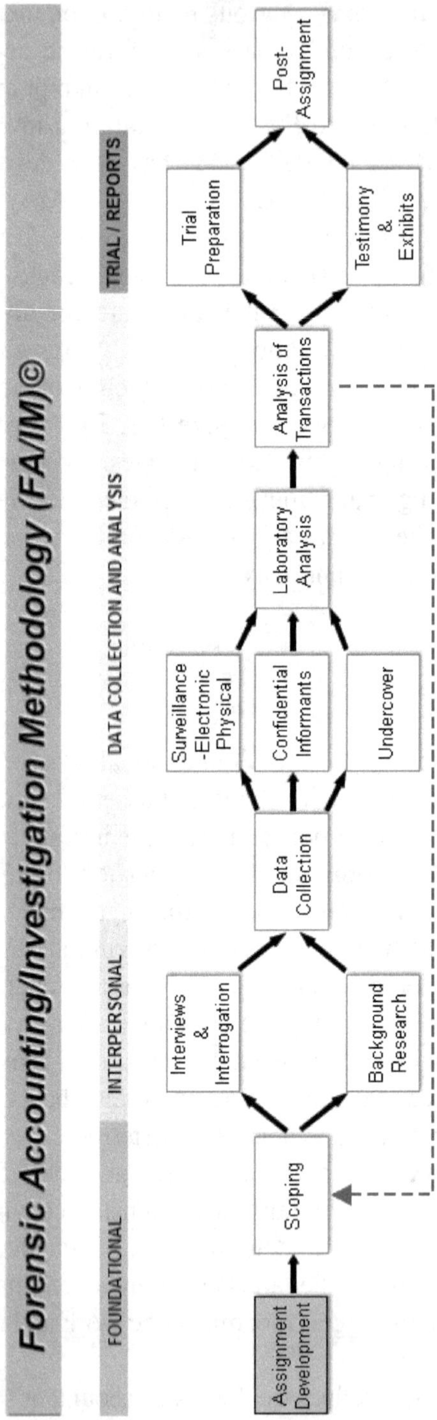

performed. Budget limitations almost always come into play here. Often, the client, attorney, and accountant, as a team, must narrow the scope to encompass only the most important objectives. For example, if there are more documents than can be reviewed and more analysis than can be done with the limited amount of resources, the team could collectively agree that the CPA should review tax returns and then focus efforts on financial records for only the two years prior to the divorce filing, after which the team would regroup and reassess.

2. **Interpersonal Communications Phase.** As the engagement begins, the CPA should question everything and everyone. This serves two purposes. First, it helps the accountant gather the factual background that will provide additional meaning to the numbers in the case. Second, it helps the accountant meet his professional duty to remain objective. Follow-up could include questioning key witnesses and completing background research. Number crunching may come later. The accountant must put the assignment into the context of the known facts, which may or may not need to be independently verified. These steps are categorized into two key areas.
   a. **Interviews and Interrogation.** Interviews consist of face-to-face contact with parties and key witnesses. In divorce litigation, there can be low-conflict interviews over the phone or high-conflict depositions. In business valuation cases, management interviews can be high stress or low stress, even though no one is under oath.
   b. **Background Research.** Research generally involves independent verification of information and certain claims made by the respective parties. CPAs can look to key public sources of information and can search many different databases, including but not limited to the following:
      i. Local business journals and newspapers;
      ii. County registers for real estate deeds and UCC-1 filings;
      iii. Secretary of state records concerning corporate entities, LLCs, and other state-law-formed entities;
      iv. Copies of filed federal and state tax returns;
      v. Civil lawsuit and criminal court records;

vi. Bankruptcy court filings;
vii. General people research databases (such as Accurint from LexisNexis);
viii. General Internet searches on Google; and
ix. Pleadings and discovery.

3. **Data Collection and Analysis Phase.** As financial documents are assembled, the forensic accountant begins to apply various quantitative and qualitative analyses to data obtained during the earlier phases. Through this process, the forensic accountant develops supporting observations and narrows supportable conclusions.
   a. **Data Collection.** In divorce cases, collecting financial records begins with documents presented by the client, obtained in discovery, and collected in research. The process is completed with supplemental discovery tools, such as depositions and subpoenas.
   b. **Surveillance: Electronic and Physical.** In divorce cases, it is not uncommon for private investigators' reports to assist with understanding behavioral aspects of the persons involved. Sometimes, understanding why people spend money the way they do helps put into context motives and the timing of transactions. This can illuminate the importance of spending patterns, asset acquisition, and financial records manipulation.
   c. **Confidential Informants.** While usually thought of in the context of criminal investigation, information from confidential informants is used in many divorce cases. It is not unusual for someone who wants to remain anonymous to report to the client unsavory behavior by the other spouse. Some witnesses are willing to divulge unverifiable data for undisclosed reasons. Forensic accountants should always remain skeptical of information obtained from known or unknown sources, especially if unverifiable claims are made.
   d. **Undercover.** Lawyers should be familiar with pretextual interviews and understand their state's ethical limitations on actions of private investigators undertaken on their or their client's behalf. If the forensic accountant relies on such information, the source may be discoverable.

e. **Laboratory Analysis.** For most forensic accountants, analysis can involve the use of many different techniques, including statistical analysis. Determining whether certain data tend to support, or not support, certain possible conclusions is a key function of any expert witness.
f. **Analysis of Transactions.** In divorce, analysis of transactions is where the rubber meets the road. Forensic accountants choose techniques, depending on their professional judgment, based on facts, information, and directives supplied, uncovered, and developed by the lawyer/client/accountant team.

4. **Trial Phase.** The trial phase encompasses all aspects of delivering the results of forensic accountants' work. Written report requirements depend on state law. In general, reports can include an opinion, an executive summary, a description of facts and documents presented, a supporting analysis, and explanations. From there, attorneys and clients read reports and either settle or head to depositions. Many family law matters are settled based on the strength and thoroughness of reports and the relative skill of the expert in defending the report at deposition.
   a. **Trial Preparation.** Completing discovery, depositions, and mediation almost always firms up testimony and trial strategy. The final efforts focus on advocacy and clarity of presentation on core issues. Lawyers should prepare the expert witness for direct and cross-examination. This preparation can include scripting out testimony establishing the expert's credentials, explaining work performed, and seeking admission into evidence of the expert's opinion.
   b. **Testimony and Exhibits.** Even with irrefutable foundational analysis, all the intense effort can be wasted if direct testimony is poorly delivered. Most effective trial testimony requires exhibits and schedules that support and simply and concisely help explain the expert's opinions. Normally, the report will include the most important schedules, which become exhibits at trial.
   c. **Post-Assignment.** Forensic accountants should always critically review the engagement, determining what aspects of their performance can be improved upon in future engagements. They should seek input from the lawyer and client as well.

Investigation

Investigation is a critical component of methodology. The more complete the CPA's understanding is of the facts early on in the case, the more efficient the engagement will likely be. In family law cases, the investigation normally begins with the client. What is known? What is suspected? What documents are possessed? What can public documents tell the forensic accountant? Then, the focus normally turns to written discovery. Interrogatories and requests for production of documents must be crafted, reviewed, and issued. From there, subpoenas may be needed to confirm or refute written discovery. Interviews of key persons may be needed. For those who will not be interviewed, depositions may be required.

The most common limiting factor of most investigations is cost. In high-asset, high-conflict cases, investigation may be a vital part of the case. To what bank or banks should subpoenas be issued? Should the client hire a private investigator? Who is the potential key witness/deponent who won't lie for the business-owner spouse? Should the spouse request copies of the filed federal tax returns to confirm that the copies of those returns provided in discovery were the ones actually signed and filed with the IRS? All these actions require time and money. Often, both are in short supply.

The second most common limiting factor is the creativity of the forensic accountant/lawyer team. Where is the "smoking gun" that will settle the case? Is it buried deep in a tax return's unproduced supporting schedule? Is the smoking gun on a business expense reimbursement form submitted to the spouse's employer? Is it in an e-mail or a cell phone bill? In almost all family law cases in which a smoking gun is found and exposed, it was there all along, just waiting for the forensic accountant to ask the right question.

Techniques

In forensic accounting, there are too many techniques to identify and categorize them all. Each day that passes, more techniques are written about in books and articles.[3] They can be simple, routine accounting

3. There are many excellent books describing forensic accounting techniques. Leading books include, but are not limited to, the following: D. LARRY CRUMBLEY, LESTER E. HEITGER & G. STEVENSON SMITH, FORENSIC AND INVESTIGATIVE

processes or complicated statistical analyses. Techniques are like tools for a carpenter. Some are common, like the saw. Other tools must be invented and handcrafted to address specific problems.

In this section, the techniques discussed are common to family law engagements. Forensic accounting techniques do not have official names. Accountants often use different names to describe the same techniques. Know that the same results can be reached through different techniques. For example, if the key questioned dissipation transaction is a below-fair-market sale of real estate purchased by a husband's golfing buddy, it doesn't matter whether the transaction was discovered while reviewing a bank reconciliation or analyzing capital losses reported on the tax return.

Many books, articles, conferences, and seminars are devoted to the profession of forensic accounting. The profession does not require particular techniques for particular situations. In this sense, forensic accounting is an art. For example, IDEA®[4] is software originally developed for fraud investigation, but it could easily be used in many different divorce litigation applications. The CPA who normally practices forensic accounting in the divorce litigation area, but does not attend conferences discussing fraud, may be losing ground professionally. He may not have heard of IDEA® and may not be aware of its capabilities. On the other hand, forensic accountants are like mechanics. Getting the

---

ACCOUNTING (CCH 4th ed. 2009); STEVEN L. SKALAK, THOMAS W. GOLDEN, MONA M. CLAYTON & JESSICA S. PILL, A GUIDE TO FORENSIC ACCOUNTING INVESTIGATION (John Wiley & Sons 2nd ed. 2011); and GEORGE A. MANNING, FINANCIAL INVESTIGATION AND FORENSIC ACCOUNTING (CRC Press 3rd ed. 2011). One of the best books specific to family law written for forensic accountants is DONALD A. GLENN, THOMAS F. BURRAGE, DONALD J. DEGRAZIA & WILLIAM B. STEWART, JR., FAMILY LAW SERVICES HANDBOOK: THE ROLE OF THE FINANCIAL EXPERT (John Wiley & Sons 2011). Its authors are considered four of the leading forensic accountants in the nation.

4. IDEA® is software for the accountant for use in review of internal controls in an audit, fraud investigation, forensic accounting, and more. According to the CaseWare website, "With IDEA®, you can lower your cost of analysis, add more quality to your work and meet the new professional requirements regarding fraud and internal control by putting the power of IDEA to work for you. IDEA can read, display, analyze, manipulate, sample or extract from data files from almost any source—mainframe to PC, including reports printed to a file." *See* www.Caseware.com, June 21, 2010.

job done right does not always require using the best, newest, and most expensive tool.

A short list of forensic accounting techniques used in divorce litigation includes the following:

1. The eyeball and smell test,
2. Transaction detail listing and analysis,
3. Reconciling tax returns and financial statements,
4. Proof of cash,
5. Reviewing files created by Quicken/QuickBooks,
6. Horizontal analysis,
7. Vertical analysis,
8. Ratio analysis,
9. ICE,©[5]
10. SCORE,©[6] and
11. Transaction sampling and testing.

1. The Eyeball and Smell Test

One obvious job of the family lawyer is to read all discovery responses. Generally speaking, it is helpful for one single person to perform the following tasks:

1. Reading all documents and financial information provided by the client,
2. Reading interrogatory answers from both parties,
3. Reviewing all documents exchanged between the parties, and
4. Reviewing all subpoena results.

These tasks may be performed by the lawyer, a skilled paralegal, or the forensic accountant. Whether or not you delegate these tasks, there is always a risk that something will be missed. The advantage of having one person review everything is that the risk of a loose end or red flag

5. Copyright by Darrell D. Dorrell, CPA/ABV, MBA, ASA, CVA, CMA, DABFA, Lake Oswego, Oregon. Reprinted by permission.
6. Copyright by Darrell D. Dorrell, CPA/ABV, MBA, ASA, CVA, CMA, DABFA, Lake Oswego, Oregon. Reprinted by permission.

being missed is significantly reduced. Some tasks may not always be complicated, but most require management of a tremendous amount of detail, including the following:

1. Identifying all assets and debts, including searching for hidden assets;
2. Classifying all assets and debts as marital or separate (community or separate);
3. Reviewing all valuations of marital or separate property, as well as the appreciation of separate property;
4. Determining income and earnings capacity for temporary support, child support, and alimony;
5. Organizing alimony claims and defenses;
6. Creating a list of suspicious transactions for possible dissipation claims; and
7. Determining if commingling or transmutation claims or defenses are at issue.

In many cases, party depositions take place after settlement negotiations. In others, depositions come before proposed settlements are created. In either circumstance, it is the better practice for one set of eyes to see every important piece of information to put all of the financial information in context and determine if additional investigation is needed. Sometimes, by staring at enough documents long enough, lawyers or forensic accountants can determine if something smells wrong.

Forensic accountants are exceptionally gifted "smellers." For almost any given level of net worth and corresponding income level, they know what the tax returns should look like. Correspondingly, from the tax returns, forensic accountants have an idea of what the net worth statements should look like. In their careers, most forensic accountants have reviewed thousands of brokerage account statements, capital gains transactions, and 401(k) statements. CPAs also know what spending levels are common and what deductions should or should not exist. They can look at personal and business financial statements and question whether debt is overstated, uninvested cash is too high, or reported income has been manipulated.

If something smells wrong, forensic accountants can best determine the scope of what additional work should be done. Experienced family lawyers know the value of asking the forensic accountant to look over everything, identify potential problems, suggest additional investigation, and recommend if additional discovery is needed or specific techniques should be applied to a particular case. This may be the most valuable service a forensic accountant can perform.

2. Transaction Detail Listing and Analysis

When it comes to money, most people can't add up in their head what they spend. This is true for both stay-at-home parents and corporate executives. This is also why personal accounting software such as Quicken and QuickBooks is so popular. Too many people spend more money than they have because people don't realize how much they spend. The only way to really know what a person spends is to add it up transaction by transaction, check by check, and credit card charge by credit card charge.

On a spreadsheet, the creator lists all known transactions. Each row contains all known facts for one particular transaction, such as date, payee, amount, source document, account, and description. Details may be added, such as expense category or commentary. See Example 6-2. By sorting transactions by date, amount, or category, the data tells the story.

Example 6-2
Detailed Transaction Listing

As part of the divorce process, there are many reasons why lawyers may want to know the amounts earned and spent during three critical time periods:

1. Prior to separation (actual historical lifestyle),
2. Following separation but prior to the divorce, and
3. Projected future expenses.

In almost all states, if temporary support or alimony is at issue, the spouses will need to create, exchange, and/or file a complete statement of income and expenses. A less formal version of the statement of income and expenses may also be requested in an interrogatory. In response, what do most family lawyers do? Hand the divorce client a form to fill out showing categories of income and expenses on

Example 6-2
Detailed Transaction Listing

	A	C	E	F	H	J	K	M	O
1	**BORG TRANSACTION DETAIL**								
2									
3									
4									
5	Date	Amour	Institution	Chec	Category	Payee	Accou	Source Document	Memo
6	3/26/2018	43.00	Credit Card		Subscription	Business Week	x0650	Visa Statement Dated 4/15/18	
7	5/4/2018	12,000.00	Credit Card		Transfer	Chase	x6190	Galaxy Statement Dated 5/6/18	
8	5/4/2018	3,000.00	Credit Card		Transfer	Citibank Cards	x6190	Galaxy Statement Dated 5/6/18	
9	5/8/2018	(43.00)	Credit Card		CC Payment	Visa	x0650	Visa Statement Dated 5/15/18	
10	5/27/2018	1,804.60	Bank	1001	Residence	National Mortgage	x2860	Jonathon's Check Register	
11	5/27/2018	1,500.00	Bank	1003	Wedding	Emerald Flowers	x2860	Jonathon's Check Register	Wedding
12	5/27/2018	250.00	Bank	1004	Wedding	Tim Johnson	x2860	Jonathon's Check Register	Wedding Cake
13	5/27/2018	295.00	Bank	1005	Residence	Terminix	x2860	Jonathon's Check Register	
14	5/27/2018	148.46	Bank	1006	Residence	MLG&W	x2860	Jonathon's Check Register	
15	5/27/2018	600.00	Bank	1007	Residence	Ashville	x2860	Jonathon's Check Register	
16	5/27/2018	1,804.60	Bank	1008	Residence	National Mortgage	x2860	Jonathon's Check Register	
17	5/27/2018	2,000.00	Bank	1009	Home Repair	Deanna Troi	x2860	Jonathon's Check Register	Contractor
18	6/1/2018	(500.00)	Credit Card		CC Payment	Galaxy	x6190	Galaxy Statement Dated 6/6/18	
19	6/6/2018	19.00	Credit Card		Memberships	Galaxy	x6190	Galaxy Statement Dated 6/6/18	
20	7/4/2018	(500.00)	Credit Card		CC Payment	Galaxy	x6190	Galaxy Statement Dated 7/6/18	
21	7/11/2018	19,183.06	Bank	1011	Home Repair	Deanna Troi	x2860	Jonathon's Check Register	Appliances
22	7/12/2018	3,500.00	Bank	1012	Home Repair	Deanna Troi	x2860	Jonathon's Check Register	Tile/Paint
23	7/19/2018	800.00	Bank	1013	Home Repair	Bottle Shock Design	x2860	Jonathon's Check Register	
24	7/19/2018	257.61	Bank	1014	Residence	Town Community Assoc	x2860	Jonathon's Check Register	
25	7/22/2018	4,475.00	Bank	1015	Home Repair	Deanna Troi	x2860	Jonathon's Check Register	Paint
26	7/27/2018	600.00	Bank	1016	Home Repair	Deanna Troi	x2860	Jonathon's Check Register	Electrician
27	7/30/2018	3,450.00	Bank	1017	Home Repair	Deanna Troi	x2860	Jonathon's Check Register	Contractor
28	7/31/2018	(500.00)	Credit Card		CC Payment	Galaxy	x6190	Galaxy Statement Dated 8/6/18	
29	7/31/2018	5,358.00	Bank	1018	Home Repair	Deanna Troi	x2860	Jonathon's Check Register	Contractor
30	8/6/2018	9,494.75	Bank	1020	Home Repair	Deanna Troi	x2860	Jonathon's Check Register	Contractor
31	8/13/2018	15,675.00	Bank	1021	Home Repair	Deanna Troi	x2860	Jonathon's Check Register	Contractor
32	8/13/2018	1,804.60	Bank	1019	Residence	National Mortgage	x2860	Jonathon's Check Register	
33	8/17/2018	15,000.00	Credit Card		Transfer	Trust One Bank	x6190	Galaxy Statement Dated 9/6/18	
34	8/17/2018	29.00	Credit Card		Bank Fee	Late Fee	x6190	Galaxy Statement Dated 9/6/18	
35	8/17/2018	8,132.00	Bank	1022	Home Repair	Deanna Troi	x2860	Jonathon's Check Register	Contractor
36	8/26/2018	7,255.00	Bank	1023	Home Repair	Deanna Troi	x2860	Jonathon's Check Register	Contractor
37	9/4/2018	8,922.00	Bank	1024	Home Repair	Jordi Jones	x2860	Jonathon's Check Register	sofa/bedroom
38	9/4/2018	1,200.00	Bank	1025	Home Repair	Jordi Jones	x2860	Jonathon's Check Register	
39	9/7/2018	806.24	Bank	1026	Residence	Hamilton Grill	x2860	Jonathon's Check Register	
40	9/8/2018	10,000.00	Bank	1027	Home Repair	Jordi Jones	x2860	Jonathon's Check Register	
41	9/9/2018	(500.00)	Credit Card		CC Payment	Galaxy	x6190	Galaxy Statement Dated 10/6/18	
42	9/12/2018	3,972.06	Bank	1028	Home Repair	Deanna Troi	x2860	Jonathon's Check Register	chairs
43	10/1/2018	(1,066.00)	Credit Card		CC Payment	Galaxy	x6190	Galaxy Statement Dated 10/6/18	
44	10/6/2018	227.64	Credit Card		Finance Charge	Finance Charge	x6190	Galaxy Statement Dated 10/6/18	
45	10/31/2018	100.00	Bank	1030	Lawn Care	Raydon Sommers	x2860	Jonathon's Check Register	
46	11/4/2018	(350.00)	Credit Card		CC Payment	Galaxy	x6190	Galaxy Statement Dated 11/6/18	
47	11/6/2018	229.41	Credit Card		Finance Charge	Finance Charge	x6190	Galaxy Statement Dated 11/6/18	
48	11/14/2018	273.00	Bank	1131	Residence	T&C Locksmith	x2860	Jonathon's Check Register	
49	11/18/2018	2,785.00	Bank	1132	Home Repair	Binswanger Glass	x2860	Jonathon's Check Register	

a monthly basis. Few additional directions are provided. The client returns the form filled out, and a legal assistant types it up. Some lawyers never even review the completed form with their client. This can be a huge mistake.

What happens if a client seriously understates her monthly expenses? Generally, if opposing counsel knows that, there may be no additional follow-up questions. Temporary support and alimony determinations are decided based on statutory factors. Usually, need and ability to pay are the two most important. Understating expenses is almost always an advantage to the opposing party because it results in less need or a greater ability to pay.

What happens if a client seriously overstates her monthly expenses? The opposing attorney can and should challenge the claimed amount. If the amount is claimed to be an exaggeration, the court will determine whether the claimed need is overstated or the spouse's ability to pay is understated. Either can result in a serious credibility problem for the overstating spouse.

Without expert testimony or a formal analysis of actual historical spending, cross-examination may end in an argument that the lawyer loses:

Attorney:	How much do you claim you spend on unreimbursed business meals eating out?
Opp. Party:	$700 per month.
Attorney:	Come on. That's a lot. You spend less than that, don't you?
Opp. Party:	No.
Attorney:	Yes, you do.
Opp. Party:	I know what I spend. $700 is an estimated average.
Attorney:	Let's look at your March 2018 credit card statement. You have only three charges. All three are between $75 and $110.
Opp. Party:	So?
Attorney:	You spent only about $225 in March 2018.
Opp. Party:	That was an unusual month. I was told by my lawyer to put down on her form an estimate of what I spend in an average month.
Attorney:	Uh-huh. So it is your sworn testimony you spend $700 per month eating out even though you only spent $225 in March 2018?
Opp. Party:	Yes. In March, that is the total on my credit card. I may have also paid for some dinners in cash.

If the family uses Quicken or QuickBooks, your client may be able to copy the entire program and the data and hand it to the forensic accountant for analysis. If parties don't have personal accounting software, the details of all transactions can be entered into a spreadsheet. From that detailed list of transactions, many different types of analyses can be performed.

With a detailed transaction listing and analysis or a Quicken report, the cross-examination might be very different:

Attorney: How much do you claim you spend on unreimbursed business meals eating out?

Opp. Party: $700 per month.

Attorney: Now, please review this summary report of your unreimbursed business meals for the last 12 months prepared from your family's Quicken reports, canceled checks, and credit card charges. We sent this list to your lawyer last week. Did you read it?

Opp. Party: Yes.

Attorney: Is it accurate?

Opp. Party: I don't know.

Attorney: Fair enough. Do there appear to be any additional unreimbursed business meals not listed in the summary?

Opp. Party: No.

Attorney: Did you read the summary of transactions?

Opp. Party: Yes.

Attorney: Did you notice that any transactions were omitted?

Opp. Party: No.

Attorney: Did you see any mistakes?

Opp. Party: No.

Attorney: Please review the summary. It shows that, for the 12 months from April 2017 through March 2018, you spent, on average, only $314 per month. Isn't that correct?

Opp. Party: Yes.

Calculating actual historical spending is only one function of the transaction detail listing and analysis. It is a tool that can also be used to help impute income, identify and classify assets, determine dissipation, identify commingling, argue transmutation, and calculate appreciation of separate property. For all these important issues, tracing transfers between accounts can be very important. The spreadsheet is a great tool for that, too. When the spreadsheet is completed, tracing a check from one account to another takes little or no time at all.

Suppose John Smith wrote a $5,000 check drawn on his brokerage account dated April 15, 2018, with the payee being "John Smith." What did John Smith do with the check? If there are five other accounts (checking, savings, and other brokerage accounts), how else do you prove he cashed the check? The forensic accountant must check all accounts, but for how long beyond April 15, 2018? Most checks/deposit transfers happen around the same time; however, no one is required to deposit checks by any sort of deadline if there is no objection or no one cancels the check. John Smith may have written the check, recorded it, and simply not deposited it—just waiting for the divorce to be final to deposit it. The detailed transaction listing helps prevent this type of fraud. By loading all transactions from all accounts, sorting the data by date and amount is easy. When sorted by date or amount, finding "loose" transactions is much easier than digging through months of statements for several different accounts.

Finally, the detailed transaction listing spreadsheet is also a great tool for the lawyer to help organize party deposition questions. Sorting the transactions by amount, highest to lowest, can highlight those transactions involving larger amounts of money. For example, if there are 30 transactions over $3,000, that would create a nice checklist to review at deposition. Obviously, there could be 200 transactions, each transferring to the spouse's brother varying amounts under $150. In total, yes, that could add up to a greater amount. Hopefully, in creating the spreadsheet, multiple transactions like these will be noticed. But in a divorce action, keeping it simple most often pays greater dividends.

Creating the detailed transaction listing spreadsheet can be time consuming and tedious. The CPA can delegate creation of the spreadsheet to a staff person at a lower hourly rate. In forensic accounting terms, this can also be called "litigation support." Or the family lawyer can delegate the data entry to a paralegal or legal assistant. In general, if the spreadsheet is well designed and the data entry person has the divorce client's assistance with categorizing the needed information, the spreadsheet creation process can actually run quite smoothly.

3. Reconciling Tax Returns and Financial Statements

Reconciling tax returns and financial statements is one of the CPA's favorite techniques. Comparing income and expenses reported on tax returns and financial statements can tell a CPA the truth. All taxpayers are motivated to report less income on tax returns. Borrowers usually want to report higher net income to lending institutions on credit applications. The difference usually tells a story. Is there deferred income? Are certain expenses claimed only for tax purposes? Were there adjustments based on depreciation or bad debt expense? Only a CPA can determine this. This technique is in the CPA's wheelhouse. There are many legitimate reasons for a discrepancy; however, uncovering questionable accounting practices can be devastating to a business owner spouse's credibility. Many triers of fact will assume a nefarious purpose if the transactions in question occurred only in the divorcing period. Also, if there is a major discrepancy that can result in a meaningful adjustment to the opposing spouse's reported taxable income, the impact can be very beneficial for the client. More details about looking for assets by reviewing tax returns can be found in Chapter 7.

4. Proof of Cash

Proof of cash means performing bank reconciliation with four columns and a different assumption. In most business situations, accountants assume the books are accurate and check only whether the bank is correct. In proof of cash, the accountant is testing the business's or party's books against the records from the bank. The reason for this paradigm shift is that proof of cash is a technique specifically designed to sniff out manipulation. See Example 6-3.

In proof of cash, the books' balance is reconciled with the bank statements for each month. The first column is the beginning of the month. The second and third columns itemize total receipts and disbursements. The final column is the end-of-the-month balance. This reconciliation process spotlights cash in and cash out. If the receipts and disbursements have been misreported, the proof of cash will illuminate the manipulation because there is no way to alter the bank records unless the bank statement itself is altered. If the bank statement is altered, it must be altered each and every month, accounting for all prior manipulation. That takes time and discipline.

Example 6-3
Proof of Cash Data Table

Description	Line	Column 1 Beginning Bank Reconciliation 12/31/2017	Column 2 Receipts	Column 3 Disbursements	Column 4 Ending Bank Reconciliation 12/31/2018
Balance per Bank:	1	1,250	10,305	(9,830)	1,725
Deposits in transit:	2				-
December 2017	a	335	(335)		
December 2018	b	*	450		450
Outstanding Checks:	3				
per list 12-31-2017	a	(25)		25	
per list 12-31-2018	b			(265)	(265)
ADJUSTED BALANCE	4	1,560	10,420	(10,070)	1,910
Balance per Books:	5	1,560	10,170	(10,100)	1,630
December Service charge:	6			(25)	(25)
NSF Checks returned:	7			(70)	(70)
Bank transfers, errors in recording, other adjustments	8		200	125	325
Interest posted, by bank:	9		50		50
ADJUSTED BALANCE	10	1,560	10,420	(10,070)	1,910
(same as line 4)		*shaded areas should not need an entry			

5. Reviewing Quicken/QuickBooks Software

Every financial planner will tell you that the first step to financial success is a personal budget. But no budget is helpful unless actual revenue and expenses are compared to it. For recording revenue and expenses and comparing them to a budget, there are no better software tools than Quicken and QuickBooks. They do everything. They record everything. They analyze the data six ways from Sunday. Personal financial software can contain the mother lode of evidence for the forensic accountant.

There is another key tool, however, which not everyone knows about. In both software programs, there are built-in audit functions. If one of the spouses has deleted some transactions, the CPA may be able to determine what was deleted. In many extramarital affairs, cell phone records and credit card charges tell the tale. If the parties record all transactions (checks and credit cards), some evidence may be recorded before the cheating spouse figures out the need to be more careful.

If you represent the spouse suspecting personal financial manipulation or an affair, encourage your client to copy the entire program and data contained therein. It's simple and doesn't take much time. From there, the forensic accountant may already have a copy of the program and may be able to load the data. Even if the financial information loaded is not current, it may not matter if the needed information is recorded. In divorce, like life, one never knows what information may be important until after it is gone (or deleted). The forensic accountant can review the financial information and let you know what, if anything, is useful evidence.

6. Horizontal Analysis

Horizontal analysis is a fancy phrase that describes comparing key account information over multiple time periods. Most horizontal analysis compares years or quarters. Examples of accounts typically analyzed include gross sales, officer compensation, travel and entertainment, and nonoperating assets. Nonoperating assets are assets that are owned by a business but don't generate income or add anything to the bottom line. Examples of nonoperating assets include the condominium purchased by the business or the chief financial officer's newly leased Infiniti. Account changes over time can help identify trends indicating the need for additional investigation. Typically, these comparisons measure changes in dollars, but some CPAs will also look at percentage changes over time, comparing changes in proportion to gross revenue. This can also be considered the same technique as ratio analysis, described under heading 8.

7. Vertical Analysis

In vertical analysis, each expense item in an income statement in a given period is divided by net sales. This percentage may rise or fall over multiple periods. Using this process, the accountant is looking for trends that do not make sense. Given the accountant's understanding of the business and industry, some expenses should rise or fall more quickly than others for specific time periods. For example, total commissions earned should increase about the same as net sales. But if net sales decrease and inside commissions increase, what happened to outside sales commissions? Was it that the outside sales force was reduced in favor of inside sales? Or is the owner's paramour now on the payroll and receiving phantom commissions?

8. Ratio Analysis

In college, finance majors learn all about ratio analysis. They must memorize hundreds of seemingly meaningless ratio formulas. Well, if you were a finance major, congratulations! You may now have your first reason to be glad you went to your college's business building for four years. To compare one business to another, ratio analysis is the starting point. For many industries, there are benchmark ratios. Benchmark ratios are averages for a group of companies in a particular industry. In retail companies, gross profit margin is important, measuring the percentage of profit of sales (all items sold). For example, if a sporting goods store buys a baseball for $1.00 but sells the baseball for $4.00, the gross profit margin is 75 percent. ($4.00 sales price less $1.00 cost of goods sold equals $3.00. The gross profit is $3.00. Profit compared to gross sales is $3.00 divided by $4.00, or 75 percent.) The higher the gross margin, in theory, the greater the profitability of the business. The gross margins at Saks Fifth Avenue should be different than those at Walmart. But what tells the story is how this ratio evolves over time.

To forensic accountants, ratio analysis is neither boring nor endless. Ratio analysis allows the accountant's creativity to shine. Before a forensic accountant discovers a ratio that illuminates an important issue, he may try many different ratios. The key is seeing patterns comparing the ratios of the subject business to industry averages and ignoring what does not really matter or appears appropriate. The goal is to find what does not make sense over a period of time. Again, that is why knowing the personal side of the divorce history makes sense. If the marriage became shaky two years prior, the forensic accountant may need to go back in time three or four years to determine "normal" operational ratios.

A few examples of more commonly seen ratios include the following:

Net profit margin	=	Earnings available for owners Sales
Earnings per share	=	Earnings available for owners Number of common stock shares
Return on assets	=	Earnings available for owners Total assets
Current ratio	=	Current assets Current liabilities

Current assets are those liquid assets that can be used to pay short-term debt and are used to measure a company's ability to pay its immediate debt.

Quick (acid test) ratio = Cash + s/t investments + accounts receivable
Current liabilities

The quick ratio is another test of a company's ability to pay its bills but excludes inventory and other current assets that are not as liquid.

Inventory turnover = Cost of goods sold
Inventory

If a company has a higher inventory turnover ratio compared to prior periods or other companies in the industry, it means inventory takes longer to be sold and may spoil or cost more than necessary.

9. ICE

ICE is a well-known concept to auditors, although it is not labeled as such. The forensic accountant compares and contrasts documents purporting to represent the same financial information for the same time periods but that are obtained from different sources or reported to different users. The three categories of sources and users include:

(I) Internal reports to management (e.g., cost accounting reports),
(C) Control reports from third parties (e.g., bank statements), and
(E) External reported financial information (e.g., tax returns filed with the IRS).

In general, financial statements, bank statements, and tax returns all report some amount of gross income. On financial statements, there are many reasons why income may not be reported during the period, even though cash was received by a business. For example, magazine subscription revenue received may be deferred to the following year, when the magazines are actually created, printed, and mailed. Bank statements show all revenue received, but there are other major sources of revenue than magazine sales and advertisements. Owners may loan the business money, or the business may sell a piece of equipment it no longer needs. Also, for tax purposes, some gross income can differ from the financial statements because income has been deferred to the following year, or income deferred from a prior year may be recorded in the current year.

Certainly, there are many legitimate accounting reasons why gross income, cost of goods sold, and expenses may differ among the three categories. For tax minimization reasons, businesses should look for legal ways to defer income to later periods and expense as much as soon as possible. In any event, the forensic accountant is attempting to determine why the numbers differ among internal, control, and external reports. It is the reconciliation process—determining why the differences exist—that may uncover manipulation of financial data. During this process, the forensic accountant learns about the business, its management, and its ownership. If there are problems, ICE is a useful tool with which to begin the investigation.

10. SCORE

SCORE is a technique by which the forensic accountant compares and contrasts the flow of money and units among the following sources and recipients:

(S) Suppliers (inflow of goods and receipt of cash),
(C) Customers (inflow of money and receipt of goods),
(O) Owners (inflow and outflow of cash),
(R) Regulators (payment of cash for taxes, fees, or licenses), and
(E) Employees (payment of cash).

By understanding the relationship among these groups and defining expectations for their financial correlations, the forensic accountant can look for anomalies. If an anomaly is unexplained or contrived, the result can be a more narrowly defined scope for additional investigation, allowing for more targeted specific transaction sampling and testing.

For example, for a particular wholesaler, the forensic accountant knows the business reported $1 million in gross revenue. To generate that amount of sales, 10,000 units must have been sold. Each unit sells for around $100. On average during the period, units cost around $35. After sales commission, marketing, and delivery, each sale generates a gross profit of around $50. All other costs, such as administration and overhead, eat another $20 in profit. For the five years immediately prior to the filing of the divorce, the business generated a net profit of around 30 percent of gross revenue. The forensic accountant can cross-check the number and cost of units purchased in the divorcing year with the number of units purchased by customers. From there, the accountant can determine what profits were paid to the owners and cross-check the amount reported in sales tax paid to the state. Finally, what were the employees paid? Of special importance, the forensic accountant will look at sales commissions paid as a percentage of sales. More often than not, these relatively simple correlations will translate more than just statistics to the forensic accountant. Once the forensic accountant observes something that just doesn't quite fit, specific testing can begin.

11. Transaction Sampling and Testing

CPAs are very familiar with the concept of sampling. All CPAs are trained to sample in auditing. While not every forensic accountant will have a strong background in auditing, many do. Sampling means looking at a particular type and series of routine transactions and testing them. It is also a method by which auditors test the strength of internal control. Internal control is a general term by which accountants gauge the reliability of the accounting information system itself.

There are two categories of tests. One tests dollars, and the other tests procedures. To test dollars, the forensic accountant may determine a sample. For example, if there are 1,000 sales transactions in a year, the CPA may statistically choose to test as few as 10 to 20 transactions. The first type of test may be very simple and straightforward. From beginning to end, the CPA reviews the receipt of revenue and determines if the amounts received were recorded accurately. The second type of test looks at the procedure and determines if the proper internal control procedures were followed when recording the transactions.

For example, from the sales ledger (at the sales department), the CPA requires the business to produce the purchase order received, invoice created, packing slip (at the warehouse), and bill of lading (in the shipping department). At the collections department, the CPA cross-references the accounts receivable ledger. Either the receivable was collected or it was not. If it was collected, it should be recorded as revenue. If the revenue was not collected, it should be recorded in an outstanding collections summary. Finally, the item is either sent to an outsourced collections firm or written off as bad debt. If the sales item (dollars generated) cannot be traced completely through the business's accounting information system to the general ledger, there is a problem. In theory, if there is a major problem and enough transactions are tested, inaccuracy in revenue recorded may appear within the sample.

Internal control is also tested. The accountant tests procedure. Who can write checks? Who signs the checks? Who can approve new vendors? Who approves payment to vendors? Who opens bank statements? Who reconciles bank statements? Can the same person who approves new vendors also open bank statements and reconcile them? Were the bank reconciliations actually completed? Were the bank reconciliations performed by the same person with the authority or responsibility to do any or all of the above? If so, you've got a recipe for disaster. If the same person has the ability and/or responsibility to do one or more of the foregoing, that person can steal with little chance of getting caught.

Think about a law firm. As lawyers, most of us have probably heard about legal administrators having stolen large amounts of money from prominent law firms. How does that happen? There are very simple ways to steal money right under the noses of business owners, especially lawyers who trust legal administrators and are too busy to check their work. Legal administrators can create fictitious vendors and payment records for dummy invoices. They may even sign the checks to the fictitious vendors. Legal administrators can pay fictitious vendors with names similar to "Lexis" or the firm's copier repair companies. Or legal administrators can steal checks from clients. They reconcile the bank accounts and can manipulate clients' payment records so that the records clients see are accurate. If clients always see accurate invoices, they will never complain about being shorted. Or legal administrators can create fictitious employees, pay themselves directly, alter bank statements, and manipulate the bank balance during the reconciliation process. This is all possible because legal administrators open the bank statements and also perform the reconciliations. If there is a different person who opens bank statements and copies them as received, there will be a copy of the bank statement the managing partner can use to compare to the legal administrator's reconciliation. This is a very important step in internal control procedures. It's so simple, it's stupid that most lawyers (and many business owners in general) refuse to take the time to watch their own cash in and out or pay an outside CPA to help.

Just as there as hundreds of ways to steal from a company, there are as many ways an owner can remove assets from the business and manipulate the financial records without getting caught. In most business situations, though, most basic forms of manipulation require assistance from someone inside the accounting information system. The smaller the business, the less assistance an owner may need.

By sampling and testing internal controls, if there is manipulation, the forensic accountant has a sporting chance to figure out how the manipulation takes place. If the business employs a CPA, the company's CPA may know what is going on. Often it is the company's CPA who should set, test, and advise about internal controls to prevent theft. Manipulation generally requires circumvention of some aspect of internal control. If there is an internal control weakness, that is the most likely source of the manipulation. And transaction testing is the tool to find it.

Conclusion

Investigation helps identify what tools or techniques should be used. The methodology describes the process by which accountants exercise professional care and independent judgment. An accountant who believes everything a client says is not objective and independent.

You should try to understand the big picture before launching an attack on any opposing expert. All the concepts interrelate. A lack of understanding of these concepts gives the upper hand to experienced opposing forensic accounting experts. Having a basic understanding of the methodologies, investigations, and techniques will help level the playing field.

Case Example: Methodology Made Simple Wins

In a 2018 unpublished opinion,[7] a California court distinguished reasonable compensation from working capital in divorce.

The wife's forensic accounting expert, Michelle Ellis, testified on unearned compensation, spousal support, and property valuation. The husband's dual experts seemed to have played a lesser role at trial on the latter two issues. Overwhelmingly, Ellis was the expert authority relied upon by the trial court. The husband appealed the distribution of assets, among other things. The wife's costs of appeal were recoverable, a clear indication that review did not go favorably for the husband. The court affirmed the judgment in large part, reversing and remanding for further proceedings on valuation of a company. The trial court erred in calculating the value of the couple's company, LEI, Inc., as $1,033,500 when the spouses' agreed valuation was $803,036.

7. LaSalvia v. LaSalvia, No. F074023 (Cal. Ct. App. Feb. 6, 2018). Although not precedential, the opinion sheds light on various financial concepts with lessons from the court's analysis.

This husband petitioned for divorce in 2010, the decree ending a 34-year marriage. With ownership interests in several slaughterhouse-related businesses, the couple enjoyed a high standard of living in California, traveling extensively in the United States and abroad. They owned their 5,000-square-foot marital home along with a vacation house in Santa Cruz.

The $7 million marital estate was divided according to community property law. Included in a community income analysis were earnings from the family slaughterhouse business. In 1950, the husband's father began operating LBA slaughterhouse in Los Banos, California, just south of Modesto. Between 1976 and 2010, LBA's annual sales ranged from $4 million to $13 million.

The spouses' divisible marital property also encompassed LEI, Inc. and LaS, LLC, both of which had substantial real estate holdings. As a processor and seller of animal byproducts, LEI's lab was used to "isolate blood serum and obtain[] rennet from calf blood and gullets"—remains of the day from the Los Banos slaughterhouse.

The husband already owned 50 percent of the LBA stock when his father died in 1986. The decedent's 50 percent share of LBA stock then funded three testamentary trusts benefiting the surviving spouse and decedent's children (survivor's trust, exemption trust, and marital deduction trust). Wearing two hats, the husband was chief executive officer (CEO) of LBA and co-trustee with his mother on all three trusts. Marital earnings, or lack thereof, proved problematical for the husband.

The trial court determined, first, that LBA undercompensated its CEO—who was "doing the work of two men"—by $912,000. Second, the husband did not collect allowable administration fees as trustee. Given a trustee's entitlement to earnings, the trial court added $832,000 to the husband's marital earnings in unpaid trustee fees. Michelle Ellis, the wife's valuation expert, opined on the reasonable rate of compensation based upon trust language and industry standards: 0.5 percent annually of the fair value of the trusts' assets ($4.6 million to $8.9 million for the relevant years). The husband's forensic accounting experts did not testify regarding the reasonable value of trust administration. The trial court adopted Ellis's total reasonable compensation value of $832,000, finding her methodology and valuation calculations "acceptable and reasonable." The wife's community share included an equal interest in the husband's constructive marital earnings as trustee. The valuation was affirmed on appeal, as there was substantial evidence supporting the trial court's valuation of reasonable trustee compensation.

Valuation of the husband's unearned income was the heart of this appeal. The trial court heard testimony from several valuation experts with varying levels of experience, all credible witnesses, as was the wife. By contrast, the husband was impeached several times by his contradictory prior statements and documents, some in his own hand. The trial court's credibility findings stated, "The inconsistent actions/ testimony by Husband draws into serious question the accuracy and veracity of his proffered evidence." The husband's lack of credibility tarnished his experts' opinions and conclusions, negatively influencing the weight of the evidence. The trial court "questioned the accuracy and the reliability of the data husband provided to his expert and expressly questioned husband's credibility on financial issues."

On marital wages, the Supreme Court of California previously held the "community is entitled to the portion of the profits fairly attributable to the time, talent, and personal effort of the spouse, as distinct from profits attributable to the separate capital of the business."[8] California's Family Code § 770 identifies income from one spouse's separate property as separate along with any "intrinsic increase" in value. That is to say, the capital profits attributable to the separate capital of the business are likewise separate. Under the rule of marital property, the fruits of this husband's "expenditure of time, talent and labor are community property" and must be distributed in divorce.[9]

To calculate the value of marital earnings, two California methods are used when a spouse operates a business that is separate property. In establishing the reasonable value of the husband's community investment of skill, effort, and industry in his separate business prior to marital division, these spouses stipulated to applying the *Van Camp* apportionment method or formula. (The *Pereira* apportionment method is the alternative.) Basically, business income during the marriage is community in nature, and business profits before, during, and after the marriage are separate in nature. In divorce, the trial court must attribute income and profits to either the community or the separate estate of the business-owning spouse.

8. Beam v. Bank of America, 6 Cal. 3d 12, 490 P.2d 257, 98 Cal. Rptr. 137 (1971).
9. Citing *In re* Marriage of Dekker, 17 Cal. App. 4th 842 (1993).

To determine whether the husband had been adequately compensated as LBA CEO, Ellis started with LBA's gross revenue. She looked for salary trends between 1976 and 2010. Ellis found the husband's 2003 to 2010 salary to be "adequate" in keeping with Economic Research Institute (ERI) data. She included salary-survey data of executive compensation from nearby Modesto, Fresno, and Stockton. A recent seminar Ellis attended confirmed the "percentage of gross revenue was a good metric to use to determine executive level salaries." Although the gross metric was not required, she explained how executive-level employee compensation is often tied to a proportion of the company's gross. Significantly, Ellis expressed skepticism over the accuracy of LBA's alleged net income and losses "[b]ased on her professional experience." (Look at how the business was formed. Look at LBA's incentive to reduce taxable income. How could LBA maintain so much business capital if true annual economic losses actually occurred?)

Ellis calculated the husband's adequate salary at approximately 2.8 percent of LBA's gross revenue for the relevant period. His 2003 to 2010 salary would serve as the benchmark for comparing salaries earned in previous years. Using this benchmark, she determined undercompensation from 1986 to 2002. For a total underpayment, Ellis gradually increased the husband's salary by about two-tenths of 1 percent of gross revenue each year over 10 years (1987 to 1997) until it matched the benchmark 2.8 percent of gross revenue. Ellis's "conservative" estimate of the husband's undercompensation from 1987 to 2002 resulted in total unpaid compensation of $912,172 (not including interest). In comparing LBA's working capital from 1987 to 2002 to what like businesses would normally keep in reserve, Ellis further determined that LBA had sufficient excess working capital to pay the additional compensation without detriment.

The husband offered two valuation experts, forensic accountants Stephen Zamucen and Michael Smith. Zamucen used LBA's net income but admitted to using the gross revenue metric himself and to observing other forensic accountants using it to calculate compensation. Zamucen opined that the husband was either reasonably compensated or overpaid given LBA's negative net income and marginal profitability for the relevant period. He testified that paying the husband the additional compensation (equivalent to LBA's net income for the same period) would have bankrupted the company. LBA had "several unprofitable years between 2003 and 2006 in which the company suffered over $400,000 in losses."

Using national salary survey data from *Meat & Poultry Magazine*, ERI, and other sources, Zamucen estimated the husband's reasonable compensation for 2010, added a California wage premium of 15 percent, and reduced it by 4 percent per year for inflation. He also testified that LBA paid $566,000 in dividends from 1995 to 1998 and, from 1990 to 1994, contributed $71,000 to its profit-sharing plan. If dividends and profit-sharing contributions had been reduced, argued the wife, then the husband's salary could have been increased without overburdening LBA.

Forensic accountant Stephen Smith opined that the husband was overcompensated during the marriage. He testified that the husband's 2010 salary of $216,000 was reasonable and applied an inflation index to reduce the salary amount for each preceding year. However, Smith's report did not explain how he arrived at that amount.

The trial court adopted the gross revenue metric as more reliable in determining the husband's reasonable compensation. The court affirmed on appeal. Specifically adopting Ellis's findings, the trial court found her graduated increase in wage application method to be "reasonable and credible." The trial court concurred with Ellis in how "net incomes can and are, at times, manipulated by various tax strategies, including but not limited to increased and advanced expensing through the corporation, which result in a reduced net income thereby skewing its reliability for the analysis before the court." It found Ellis credible and her methodology and calculation "better reasoned" than the husband's dual experts. What Ellis may have lacked in accounting experience, she made up for with the better-reasoned analysis.

Emphasizing a complex 15-day trial and inclusive 28-page ruling, the court held there was no error in the lack of specific findings regarding LBA's ability to pay the additional compensation. Even if a material omission, it was a harmless error. Nor did the trial court err in adopting Ellis's expert opinion. There was substantial evidence to support the trial court's use of the gross revenue metric. The trial court did not abuse its discretion in relying on Ellis's opinion and calculations that LBA undercompensated the husband by $912,000.

Notably, the wife's expert testified that LBA's alleged net income and losses may not have been accurate based upon her "professional experience." This phrase is very similar to "professional judgment" based upon the expert's education, training, and experience. An important lesson to be learned from this case is the need for the forensic accountant to testify credibly, confidently, and clearly. The trial court gave greater weight to the less-experienced forensic accountant because her analysis and methodology were easily explained. Clarity of analysis and methodology can win the day.

Family lawyers should coach forensic accountants to be comfortable stating in court that opinions are based on "professional judgment." And then they need to be ready to follow up by explaining how and why professional judgment is important to the particular issue.

Case Example: Methodology Must Be Understood

Forensic accountants must be able to explain how an amount is calculated. The ability to explain a forensic accountant's methodology for an analysis is just as important for the family lawyer as it is for the forensic accountant. It is important to keep explanations simple. If a complex tax and financial analysis is at issue, be prepared to spoon-feed your trial judge. One way to accomplish this may be to write down the methodology for the calculation in as simple of terms as possible so that the court may quote it in its findings of fact and conclusions of law. That way, if there is an appeal, the record is complete.

The husband and wife in this Oregon divorce case[10] were married in 1952 and separated in 2010 when both were 84 years old. During the marriage, the husband worked as a log truck driver and excavation operator, and the wife was a homemaker and caretaker for the five children, all of whom were adults at the time of the parties'

10. *In re* Marriage of Johnson and Price, 280 Or. App. 71, 380 P.3d 983 (2016).

separation. They operated a 137-acre ranch where the husband raised bison, produced hay, and received rental income from a mobile home.

At the time of trial, the wife was suffering from dementia and vertigo and living in an adult foster home. There was also some evidence that the husband had difficulty caring for himself, although he was generally in good health.

The trial court ordered that the husband pay maintenance spousal support of $2,600, increasing to $3,000 per month the following year. This amount was intended to cover the wife's foster care expenses. The trial court then ordered the husband to sell as many bison per month as were necessary to fund the maintenance. This was to continue until the first sale of real property.

The trial court awarded particular lots to each spouse and, between the value of the real property and the personal property, attempted to equalize the award to each spouse. To equalize the amounts, the wife was awarded an additional $83,000. The three lots awarded to the wife were valued at about $619,000.

The wife had requested that the court take into consideration the tax consequences of the sale of her property, whereas the husband did not make this request. Therefore, the trial court credited the wife with $119,000 in tax consequences based upon the immediate sale of the parcels awarded to her. It did note that the wife might not make an immediate sale, whereas the husband might be more able to do so. Therefore, the lower court recognized that the wife might "end up with the long half of the marital estate."

In computing the tax consequences, the lower court stated that the tax liability was based on the opinion of the wife's tax expert. However, the trial court noted that it was unable to discern the methodology that the expert had used to arrive at the tax basis for each parcel. However, despite being unable to compute the capital gains, the lower court found that $119,000 was an adequate adjustment for potential tax liability, especially since it was unlikely that the wife would sell all three parcels immediately.

The husband appealed to the Oregon Court of Appeals, raising a number of issues. The appeals court first held that the lower court had improperly awarded spousal support, since the sale of the bison necessarily reduced the size of the husband's share of the marital estate. Essentially, when setting spousal support, by requiring the husband to tap into his share of the property distribution, the lower court had ignored the husband's ability to pay.

The appeals court then addressed the husband's argument that the court should not have revoked a trust in order to make the property division. However, the court of appeals held that this was proper, since the trust assets were reachable by the husband.

The husband next argued that the lower court erred by miscalculating the wife's tax burden and subtracting that amount from the value of her property award while failing to do the same thing with respect to his share. The wife first pointed out that the husband did not present any expert testimony to challenge her expert's methodology and that the final value was reasonable despite not being computed to complete certainty. She also argued that the husband had the burden of proof to establish his own tax liability and that he had failed to offer any evidence of the amount.

Citing a 1997 case, the appeals court first noted that a court may adjust a property division based on tax consequences but there must be evidence to demonstrate a reasonable and supportable basis for the likely tax liabilities. The amount of potential tax liability must not be speculative.

Applying that standard, the appeals court held that the wife had not met her burden. Specifically, the wife's expert testimony as to taxes did not relate specifically to the parcels that she was ultimately awarded. Instead, the testimony had focused on the parcels that she had hoped to receive in the property division. There was actually no evidence on which to base the tax calculation for the parcels ultimately awarded. Indeed, in arriving at an award, the trial court had conceded that it was unable to perform the computations of the capital gains on those parcels.

Despite this admission, the trial court had set the tax adjustment at \$119,000 without any evidence. The appeals court held that this was speculative and that the lower court's finding would need to be reversed for that reason.

However, the court did agree with the wife that the husband's claim for credit for tax liability failed for the same reason since he had presented no evidence whatsoever to allow for such consideration.

Finally, the husband appealed the distribution of certain personal property, such as a piano, and the appeals court agreed with the husband that this distribution needed to be revisited. For these reasons, the court of appeals vacated the property distribution and remanded the case.

Case Example: Methodology Survives Challenge

In a 2018 Texas divorce[11] from a brief four-year marriage, the challenge by pretrial motion and then on appeal was to the forensic accountant serving as the expert witness. While there was no serious objection to qualification of the forensic accountant testifying as an expert witness, the wife challenged the expert's foundation for the particular testimony offered.

Married in January 2011, this Canadian couple relocated to Friendswood, Texas, with their children in late 2013 for the husband's employment. They separated in March 2015, and a December jury trial followed. In a

11. Mugford v. Mugford, No. 14-16-00436-CV (Ct. App. Tex. May 22, 2018). Although this was a memorandum opinion, it still has precedential value under the Texas Rules of Appellate Procedure. Memorandum opinions are published and made available to the public, as are all other appeals court opinions in Texas. The distinction between opinion and memorandum opinion is simply length, breadth, and depth. A memorandum opinion is abbreviated because the court believes the issues are settled, which makes writing a lengthy opinion unnecessary. *See* Tex. R. App. P. 47.4.

Texas divorce, the jury is the fact finder with the judge deciding all remaining issues. This jury found grounds for divorce based upon the husband's adultery and both spouses' cruel treatment. Among other findings, the jury determined the characterization of eight property items. The wife appealed on six.

The wife's key challenge was to admission of one expert's testimony. The husband's forensic accounting expert, William Stewart, CPA, testified at trial regarding his analysis of certain financial records pertinent to property characterized as marital or separate. The presumption in Texas is that all property possessed by a spouse during the marriage or upon dissolution of marriage is community property. To claim an asset is separate property, the spouse rebuts the presumption with clear and convincing evidence.

The wife contended that the trial court abused its discretion by allowing Stewart to testify on tracing the husband's lines of credit used in purchasing the Friendswood house with $985,000 of his separate funds. (Stewart traced $12,000 to community funds for reimbursement to the marital estate.) Taking issue with Stewart's methodology in attempting to preserve the presumption of the Friendswood house as marital property, the wife disregarded Stewart's experience and training in tracing financial assets in divorce.

She contended that Stewart "never read those notes and/or contracts and they were not produced prior to trial pursuant to requests for discovery." She argued that Stewart's testimony and report should not have been admitted because he "erroneously characterized" a bank loan as the husband's separate debt and resulting loan proceeds as the husband's separate asset and that Stewart's misstatements of law rendered his opinions "incorrect, unreliable and misleading." She essentially contended that Stewart's tracing methodology was flawed and unreliable.

There are two ways to challenge expert testimony. The first is by objecting to admissibility by challenging the expert's qualifications. The second is by objecting to the expert's opinions, which goes to the weight accorded such testimony by the trial court. Objections to qualification must be made prior to the expert testifying. Otherwise, challenging the particular opinions formed will almost always be considered going to the weight of the evidence and not to admissibility.

After the hearing, the trial court overruled the wife's pretrial motion to exclude Stewart's expert testimony. Her complaint that Stewart's expert opinion evidence should be inadmissible as unreliable was preserved for appeal because she properly objected to the evidence either before trial or when offered.

For Stewart's testimony to be admissible, he must be "qualified" and his testimony must be "relevant and based on a reliable foundation." The wife challenged Stewart's foundation but not his qualifications. The Texas Supreme Court set forth six factors for determining whether an expert's testimony is reliable:

> *(1) the extent to which the theory has been or can be tested; (2) the extent to which the technique relies upon the subjective interpretation of the expert; (3) whether the theory has been subjected to peer review and/or publication; (4) the technique's potential rate of error; (5) whether the underlying theory or technique has been generally accepted as valid by the relevant scientific community; and (6) the non-judicial uses which have been made of the theory or technique.*[12]

The court noted how the *Robinson* factors were not always useful in assessing reliability of a CPA's proposed testimony on his or her analysis of financial records—namely, when the expert relies on experience and training rather than specified methodology.[13] *Paschal* re-emphasized the supreme court's position that the *Robinson* factors were nonexclusive. Rule 702 of the Texas Rules of Evidence contemplated a "flexible inquiry." The Texas Supreme Court provided the following "general reliability" test:

> *When experts rely on experience and training rather than a particular methodology to reach their conclusions, reviewing courts determine whether there may be "simply too great an analytical gap between the data and the opinion proffered" for the opinion to be reliable.*[14]

There must always be some basis for the opinion offered to show its reliability.

---

12. E.I. du Pont de Nemours & Co. v. Robinson, 923 S.W.2d 549 (Tex. 1995).
13. Citing Paschal v. Great Western Drilling, Ltd., 215 S.W.3d 437 (Tex. App.-Eastland 2006, pet. den.).
14. Gammill v. Jack Williams Chevrolet, Inc., 972 S.W.2d 713 (Tex. 1998).

The court held no abuse of discretion by the trial court in concluding Stewart's testimony was reliable based on the facts that (1), the tracing methodology Stewart performed along with his report were before the trial court, and (2), the hearing record showed Stewart's experience and training were considered, particularly his "experience tracing financial assets."

Successfully challenging the weight of a forensic accountant's testimony, and not its admissibility, almost always requires testimony from a competing expert witness who identifies flawed assumptions and methodology. However, that did not happen here and the results reflected that.

Case Example: Sound Methodology Wins the Day

Family lawyers should always ensure that the judge understands a forensic accountant's methodology even if it is as simple as how a particular amount was calculated. In some situations, a forensic accountant may be required to calculate and testify to an amount of money even if the accountant has not been provided with adequate financial records to determine a precise amount.

The husband and wife getting this California divorce[15] had been married almost 17 years. The husband was a physician whose practice had been carried out through a medical corporation, Inland Neurosurgicare, Inc. During the marriage, the couple had amassed considerable assets and formed various corporations. Most of these assets constituted community property under California law.

In 1999, the husband filed for divorce in state court. At the time the husband filed the divorce petition, he also began looting the marital estate by transferring community

15. Abu-Assai v. Abu-Assai, No. EDCV 01-0153 GAF (SGI.x), 2010 WL 11508162 (C.D. Cal. Feb. 8, 2010). This is a federal district court ruling, not a state appellate court ruling.

property to third parties, including his parents. He transferred additional assets to companies that he and his parents controlled. As a result of these transfers, it appeared that the couple owned few community assets at the time of the divorce.

The wife later discovered the fraud and filed a federal lawsuit against the husband and the other parties in federal district court. In her lawsuit, she alleged that the husband had fraudulently transferred millions of dollars in community property and had violated the Racketeer Influenced and Corrupt Organizations Act (RICO). She also included claims for slander of title, fraud, and breach of fiduciary duty.

At some point, the husband fled the country to avoid the obligations imposed by the state court and was then considered by California law enforcement to be a fugitive. The court noted that some documents in the case had apparently come by fax from Cairo, Egypt.

In 2007, the court clerk's office entered a default against the husband, and the wife went to court asking that the court grant a default judgment. The federal court decided that motion in early 2010, 11 years after the divorce had begun.

To obtain a default judgment, the wife was required to establish a number of factors, including the merits of her claim and the amount of money at stake. She was also required to address the possibility of the material facts being disputed and whether the default was due to excusable neglect.

By the time the default judgment hearing was held, the case had been in litigation for years, and the court had already conducted numerous hearings on other issues. Therefore, the court quickly concluded that the wife had made sufficient allegations to support her claims. It also concluded that there was no real possibility of dispute and that the husband's failure to defend was not a case of excusable neglect. Then it turned to the question of how much money was at stake.

The court noted that in ruling on a default judgment, it was important that the judgment not be too large or unreasonable in light of the defendant's actions. The wife was claiming damages of $30 million, which included actual damages as well as treble damages under RICO. Given the circumstances of the case, the court ruled that this was a reasonable request and thus undertook an analysis to determine the amount of damages to be awarded.

The court noted that, even in a default case, the court should not automatically presume the truth of the plaintiff's allegations. Instead, the plaintiff must "prove up" the damages, and the wife was required to prove her claimed actual damages of $10 million, as well as her entitlement to treble damages under RICO. Therefore, the court closely scrutinized the wife's proof of damages, which included a declaration made by her expert witness, forensic accountant Donald T. Fife.

The court commended Fife on his attention to detail and noted that his review of the bank accounts and financial records had been "through and substantially accurate." Fife had reviewed 70 boxes of financial information regarding both the husband and the various business entities. He had also consulted with Jan Alexander, the family law court's accountant in the divorce case, as well as Eugene Platt, who had served as an accountant for the husband's medical practice, Inland Neurosurgicare, prior to that company going into bankruptcy.

The court first turned to Fife's analysis of various transfers from joint bank accounts as well as the husband's bank accounts. These transfers had been made to the husband's parents or to corporations controlled by them.

Fife concluded that such transfers totaled over $5 million and that there was absolutely no evidence showing that these transfers had any legitimate purpose. Some of the canceled checks had a notation of "loan," but Fife's search of the records failed to find substantiation that any loans had ever been made. Fife further testified that these monies had never been recovered and that he was unable to determine the current location of the money, although there were indications that it had been transferred overseas.

Fife analyzed all these transfers, and the court carefully reviewed all his conclusions. It began its analysis by reviewing about $1.7 million, which had been disbursed from the couple's joint bank accounts to a company called Advanced Child Development Systems.

Another half million dollars had been transferred from the joint accounts to an entity called Nile Import & Export, Inc. in which the husband had an ownership interest. Another company named Nile Oil Company was the recipient of over $600,000 from joint accounts, and LNMN Investments received over $700,000 from joint accounts. An additional $167,000 went from the joint accounts to Tender Care Children's Center, another company affiliated with the husband's family. Almost $1 million from the joint bank accounts went to United Child Development Group. Fife also found transfers from the husband's personal bank account. Of those, $225,000 went to Inland Child Development Center, one of his entities.

Finally, Fife found a number of transfers directly from the husband to family members. For example, he found payments of $106,000 to the husband's mother and over $19,000 to his father.

After reviewing all of Fife's analyses of the cash transfers, the court agreed that they established damages exceeding $5 million.

Fife had next analyzed payments made by Inland, the husband's medical practice, to various entities. Fife discovered payments of over $900,000 from the medical practice to one of the husband's companies. Based upon Fife's analysis, the court held that these amounts constituted earnings, which would have normally been paid out. Thus, they constituted community property, and therefore, this sum was also approved as damages.

Fife next analyzed transfers of over $2.3 million that the husband had made from mutual funds. In addition, the husband had liquidated about $160,000 that had been received as 1998 tax refunds. Here, the court concluded that some of the proof was lacking. In particular, the court held that about $500,000 was not adequately shown to have been liquidated during the husband's fraud. Therefore, the court allowed only about $1.8 million in damages for the transfers of mutual funds and tax refunds.

Finally, Fife analyzed the business expenses of the husband's medical practice. He noted that prior to July 1999, around the time of the divorce petition, all disbursements made appeared to be legitimate business expenses. However, after that date, there were check and credit card disbursements for things such as car expenses, airline tickets and hotels, Los Angeles Lakers basketball tickets, yacht expenses, and equestrian costs. The court examined these expenses and agreed with Fife that over half a million dollars in such expenses constituted fraudulent transfers and was properly included in the wife's damages.

The analysis of the business expenses was complicated by the fact that there had been a bankruptcy and that, following the bankruptcy, the husband practiced under the name of a new medical corporation, Neuro Surgical Associates Medical Corporation. Fife did not have full access to the business records for the new corporation. Instead, he used the nine months of bank records that he had available and extrapolated this using what the court called a "complex formula" to reach the conclusion that the new corporation had $880,000 in cash available to the husband. The court agreed that Fife had used sound methodology in coming up with this figure and approved it as damages as well.

After considering all of Fife's testimony, the court approved a total of over $8 million as being supported by the evidence. It went on to hold that treble damages under RICO were appropriate in this case and thus increased the amount of damages to over $24 million. Therefore, it awarded the wife a default judgment for the $24 million.

7 Asset Identification, Classification, and Valuation—From Simple to Complex

Some clients may first walk into your office having already thought about property division in terms of particular assets: "I want my car, half the equity in the house, my IRA, my grandmother's antiques I inherited, and my jewelry." Other clients know there is more to consider and rely on you, their lawyer, to explain the process. Before you advise what a reasonable settlement may be, you must determine what comprises the estate. Clients and lawyers should know the size of the pie before cutting into it.

Depending on the mix of assets that comprise the marital estate, there are almost always trade-offs. Consider the following proposal: "You take your pension, and I'll keep my IRA." If the estimated present value of the pension interest is much greater than the individual retirement account (IRA), this could cause a seriously one-sided divorce. Also, if a stock portfolio is chock-full of built-in capital gains, exchanging a stock portfolio for an equal amount of cash may make little sense.

As assets become more complex, so does your job, especially when clients ask questions like the following:

- What is the timeshare worth? If I receive it, can I sell it?
- What should we do with the kids' education saving accounts?
- I don't even know what a 403(b) is. Do you?
- How do we handle my husband's deferred compensation?
- What is my wife's pension worth?
- My husband says his stock options are "underwater" and are nontransferrable, so he says he gets to keep them. Is that true?
- My friend who's a stockbroker tells me to keep the Roth IRA and give away the regular IRA. Does that make sense? Why?
- My wife gets paid her sales commission bonus in February every year. Should we settle the case before the kids go back to school in January, even though she may get a big bonus?

The place to start is to create a marital balance sheet (MBS). The MBS lists all of a party's assets and debts. It should be compiled in a spreadsheet so that the totals add automatically and ratios are calculated instantaneously. It is the cornerstone of all financial analysis. To answer your client's key questions, you must have an overall mutual understanding of what comprises the marital estate. Without an understanding of the ratios—each spouse's relative share of the estate—you are only guessing. Many lawyers routinely create their own MBS. But some of the more technical aspects may need to be completed with help from the certified public accountant (CPA).

Before trial and settlement offers are prepared, the MBS creates a framework for other tasks. As the case progresses, new information can be easily compared with existing information, placing a spotlight on conflicting information. The MBS can also be used as a checklist for drafting deposition questions, answering discovery, and sharing information with the mediator.

Without a complete listing of assets, debts, their classification, and their valuation, there is no way to analyze and compare settlement proposals. Granted, both parties may be working from a completely different set of valuations. Being able to calculate each party's share based on the different valuations is important. Consider the following example:

Based on Mary's valuations, she offered a settlement proposal with a proposed distribution percentage of 52 percent to herself and 48 percent to her husband, Harry.

Harry responded with a counteroffer containing a proposed distribution percentage of 49 percent to Mary and 51 percent to himself at Mary's valuations. Using Harry's valuations, his counteroffer proposed a distribution of 45 percent to Mary and 55 percent to himself.

These numbers won't tell Mary or her lawyer what a reasonable settlement may be or what her response to Harry's counteroffer should be, but they do give both benchmarks for comparison. Assuming Mary is comfortable with the valuation differences being split in half, and assuming she is targeting a 50/50 property division, she can determine how far she may be from that desired settlement and respond accordingly.

This chapter provides a starting point for the family lawyer to begin looking at asset division in both the big and small picture. The process is very important. Understanding the ratio of proposed property division is vital for giving advice to clients. With the MBS as a tool, you can do more for clients in a shorter period of time. Compressing time can be critical in making decisions in a high-pressure mediation and in other settlement negotiation situations.

Organizing Assets and Debts

Almost all state laws have a set structure for the divorce trial process. At trial or in a settlement, there must be a determination or agreement of jurisdiction, a division of real and personal property, an agreement on temporary and permanent spousal support, a custody decision, a parenting-time structure, and an allocation of attorney's fees and court costs. Property division is usually based on factors that are statutory or derived from case law and that cover almost all aspects of the marriage. Very few facts are left out of the analysis. But the first step in all property division must include:

1. An identification of assets and debts,
2. A classification (marital/community or separate), and
3. A valuation.

You must explain to your clients that these steps aren't suggestions—they are mandatory tasks. In a trial or settlement, your primary responsibility as an attorney is to present evidence pertaining to each of these categories or list all of the parties' assets in the settlement agreement. At trial, if a party fails to present evidence on these issues, courts are generally free to do what they want with the other party's proof. In settlement, if an asset is left out, that asset could be lost forever.

The best tool for managing the list of assets is the MBS. See Example 7-1, a sample MBS. CPAs love spreadsheets because they have lots of straight lines and right angles, and if you load the formulas correctly, they will always add accurately. To CPAs, it's almost romantic what a spreadsheet can do. As a divorce lawyer, if you don't know how to run and manipulate an Excel spreadsheet, you are missing out. Consider reading a book or taking a course.

Here are some tips for building the MBS:

- Start the MBS at the very beginning of the case. Don't procrastinate. Like in law school, it is much easier to begin preparing for finals by attending classes and taking notes than by trying to read everything the night before an exam. Building the MBS is a daunting task if you wait to receive every piece of information before starting.
- Use the MBS as a cross-reference tool. If your client supplies information and the other spouse provides contradictory information in discovery, more investigation may be needed. One spouse may be right, and the other may be wrong.
- Show your client the MBS. It should be a concise document confirming a mutual understanding of the marital estate. The client can help spot errors. No matter how attentive you or your staff may be, there can always be mistakes. Discovering a miscommunication early in the process is always much less embarrassing than discovering it later during a court hearing.
- List only accounts' last four digits in case a copy is lost or stolen.
- List each asset's formal name. The formal name will be needed for the settlement agreement (e.g., Merrill Lynch Brokerage Account #3441).
- Also, list each asset's name as the parties call it, such as "Daddy's old stock account." Be vigilant. What spouses call accounts often differs from their formal names. Because clients get confused on this, lawyers will, too. If the property settlement agreement is inaccurate, this can cause serious problems.

- List closed accounts. Note the date accounts were purportedly closed. It is a good reference to double-check in the event a transaction is found after the date the account was supposedly closed.
- List statement dates or valuation dates and source documents. Update those as they are received. For a stock brokerage account, list these as follows: "Per Wells Fargo Quarterly Statement dated 3/30/2018."
- List all persons named on accounts.
- In the comments, list important reference information and comments from the client. For example, "Cash surrender value per 8/30/2018 statement is $53,000," and "Husband prefers to receive this in settlement."
- List both parties' valuations in the comments section. Keep it simple. For example, for the husband's 1974 Corvette, "Wife valued by kbb.com at $23,000 on 4/12/2018. Husband valued in interrogatory answer #20 at $20,000 on 3/28/2018."
- When printing an MBS to share at mediation or in court, be very careful to keep confidential any attorney's mental impressions and other work product, as well as any client confidences, noted in the comments section.
- Get a jump start on the calculation of estimated pension values and other complex retirement and compensation assets, such as stock options, as soon as possible. Determine early on whether a forensic accountant is needed.
- For pensions, review the summary plan description as soon as possible and determine whether the pensions can be divided.
- Determine early in the case whether assets such as real estate or personal property need to be appraised.
- Note if the asset has built-in capital gains or other special tax treatment considerations, especially stock portfolios, real estate portfolios, and second homes. Understand that the tax basis is not always the same as the original purchase price.[1] Consider consulting with your client's forensic accountant on these issues.

---

1. *See generally* IRS Publication 551, *Basis of Assets*, available at www.IRS.gov.

Example 7-1
Sample Marital Balance Sheet

J. L. Picard v. Beverly C. Picard, M.D.
Marital Balance Sheet

#	Net Value	Separate Property: Wife	Separate Property: Husband	Marital Property	Division of Marital Property: Wife	%	Division of Marital Property: Husband	%	Comments
9									
10	295,000	-	-	295,000	295,000	100%	-	0%	Titled in both parties' names as JTWROS; purchased 5/15/15 for $779,000.00; appraised for Husband by Leonard H. McCoy for $850,000.00 on 9/12/18; appraised for Wife by Tiberius Kirk for $830,000.00; mortgage balance with Enterprise Mortgage $555,000.00; net equity $295,000.00 per
11									
12	20,000	-	-	20,000	20,000	100%	-	0%	Husband's value $20,000.00; Wife's value $5,000.00
13	25,000	-	-	25,000	25,000	100%	-	0%	Wife drives; jointly titled; Kelley Blue Book new car value $25,000.00
14	30,000	-	-	30,000	-	0%	30,000	100%	Husband drives; in Husband's name; Kelley Blue Book trade-in value $30,000.00
15	2,000	-	-	2,000	-	0%	2,000	100%	his answer to Interrogatory No. 7; Wife's value $20,000.00 per her answer to Interrogatory No. 12
16	COUNTS:								
17	7,000	-	-	7,000	7,000	100%	-	0%	Joint account; balance $5,000.00 per 12/16/18 statement; W primary user of this account
18	10,000			10,000	-	0%	10,000	100%	Husband's account; balance $10,000.00 per 12/7/18 statement; Husband opened account after the parties separated; Husband deposits his paycheck into this account
19									
20	15,000	-	-	15,000	15,000	100%	-	0%	**Policy Owner:** Wife; **Insured:** Husband; **Beneficiary:** the parties' children; **Cash Surrender Value:** $15,000.00; **Face Amount:** $150,000.00; $15,000.00 cash surrender value per 6/30/18 annual statement
21	-	-	-	-	-	0%	-	100%	**Policy Owner:** Husband; **Insured:** Husband; **Beneficiary:** **Wife**; **Cash Surrender Value:** $0.00; **Face Amount:** $500,000.00; benefit provided by Large Public
22	TMENT ACCOUNTS:								
23	75,000	-	-	75,000		0%	75,000	100%	Joint account; balance $75,000.00 per 11/30/18 statement
24	145,000	-	-	145,000	-	0%	145,000	100%	Husband's account; balance $145,000.00 per 11/30/18 statement
25	PLANS:								
26	165,000	-	-	165,000	123,750	75%	41,250	25%	Wife's account; balance $165,000.00 per 11/30/18 statement
27	255,000	-	82,992	172,008	-	0%	172,008	100%	Husband's account; balance per 6/30/18 annual statement
28	1,044,000	-	82,992	961,008	485,750	51%	475,258	49%	
29									
30	-	-	-	-	-	100%	-	0%	Joint mortgage secured by 1925 Vulcan Way, San Francisco, Mississippi; balance $555,000.00 per 11/30/18 statement
31	2,000	-	-	2,000	-	0%	2,000	100%	Husband's account; balance $2,000.00 per 12/7/18 statement
32	12,000	-	-	12,000	12,000	100%	-	0%	Wife's account; balance $12,000.00 per 12/23/18 statement
33	14,000	-	-	14,000	12,000	0%	2,000	0%	
34	**1,030,000**	**-**	**82,992**	**947,008**	**473,750**	**50.0%**	**473,258**	**50.0%**	

- Include airline miles, credit card points programs, and other business perks in the MBS.
- Know that it is easy for the spreadsheet formulas to get out of whack. Double-check them with a calculator.

Identification

Have you ever worried that the proposed settlement agreement you just drafted left something out? Have you ever wondered what would happen if your client missed it too? Have you ever worried that you were moving too fast at a mediation and were afraid you were missing something? Every asset is listed on the MBS. Every suspected asset is listed. Closed accounts are listed with zero balances. Everything can be cross-referenced. From the minute the client hands you or your paralegal the first bank statement, the asset should be recorded. Also load the results from the opposing party's discovery answers and produced documents into the MBS. Be thorough from the beginning of the case.

Classification

Many lawyers forget that the valuation of assets at the date of acquisition (or marriage) can be just as legally relevant as the valuation at the distribution date (separation or divorce). It is not only legally relevant but also essential. The calculation of the appreciation of separate property begins with the current value of an asset and is reduced by its value as of the date of the marriage or acquisition. This sounds simple enough. But some lawyers only worry about proof of valuation at mediation or trial. Often, that's too late.

Additionally, CPAs don't always understand that the calculation of the appreciation of separate property can be the forensic accountant's full employment act. Divorce lawyers must have a good handle on their particular state's classification law. It is the lawyer's job to educate the accountant on what must be proven. CPAs can often take it from there.

Consider a simple example: In year five of a marriage, the wife, Sarah, inherited $300,000. To keep the asset separate, Sarah deposited the money in a brokerage account listed in her name only. Over the next six years, the account grew by $175,000. During that time, the brokerage account generated interest, dividends, and capital gains and losses. That taxable income flowed into the parties' joint tax return.

The husband, Joe, earned income used to pay the taxes. Under that state's law, because Joe made a substantial contribution to the preservation or appreciation of the asset when he paid the taxes, the $175,000 gain is now a marital asset, even though the original $300,000 remains separate.

Valuation

Valuation is always a struggle and requires patience. Some assets, such as brokerage accounts, come with monthly statements. Other marital assets, such as businesses, have no such statements. Balance sheets do not reflect a business's fair market value. If the case is tried, both parties most likely have a duty to value all assets. If your client fails to present evidence of value for an asset, the court may accept the other party's value without argument. For settlement, how do you calculate the client's percentage of marital assets without knowing the value of all the assets in the estate? You can't.

Some cases present a combination of classification and valuation problems. For example, at the time of the marriage, Carol owned a business. At that time, it employed 15 people. Over time, it grew, and ten years later it employed 40. Then Carol and Fred divorced. Carol and Fred must determine the value of the business at the time of the divorce and at the time of the marriage. The difference is appreciation of separate property. Valuing any asset in the past is challenging, but as long as the right documents still exist, the business valuation expert can do the job.

Clients always underestimate the challenges of valuation. Sure, clients can testify as to the value of assets they own, but who should really believe their opinion if the asset is significant? Parties' opinions are assumed to be biased. And some judges are apt to value assets in their own mind, regardless of the testimony offered. Nevertheless, whether at trial or during settlement negotiations, the spouse submitting the more credible evidence of value usually has a serious advantage.[2]

2. All family lawyers should consider purchasing SHANNON PRATT & ALINA V. NICULITA, THE LAWYER'S BUSINESS VALUATION HANDBOOK (ABA 2nd ed. 2013).

Hire the best valuation expert the client can afford. Do your homework. Learn about the different business valuation experts' credentials.[3] Narrow the potential experts to two or three. Interview the experts with the client present and then get going. Completing valuations before the other spouse can become an important strategic advantage. It sets the tone for negotiations, and the opposing party may even agree to the early valuation—your evaluation—especially if the valuation professional is well respected.

The Information Needed Depends on the Assets and Debts

What information should be loaded into the MBS? Everything that's relevant to identify, classify, and value assets. Listed below are some of the more common assets and the detailed information relating to them that needs to be loaded into the MBS.

For **real property**, provide the equity of the parties' primary residence and any second homes (fair market value less all debt secured by the real property). The secured debt should almost always be the responsibility of the party receiving the asset. In the debts section, list the mortgage, home equity lines of credit, and second mortgages separately with the zero balances but cross-reference the properties and amounts in the comments column. Be careful not to list both the equity value and the debts. This will double count the debt.

In the description for real property, describe the asset as the marital residence, second home, or investment real property and include the property's street address or location. In the Comments, list the asset's fair market value less its secured debt. Know your state's law regarding sales costs and tax treatment. If the property is likely to be sold by either or both parties, you may need to list the equity net of sales commission, estimated closing costs, and capital gains taxes. Also, list the source of information for the fair market value and the date. For each secured debt, list, describe, and provide its current balance separately, as well as the date of the amount.

For **tangible personal property** (aka "the stuff"), list all important or valuable individual personal property items. The client will want to see them there and see them accounted for in the settlement. Examples

3. *See generally id.*, Chapter 2.

include Grandmother's rocking chair, the Rolex watch, Auntie's diamond and pearl earrings, and the collector's-grade coin collection. In the description column, list how the item is commonly described and note its location, if anywhere other than either party's residence. For jewelry, list the appraiser and date of appraisal. If it's separate property, list details of the transfer, such as "Valentine's Day 2014 Gift from Husband." Other assets may be grouped together as "household contents."

For **cars, boats, and airplanes**, list in the description column their make, model, year, serial number, primary driver or operator, and location, if anywhere other than either party's residence. Also, if any of them are leased, note that fact. In the comments column, record each party's valuation and desired distribution. Always keep in mind that, if the matter must be tried, the client may need to testify to their value if the cost of an appraisal will exceed the appraised value, as is often the case.

For **checking and savings accounts**, record in the description column the name of the institution and type of account, the name(s) on the account, a description of the type of ownership (e.g., "joint" or "joint tenancy with right of survivorship"), and the last four or five digits of the account number. In the comments column, list the balance, the source document for the balance, and the date of the statement. Listing dates of statements makes the MBS much easier to update.

For **life insurance**, list all policies owned, regardless of whether the policy has a cash surrender value. Often, spouses may keep older policies active without the other's knowledge, permission, or consent. Lawyers and paralegals should learn about life insurance policies and the meanings of their terms. Consider inviting a trusted insurance professional to visit with your team and present a seminar on the basics of life insurance. Most will be flattered and may even refer you a case someday. In the description column, list the insurance company, type of policy (e.g., term, whole life, universal), and last four digits of the policy number. In the comments section, list details, including the policy owner(s); the insured; the beneficiary and face amount (benefit); the cash surrender value, if any; the source document; and the date.

For **investments, complex compensation and bonus packages, and retirement assets**, list in the description column the name of the institution holding the asset, the title and type of account, the owners, and the last four or five digits of the account number. In the comments section, note the balance; the source document; the date; the owners and authorized parties, if different from the owners (e.g., "joint owners, two signatures required"); the type of ownership (e.g., "joint tenancy with right of survivorship"); the tax basis; the valuation; and the date of valuation. For pension and 401(k) plans, also list whether the asset can be divided. Some can't. Also, note whether the stock options are nontransferable.[4] If you need help, forensic accountants call this aspect of their services "litigation support."

Calculating Estimates of the Value of Deferred Pension Benefits

Most lawyers say "pension valuation" when they mean to describe the process of calculating estimates of value of deferred pension benefits. "Pension valuation" is not a technically correct term because forensic accountants are not valuing the pension. Instead, they calculate an estimate of value of the participant's interest. Whatever family lawyers may call it though, the entire process of dealing with pensions is a bugbear.

Most QDRO (qualified domestic relations order) seminars are taught by pension lawyers. Pension lawyers make dealing with pensions sound easy because they read, draft, and use pension terms daily. Most family lawyers feel uneasy from the very first QDRO seminar session. Sure, like all lawyers, family lawyers made good grades in college, went to law school, passed the bar, and all that. But at the end of the day, it takes years of experience and regular attendance at annual ERISA (Employee Retirement Income Security Act of 1974) updates to feel comfortable handling transactions involving pensions and drafting important documents dividing hundreds of thousands of dollars with QDROs. The ABA Family Law Section publishes a very important book, *The Complete QDRO Handbook* by David Clayton Carrad. Buy it. Read it. At a minimum, family lawyers must read and understand the first six chapters—no exceptions. Even if you are like many family lawyers and choose to direct clients to retain outside pension counsel, you really need to read and understand the first six chapters. Reading the rest of the book is a good idea too.

---

4. Almost no employer-issued stock options can be transferred. *See* Lester Barenbaum, Walter Schubert & Robert Feder, The Family Lawyer's Guide to Stock Options (ABA 2007).

Nevertheless, after having read the first six chapters of *The Complete QDRO Handbook* and having attended a few seminars on the topic, you should start to realize some startling and disturbing truths about family lawyers' handling of pensions:

1. Pensions can be worth hundreds of thousands of dollars.
2. Pensions are hard to handle,[5] and QDROs can be costly to prepare for many reasons.
3. Mishandling QDROs can be malpractice, and family lawyers do mess up QDROs every day.
4. Even if all your client wants is the ubiquitous "just half," there is still plenty of work that must be done.
5. There are so many different types of plans that it is tough to get enough repetitions to become comfortable working with QDROs, and at least one odd exception often seems to apply.
6. For every state, specific property division laws apply, and you've got to know your state's law to negotiate the classification, valuation, and division of pension benefits.
7. A few problems don't have simple, clean solutions, and it is your job to make lemonade out of lemons.
8. Learning about pensions is nonlinear. You may need to read, consult, and think about the same problem from many different perspectives.
9. How you handle a particular pension situation may depend on whether you represent the participant spouse (employee) or the alternate payee spouse (nonemployee).
10. You must know what's what with all possible elections, especially the pension's particular survivorship elections options.[6]
11. As a concept, every family lawyer should understand "present value."[7]
12. You must know about separate interest, shared interest, and offset methods.

---

5. *See The Top Ten QDRO Mistakes and How to Avoid Them*, in Chapter 1 of David Clayton Carrad, The Complete QDRO Handbook (ABA 2004).
6. *Id.*
7. Present value is discussed later in this chapter.

Of all the mistakes a family lawyer can make, the one that can be most easily avoided is waiting to handle a pension at the last minute. All family lawyers make this mistake at some point, often resulting in unpleasant complications. For instance, suppose you start to open the file to draft the proposed pension division provision, whereupon you realize you don't have the summary plan description and can't determine whether a QDRO will be accepted. It may take weeks to get a copy of the summary plan description in your office, even if your client is the employee/participant. Or worse, suppose you are at mediation, and the mediator asks you in front of your client, "Have you reviewed the plan administrator's QDRO procedures to see what elections must be considered?" When your client looks at you, she knows that the look on your face means you haven't done something you should have. In a worst-case scenario, suppose the divorce settlement failed to address the survivorship election and the opposing party refuses to allow the survivorship election to be shown in the QDRO because it had not been negotiated. If you procrastinate often enough, you'll eventually hurt a client's case by causing significant delay waiting for necessary documents that could have been requested earlier in the representation or by making a mistake in a rush just to get the case completed.

Calculating the estimated value of a pension interest to a participant and what part of that is marital property can be crucial. For example, what if at mediation the participant spouse offers to offset the value of the pension with equity in the house, but you don't know whether the amount of the offered offset is reasonable because you have no expert report? Or what if the client is tempted to accept the offer because all the client wants is to end the divorce at any cost, and you cannot advise whether the offer makes financial sense? Or even worse, what if the opposing party's forensic accountant has prepared a report calculating the estimated value of the marital portion of the pension and you have no idea whether the calculated estimated amount is reasonable? Do you know your state's case law regarding determining the marital portion and valuation methods well enough to review the opposing expert's method of calculating marital versus separate property interest? Below, you will learn that the calculation of value is never accurate but instead is an estimate for at least two important reasons. First, no one knows exactly when the participant will die. Second, judgment is always involved when determining a discount rate. Regardless, in every case, you and your client should plan and discuss whether the cost of the calculation and the likelihood of its being needed justify having it done.[8] Some cases will not need any calculation if a settlement can be reached that divides the pension without the need for an analysis of its impact on the estate. Unfortunately, family lawyers don't always know that until they're in the midst of settlement negotiations, when the calculation is either needed or not needed and it's too late to have one done.

The overall process of handling pensions, determining their financial impact, negotiating a settlement, and handling the QDRO from start to finish is counterintuitive and backward. For example, what if the pension can't be divided by a QDRO yet the settlement agreement says you are to divide it 50/50? Also, what if you settle at mediation agreeing for the parties to execute a 50/50 division of the pension; fail to list in the settlement how any of the elections are to be handled; draft the QDRO stating that your client, the alternate payee, shall receive a joint and survivor annuity option; and opposing counsel then refuses to agree to your proposed QDRO with that provision included? Preventing these problems is often more easily accomplished than solving them.

Preventing problems means you can't just take one step at a time. You must see the entire journey before taking a single step. As with building a swing set, even if you intend on reading the instructions, you must begin well in advance of the child's birthday to start assembling it. Because you are a responsible parent, you should make sure all the parts and tools are on hand well in advance of tackling the job. When building a swing set, if a part is missing or you don't have a needed tool, you can't finish the job in one session. You may need to order a missing part or go to the store for a special tool. Similarly, when handling pensions, if a document is missing, it may take weeks to get your hands on it because it may need to be requested from the participant's human resources (HR) department or the plan administrator. In the meantime, if a necessary document is missing, clients are inclined to ask the pesky question, "Why didn't we (meaning *you*) get this document in already?" Clients are rarely fans of avoidable delay.

Handling the pension division process is a complex, time-consuming, and often expensive job. Feel free to blame Congress and its ERISA and tax laws. In the same breath, though, you should be able

8. Shop and price local forensic accounting and actuary experts for this service.

to explain why the cost is worth it. The estimated net present value of the benefits may be worth hundreds of thousands of dollars and is often the most valuable asset in many marital estates. As a matter of overall value, you are doing the equivalent of handling the closing on a very complicated house. Receiving part of the pension benefits, however, may be better than owning a house because a house won't pay your client cash every month. Pensions do.

Key pension documents include the following:

1. The summary plan description,
2. The most recent annual benefits statement,
3. The plan administrator's QDRO procedures and instructions,[9]
4. The plan administrator's sample QDRO form,[10] and
5. The text of the pension plan.[11]

Memorize this list.[12] These documents are needed to calculate the estimated value of a participant's pension interest, advise the client, handle the negotiations of the pension division, draft a thorough settlement agreement, and draft or review the proposed QDRO. Ask your client for these documents. Ask for them in correspondence to

9. QDRO instructions are wonderful if they were drafted by a plan administrator who chooses to explain the common mistakes made by divorce lawyers who are unfamiliar with pension law.

10. QDRO forms should give the divorce practitioner a road map about the various important elections that should be decided when drafting specific settlement terms.

11. If you have the other four, you may not ever need the complete text of the plan itself. So, always at least ask for it. Sometimes, the text of the plan is available for download on a website to which your client has access. If so, grab it. You may never need it, but occasionally a summary plan description may reference a term with a definition found only in the text of the plan document.

12. Seriously. Memorize all five and what important information they convey. Make sure your request for documents asks for all of them. If you are required to argue a motion to compel document production in discovery, be prepared to explain to your judge what vital information each document contains and why you require all of them. For example, "Your Honor, I want to settle this divorce and get this off Your Honor's docket for good. I can't even write up a settlement offer without reviewing them. I promise that within ten days of receiving these documents, I will send opposing counsel a written and complete global settlement offer."

opposing counsel, document requests, and subpoenas to employers. Simple enough? Evidently not. For a variety of reasons, experience teaches that getting these documents is a much more difficult process than it needs to be. Often, it doesn't matter whether you represent the participant spouse or the alternate payee.

Most summary plan descriptions will tell you everything you need to know about the pension, the definition of terms, and the basics for its division. But unfortunately, not all will. Pension plan terms have definitions specific to the particular plan in which they are used. If you need to research the plan's exact definition of a term or treatment of a particular situation related to the alternate payee's interest, you may need the text of the pension plan, also called the "plan document." The plan document may be hundreds of pages long. If the plan administrator has a scanned version of the plan document, ask for that via e-mail. In the meantime, if you have the summary plan description, see if you can get by with just that, along with the QDRO instructions.

Most pensions' annual benefits statements are given to employees. Most employees will keep them. Some may not or claim they didn't keep them. Nevertheless, employees should be able to get copies. Some may be available online. Annual benefits statements usually show the employee's basic information, pension benefits accrued to date, vesting analysis, expected benefits, and other statistical information. Experienced lawyers suggest asking for the three most recent annual benefits statements and any supplemental statements (quarterly or semiannual), reviewing them, and looking for any important changes in the plan's administration. But know that not all financial information on the annual benefits statements can be trusted or understood from the face of the documents. Some annual benefits statements have feel-good calculations showing what the pension benefits are worth given certain assumptions. Unfortunately, those assumptions are not always listed and may or may not be realistic. So if an annual benefits statement shows a "calculated value," don't trust it. Also, tell your client not to trust it. Certainly, don't rely upon the listed calculated value to offset against other marital estate assets in a proposed settlement division without an expert's opinion clearly stating you can do so.

It should be common sense to obtain and read the plan administrator's QDRO instructions and sample form. If you don't understand the wisdom of doing so, read the first six chapters of *The Complete QDRO Handbook* again. But some plan administrators have had enough experience with less-than-knowledgeable family lawyers and, therefore, have taken the time to write down helpful instructions and tips. Other plan administrators may choose to be unhelpful because many believe offering any advice creates a conflict of interest. From the pension plan's perspective, most plan interpretations are a zero-sum game. If a particular sentence is interpreted in a particular way, it will be helpful to one spouse and detrimental to the other. And if a spouse's lawyer who drafts the QDRO fails to use the plan's sample form (or fails to make a certain election that that spouse really should be making if that spouse's lawyer knew better), the pension plan administrator will not help correct such errors. Once the QDRO is accepted, the QDRO will be interpreted in accordance with the terms of the plan—period.

Negotiating a pension deal in a divorce means understanding the proposal. Understanding the proposal means understanding the money. Understanding the money means knowing the math. Luckily, the math is not really that tough—if you understand present value. If necessary, ask a forensic accountant to help explain present value. Before considering the math of calculating estimates of value, though, it is important to understand that there are three ways pension divisions are handled:

1. **Separate interest** divides the interest completely between the spouses. In the majority of cases, if offset is not chosen, this is the preferred option. If the marital interest is divided equally or proportionately, there may be no need for the calculation of the estimate of the value of the pension interest to divide it. But it is not that unusual these days for both spouses to have pension interests. If so, calculations of value can be completed just in case, during settlement negotiations. One party offers, "Why don't you just keep yours, and I'll keep mine?" If your client's interest is worth significantly more and the offering party's lawyer has no clue, why not agree?

2. **Offset** leaves all the pension interest in the hands of the participant spouse, and other assets are exchanged of an equitable value. If offset is used, your client must have competent advice about the calculated estimate value.

3. **Shared interest** means not dividing the asset. The participant receiving the pension must pay the former spouse a certain sum following the beginning of the payout. This option is also described as "deferred jurisdiction" or "deferred distribution"

and is almost always chosen only as a means of last resort. Shared interests most often occur only when the pension interest cannot be divided and there are not enough assets to complete an offset. Although a shared interest does not necessarily require an estimated calculation of value, it can be very helpful in explaining to the trier of fact the importance of handling the transaction correctly.

Calculations of estimates of value can be done by actuaries or forensic accountants. Actuaries will almost always charge significantly more, and they are often harder to find. There are two basic methods of estimating value. The mortality method takes into consideration probabilities of death, is considered more precise, is much more complicated and difficult to explain, and is almost always handled by actuaries. The more common life expectancy method, also called the discounted present value method, is the method much more commonly used by forensic accountants. Some states require the calculated estimate of value to include the probability of the employee's death, disability, or leaving employment.

Example 7-2 is a sample report by Robert Vance, CPA, ABV, CFF, CVA, CFP, a forensic accountant practicing in Memphis, Tennessee.

Reports can be unwieldy, multiple-page discussions of the calculations, sources of information, analyses, judgment calls, and applicable theories used in determining a pension's value. The sample report provided, however, is a "one pager." In many cases, judges, lawyers, clients, opposing counsel, and opposing parties equate reliability with simplicity. There are a few concepts lawyers should really know before tackling the calculation itself.

1. **Present value.** If you don't understand present value, you aren't alone. This means you probably didn't take an undergraduate course in finance. If you did, you probably didn't get a good grade without understanding present value. Present value describes what money to be received in the future is worth today. Simple, right? If you buy a CD paying 5 percent interest per year, investing $100 today will yield you $105 a year from now. Assuming a 5 percent discount rate (the reverse of interest), the present value of receiving $105 a year from now is $100. Present value calculations require a spreadsheet program such as Excel, a calculator, or printed tables (old school).

Example 7-2 Calculation of Estimated Value of Defined Benefit Pension Plan Interest

Calculation of Estimated Value of Defined Benefit Pension Plan Interest

Case Information		Plan Information	
Case Style:	Picard v. Picard	Employer:	Large Public Enterprise, Inc.
Plan Participant:	J.L. Picard	Plan name:	Large Public Enterprise, Inc. Retirement Plan
Sex:	M		
Race:	W	Payout Method for Monthly Benefit:	Single Life Annuity
Date of Birth:	12/1/1958	Date of Retirement:	1/1/2023
Age at Date of Valuation:	51.7	Age at Retirement:	65.0
Date of Valuation:	8/31/2010	Date of Hire:	10/1/1986
Date of Preparation:	8/31/2010	Date of Plan Participation:	10/1/1986
Date of Marriage:	9/21/1990	Years in Plan as of Date of Valuation:	23.9
Years of Marriage:	19.9	Ratio of Benefits During Marriage:	83.3%
		Vested Percentage:	100.0%

Calculations

Pension Plan Valuation Timeline

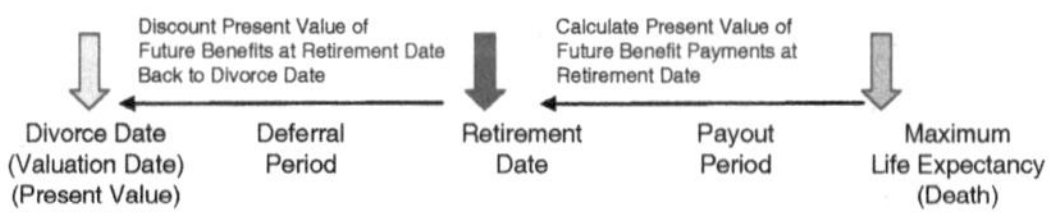

Monthly retirement benefit	$2,850.00	a.	Per pension benefit statement dated 6/30/10
Retirement age used in this calculation	65.0		Per pension benefit statement dated 6/30/10
Life expectancy at valuation date[1]	28.2	b.	
Number of years to retirement age (deferral period)	13.3	c.	
Years of life expectancy beyond retirement age (payout period)	14.9	d.	b. - c. = d.
Discount rate for payout period[2]	4.50%	e.	
Present value of monthly benefits at retirement date	370,808	f.	Present value of a. discounted monthly with d. & e.
Discount rate for deferral period[2]	4.50%	g.	
Present value of retirement benefits at valuation date	206,492	h.	Present value of f. discounted annually with c. & g.
Ratio of total benefits during marriage	83.3%	i.	Married after plan participation started
Marital value of retirement benefits at valuation (divorce) date	**$172,008**	j.	h. x i. = j.

Notes

1) Life Expectancy Tables: "United States Life Tables, 2004", National Vital Statistics Reports, Vol. 56, No. 9, Dec. 28, 2007, National Center for Health Statistics; Life Table for white males.

2) Derived from Federal Reserve Statistical Release as of 8/31/10; 20 Year, U.S. Government Securities, Treasury Constant Maturities, plus a factor for risk

Prepared By:
Robert Vance, CPA/ABV/CFF, CVA, CFP
Forensic & Valuation Services, PLC
Memphis, TN
www.ForensicVal.com

2. **Discount rate.** To calculate present value, a discount rate must be chosen. Discount rates (and interest rates, for that matter) reflect an assessment of risk. For pension calculations, risk is determined by adding the "safe" rate, or "risk-free" rate, which is usually the rate guaranteed by the U.S. government

for investments for that length of term and the amount of risk related to the particular pension plan. This risk related to the particular pension plan considers the likelihood that the pension benefits will not be paid due to a financial collapse of the plan. This involves a judgment call made by forensic accountants and can be the simplest way to manipulate the results. How could a forensic accountant manipulate results? The greater the discount rate, the less the estimated net present value of expected benefits. This judgment call can have a huge impact on the calculation of estimated value. Without your client's having her own forensic accountant's report, are you really able to effectively argue that the other expert's opinion is materially overstated or understated? Probably not.

3. **Present value of an annuity.** Annuities pay money in regular intervals, usually monthly, and so do pensions. The present value of a future stream of payments is often called "present value of an annuity." It describes what an ordinary investor would pay today for that stream of payments. Again, a discount rate is utilized, and risk is considered in its determination.
4. **Life expectancy of the participant** is always unknown. On Example 7-2, see "life expectancy at valuation date." Pension benefits are usually paid until the participant dies. Since they have no way of knowing how long someone will live and receive payments, forensic accountants look to mortality tables for answers. Since there are many mortality tables to choose from, you may want to challenge the opposing expert's choice of mortality table. In general, the more current and detailed the table chosen (i.e., including gender and race), the more reliable the life expectancy determination.
5. **There are two present value calculations.** It may be helpful to know that the calculations occur in reverse chronological order. First, the length of time for which the pension benefits are expected to be paid is determined. On Example 7-2, see "present value of monthly benefits at retirement date." The calculation of the present value of the future stream of payments is calculated to the date of retirement. This is expressed as a lump sum. Second, the present value of that lump sum must be calculated as of the date of the report, separation, or trial. On Example 7-2, see

"present value of monthly benefits at valuation date." Consider asking your client's forensic accountant to check the opposing expert's math. Even if the opposing expert uses different assumptions, which is likely, the math could still be wrong. Accountants hate to be wrong on math, but it happens.

6. **"Coverture factor"** describes the formula for the determination of what portion of the benefit is marital property and what portion is separate property. On Example 7-2, see "ratio of total benefits during marriage." Research and know your state's exact applicable law and definitions. If your expert doesn't know it exactly, you should provide it. A great deal of money can change hands based on your understanding of the law and calculations (or lack thereof).

Once you receive your forensic accountant's report, you can analyze how the estimated pension interest's value fits within the overall estate and begin to formulate an overall negotiating strategy.

Complex Compensation, Bonus Packages, and Perks

Major corporations may have layer upon layer of complex compensation and bonus packages. For highly compensated executives, bonus packages may comprise as little as 10 percent to more than 300 percent of their total annual compensation, compared to their base salary. For a very predictable, self-interested reason, executives hate disclosing these bonuses and perks during a divorce. Luckily, many executives' spouses have overheard conversations about the bonuses throughout their years of marriage. Or the spouse's claimed annual income for the current year is a fraction of the previous years' taxable income. In any event, identifying spouses who have these complex and possibly covert deals is the first step.

Some packages are based on annual calculations, and others may involve multiple years. If so, know your state's law on vested and unvested benefits. Usually, bonuses are based on some company metric. "Metric" is a general business term describing a performance indicator, usually a calculation or ratio, that the business is focused on improving. For example, one metric may be an increase in sales over prior years. Or it could be a moving average of certain financial statistics. In any event, know that, if the terms of the compensation package are written, they might be described in a one-sentence letter or involve a documented formula that is as complex as any rotisserie baseball league nerd could invent.

Almost all packages are in writing, but they don't have to be. The smaller the business, the more likely such deals are not written. Many sales commissions may be handshake deals, even though the commissions themselves may be well-defined. For example, an opposing spouse works as a commissioned salesperson for Bob, the business owner. Bob trusts his sales force, and his sales force trusts him. For the last eight years, Bob has given a 50 percent bonus on top of commissions and base salary to all sales professionals, but only if sales increased at least 18 percent annually or more, and a 60 percent bonus if sales increased 25 percent or more. But nothing is written down documenting this deal. Since Bob's brother went through a divorce eight years ago and half of the sales force pays child support, Bob and his sales force see this handshake deal as a special perk. Every member of the sales force can say under oath, "We never know when or how much of a bonus we will receive. Bob unilaterally decides bonuses. We are never allowed to see the company's numbers—we only see our own. My sales are down, and I'm told the company's sales are down. It doesn't look good that I will receive another bonus this year, even though last year was my biggest year ever. Likely, the only earning I will have is my basic draw." When the follow-up questions are asked, the salesperson can say, "No, there are no documents supporting what I said. We must trust Bob. He makes the final decision, and we have no access to any of the company's financial information." The only way to get the necessary information may be to depose Bob. But Bob is also unlikely to provide helpful documents or evidence.

Larger companies can present the same problem but add layers of bureaucracy. Because several corporate departments may have a hand in the bonus decisions, HR departments may claim to not have knowledge of or access to the appropriate or complete set of documents. So issuing a subpoena for the employee's entire employment file may not result in obtaining a complete set of documents.[13] The company's accounting department could have some of the necessary documents, or the

13. As you draft your subpoena, consider your state's authentication requirements. Check out your state's equivalents to the Federal Rules of Civil Procedure 901 and 902.

employee's department head could. If the opposing spouse is the department head, the person with the necessary documents could be the chief financial officer or the chief executive officer. In these situations, grinding out discovery may be required, which means writing letters, making phone calls, and when all else fails, filing a motion to compel. The head of HR may need to be deposed. You may need to determine which corporate bureaucrat *doesn't* want to be deposed and issue a subpoena for *that* person for the necessary documents to be produced. Obviously, waiting until the last moment to try to find this person is a bad thing. Grinding out discovery takes time. Start as soon as possible. Larger corporations can be incredibly talented at delaying and deflecting the discovery efforts of divorcing spouses' lawyers, especially if they are practiced at it.

Because most forensic accountants have at least a working knowledge of tax law, most have worked with many different types of benefits packages for tax clients. With such benefits and plans, the terms used are not always consistent or even defined. But CPAs can usually figure it out better than "history major" attorneys. Give the CPA a chance. If the CPA is not completely comfortable with his understanding of the benefits package, strongly consider deposing someone with the company to get answers to all the important questions. If you don't know what questions to ask, the forensic accountant will.

Don't forget the perks. "Perks" is short for "perquisites." Perks can be any type of extra benefit, from discounts on company-made shirts or tickets to pro basketball games to the more exotic perks, such as country club memberships and access to luxury vacation time shares. Perks don't always show up on W-2s, even when they should. Airline frequent flyer miles earned on company credit cards can add up, too. Experienced family lawyers suggest never underestimating their value. Sometimes, placing a value on them is not as important as making sure they are listed in the assets to be divided. For example, if Bill used 25,000 miles to visit a cousin in Boston a month ago and the plane ticket would have cost $450, it seems that 250,000 miles ought to be worth around $4,500. Value can also be negotiated in a good, old-fashioned way: "Well, Bill, if the airline miles aren't worth anything, why can't I have them?"

Stock Options

If you represent the nonemployee spouse and do not know how to handle stock options, the employee spouse may very well figure that out.

From the very beginning, you need to request the right documents. An employee spouse with stock options almost always knows a great deal about them and may try to test you by failing to provide the necessary information to handle them, especially if the right documents aren't requested. In almost all cases, it's a big mistake to wait until settlement negotiations begin to figure out what needs to be done.

The Family Lawyer's Guide to Stock Options[14] is a great place to start learning. It's not a large book and contains calculations and explanations. Just flip through the book for five minutes, and you will quickly see the value in having an experienced forensic accountant to help you with stock options.

Each company creates its own stock options. Rarely will two different companies' stock option plans look alike. Stock options allow employees to share in the growth of a company's value. They can be very valuable and are almost always not assignable to the nonemployee spouse. Because options are rarely assignable, the nonemployee spouse must be vigilant to obtain offset value from the marital estate. At a minimum, the nonemployee spouse should calculate the value of the options and determine whether the income from the options should be included in income for spousal and child support. Normally, short-term options can be applied to the year in which they are earned. If the options are earned over a multiyear period, the income may need to be averaged over the relevant time period.

Documents You Need for Stock Options

Determining what documents you need may be a challenge because every company's stock option plan is different. Even in large companies, stock option grants may be described in a letter only a few paragraphs long. In others, there may be a very detailed and lengthy written plan. Assuming you issue written discovery, you should ask the employee spouse for a copy of the stock option plan and a summary of stock options that have been granted. You should then take the produced documents to the forensic accountant and ask if the information provided is enough. Regardless of the answer from the accountant, you may choose to issue a separate subpoena to the employer to confirm you obtained complete and accurate documentation. Experience teaches that many employee spouses claim

14. *Supra* note 4.

not to possess key documentation, even when the documentation may be readily available upon request. Depending on the level of conflict and the honesty of the employee spouse, issuing a subpoena to the employer early in the divorce process can actually save time and money.

In crafting the subpoena document request, consider asking for the following:

1. Stock option grants, agreements, and amendments for both employment service already rendered and future employment, including but not limited to stock option plans, summary plan descriptions, employment contracts, amended employment contracts, and letters or memoranda offering employment;
2. Schedules of vested and unvested granted stock options with all conditions listing number of options, exercise dates, exercise price, expiration dates, and vesting dates;
3. All company information, whether provided to employees or not, describing the purpose of the grant or award and calculations of the value of the options;
4. All other documents describing the employee's compensation package, including short-term and long-term incentives;
5. All award and grant letters and correspondence to employees regarding stock option grants available to the employee spouse;
6. Employment manuals, agreements, handbooks, memoranda, and company plans describing or detailing stock options and employees' rights to benefits, including reload and replacement provisions;
7. The employee's employment and personnel records showing the name(s) of the employer(s),[15] date of hire, positions held, salary history, titles, and job descriptions; and
8. All benefits statements, whether issued annually, semiannually, quarterly, or monthly.

If the employer is a publicly traded company, consider also requesting (or researching) and reviewing all public documents, such as the

15. Don't forget to consider that the current employer may honor and pay benefits to employees of businesses acquired by the current employer or with which the current employer merged.

company's annual reports, Securities and Exchange Commission Form 10-K, quarterly Form 10-Q, and special events reports on Form 8-K. These documents may contain notes with helpful information about executive stock options. Finally, understand that different stock option plans are often offered to various tiers of management. The higher the employee is within the company, the greater the likelihood that the stock option is more lucrative.

Stock Option Valuation

The value of stock options can be simply calculated using the intrinsic value method, or not so simply using the much more complicated binomial models or the Black-Scholes option pricing model. The intrinsic value method calculates the difference between the current share price and the exercise price. If the existing stock price is below the exercise price, the employee spouse will argue there is no value. This situation is commonly described as the option being "underwater" or "out-of-the-money." Even if the options are underwater, they may have value because the stock price *might* rise above the exercise price over time prior to the expiration date.

The intrinsic value calculation is straightforward but does not take into consideration important variables, unlike the binomial and Black-Scholes models. The binomial model considers different pricing likelihoods as a function of time. The Black-Scholes option pricing model uses a very complicated formula considering several variables, including risk-free rate and stock price volatility, and is based on several market-related assumptions, which arguably may not apply in a divorce.

Exactly which method is required or appropriate may be dictated by your state's case law. If your state's case law does not mandate a particular method, it may authorize one or more methods. Of the authorized methods, you should consider what is in the best interest of your client. The forensic accountant should be able to adequately advise your client on the relative strengths and weaknesses of the varying calculation methods and resulting comparative values. Keep in mind that the valuation of stock options can be very important because stock options are almost always nontransferrable. This means they are part of an offset calculation, rarely a simple "you take half and I'll take half" type of division.

Note that many experienced forensic accountants may not be comfortable working with the Black-Scholes or binomial models. Both involve complicated calculations, and each input variable requires research and judgment. If your client's forensic accountant is uncomfortable performing the calculation, you may need to consider finding an additional expert just for this aspect of the case. Only in the rarest of circumstances should your client rely upon a calculation performed by an opposing expert witness without having had an experienced financial expert review it.

Reload Provisions

When reviewing stock options, you must look for "reload" provisions. Reload provisions can allow for the exercise of stock options using stock currently owned and result in the employee obtaining new options. Reload options may be separately valued. What makes reload provisions particularly worrisome is that the employee spouse could exercise existing stock options, keep the benefit in the form of the new options, and fail to disclose the transaction. In the terms of the settlement agreement, consider requiring an employee spouse to disclose the existence and exercise of reload provisions and deal with that contingency. Also, when deposing the employee spouse, always ask if any reload provisions have ever been granted.

Time Rule Formulas

Know your state's law regarding stock options in general and calculations for valuation. Also, know your state's law as it relates to options issued prior to marriage and determine if the employer requires continued employment for a period of time after the divorce. Often, you may be required to determine which portion of the value to be received is marital property. These classification determinations are described as time rule formulas.[16] Time rule formulas require consideration of

16. *See* Donald C. Schiller, *Stock Options: Be Aware/Beware*. In Gregg Herman (Ed.), 101+ Practical Solutions for the Family Lawyer 395–97 (ABA 2003). *See also* Lester Barenbaum, Walter Schubert & Robert Feder, The Family Lawyer's Guide to Stock Options, Chapter 1, Section D (ABA 2007), discussing time rules.

the length of the marriage and compare that to the length of employment. If there is an important factual difference between leading cases in your jurisdiction and the client's situation, it may make sense to consider advocating that a more advantageous formula should apply. If your state does not specify which time rule formula applies, you should advocate for the time rule formula that is in the best financial interest of the client.

Tax Issues

For tax purposes, know that not all stock options are treated equally. If the company set up and handled the plan correctly, incentive stock options (ISOs) can result in significant financial benefits to employees because ISOs are designed to result in no taxable income for the employee spouse. This is completely different for non-qualified stock options, which do create taxable income for employees at the time of their grant or exercise. The tax rules for each can be complicated. Most experienced family lawyers prefer to request that the forensic accountant or client's tax advisor provide specific advice regarding the tax consequences of a possible or proposed negotiated settlement of stock options.

Deferred Distribution Approach

Almost all stock options are nontransferrable. As such, the nonemployee spouse should negotiate to receive cash or other assets in exchange for the stock options. This is often called the "immediate offset" approach to division. In some cases, if the options are underwater and the employee spouse refuses to exchange other assets for the value of the employee spouse's stock option, the default option is for the employee spouse to agree to pay cash to the nonemployee spouse "if, as, and when" the options are exercisable after the divorce. This is called the "deferred distribution" or "deferred jurisdiction" method because the court must retain jurisdiction over this aspect of the property division in the event the options become exercisable.

Appendix 4-A of *The Family Lawyer's Guide to Stock Options* provides sample language for the deferred distribution of stock options and discusses use of a constructive trust. This sample language is very well considered but complicated. If necessary, the forensic accountant should be enlisted to help answer the client's questions and tailor the sample language to the particular nuances of the stock option plan at issue. You must advise the client of the pros and cons of negotiating a deferred distribution approach. Divorce clients often shudder at having to return to court if there is a dispute after the divorce is final.

Negotiating

Negotiating value for the client in excess of the employee's stock option's intrinsic value is part science and part art. Publicly traded stock has an unknowable potential increase in trading price. Any efforts you expend must be well considered. Keep in mind that some people have gotten filthy rich on stock options. Whether or not the employee spouse will see any financial benefit after the divorce is not calculable. No family lawyer wants to be responsible for predicting the future. One thing is for certain though: in negotiations, the employee spouse will poor-mouth the stock's future.[17]

After obtaining the necessary documents, you will likely need a written report from the forensic accountant. If the calculation method used is approved by state law, the better practice is to include that in the report. The issuance of the report sends an important message to the employee spouse that the nonemployee spouse is serious about negotiating value for the stock options. In the nonemployee spouse's initial proposed settlement, the choice must be made to propose an offset for the stock options or propose deferred distribution. Usually, an offset of cash (i.e., equity in the marital residence) is proposed to keep it simple. In any event, counsel for the nonemployee spouse can expect resistance. This is the point in time when the art of negotiating must be asserted.

If the exercise of the stock options is contingent upon continued employment and you represent the nonemployee spouse, you must develop a strategy for dealing with that fact. What if the employee spouse's employment is terminated prior to the options achieving value? What if the termination is voluntary? What if the employee spouse is terminated for cause? Will the employee spouse agree to a reasonable

17. If you have a friend who is a stockbroker, consider asking the broker for positive research on the stock that predicts a bright future.

or meaningful financial penalty for failure to continue employment? Is there another asset that can be exchanged instead?

Advice Regarding Deferred Distribution Division

When drafting stock option deferred jurisdiction provisions, be patient. These provisions are challenging and difficult. Don't procrastinate. Learn what is needed to be learned. If you need help, ask an experienced lawyer to help you. Also, the client's tax advisor or the forensic accountant can help with many aspects of the proposed provision, including tax considerations.

Be very clear in declaring the overall intent of the parties. State exactly what is marital property and what is nonmarital. After the divorce, if there is an ambiguity in the interpretation of the provision and the court is tasked with interpreting a technical aspect of the proposed division, the court should seek to rule consistent with the parties' intent. Some opposing counsel may seek to strike language describing intent. Be firm. It may save the client.

The Best Way to Handle This Problem May Be the Stock Option Trust

Jeffrey D. Urbach, MBA, CVA, CFE, CPA/ABV/CFF,[18] an experienced forensic matrimonial accountant in New Jersey, observed that valuations of stock options are infrequently seen during a divorce. While it is theoretically possible to value stock options, doing so is difficult because of the various inputs needed to run a model. Urbach adds that the preferred way of handling stock options is sometimes called a "Callahan trust," in reference to the 1976 case *Callahan v. Callahan*.[19] Constructive trusts are created under a marital settlement agreement, effecting a deferred distribution. The holder of the stock options must

18. Jeffrey D. Urbach has over 40 years' experience in financial forensics, divorce taxation, business valuation, and general accounting. Urbach has qualified in New Jersey courts as an expert witness and is a nationally recognized speaker, instructor, and author. His company, Urbach & Avraham, CPAs LLP, practices out of Edison, New Jersey. For more information about his practice, see www.ua-cpas.com, or read Urbach's bio on LinkedIn at https://www.linkedin.com/in/jeffurbachcpanj.
19. 142 N.J. Super. 325 (1976), 361 A.2d 561.

maintain full transparency, usually by sharing quarterly statements from his or her company's HR department. As long as the option's not underwater, it can be tied to certain trigger dates, such as college tuition payments for children of the marriage, or it can be left to the joint discretion of the parties. With this method, both spouses share the market risk equally. Callahan trusts are also often used for stock appreciation rights, restricted stock, and similar financial instruments.[20]

Urbach also says that running a valuation model is the easy part when it comes to dividing stock options, mostly due to the software that is available for the task. It is testifying about the results that can be the difficult part. Testifying experts need to be sure they can explain the complicated intricacies involved in valuation models, including the detailed statistics. Urbach confides that he has only once encountered a case where the parties involved insisted on a court-ready valuation. Urbach declined but located a finance PhD and professor who specialized in option modeling. Eventually, however, a Callahan trust was used, which saved both parties a good deal of money in PhD expert witness fees.

Buffet of Employment Benefits and Retirement

When thinking of employee retirement benefits; individual retirement savings; good, old-fashioned, nontax-deferred incentives; and perks, anyone can get lost. Lost is bad for lawyers. Just staring at a benefits statement is not enough—it won't tell you what you need to know. Whether you have practiced family law for 15 minutes or 15 years, keeping this all straight in your head is challenging.

If you personally don't have a financial plan, get one. If you don't know what financial planning is, learn. If you want financial planning help, people will help you just because you're a lawyer. As with anyone who first talks with a financial advisor, you will likely feel uninformed and embarrassed you don't know the financial terms you think you should. You may also feel guilty about money you have spent but should have saved. If you know yourself well enough to feel sure that

20. For an excellent and very detailed discussion of trusts used to settle stock option divorce problems, see Charles F. Vuotto, Jr., Esq., and Jeffrey D. Urbach, MBA, CPA/ABV, CFE, CVA, *Stock Option Distribution via Constructive Trusts in Divorce Settlements*, The Value Examiner (January/February 2006). The Value Examiner is a National Association of Certified Valuation Analysts publication.

you aren't going to go to a financial advisor, for whatever reason, consider buying and reading Dave Ramsey's book *Financial Peace Revisited*[21] and listening to his nationally syndicated radio show. If you have no retirement investment opportunities at your firm, take $1,000 and open a Roth IRA at a discount brokerage firm. From there, consider taking Dave Ramsey's 13-week course, Financial Peace University. Learn basic investors' language your clients know (or should know), such as "budgeting," "saving," "Roth IRAs," and "compounded interest." Everything you learn will help you in your career as a family lawyer, as well as help you as a spouse or parent.

When you are negotiating a divorce settlement, there's a very simple concept you should always keep in mind: the value of money, investments, and retirement assets cannot be compared based on dollar amount alone. For example, $100 in cash does not have the same value as $100 in Disney stock, $100 in Disney stock does not have the same value as $100 in a 401(k), and $100 in a 401(k) does not have the same value as $100 in a Roth IRA. Sometimes, numbers on a page are not numbers on a page. Understanding the relative value of each requires consideration of the following:

1. Investment risk,
2. Built-in capital gains,
3. Tax deferral on original investment, and
4. Tax deferral on income from an original investment.

For example, cash invested in a money market fund will have little risk and will not have a built-in capital gain, but it generates taxable interest in the period in which it is paid. A purchase of Disney stock as a good, old-fashioned investment (and outside a retirement plan) will likely appreciate, and that appreciation will be taxed when sold as a capital gain. The part of the sales price that was the original investment, or its basis, will not be taxed. But as the Disney company issues dividends, that income will be taxable in the year in which it is distributed.

If the Disney stock was purchased within a traditional IRA (discussed in more detail below), the original contribution to the IRA was deducted from that year's current income, but all of the appreciation and dividend income will be fully taxed at distribution, albeit at retirement.

21. Dave Ramsey, Financial Peace Revisited (Viking Penguin 2003).

When planning a proposed property division, another important consideration is that one asset may be much more valuable to a particular client than another, based on age and savings discipline. From a savings and retirement planning perspective, a disciplined and investment-savvy client will very likely have a financial plan and will consider the mix of assets carefully, depending on how close the person may be to reaching her financial goals. Generally, a disciplined client is likely to seek financial advice. An uninformed divorce client prefers to receive cash in the divorce and then spend it. Family lawyers should not be in the financial advice business. Family law is hard enough.

For tax-deferred retirement accounts, the amounts withdrawn at retirement are almost always taxable income. Assets received pursuant to a divorce decree are not taxed. From a financial planning perspective, having tax-deferred retirement savings may be more valuable than cash. Income from cash, presumably subsequently invested in stocks, bonds, or mutual funds, is taxable in the year earned. But receiving and spending the cash immediately does not result in a taxable transaction. Immediate cash-flow needs must be balanced against long-term savings and retirement-planning needs.

Qualified versus Nonqualified Plans

Qualified plans are established pursuant to tax rules, ERISA, and the Department of Labor. Employers and employees prefer to have contributions made pursuant to qualified plans because both receive favorable federal income tax treatment at the date of distribution, and income to the employee/participant is shielded from taxation over time. Then why do employers even have nonqualified plans? In almost all cases, nonqualified plans are incentives for upper management where tax treatment for the employer and employee is not a major consideration. For almost all qualified plans, the contributions should be noted on the employee's W-2.[22] For more detailed information on W-2s, please see Chapter 8. Just keep in mind that not all smaller businesses prepare

22. To determine which box records what source and type of income when reading a W-2, see IRS General Instructions for Forms W-2 and W-3. This, or a very similar publication, is updated annually and tries to include as easy instructions as possible. Also, you can cross-reference the "codes," which should be recorded on the reverse side of the W-2. So, when reviewing a W-2 for income determination purposes, always ask to receive a copy of both sides of the W-2.

W-2s accurately and completely. If an in-house bookkeeper prepared them, the likelihood of an error is much greater than if an outside CPA firm prepared them.

Defined Benefit Plans

Defined benefit plans are sponsored by employers and pay employees particular dollar amounts upon retirement. Employers, not employees, are in control of the investment portfolio. Defined benefit plans include pensions and annuities.

1. Pension, Also Called Traditional Pension

A pension is generally a series of definitely determinable payments made to employees upon retirement. Pension payments are made regularly and are based on such factors as years of service and prior compensation. They are discussed in more detail in the following section.

2. Annuity

An annuity[23] is a contractual right to receive a series of payments at regular intervals over a period of more than one full year. The amounts to be received are either fixed or variable. The contract can be bought by the employee alone or with the help of the employer. Many financial advisors don't favor annuities as an investment option because overall returns on investment are considered lower than for other opportunities, even those with greater risk. If a marital estate includes annuities, you may want to inquire how and why those annuities came into existence.

Defined Contribution Plans

All "plans" are created by an employer. Defined contribution plans are those where you can look at a statement and see the balance. Most

23. Annuities can be very dangerous for the family lawyer. If you are not experienced working with them, seriously consider consulting with a very experienced financial advisor. You must worry about surrender penalties and other division problems. Some annuities are just flat out mechanisms for stealing money from unsuspecting investors because sales commissions can be ridiculously high and investment returns can be low. The family lawyer must always worry whether an annuity can be divided. If the annuity cannot be divided, you need to know that as soon as possible because a great deal of wealth could be locked up in it.

defined contribution plans do not require QDROs, but some do. Always check the summary plan description. Generally, transferring balances is not tricky, but as a family lawyer, you must deal with gains and losses. If you are transferring a particular balance to the nonemployee spouse, the balance as of the date of the agreement will differ from the date of distribution, and the agreement should reflect that aspect of the deal. The following is a discussion of the most common defined contribution plans.

1. 401(k)

A 401(k) plan is a qualified profit-sharing or stock bonus plan under which an employee can elect to have the employer contribute a portion of the employee's cash wages to the plan on a pre-tax basis. It can also consist of a pre-ERISA money-purchase pension or a rural cooperative plan. Employers may choose to match a certain amount of the employee's contributions. These deferred wages, called "elective deferrals," are not subject to federal income tax withholding at the time of deferral, and they are not reflected as taxable income on the employee's Form 1040, U.S. Individual Income Tax Return. The employer reports these contributions on the employee's W-2. The W-2 is copied to both the employee and the IRS. Although these amounts are not treated as current income for federal income tax purposes, they are included as wages subject to Social Security (FICA), Medicare, and federal unemployment taxes (FUTA). As income is generated within the plan, the taxation of earnings is deferred until distribution at retirement. While some plans allow for borrowing against money in the plan, failure to abide by applicable rules and restrictions could cause interest and penalties to be assessed against the borrower.

2. 403(b) Tax-Sheltered Annuity Plans

A 403(b) tax-sheltered annuity (TSA) plan is a retirement plan offered by public schools and certain tax-exempt organizations.[24] Generally, these annuities are funded by elective deferrals made under salary reduction agreements and nonelective employer contributions. Just as with a 401(k) plan, a 403(b) plan lets employees defer some of their salary. Employees' deferred income goes to a 403(b) plan sponsored

24. For more information, see IRS publication 571, *Tax-Sheltered Annuity Plans (403(b) Plans),* which is available at www.IRS.gov.

by the employer. The investments may be held in an annuity contract through an insurance company, a mutual fund custodial account, or another retirement account for church employees. The deferred earnings generally are not taxed by the federal government or by most state governments until they are distributed.

3. Section 457 Deferred Compensation Plans

Employees who work for a state or local government or for a tax-exempt organization may participate in section 457 deferred compensation plans. Employees are not taxed currently on pay that is deferred or on earnings from the plan's investments. Employees are generally taxed on amounts deferred only when those amounts are distributed from the plan or otherwise made available to employees.

4. Profit-Sharing Plans

As with 401(k) plans, profit-sharing plans can be simple or complex. Certain less complicated and pre-approved profit-sharing plans are much less costly to administer than pension plans. Only employers contribute to profit-sharing plans, and the amounts are predetermined by a set formula. This money then goes into a separate account for each employee. There are contribution limits set by federal income-tax law. Check the employee spouse's W-2s, box 13, to determine if a profit-sharing plan is recorded.

5. Money Purchase Pensions Plans

With money purchase pension plans (MPPPs), both employers and employees can make contributions, but employers are required to make a contribution to the plan on behalf of the participants each year. The plan states in advance the contribution percentage that is required. A participant's benefit is based on the amount of contributions to her account and the gains or losses associated with the account at the time of retirement. Again, annual contribution limits apply, and in-service withdrawals are not allowed.

6. Employee Stock Ownership Plans

Employee stock ownership plans (ESOPs) are formal arrangements made by corporations for employee participation and ownership. Employees are usually given stock ownership in the corporation after a certain length of employment and can then buy shares at any time under favorable terms. A corporation owned entirely by its employees will not, therefore, have its shares publicly traded. Employee-owned corporations may adopt profit-sharing options in which all the profits of the corporation are shared with the employees. In those cases, the companies' boards may be elected by the employees.

7. SIMPLE IRA and SIMPLE 401(k)

There are two types of SIMPLE (Savings Incentive Match Plan for Employees) plans, the SIMPLE IRA plan and the SIMPLE 401(k) plan.[25] SIMPLE plans were created for small businesses as a cost-efficient way to offer retirement benefits to employees. Employers and employees may both contribute. Qualified plans are more complex and, therefore, more costly to administer than simplified employee pension (SEP) and SIMPLE plans. The employer is required to make employer contributions that are fully vested. As of 2009, SIMPLE plans are available to employers with 100 or fewer employees who received at least $5,000 in compensation from the employer for the preceding calendar year. Employees who are eligible to participate in a SIMPLE plan may not receive any contributions or benefit accruals under any other plans of the employer. For withdrawals, SIMPLE IRAs and SIMPLE 401(k)s are subject to regular IRA and 401(k) tax rules. Withdrawals are taxed in the year received.

8. SEP Plans and SEP IRAs

A SEP plan is a qualified plan.[26] Under a SEP, employers make contributions to traditional IRAs set up for employees (which can include self-employed individuals), subject to certain limits. The SEP IRA is owned and controlled by the employee. To establish a SEP, a business can be any size, and self-employed persons can also set up a SEP. The business must adopt a SEP plan document and generally cannot have any other retirement plan.

---

25. To learn more about SEP, SIMPLE, and qualified plans, see IRS Publication 560, *Retirement Plans for Small Businesses*, which is available at www.IRS.gov. For challenging cases, you may want to review associated IRS forms to confirm important financial information.

26. A SARSEP (salary reduction simplified employee pension) is the same thing as a SEP but would have been set up before 1997 and would have different restrictions.

9. Stock Bonus Plans

Stock bonus plans are just like profit-sharing plans, except employer contributions are made in stock.

10. Thrift Savings Plans

Civilians employed by the government and military service members are eligible to participate in thrift savings plans (TSPs). These are voluntary contributions. TSP benefits are offered in addition to Federal Employees' Retirement System or Civil Service Retirement System annuities.

Investments Unrelated to Employment

A number of common investment opportunities exist that are unrelated to employment. Evidence of the existence of these investments is not found on W-2s, but such evidence may be found within brokerage account statements and tax returns.

1. IRAs

An individual retirement arrangement (IRA)[27] is a trust or custodial account created for the exclusive benefit of individuals. The account is created by a written document, and the trustee or custodian must be a bank, a federally insured credit union, a savings and loan association, or an entity approved by the IRS to act as trustee or custodian. The trustee or custodian generally cannot accept contributions of more than the deductible amount for the year. However, rollover contributions and employer contributions to a SEP can be higher than this amount. Contributions, except for rollover contributions, must be in cash. The individual must have a nonforfeitable right to the amount at all times, and the amount cannot be used to buy a life insurance policy. Assets in the IRA cannot be combined with other property, except in a common trust fund or common investment fund. The owner must start receiving distributions by a certain age. As with all investments receiving

27. For more information, see IRS Publication 590A, *Contributions to Individual Retirement Arrangements (IRAs),* which is available at www.IRS.gov. While it is most commonly described as an individual retirement account, know that the IRS calls it an individual retirement arrangement.

favorable tax treatment, know that restrictions and requirements can change over time.

2. Traditional IRA

A traditional IRA is any IRA that is not a Roth or SIMPLE IRA. Contributions made to a traditional IRA can be fully or partially deductible, depending on the circumstances. Amounts in the traditional IRA (including earnings and gains) are not taxed until distributed upon retirement.

3. Roth IRA

A Roth IRA differs from a traditional IRA in that contributions to it are *not* tax deductible, but there are fewer restrictions and requirements on withdrawal. The Roth IRA's most important advantage is that appreciation and income earned within the account accumulate tax free, and if all requirements are satisfied, Roth IRA distributions during retirement are tax free.[28]

Other Investments Not Related to Retirement or Employment

1. CDs, Stocks, Bonds, Mutual Funds, Stock Options, Futures, Derivatives, and Exchange-traded Funds

Luckily, family lawyers don't have to be experts on investing to practice their craft. You should learn the language of investing, though. Explaining basic investment terms is beyond the scope of this book. What you must seek to understand is the degree of risk associated with each type of investment and its tax treatment—especially with respect to built-in capital gains. When in doubt, ask the forensic accountant or make friends with a financial advisor. An important consideration is whether the risk associated with a particular mix of investments makes sense for that particular marital estate. If the risk associated with the mix of assets makes no sense for the investor(s), you really need to

28. Tax-free distributions are unique. If the taxpayer has significant income from a job or other investments, tax-free distributions upon reaching retirement age can be very beneficial.

understand how that happened.[29] For example, most investors should not be trading options contracts. If one or both of the parties' financial advisors are responsible for that type of risk assumption, that could be a red flag suggesting a need for additional investigation.

2. 529 College Plans (Children)

Formerly known as qualified tuition programs, or QTPs, 529 plans are programs established and maintained by states that allow a parent to either prepay or contribute to an account for paying a student's qualified education expenses at a postsecondary institution (college/university). Eligible educational institutions may establish and maintain programs that allow parents to prepay a student's qualified education expenses. If tuition is prepaid, the student (designated beneficiary) will be entitled to a waiver or a payment of qualified education expenses. Payments or contributions to a 529 plan are not deductible, but no tax is due on a distribution from a 529 unless the amount distributed is greater than the beneficiary's adjusted qualified education expenses.

3. UGMA and UTMA (Children)

The Uniform Gift to Minors Act (UGMA), supplemented by the Uniform Transfers to Minors Act (UTMA), is codified on the state level and comprises fairly simple laws by which contributions to funds benefiting minors are regulated and taxed. Once an account is designated to a minor beneficiary under UGMA/UTMA, it is irrevocable, so neither parent can take back the money. Earnings are taxed to the beneficiary. Typically, the funds are in the name of the minor, with at least one parent serving as a custodian. When the minor reaches 18 years of age, she usually gains full control of the funds, which can then be used, usually for any purpose. The better practice in divorce settlements is to address anticipated disputes over future decisions, such as use of UGMA/UTMA funds and investing options, even though the assets aren't technically part of the parents' marital estate.

---

29. Over the last 20 years, many investors began handling their own accounts, and some even "day trade," which means the investor seeks smaller, shorter-term returns. You should look for investment failures under the control of one spouse and determine whether they constitute dissipation of the marital estate. There aren't that many successful day traders, but some do exist.

Debts

On the marital balance sheet, show all debts and credit accounts. As discussed previously, even if the asset is listed net of the debt, all debts should be listed in the settlement agreement and assigned to one party or the other. Plus, know your state's factors for debt division. Most are fairly straightforward. The party receiving a corresponding securitized asset, such as a car, will usually be responsible for that debt.

Create a protocol for clients to run their own credit report or obtain permission to run it for them. Review the credit report. If the client can close open joint accounts, consider instructing her to do so. Make sure all open accounts are addressed in the property settlement agreement, even if the account has no balance. Many credit accounts lie dormant. For example, it is not unusual for a Macy's account to have no balance until the beginning of the school year, when new school clothes are purchased. So if the divorce takes place in August or September, make sure the open Macy's account is addressed, or the client may end up jointly responsible for a bill that is charged to the joint account as the divorce is being settled.

Importance of Financial Statements

Finding personal financial statements is often the most important discovery for family lawyers. Personal financial statements list individuals' claimed income and net worth. Very few individuals compile personal financial statements for fun.[30] They are almost always compiled to be shown to lenders. Business owners need lines of credit from banks and other lending institutions. Homeowners need them for mortgages and second mortgages. Even some companies making car loans may require the completion of a personal financial statement.

On tax returns, taxpayers seek to legally record as little income as possible and deduct as much as possible. Plus, not all income must be reported as taxable income. One example is 401(k) contributions. Employee and employer contributions are not required to be shown as taxable income on the returns because the money will be taxed upon withdrawal at retirement. But with personal financial statements and disclosure of income and net worth for loan applications, most debtors are motivated to list every last dime of income and show as high a net worth as possible. In most cases, loan recipients will list optimistic fair

30. But many may as part of personal financial management, planning, and budgeting. Of those, most will use a program such as Quicken or QuickBooks.

market values on certain real estate and business interests. Practical reasons for overstating income and net worth may also include qualifying for more debt or lower interest rates.

When investigating real estate ownership and associated debt, find creditors and issue subpoenas to them demanding copies of personal financial statements and/or loan applications submitted by the spouse. In some cases, when representing spouses of business owners, you may even want to issue subpoenas to banks you suspect may have loaned the owner money. Remember from your real property class in law school that a person can own unrecorded interests in real estate by taking possession of deeds even if they are not recorded. But for most transactions, closing attorneys record the deeds, especially if money was loaned to purchase them. If the deeds were not recorded, the loan would not be properly securitized.

Know that the law of many states makes providing a false financial statement to a financial institution a crime. Also, on certain loan forms, the information may be provided under oath. Either way, a loan applicant's overstatement of income or net worth can be potentially devastating in the courtroom.

Business Valuations

If you have ever worked a divorce case with a business valuation expert, you already understand business valuation cases are some of the more complicated matters a family lawyer can handle. Business valuators have their own language and have very set rules. If you plan on a career in family law, you will eventually need the services of such an expert. Many forensic accountants are also business valuation experts. In most divorces, there is no reason why one expert can't serve as both.

Buy and read *The Lawyer's Business Valuation Handbook* by Shannon Pratt. It is an ABA publication and a great place to start learning. In the meantime, look up forensic accountants and business valuation experts in your area. Places to start are the websites of the American Institute of Certified Public Accountants (AICPA), NACVA, the Institute of Business Appraisers, and the American Society of Appraisers. They list professionals who are members, and many forensic accountants and business valuation experts are members of both the AICPA and NACVA and may be members of one of the other two as well.

Ask around. Look up some appellate opinions. Take a business valuation expert to lunch. He will be glad to meet with you. Even if you're young and inexperienced, you're a family lawyer. Family lawyers refer expert's work. In all likelihood, the expert may even pick up the tab. Before lunch, read the expert's website. Print and read a copy of his curriculum vitae. Take the opportunity to ask questions like the following: "How did you get started in such a fascinating career?" "What do you like best about expert testimony?" "If you were me, what questions would you ask you?" "What types of cases do you want referred to you, and what cases do you not want referred to you?" "How much do you charge?" At the end of the lunch, invite the expert to put you on his mailing list. Someday, you may need to make the call.

Reading a Tax Return and Discovering Assets

Hiring a forensic accountant to review a party's individual and business tax returns can have several advantages. First, a CPA can often perform the review in less time. Often, lawyers will put a client's tax return review at the bottom of the "to do" pile. Second, the CPA will likely have a sense of whether everything smells right. If it doesn't, the CPA will know where to look next. Finally, attorneys cannot testify. A CPA may be required for that purpose. Even if the client can testify regarding her own tax return, rarely can a client handle cross-examination of the ins and outs of tax returns.

Even though forensic accountants are the best professionals for reviewing tax returns to find assets, every member of the divorce team can learn to read tax returns and supporting documents. Finding hidden assets on tax returns is not rocket science. Furthermore, identifying an asset listed on a tax return but otherwise omitted from financial disclosures can be very powerful. Once an asset is found, it should be cross-referenced or recorded on the marital balance sheet. The tax return checklist provided below is designed to illustrate most common opportunities for uncovering the nondisclosure of assets and to assist you and your paralegals in communicating with experts.[31]

As a family law attorney, you should understand why reviewing tax returns is so important. In most cases where tax returns are reviewed in detail, you are investigating a spouse suspected of hiding assets. Therefore, you should learn the most obvious ways to hide assets, even

31. Two other helpful resources are JACK ZUCKERMAN & WILLIAM F. WOLF, THE BUSINESS TAX RETURN HANDBOOK (ABA 2nd ed. 2004), and JACK ZUCKERMAN, THE 1040 HANDBOOK: A GUIDE TO INCOME AND DISCOVERY (ABA 6th ed. 2015).

though there are many more ways to go about it than any one book can address. For example, one of the most common schemes is converting tangible assets to cash. In order to do this, most situations require the schemer to sell an asset. The sale of an asset, however, can result in a taxable transaction. Because federal tax law is very thorough, the transaction may be reported to the IRS by the purchaser of the asset. If that is the case, the schemer must choose either to report the transaction on his return or to commit federal tax fraud. Fortunately for the divorce team, many spouses report tax liability honestly. The spouse who is honest with the IRS (but lies or omits key information in discovery) is betting that the spouse's legal team is not smart enough or thorough enough to discover the plot.

All line numbers cited herein apply to the 2017 IRS 1040 form.[32] The 1040 is the most common personal income tax return form. Line numbers may be different from year to year. For more information about particular line items, search the IRS website (www.IRS.gov) for instructions for taxpayers related to specific forms. Specific helpful resources include the following:

- Instructions—for almost all forms, including the important 1040 and W-2; and
- Publications—for many typical situations, see Publication 504, "Divorced or Separated Individuals," and Publication 551, "Basis of Assets."

The following is a tax return checklist for your legal team:

A. Determine whether you possess all the documentation you have requested and need. The term "tax return" is vaguely defined. Depending on the user, specific documents called "tax returns" can include the following:
   1. Federal tax returns, also called by their form numbers—the 1040,[33] 1120,[34] and 1165.[35]

32. As of the date of writing, the 2018 federal income tax forms have not been released subsequent to enactment of the Tax Cuts and Jobs Act. Line numbers for particular tax return items can and do change. So, again, review current IRS instructions and publications available at www.IRS.gov.
33. For individuals.
34. For corporations.
35. For partnerships and LLCs.

2. State tax returns—Although not all states have a tax on earned income, there can be state returns that must be filed to record dividend and interest income.
3. All amended returns—If a taxpayer amended a return, try to obtain both the original and amended versions because the forensic accountant may find something interesting.
4. State excise tax returns, which have a tax on assets, for owners of businesses, such as LLCs and corporations.
5. Copies of tax checks paying estimated payments, annual tax liability, and tax refund checks from the IRS to the taxpayer.
6. Sales tax and personal property tax returns for businesses.
7. Schedules—The 1040 may also include some of the following most commonly used schedules (which should be attached to the return and cross-referenced):
   a. Schedule A—itemized deductions (1040, line 40);
   b. Schedule B—interest and dividends (1040, lines 8 and 9);
   c. Schedule C—business income (1040, line 12);
   d. Schedule D—capital gains and losses (1040, line 13);
   e. Schedule E—rental real estate, royalties, partnerships, S corporations, estates, trusts, real estate mortgage investment conduits, etc. (1040, line 17); and
   f. Schedule F—farm income (1040, line 18).

   Make sure all schedules are attached. Look at the 1040 and cross-reference descriptions and listed amounts. In discovery, it is common for spouses to omit schedules and wait for the opposing counsel to demand to see them.
8. Attachments—Also make sure the federal tax return includes the following attachments:
   a. W-2s—issued by employers to employees (Practice tip: When copying W-2s, always copy both sides of the form!);
   b. 1099s—issued by businesses to independent contractors (later cross-reference that all projects and work-in-progress items are disclosed);
   c. K-1s—issued by partnerships to partners and LLCs to members listing income attributable to individual partners from the partnership;

d. W-2Gs—income from gambling; and
e. Miscellaneous supporting subschedules, reports, and worksheets—Not every piece of paper filed with a return must be on an IRS form. Often, tax professionals and tax return preparation software will create (and preparers will attach) additional schedules, reports, and worksheets. Those not attached to the return are generally kept with the supporting documents maintained by the taxpayer and/or preparer in the event of an audit.[36]

B. Know that, in general, there are as many as five different sources of tax returns you can tap:
1. The client—Regardless of the number of years of tax returns there may be in existence, make copies of them all. If you don't copy or scan one old tax return, it seems that is always the one that is needed later!
2. The parties' home computer—Even if hard copies of the returns are not available, try to obtain copies of any personal tax return preparation data; all information entered into the program; and all reports, subschedules, and worksheets generated by the program. When in doubt, ask a forensic accountant or computer consultant to assist.
3. Discovery—Definitely compare what documents have been provided to what was requested. In the comparison, determine whether all of the requested years are included in the production. If the marriage lasted longer than four years, at least five years should be requested. Also, advise the client whether the document production is "under oath" and what legal ramifications may befall the spouse who produces false or misleading information as part of the discovery process.
4. The spouse's CPA—If the parties' CPA prepared joint returns, either party may request copies be provided by the CPA. One strategic advantage to issuing a subpoena is that, if all financial records are requested in the subpoena, CPAs

---

36. Note that some tax preparers may not give clients copies of all supporting schedules, especially if the schedule was not filed with the tax return itself but created and maintained in the event of an audit. This is another reason to consider issuing a subpoena *duces tecum* to the tax return preparer.

are very unlikely to shred documents before production. In cases in which the parties' CPA is a close personal friend of the opposing spouse, consider issuing a subpoena earlier in the case than normal.

5. The IRS—If hiding assets is suspected, definitely request documents directly from the IRS. Obtaining a copy of the return allows for confirmation that the return produced in discovery was, in fact, the return submitted. Often, unsigned tax returns are produced in discovery.[37] A nefarious spouse can fairly easily present a false tax return to the unsuspecting spouse for signing on page two and actually submit a completely different version of the rest of the return to the IRS. In addition, even if the return presented to the spouse was the version submitted, a nefarious spouse could also change an amount on the return after it's filed, print it out, and submit that as a copy for divorce discovery.

C. There are two options for obtaining information directly from the IRS. First, complete and mail IRS Form 4506, "*Request for Copy of Tax Return*," available at www.IRS.gov, along with a check or money order for $50 per tax year made payable to the United States Treasury. Allow approximately 60 calendar days to receive the copies. The second option is to obtain a tax return transcript, which can be quicker and is free of charge. A tax return transcript shows information from the return as it was originally filed with the IRS. A tax return transcript should also show any later adjustments either the taxpayer or the IRS made after the tax return was filed. A transcript can be obtained by mailing IRS Form 4506-T, "*Request for Transcript of Tax Return*," to the address listed in the form's instructions or by calling the number also listed there. Transcripts should be received within two weeks after the IRS receives the request. Transcripts can also be mailed by the IRS to a third party, such as an attorney or forensic accountant, rather

---

37. If a CPA prepares a return and e-files it for the client, many CPAs routinely deliver a hard copy to the client. There is likely no signature appearing on the copy provided to the client(s). This means a family lawyer should always be skeptical about receiving tax returns directly from an opposing party who has an incentive to provide a tax return showing less income than what was actually reported to the IRS.

than to the taxpayer if that is properly specified on the form, but they may take longer to receive if this is done. The taxpayer must sign and date the form authorizing the disclosure. Definitely read all IRS forms' instructions to understand exactly what is required and what to expect.

D. A clever way of hiding an asset in plain sight is to overpay estimated payments on a married-filing-separately return and carry that overpayment into future years. Review total tax payments, reported on line 74. Compare that to the amount owed on line 78. Overpayments appear on line 75. Refunds appear on line 76. But also see line 77, showing the amount applied to a future year's estimated tax. Any prepayment may be a marital asset. If discovered, the hiding spouse may claim, "I forgot."

E. Check the W-2 and look for a 401(k) or pension. If line 1 of the W-2 is different from line 5 (Medicare wages), then check to see if the line 13 box is checked. If the lines are different or box 13 is checked, then the employee has a retirement, 401(k), or other important asset. Record that as a follow-up item. Also, when requesting W-2 forms, make sure the request or subpoena asks for copies of both sides. The reverse side can contain codes or other helpful information. For more information, see Chapter 8's detailed discussion of reading W-2s, or see the current "Instructions for forms W-2 and W-3" available at www.IRS.gov.

F. Look on the 1040, line 32: "IRA deduction." If there is an amount listed, this means the taxpayer contributed to an IRA for that tax year and claimed the amount as a deduction from income. Keep in mind that a crafty spouse planning to avoid disclosing an IRA may choose not to contribute to an existing IRA in the tax year prior to the divorce or may make a contribution after the year of the tax return. Check prior years' tax returns, too. Confirm the balance of the IRA asset by reviewing the most recent monthly statement. In addition, while reviewing the 1040, also check line 28, "Self-employed SEP, SIMPLE, and qualified plans." Finally, investigate any amounts included on line 30, "Penalty on early withdrawal of savings."

G. If there are significant gambling winnings, W-2Gs may be included. Always consider that winnings (or any other money for that matter) may be placed "on account" with casinos. If your local casinos will honor them, consider issuing them subpoenas for player's card information and disclosure of amounts held on account. Regular ATM withdrawals located at or near casinos may also be a red flag.

H. Know that, when a taxpayer takes advantage of itemized deductions, shown on Schedule A, the amount was compared to the "standard deduction." The standard deduction is an amount that can be placed on the 1040 on line 40 whether or not itemized deductions can be taken. The amount of either the itemized deduction or standard deduction, whichever is greater, is used to reduce income upon which taxes are calculated. Examples of itemized deductions include medical and dental expenses, unreimbursed employee business deductions, and other deductions listed below. Always review Schedule A's listed itemized deductions because they may provide other helpful clues.

   1. When a person owns real property and borrows money secured by her primary residence, the interest paid can appear on Schedule A under "Home Mortgage Interest." The amount of interest paid in a year is reported to the homeowner on Form 1098. When reviewing the return, compare the 1098 to the amount on the return. If the amounts do not match, learn why. One reason for a difference could be that there is more than one piece of real estate for which interest is being deducted, even if the deduction is wrongfully taken. Determine whether all real property is accounted for or if a parcel of land has not been disclosed.
   2. As with the home mortgage deduction, compare the amount of real estate taxes deducted on the tax return with the supporting documentation. Determine whether all real property is accounted for or if there is a parcel that has not been disclosed.
   3. If there is a casualty loss deduction, investigate what this deduction represents. Depending on the asset loss or amount deducted, it could be important.
   4. Under certain circumstances, costs associated with certain types of investments may be deducted. If a party deducts investment expenses, the team should investigate to which property the expenses relate. Examples include the cost of subscriptions or interest on a margin account.

I. On Schedule B, taxpayers must report interest and dividend income. Many bank accounts, savings accounts, mutual funds, and other investment vehicles generate interest that is paid to depositors or investors. The interest income paid during the year is reported by the financial institution to the taxpayer on a form called the 1099-INT. A copy of that form is also forwarded to the IRS for cross-reference. Corporations can pay their after-tax earnings to stockholders by payments called dividends. Most stock mutual funds generate at least some dividend income every year. Dividend income paid to owners is reported to the taxpayer and the IRS on the 1099-DIV form. Every asset generating interest or dividend income listed on Schedule B should be added to and cross-referenced on the MBS. Also, know that, with ownership of many mutual funds, interest and dividend income can generate income that is reinvested and *not* distributed to the taxpayer, but this income may result in taxable income. In addition, if an exemption is claimed, examine that as well. The exemption may be related to government-issued savings bonds. Finally, this form also requires reporting income related to foreign trusts and accounts. It is located at the bottom of the form and should not be overlooked.

J. Another clever and devious way of hiding an asset's existence from a spouse is to "accidently" leave off of the return income generated from a recently acquired investment asset. In this plan, the devious spouse completes the tax return, leaving off the asset's income, obtains the spouse's signature on the joint return, and submits the actually filed return in discovery. If the asset is jointly held by a financial institution, that institution has likely generated and issued 1099-INTs and 1099-DIVs. The IRS will eventually discover the "error" and can assess additional taxes owed, interest, and penalties. If the devious spouse can settle the divorce quickly enough, the spouse can possibly amend the return (forging the signature of the spouse or former spouse) and pay the associated taxes, interest, and penalties, and no one will be the wiser. For some spouses, this is a small additional price to pay to secrete a significant amount of money from disclosure. If you suspect that the spouse has done this, consider ordering the tax return transcript discussed previously because it should show post-filing adjustments made by the IRS and amendments.

K. Schedule C reports income or loss from a business or profession if it is operated as a sole proprietorship. Hobby income may not be reported on Schedule C, but see Form 1040, line 21, for "other income." If there is a Schedule C, determine whether the business must be valued and whether additional discovery may be required. If the business is not owned within a separate legal entity, like a corporation, the business will be considered owned by the individual taxpayer. In any event, almost all businesses have some "separate" assets, such as cash, inventory, equipment (leased or owned), accounts receivable, and real estate. Schedule C is a very important document for you and the forensic accountant to review. Note that, if a business reports its annual income on a cash basis, accounts receivable will not be reported, even though they may exist. Also, always keep in mind work in progress, which also may not be reported on tax returns because the income has not been realized.

L. In many situations, if a taxpayer sells property and investments of any kind, the sale likely results in a capital gain or loss. Schedule D is used to report the sale or exchange of a capital asset, gains from involuntary conversions not held for business or profit, capital gain distributions not reported directly on Form 1040 (line 13), and nonbusiness bad debts. At a minimum, know these helpful definitions:
    1. Capital asset—most property owned and used for personal purposes, pleasure, or investments.
    2. Basis—the amount of the investment in property for tax purposes, subject to certain adjustments depending on the type of property.
    3. Capital gain or loss—the difference between the sales price of a capital asset and its basis.
    4. Short or long term—if a capital asset is owned one year or less, its sale will result in short-term gain or loss. Short-term and long-term transactions can be taxed differently.
    5. Passive activity loss carryforward—losses that are not deductible for a particular tax year because there is insufficient passive activity income to offset them are carried

forward indefinitely and are allowed as deductions against passive income in subsequent years. The potential tax benefit of loss carryforwards can be very valuable to divide in divorce.[38]

Very important information can be found on Schedule D, including the date an asset was purchased, its cost, the date of the transaction, and the amount for which the asset was sold. Always look for sale of stock and trace it to the brokerage account. Also, know that Schedule D provides disclosure of capital gains and losses from activities from partnerships, S corporations, estates, and other entities. If there were capital loss carryovers from prior years, definitely enlist the help of the CPA. Schedule D will not contain information about the source of money to purchase particular assets or where the proceeds from the sale can be found today. Those follow-up questions may best be asked at deposition. Transactions recorded on Schedule D are almost always the beginning of a trail, not the end.

M. Schedule E records supplemental income and loss. Rental real estate, royalties, partnerships, LLCs, S corporations, estates, trusts, real estate mortgage investment conduits, and other entities file tax returns and then report that income to the IRS and the respective individual taxpayers. Income and losses from these entities are reported on Schedule E. For example, partners and members of LLCs receive K-1s whether or not income was distributed. Draws are reported on the K-1s, line J, and page 4 of Form 1065. The information reported on a K-1 must correspond exactly to the information on the owner's individual tax return, or the IRS will look at the difference to determine if adjustments must be made to either return. Know that K-1s can be very complicated, and it is not uncommon for K-1s to be prepared incorrectly. Any tax return or form can contain an error; however, in divorce situations forensic accountants can

38. Know that passive losses require future passive gains to benefit from them. For more information, see IRS Publication 925, *Passive Activity and At-Risk Rules*, which is available for download at https://www.irs.gov/pub/irs-pdf/p925.pdf.

help look for errors. Also, recognize that owners of businesses often invest money and then legally loan money back and forth between the business and themselves. To identify suspicious transactions, you can track retained earnings, partner's equity, and loans over multiple years. Look for patterns and changes in divorcing years. Also, look for rent expenses, and other costs that can be prepaid, appearing to be a tax deduction. In reality, it is the same as a hidden asset. Like many tax forms, Schedule E can be a gold mine of information.

N. Schedule F reports farm income and expenses. Consider that a farm may be valued as an ongoing business activity separate from its real estate value.

O. Form 4797 is used to report the sale or exchange of assets used in a business, involuntary conversion (casualty or theft), disposition of noncapital assets, ordinary loss on the sale or worthlessness of a small business or investment business, and ordinary gain or loss on securities held in connection with a trading business. Any of these items will likely require some additional investigation. See 1040, line 14, "Other gains or (losses)."

Know that many types of assets can generate income for a taxpayer that does not appear on personal tax returns. For example, corporations (both foreign and domestic) and trusts pay their own taxes. Also, the sale of certain assets can result in nondeductible losses, such as the sale or exchange of property between a fiduciary and a beneficiary of the same trust, an executor of an estate and the beneficiary of that estate, members of a family, or an individual and tax-exempt organization controlled by the individual or the individual's family. As always, as questions arise, ask the forensic accountant for help.

Case Example: Tracing as a Defense to Commingling

Tracing funds can be used as a defense to commingling. Expert testimony can be the very best way to assert or defend against these claims. The best way to counteract a forensic accountant's testimony is with another forensic accountant. Family lawyers must endeavor to determine what work was performed by an opposing forensic accountant as well as to advise their client to engage his or her own expert to evaluate the analysis and possible testimony and to advise whether or not the particular issue should be challenged.

The husband and wife in this Missouri divorce case[39] were married in 1978, the day after signing a prenuptial agreement. After 30 years of marriage, they separated and divorced. The trial court held that the prenuptial agreement was valid and enforceable and divided the marital property 60 percent to the wife and 40 percent to the husband.

39. Short v. Short, 356 S.W.3d 235 (Mo. Ct. App. 2011).

Both parties then appealed to the Missouri Court of Appeals. In her appeal, the wife argued that the trial court had erred in treating much of the property as marital rather than her separate property. In particular, the lower court had found that assets had been transmuted over the years into marital property by virtue of comingling. She argued that the assets remained in her name only and remained traceable throughout the marriage—a defense to the commingled assets claim.

The appeals court first agreed with the trial court that the prenuptial agreement was valid and enforceable and upheld the lower court's $8 million valuation of a closely held corporation. However, it reversed the lower court's ruling with respect to approximately $5 million in distributions from a dissolved corporation. The lower court had held that these distributions were marital property because they had consisted primarily of the corporation's retained earnings. However, the appeals court held that they were properly the wife's separate property.

The appeals court then addressed the lower court's finding that many of the wife's assets had been transmuted into marital property by comingling. The primary asset in question was $5 million received from the corporate liquidation of a former corporation. The wife had deposited these funds into three separate accounts in her name only, and her expert witness had testified extensively as to how these funds could be traced from the time of deposit until the time of trial.

The lower court had never fully addressed the tracing of these funds. The wife's expert testimony on the issue of tracing had focused almost entirely on the $5 million, to the exclusion of other assets. The wife's accounts were "hopelessly comingled"[40] due to the length of the marriage, the number of accounts, and their level of activity. The lower court had held that the wife's expert had not presented convincing evidence to dispute the finding.

However, the appeals court noted that the issue of comingling wasn't squarely before the lower court, since it had already concluded that the bulk of those accounts, the $5 million, had been marital property in the first place. Therefore, the court of appeals, though it affirmed the lower court's ruling with respect to comingling of other assets, remanded the case and directed the lower court to reconsider the wife's expert's

40. In Tennessee, the courts refer to this as "inextricably commingled." CPAs may have a serious problem with this rather opaque standard, making this subjective standard such fertile ground for dispute.

testimony as it related to tracing the $5 million. It directed the lower court to modify the judgment accordingly after reconsidering this evidence. As to the remaining funds in the accounts—which consisted of dividends, earnings, and income—the appeals court held that there was substantial evidence to support the lower court's finding of the assets being hopelessly comingled.

Case Example: The Barren Wasteland That Is Accounts Receivable

With many businesses, accounts receivable can be a barren wasteland of money. Although the money may be owed to the business, many businesses fail to engage in any meaningful collection efforts, or they fail to write off the uncollectible debt. The amounts listed on the balance sheets could be totally worthless.

On the other hand, accounts receivable (and corresponding adjustments for "bad debt") can be a hide-in-plain-sight opportunity for crafty business owners to hide money. Never underestimate how long a business owner may have been planning a divorce. If one business owner has a strong personal relationship with another business owner who owes the subject business money, it could easily be presumed that a handshake deal has occurred agreeing that payment on an old and apparently uncollectible accounts receivable may be made after the divorce.

For all divorce engagements involving a business owner, business valuation experts and forensic accountants should strongly consider visiting the business personally and making every effort to speak with management. On cross-examination, simple follow-up questions can make financial expert witnesses who haven't done their homework look frivolous: "How do you know [list concern here]? Did you even visit the offices? Did you ever even ask to speak with the office manager? Have you ever asked anyone a single question about your concern? Why not?"

The husband and wife in this Ohio divorce case[41] were married in 1971, when the husband was finishing his last year of medical school. During this time, the wife was the primary source of income. Although she worked briefly while the husband finished his residency, she did not work later in the marriage. Instead, she stayed at home to raise the couple's three children.

In 1976, the husband specialized in obstetrics and gynecology and worked for a medical corporation owned by another physician. In 1980, the husband and another physician became equal shareholders in the corporation with the original physician, who then withdrew in 1984. At that time, the original physician received about $38,000 for his one-third interest, which included $10,000 for his share of the goodwill of the business. The second doctor later left the corporation also and received about $28,000, which included $15,000 for his proportionate share of the goodwill.

In 1990, the husband merged with another physician, and the new doctor purchased half of the corporate stock. The 1990 agreement provided that either doctor could sell out for a price equal to the fair market value of the company assets, plus the $30,000 worth of goodwill.

For the years 1989–91, the husband's income ranged from about $290,000 to $392,000 per year. He testified, however, that these figures were artificially high because a lack of physicians in the corporation forced him to work long hours. Family living expenses during that time were about $50,000 per year, which the husband described as a comfortable lifestyle.

In 1990, the parties separated, and the husband filed for divorce in 1991. The parties resolved many issues, but the sticking points were the value of the medical corporation stock, the husband's interest in the accounts receivable, and the value of the goodwill. The wife's expert witness was independent business and financial adviser George

41. Kell v. Kell, No. 92CA1931 (Ohio Ct. App. Dec. 14, 1993).

W. Baughman. He testified that the stock was valued at $75,000 and the goodwill was worth $852,000. He also testified that the accounts receivable were valued at $139,000. He based this assumption on a collection rate of 82.8 percent.

The husband's expert was forensic accountant Ralph D. Dickson, who was taking courses to become a certified business appraiser. To set the goodwill, he concluded that the $30,000 specified in the buy-sell agreement was appropriate. He also concluded that the accounts receivable were largely not collectible and therefore deducted over $300,000 from the total. He concluded that the husband's interest in the business was valued at $87,198, which included $15,000 for his share of the goodwill. He also testified that the husband's interest in the accounts receivable was about $55,000.

The trial court's findings accepted the husband's expert's view of the valuation of the medical practice and divided the marital property accordingly. The wife appealed to the Ohio Court of Appeals and first argued that the lower court had abused its discretion in accepting the husband's valuation of the medical practice.

As to the valuation of the goodwill, the appeals court noted that there are numerous methods of valuation, of which reference to a buy-sell agreement is only one. It noted that previous cases did not prescribe any flat rule for which method should be used.

In this case, the appeals court noted that the wife's expert, Baughman, had admitted that he had no formal training in business appraisal and had not followed any written standards adopted by professional appraisal organizations. In reaching his conclusion, Baughman did not visit the practice or speak with the manager or corporate accountant. The appeals court therefore held that there was sufficient evidence for the trial court to accept the opinion of the husband's expert and reject that of the wife's expert.

The wife had also argued on appeal that the husband's expert, Dickson, had "arbitrarily" disregarded over $312,000 in accounts receivable on the grounds that they were "too old" and "not collectible." The wife argued that this was inappropriate, since the buy-sell agreement did not permit such discounting. However, the husband's expert, Dickson, testified that the wife's expert, Baughman, had erred by using a percentage that was never intended to value accounts receivable such as the ones in this case, which included amounts that had been allowed to remain for years. The office manager testified that the accounts receivable erroneously included amounts that were uncollectable. The husband's version of this evidence was supported by the record, so adopting Dickson's conclusion was not an abuse of discretion.

For these reasons, the appeals court held that the lower court's ruling on the business valuation issues would be affirmed. After addressing child support, spousal support, and attorney's fee issues, the appeals court affirmed the lower court's judgment.

Case Example: Future Benefit from Prior Passive Losses

Family lawyers and forensic accountants must always be on the look out for possible post-divorce tax benefits from passive tax loss carry forward items from prior tax returns, especially for owners of real estate. Tax benefits from passive losses can be confusing and challenging. They may also possibly be speculative because they may never be used. On the other hand, they can also be very valuable. Be prepared to go the extra mile on this issue when preparing for settlement or court.

The husband and wife in this Virginia divorce case[42] were married in 1976. In 1993, the husband filed for divorce. The following year, an equitable distribution hearing was held. This hearing focused on the value of two start-up businesses owned by the husband. A decision was not rendered until 1996, after which the wife moved for reconsideration on the grounds that the valuation of the businesses could have changed considerably

42. Shooltz v. Shooltz, No. 2205-96-4 (Va. Ct. App. Apr. 28, 1998).

during that time. The Virginia Court of Appeals ultimately held that the motion for reconsideration should have been granted due to the delay.

At the hearing, the wife's expert testified as to the tax ramifications of the property distribution. The husband and wife had approximately \$1.2 million in suspended passive tax loss and \$334,000 in carried-over investment interest. As a result, the parties had the ability to apply over \$1.5 million in suspended passive losses, which could be used to offset income and capital gains taxes. According to the wife's expert, this would generate a tax benefit of \$518,000.

Six months after the equitable distribution hearing, the husband moved for permission to liquidate marital assets in order to pay about \$100,000 in taxes that had resulted from sales of stock and margin calls. The husband had sold \$750,000 in stock in a margin account to generate the \$250,000 necessary to retire a debt incurred during the marriage. The husband then asked the court to reduce the value of the marital estate by the amount of the tax liability.

The trial court heard evidence on this issue. The husband argued that the sale had generated an additional \$307,000 in tax liability. The wife's expert opined that the husband had over \$374,000 of tax benefits available due to passive losses from a defunct limited partnership. However, the husband's expert countered by testifying that most of that tax benefit was unavailable because it would need to be reduced by the husband's negative capital account in the partnership.

After considering the evidence, the trial court reduced the award from the husband to wife by \$150,000 to compensate for the tax liability.

Essentially, the trial court agreed with the husband's tax expert and rejected the opinion of the wife's expert. In her appeal, the wife argued that the husband's tax consequences were speculative, the result of the husband's unilateral actions, and offset by his accumulated passive losses.

The appeals court ruled that the trial court had acted properly because tax considerations are to be considered under Virginia law. The trial court had reviewed the parties' testimony and memoranda on the issue and made the finding that it didn't see "anything artificial or made up in this." Even though the tax returns had not yet been prepared at the time of the hearing, the trial court had found that they were "real life taxes that have to be paid."

The wife also pointed to her expert's opinion that the tax liability could be offset by the passive losses. But the appeals court noted that because two conflicting experts testified, it was within the discretion of the trial court to select either opinion. It therefore affirmed the lower court's resolution of the tax issues. Since the court of appeals had reversed other portions of the lower court's ruling, it remanded the case.

Determining Income 8

"And once more, we play our dangerous game, a game of chess, against our old adversary, the American Navy." —The Hunt for Red October, Marko Ramius, played by Sean Connery

Clients usually know right off the bat when income determination is going to be an important issue. For obvious reasons, it's most often the less propertied, supported spouse raising the concern. In those cases, temporary support also almost always seems to be an issue, and temporary support is always important because it's early in the case. And if it's mishandled, the case will become much more difficult for the supported spouse. What's the easiest way temporary support gets bungled? The supported spouse can't prove what the supporting spouse earns. The risk of not being able to prove income is always highest early in the case before the best documents have been exchanged or researched.

Depending on the level of conflict and complexity of earnings, determination of income affects the following:

1. Temporary support;
2. Alimony; and
3. Child support.

Alimony focuses on need and ability to pay. Ability to pay means available cash after taxes and expenses. Determining the obligor's ability to pay begins with income determination.

For child support, even though every state has its own guidelines, the attentive family lawyer should study, meditate on, and contemplate the sometimes subtle but important differences between her particular state's definition of income and the definition of taxable income under federal income tax law. A state's definition of income will be much broader than the interpretation of federal income. For example, take Illinois's definition of net income: "The total of all income from all sources."[1]

Tax returns are often the first documentation of income the family lawyer reviews. But tax returns don't always show the whole truth, especially for business owners and those with cash businesses. At a minimum, what documents are needed for temporary support disputes? Last year's tax return, W-2s, and a current pay stub. Obviously, more detail is better. The 1040, W-2s, and other income reported therein become the beginning of the inquiry, not the end. You must put into context the documents, their analysis, and the help a certified public accountant (CPA) may need to provide when dealing with the almost infinite number of possible legal issues. For example, in Illinois, income disbursed from a spendthrift trust,[2] IRA withdrawals,[3] and Social Security Disability benefits[4] all present unique problems. You must obtain the documents, understand them, and seek to admit evidence in the context of your state's law. For a more complete legal discussion of what is and is not includable as income for child support across jurisdictions, see Chapter 2, "Construction of the Guidelines: Defining 'Number of Children' and 'Income,'" from *Child Support Guidelines: Interpretation and Application*, by Laura Morgan, available through Aspen Publishers.

When dealing with challenging money issues, you must consider people's behavior, different types of investments, their tax ramifications, hostile motives, varying degrees of honesty, principles of finance,

1. 750 Ill. Comp. Stat. Ann. 5/505(a). Enumerated deductions areconsidered as part of the determination of income for child support purposes.
2. *Sharp v. Sharp*, 860 N.E.2d 539 (Ill. App. Ct. 2006).
3. *O'Daniel v. O'Daniel*, 889 N.E.2d 254 (Ill. App. Ct. 2008).
4. *Truhlar v. Truhlar*, No. 2-09-0536, 2010 WL 3667117 (Ill. App. Ct. Sept. 17, 2010).

and financial reporting requirements all at the same time. Looking at income from just one angle gives the nefarious spouse too much room to cheat. Comparing documents reporting the same information is one very good way to limit the cheater's room to get away with it. For many, it's a game. Luckily for family lawyers, forensic accountants love to expose cheaters.

At this point in the book, there has already been much discussion about income determination:

1. Financial statements and accounting in Chapter 3,
2. Nefarious business owners in Chapter 4, and
3. Review of tax returns for hidden assets in Chapter 7.

Know that, as you are looking for hidden assets, those assets often continue generating additional income. Also, consider that tax returns show many categories of taxable income, but not all income is taxable. The returns may, however, contain information describing assets that generate nontaxable income that can be included in income determination for support purposes. If you are looking for taxable income first, you can easily miss nontaxable income simply because it may not appear on the face of the 1040 itself. Chapter 7 provides a guideline for using the 1040, its supporting schedules, and its attachments to ferret out these assets.

Documented Income

Finding documented income is important. There are several sources for finding this income. Think of the following as pieces of a larger puzzle:

1. Tax returns,[5] W-2s, and current pay stubs;
2. Declarations of income in discovery, such as interrogatory responses and produced documents;
3. Declarations of income on statements of income and expenses submitted during the divorce process;
4. Declarations made as part of loan applications;

5. See Chapter 7's discussion of what the term "tax returns" should mean. It should always include 1040s, state income tax returns, W-2s, 1099-INTs, 1099-DIVs, supporting schedules, attachments, and so on.

5. Financial statements submitted as part of loan applications;
6. Financial statements generated as part of financial planning and budgeting found on home computer programs, such as Quicken and QuickBooks;
7. Imputed income methods discussed below, including adding up deposits on bank statements;
8. Bankruptcy filings; and
9. Past salaries listed on job applications.

Claimed Income versus Documented Income

Claimed income on discovery responses and on Statements of Income and Expenses is always an admission. Claimed income will usually be the starting point for challenging the credibility of the declaring spouse. If a spouse lies, or seriously understates income, some triers of fact will absolutely cream the spouse by discounting whatever else that spouse says during the case. Most believe that, if a spouse will lie about something as basic as income, the spouse will lie about anything and everything. Reported income refers to statements declared on external documents completed by borrowers and taxpayers. Comparing and contrasting claimed and reported income usually involves the technique of ICE (internal, control, and external documents) described in Chapter 6. Once you find conflicting statements of income, you must take advantage of that. Often, the testimony of the forensic accountant is the best way to do so.

Most of the time, reported income is factual and straightforward. Other than tax returns, income is usually declared as a part of loan applications. Financial statements and tax returns are provided as supporting documentation as well. Fortunately, borrowers normally list all income, not just taxed income. Understanding what documents lenders require is very helpful.

Loans are usually earmarked as business or personal, even though most small business loans are personally guaranteed by the owners of the business. Also, loans are often securitized by one or more assets. Almost all securitized loans will result in certain documents being publicly recorded. For example, loans securitized by real estate include documents such as mortgages and trust deeds. Regardless of how the law of your particular state describes such instruments, all loan transactions securitized by real estate should be recorded with the county register of deeds or its equivalent. If a financial institution can secure a sizable loan with real estate, it will most likely require that that be done. There's no requirement that loan applications themselves be recorded, but you should always try to learn who made the loan, when, and for how much. For example, some spouses who borrow fail to produce the loan application in discovery. That loan application may include financial statements. If it does and you can acquire it, you can then use the information to issue a subpoena to the financial institution, thereby obtaining the loan application package and any supporting financial statements submitted to the lender. Then compare the reported income to the spouse's claimed income. If there is a material difference, the spouse may have lied regarding his claimed income. That lie may be a crime in his state.

You may often use many of these same steps for business loans securitized by assets other than real estate. If inventory or other business assets are used as security, there may be a publicly filed UCC-1 or financing statement listing the securitized collateral. When filed, this legal document gives formal notice to the world that the lender has a superior right to the asset. Securing loans against other assets may be less formal or complicated. For example, a car loan will be documented by the lender's lien appearing on the face of a car's certificate of title. The loan may have been obtained by completion of an application at the car dealership. A car loan application is often comprised of a simple declaration of the borrower's income and a credit report review. Copies of car loan applications, though, may not be maintained by the borrower or the lender. Once the loan is made, the car is the security. When all payments are made, the state reissues the title with the lien removed. If payments aren't made, there can be repossession. The larger the financial institution making the loan, the more likely it has retained the application.

For most small business loans and lines of credit, all the business's assets are usually pledged, and all of the owners/borrowers are usually individually and personally liable for the debt of the business. When a business takes out a loan, it is for a specific amount of money. For a line of credit, the loaned amount can fluctuate up to a preapproved limit. The higher the limit, the higher the annual fee the business is charged. For example, with lawyers, accounts receivable may be the largest asset on the books and may be the asset primarily securitized for a business loan. Note that accounts receivable are not reported on cash-basis taxpayers' tax returns. This may mean that the list of accounts receivable must be reported separately to the lender.

Financial institutions usually have strict and formal procedures and documentation requirements for making loans, which will be adhered to unless the borrower has a long-term relationship with the lender. Having borrowed and paid back large sums of money over periods of years usually means the borrower has such a relationship. Nevertheless, business borrowers are almost always required to update financial disclosures annually. For small businesses, the annual update will usually involve production of at least the following:

1. Business financial statements (income statements and balance sheets),
2. Business and personal tax returns,
3. Personal financial statements signed by the borrowers/owners, and/or
4. Formal loan application forms listing income and net worth.

The greater the amount of the business loan, the more documentation will be required for review. The personal financial statement may or may not list income. Claimed income, in some cases, may be supported only by tax returns. But for the forensic accountant, there are two unique aspects to business loan applications that the personal loan application will not have:

1. Business financial statements are often prepared by a CPA.
2. Business and personal tax returns can be compared to financial statements.

When financial statements are issued by the business's CPA, it means that the CPA firm probably has even more in its files for the client's forensic accountant to dig through. The financial information can include tax returns, general ledgers, asset and depreciation schedules, state and local tax returns, sales tax returns, and more—and forensic accountants love this. There may be many years of this type of documentation in the CPA's files. If the personal tax returns aren't current—and for some unknowable and incalculable reason, they often seem to be late in a divorcing year—the lender usually must do something to paper its file regarding income. You can try to discover what documentation of income was provided. The client's forensic accountant can compare the completed tax returns to those years' financial statements line by line. CPAs eat up this type of financial information buffet to learn the secrets divorcing business owners don't want opposing family lawyers to know.

You can also issue subpoenas to credit card companies (or other sources of unsecured credit) for credit applications, but if you decide to do so, good luck. The consensus among experienced family lawyers is that issuing subpoenas to credit card companies for applications and statements is a hit-or-miss proposition that is mostly miss. Many credit card applications and subsequent applications for credit limit increases are taken over the phone and aren't really based on proof of claimed income but rather on credit scores. In any event, note that a business owner who has substantial credit card debt likely has that much debt for one of three reasons:

1. The business owner can't obtain conventional financing and is desperate because conventional loans are much less expensive than credit cards.
2. The business owner can't stop overspending.
3. The business owner intentionally wants to look poor and/or rack up debt to cut off his nose to spite his face.[6]

Granted, significant credit card debt and people's lives shouldn't be summed up in discrete cookie-cutter, armchair-psychologist psychobabble. But this view suggests an important facet of forensic accounting. Understanding *why* something was done can be as important as knowing *what* was done. Never lose sight of the ultimate goal in

---

6. Use of money reveals much about a person's character and decision-making values. Why would a divorcing spouse rack up debt neither spouse can afford to pay? Exploring the answer to that question could be a book in itself. Why does anyone overeat? Why does anyone drink too much? As a divorce strategy, self-destructive behavior presents its own reward, often achieving retaliation and retribution. In the movie *Tombstone*, Johnny Ringo is portrayed as a vicious, psychotic, and very quick-draw gunslinger. Near the end of the movie, Wyatt Earp asks Doc Holliday, "What makes a man like Ringo . . . do the things he does?" Doc replies, "A man like Ringo has a great empty hole right through the middle of him. He can never kill enough or steal enough or inflict enough pain to fill it." Wyatt asks, "What does he need?" "Revenge," says Doc. Wyatt asks, "For what?" Doc answers, "Being born."

divorce—a favorable settlement. To find the path to a favorable settlement, often *how* to negotiate is discovered only after understanding *why* the other party does the things he does.

Imputed Income

Imputed income is one of the most important, but challenging, calculations to get into evidence. In general, there are three ways to impute income:

1. Use of a detailed transaction listing and analysis,[7]
2. Proof of luxury spending that is clearly inappropriate for the amount of claimed income, and
3. Use of the net-worth method.

In the context of imputing income, the detailed transaction listing and analysis can be used in two ways. First, you can add up all deposits to calculate actual after-tax earnings and compare that amount to claimed earnings. Second, you can use it to compare actual spending with the obligor's claimed after-tax income. The forensic accountant can determine whether the expenses greatly exceed known sources of funds. If the proven lifestyle of the parties during the marriage is greater than known sources of income, you may be able to establish that the claimed income has been understated. The predictable problem with this method can be disproving the obligor's explanation for spending more money than what has been, or is, claimed as income. Usually, the obligor spouse's claim is that the divorcing parties overspent.

Thinking an additional move ahead on the chessboard, if the result of the claimed overspending is a bunch of debt, well, that explanation might stand unless the forensic accountant can disprove it. On the other hand, if there is little or no debt, the forensic accountant must determine whether cash assets, investments, or savings were encroached upon. Regardless, thoroughly reviewing all financial documents is necessary for disproving the obligor's claimed explanation. The forensic accountant must have sufficient relevant documents accounting for all transactions. If there are sufficient relevant documents, the forensic accountant

7. In the context of forensic accounting techniques, see the discussion of the Detailed detailed Transaction transaction Listing listing and Analysis analysis in Chapter 6 and Example 6-2.

may be able to testify that, to a reasonable degree of accounting certainty, there must be other income to explain the spending pattern.

Proof of luxury spending can be straightforward.[8] It begins with an important, but arguable, assumption: "People spend money they can afford to spend." Rolex, like many name brands companies, markets its watches to symbolize success and affluence. The consensus is that luxury-purchasing spouses who claim during the divorce to be not as wealthy as they otherwise appear to be are apt to fudge on claimed income. That fudging is more critically viewed in child support matters than alimony cases because the children are seen as victims. In any courtroom, the more outrageous the luxury item, the more difficulty the obligor may have claiming impoverishment.[9]

From a different angle, proving luxury spending can be very similar to proving unrecorded income in the form of perks paid by an employer. For example, sometimes a doctor's medical practice makes lease payments for the doctor's luxury car. The medical practice deducts the lease payments and, for whatever reason (legall or not), the lease payments are not included on the doctor's W-2 or 1099. The amount paid by the practice could be more than $1,000 per month and should be included in the doctor's income considered for support.

Net-Worth Method

The net-worth method is used to impute income based on a change in known net worth over a period of time. If someone earns a great deal of money and does not spend it, that person's net worth should increase. If the person spends more than she earned, that person's net worth should decrease. To apply the net-worth method, the forensic accountant must know several things:

1. The person's beginning net worth,
2. The person's reported income,

8. Check your state's child support guidelines to see if it references luxury spending in the context of imputing income.

9. Every experienced family lawyer has an arsenal of stories about luxury spending around the time of filing for divorce. Many of the spending binges are the stuff of melodramatic novels, such as luxury vacation time-shares, bracelets, diamond engagement rings, and elective plastic surgery.

3. The person's expenses,
4. The person's ending net worth, and
5. The appreciation of and depreciation applied to listed assets.

The IRS uses the net-worth method to catch tax cheats with untrustworthy accounting records.[10] It has also been used in family law cases.[11] One specific definition of the net-worth method is the following:

> *The net worth method calculates income by determining a taxpayer's net worth at the beginning and end of a period.*
>
> *The difference is the increase in net worth. An increase in net worth, plus nondeductible expenditures (such as personal living expenses), less nontaxable receipts, may be considered taxable income. If the resulting figure for any year is substantially greater than the taxable income reported by the taxpayer for that year, the IRS claims the excess represents unreported taxable income.*[12]

The IRS calculates unreported taxable income using the net-worth method. In family law cases, forensic accountants can use this method to calculate understated income. If the claimed amount of income cannot explain the increase in net worth, the income must have come from an unknown source. Many of the adjustments described by the IRS that relate to taxation need not be made for determination of income available for support. The net-worth method calculation relies upon the relationship among assets, debts, reported income, and expenses in order to back into, or reverse engineer, the person's total income, including

---

10. For more information about the net-worth method, see the IRS's *Internal Revenue Manual*, Part 9, "Criminal Investigation," Section 9, "Methods of Proof," available at www.IRS.gov. This is exactly the kind of financial analysis that causes forensic accountants to get all jacked up on Red Bull and party like it's 1999.

11. *See, e.g.*, Tucker v. Office of Child Support Enforcement, 247 S.W.3d 485 (Ark. 2007) (accepting net-worth method for calculation of income) and Schoenbachler v. Minyard, 110 S.W.3d 776 (Ky. 2003) (affirming trial court's rejection of use of method based on insufficient proof but impliedly stating net-worth method could be used under certain circumstances).

12. *Schoenbachler*, 110 S.W.3d at 785 (quoting *Yoon v. Commissioner of Internal Revenue*, 135 F.3d 1007, 1009–10 (5th Cir. 1998)).

unrecorded income.[13] The Supreme Court of Arkansas outlined the following procedure:

> *[F]or self-employed payors, the circuit court should first consider the last two years' federal and state income tax returns and the quarterly estimates for the current year. A self-employed payor's income should include contributions made to retirement plans, alimony paid, and self-employed insurance paid. Depreciation should be allowed only to the extent that it reflects actual decrease in value of an asset.*
>
> *If the circuit court determines that the tax returns are unreliable, then it shall make specific findings explaining the basis of its determination. The circuit court shall then proceed using the net-worth method. The circuit court shall establish a beginning net worth at the start of the relevant period and an ending net worth at the end of the period, considering living expenses and allowable deductions for the same period. Additionally, the circuit court shall consider the following factors: (1) the impact of inflation or deflation on the payor's net worth; (2) liquidity of the payor's assets; (3) the payor's cash flow; (4) the payor's current and long-term financial obligations; (5) the payor's lifestyle; and (6) any other relevant factors. After determining the payor's disposable income, the circuit court shall calculate child support in accordance with the child-support guidelines.*[14]

The net-worth method makes lots of sense to forensic accountants. Depending on the relative financial and accounting sophistication of the trier of fact, the method can be very challenging to explain in the courtroom. One important key is having a locked-down net-worth

---

13. Recall the key accounting equations:

    Assets – debt = net worth (the balance sheet equation reflects the financial positions at a moment in time, like a photo);

    Income – expenses = net income (income statement reports events over a period of time).
14. *Tucker*, 247 S.W.3d at 489–90 (citations omitted).

statement from which all other analysis can be judged.[15] There must be a point in time when a precise net worth is known. A typical way this occurs is when, on an annual basis, business owners create and produce personal net worth statements for business loan applications on which the business owner is personally liable.

The following is a hypothetical example of the net-worth method being used to prove income greater than the obligor's reported and claimed amount:

In 2015, the IRS audited Mr. and Mrs. Kirk. Pursuant to a request from the special agent, Mr. Kirk furnished a personal financial statement prepared by the parties' CPA and dated December 31, 2014. Mrs. Kirk kept a copy. At all relevant times, Mrs. Kirk was a stay-at-home mom. The parties' net-worth statement was as follows:

Assets:	
Cash	$50,000
Cars and personal property	25,000
Investments – Wells Fargo	50,000
Marital residence FMV [fair market value]	400,000
Business – FMV Spock, Inc.	100,000
Total Assets	$625,000
Debt:	
Credit card	$25,000
Mortgage	200,000
Total Debt	$225,000
Net Worth	$400,000

In 2017, Mr. Kirk filed for divorce. But on June 30, 2018, he filed a net-worth statement with his bank for a line of credit with the following information:

15. *Schoenbachler*, 110 S.W.3d at 785 n.27 (Ky. 2003) (citing *Holland v. United States*, 348 U.S. 121, 132, 75 S. Ct. 127, 134, 99 L. Ed. 150, 162–63 (1954)), which reads as follows: "We agree with petitioners that an essential condition in [net-worth method cases] is the establishment, with reasonable certainty, of an opening net worth, to serve as a starting point from which to calculate future increases in the taxpayer's assets."

Assets:

Cash	$50,000
Cars and personal property	75,000
Investments – Wells Fargo	225,000
Marital residence FMV	450,000
Business – FMV Spock, Inc.	300,000
Total Assets	$1,100,000

Debt:

Credit card	$50,000
Mortgage	190,000
Total Debt	$240,000
Net Worth	$860,000

During the relevant time frame, 2015 through 2017 and half of 2018, Mr. Kirk claimed to have earned $50,000 (after taxes) each year. Mrs. Kirk's forensic accountant can prove that, during this 3-and-a-half-year period, Mr. and Mrs. Kirk spent $215,000. This means the parties spent $40,000 more than the $175,000 ($50,000 × 3.5 years) Mr. Kirk earned. How should the situation be analyzed?

The forensic accountant first determines the change in net worth. The overall total increase in net worth is $460,000 (see below). This increase in net worth is the result of increased values of assets and payments reducing debts, or amounts spent to increase the value of investments.

Next, the analysis must consider appreciation in the claimed value of the business, investment portfolio, and house. In this case, the change in the value of the cars and personal property is a result of transactions, not appreciation or depreciation. If there were appreciation or depreciation, those amounts would have to be removed from the change in net worth. The business, investments, and house assets all appreciated, but not because of Mr. Kirk's use of income or cash used to improve the assets. Mr. Kirk claimed, and the business records confirmed, that he had not invested money in the business or withdrawn any money in the form of loans or capital withdrawals. Also, Mr. Kirk's stock portfolio showed he removed no funds from his stock portfolio at Wells Fargo but added one check of $75,000 from an undisclosed source. In order to remove the appreciation of the stock portfolio on its own, the analysis must add back the $75,000 contribution. For the investments, the change in net worth resulted from increases in the value of investments, except for the appreciation and contribution. To remove that item, it is added back to the reduction for appreciation. Finally, the FMV of the house increased $50,000, but not from an addition, improvement, or other source of income or use of funds.

Net Worth June 30, 2018	$860,000
Net Worth Dec. 31, 2014	(400,000)
Overall increase in Net Worth	$460,000
Spock, Inc. value Dec. 31, 2014	100,000
Spock, Inc. value June 30, 2018	(300,000)
Investments—Wells Fargo Dec. 31, 2014	50,000
Investments—Wells Fargo June 30, 2018	(225,000)
Investments—additional contribution	75,000
Marital residence FMV—Dec. 31, 2014	400,000
Marital residence FMV—June 30, 2018	(450,000)
Adjusted Increase in Net Worth	$110,000

In the next step, the forensic accountant adds living expenses and reduces the amount of the increase in net worth from income from known sources. Here, the known income source is Mr. Kirk's business. The business's records show that Mr. Kirk paid himself only $50,000 after taxes each year, and no other distributions of profit were made during that time to Mr. Kirk from the business. The after-tax amounts are used because the amounts paid for taxes are not available to the Kirks to purchase assets, reduce debts, or pay for living expenses. This allows the forensic accountant to reverse engineer the increase in net worth from unknown sources. The calculation looks like this:

Adjusted Increase in Net Worth	$110,000
Reported living expenses:	$215,000
Reported income (3.5 years × $50K)	(175,000)
Increase in Net Worth from Unknown Sources	**$150,000**

What about depreciation? Since the goal of this exercise is to calculate a change in net worth to determine income, depreciation of assets during the period must be excluded. But no asset depreciation was included in the example.

Mr. Kirk claimed to have earned only $175,000 during this time. But his net worth increased $325,000 after removing nonincome-related changes in net worth. Mr. Kirk must have earned an additional $150,000 from unknown sources. Assuming Mr. Kirk dared not risk perjury in the divorce (by having failed to disclose a separate source of income or cash account to which only he has access), the increase in net worth must have come from somewhere. Where? We don't know for sure, of course. Likely, though, it came from unrecorded, undisclosed, and untaxed distributions from Mr. Kirk's business. If that was the case, Mr. Kirk was willing to commit federal income tax fraud to lower his child support and alimony obligations.

Problems with Cash and Cash-Based Businesses

As described in the preceding example involving Mr. Kirk, an increase in net worth over time can occur in unexplained ways. Cars, boats, and even second homes can be purchased with income obtained with secreted cash. Restaurant and bar owners, lawn-service companies, and painting and drywall subcontractors are all often paid by customers with cash, which is often not reported on tax returns. (Unfortunately, some lawyers even transact business this way.) Understanding the type of business and how it is transacted is one key to investigating an unexplained increase in net worth. Some spouses of business owners may have a clue about this tax fraud and whether it occurs on a regular basis. During the marriage, there may have been a time when cash was paid for items in the presence of the nonbusiness-owner spouse, and the owner may have even bragged about this particular shortcut "saving" money on taxes.

Your duty, as a family lawyer, is to be a zealous advocate. Nevertheless, no matter how much information you gather in an investigation—no matter how many financial statements, general ledgers, tax returns, bank statements, canceled checks, credit card statements, and receipts you obtain and analyze—some nefarious cash-based business owners will be able to get away with seriously understating their income. There are very few feelings worse for a family lawyer than walking out of a courtroom after failing to prove the opposing spouse's cash income. Working with a talented forensic accountant who can make a professional attempt at catching the cash-based business cheat means that you know you've done everything that could have been done.

Family law attorneys representing spouses of cash-based business owners not reporting all their income on tax returns must use one of the methods of imputing income, or a combination of these methods, to prove the lie. For example, like many firefighters, Mr. Goodman cuts lawns while off duty. His customers, like most lawn-cutting customers, pay in cash. If Mr. Goodman testifies that his lawn service earnings "make an extra $4,000 maximum per summer after costs," Mrs. Goodman knows this is a lie. But how can she prove the lie?

Based on some known information,[16] the forensic accountant can estimate and assume certain facts, such as assuming that an average price for lawn cutting is around $50 per lawn, that there are around 18 or so weeks of cutting time during the season (not just the summer), and that Mr. Goodman cuts around 30 lawns per week. If these assumptions are reasonable, the firefighter earns an additional $27,000 in gross income per cutting season. Estimating costs of 25 percent for assistants, gas, maintenance, and average annual equipment replacement, Mr. Goodman is left with a net income of $22,500. Combine this with Mrs. Goodman's testimony that her husband bragged about the business earning enough for him to purchase his bass boat[17] for $20,000 cash in the fall of 2009, and the forensic accountant's testimony will likely hold water.

---

16. Owners of sole proprietorships should include business operations in Schedule C of the federal income tax return. If the spouse of the business owner signed joint tax returns with the business-owner spouse and earnings were underreported, you should refer the spouse to a competent CPA or tax lawyer for advice to discuss legal obligations and opportunities for innocent spouse relief.

17. One chancellor in Shelby County, Tennessee, who is now retired often imputed overtime income to fathers for child support purposes even if there were no additional hours actually being worked because, in his words, "Fathers can work overtime or a second job in order to buy a bass boat." With a stony glare, the chancellor would then look directly at the father, pause, and ask, "Don't you agree that your children are more important than a bass boat?"

Money In and Money Out of a Business

If a business owner wants to infuse capital into a business, there are several ways to do so:

1. Contribute cash capital,
2. Transfer noncash assets as capital or as a loan, or
3. Loan the business money or repay an existing loan.

Transfers of cash are traceable among bank accounts. Transfers of noncash assets as capital or loans to the business present some challenges. Was the transfer for fair market value? During a divorce, a great way to hide personal assets may be to transfer (sell) a $35,000 car to the business, with the owner receiving only $2,000. If her business is not valued, the owner realizes an unrecorded windfall through that business. Forensic accountants know to look for transfers, sales, and related-party transactions to determine whether the deal was conducted at arm's length. The forensic accountant may be able to testify that the transfer resulted in dissipation to the marital estate.

If a business owner wants to remove cash from a business, there are a finite number of options:

1. Compensation,
2. Loan,
3. Return of capital,
4. Retained earnings distribution, or
5. Theft.

All salary or wages paid to all employees, including owners, should be recorded on a W-2, on a 1099, as a draw on a K-1, or the like. Taxes must be withheld, either as part of the regular payroll or through estimated quarterly payments.

Businesses may loan owners or employees money. It's certainly very easy for an owner to approve a personal loan or obtain permission from co-owners for that loan. Accounting for the employee loan transaction is not terribly difficult. In general, loans to owners or employees do not result in taxable income, nor are they deductible to the business.

Return of capital is also simple. For example, if an owner contributes $100,000 to begin the business and the business loses $25,000 its first year, the business still has $75,000 of owner's equity. Note that that doesn't mean there is $75,000 of cash available. If the owner withdraws $15,000 from capital and it is not compensation, the owner's equity is reduced to $60,000. Depending on the circumstances, the owner may or may not owe taxes on the return of capital.

Retained earnings is a capital account assembling an accumulation of profits. For example, if the business with $60,000 of owner's equity earns $200,000 in net profits, the total owner's equity will be increased to $260,000. Of that amount, $60,000 is in a contributed-capital account, and $200,000 is in a retained-earnings account. If the owner chooses to distribute $100,000 in earnings, it should be removed from the retained-earnings account first, and taxes may be owed as capital gain on the excess of distribution over the original amount contributed. Without question, this is a rather simplistic example. In the real world, the tax consequences of capital contributions, return of capital, and distribution of profits and the determination of whether such transactions result in taxable income can be ridiculously complex. Tax lawyers and CPAs with tax practices get to make those calls. A good first step is recognizing when you must call for help in interpreting the ramifications of these transactions.

Theft is included in this discussion as an option because it happens. Whether a restaurant owner pulls cash out of the till or a lawyer accepts a cash fee from a client and puts it in her pocket without depositing or recording it, it's all the same to the IRS and the defrauded support obligee.

There is one final aspect of money coming into and money going out of a business that you must consider. What happens if the business owner-obligor fails to take money out of the business that he could otherwise take out? Corporations pay taxes on the income when the income is realized, and owners of corporations are taxed on income when it is paid to them in the form of dividends. If the business owner is paid a low salary and does not remove profits through the salary, the corporation retains the profits and no additional tax is charged to the owner. This is sometimes referred to as excess retained earnings. By retaining the undistributed profits within the corporation, the owner can significantly understate income reported on personal tax returns as compared to what the business and the owner earn together—the real amount of income. For purposes of support, the corporate and personal income should probably be combined. In this situation, a forensic accountant can be very helpful explaining why this is so.

Reading W-2s—The Family Lawyer's Not-So-Concealed Weapon

As a family lawyer, you should love W-2s. If the business prepared them accurately, they will give you a great deal of information that opposing spouses may not want you to know. Boxes 1, 3, and 5 are the usual places you'll see critical information. To CPAs, the necessary detail is all there. To others, it's just an indecipherable mess.

In the courtroom, it can be a challenge to prove income from a W-2. The supporting spouse may assert that income should be determined from the *lesser* of the amounts shown in boxes 1, 3, and 5. Every family lawyer needs a strategy for arguing against that sort of predictable, but misleading, tactic.

What if the client can't afford to bring a forensic accountant into the courtroom to explain the W-2? Then you must be able to explain by yourself what each box means. How do you accomplish that? Know the information cold. Luckily, the IRS has given you a great tool. Every year, the IRS publishes *General Instructions for Forms W-2 and W-3*,[18] available at www.IRS.gov.[19] The 2018 version is 34 pages long. It is designed to be a simple, easy-to-read manual for accountants and bookkeepers. For family lawyers, it can be used to help identify earnings that are not taxable but that can be included for support purposes.

Okay, but what is a W-3? It is the form the employer must complete to transmit W-2s to the IRS. So you don't need to worry about W-3s.

---

18. Warning: the W-2 form itself, including its boxes and codes described herein, and its instructions are subject to change. Always work from a current set of instructions, which are updated annually. Also, there are quick reference charts at the end that are helpful to divorce lawyers who want to figure out what's what, such as the Form W-2 Reference Guide for Box 12 Codes, Form W-2 Box 13 Retirement Plan Checkbox Decision Chart, and Nonqualified Deferred Compensation Reporting Example Chart.

19. Depending on the trier of fact and your particular state's evidence law, the *Instructions* may be admissible into evidence as a public document or simply referenced in conjunction with a request that the information contained therein be accepted under judicial notice rules.

FICA, Medicare, Self-Employment Taxes, FUTA, and SUTA

The Federal Insurance Contribution Act (FICA) is financed by the Social Security tax. The Medicare tax covers the hospital insurance part. Both are major components of employment-related taxation. For employees, these taxes are withheld from each paycheck, and employers must pay their matching contributions at the same time. Although there are a few exceptions for certain types of employers and employees, everyone must pay them. The amounts paid by employees for FICA and Medicare are not reflected on the 1040 because that form calculates federal income tax due, not Social Security or Medicare tax, which presumably has been paid already through employer deductions. Self-employment (SE) tax simply refers to the self-employed person's requirement to pay Social Security and Medicare taxes, which are reconciled as part of the 1040 federal income tax return and Schedule SE. Federal unemployment tax and state unemployment tax must be paid quarterly by employers and do not result in income to employees.

Wage Base Limit

Social Security and Medicare taxes have different rates. A "wage base limit" means that only earnings up to a certain amount are taxed. The 2018 Social Security wage base limit was $128,400. Only earnings up to that amount are taxed at the 2018 rate of 6.2 percent for both the employer and employee. The Medicare rate is 1.45 percent for both the employer and employee, and all wages are taxed at that rate. Medicare does not have a wage base limit. The wage base limit increases over time, and Social Security and Medicare rates may increase as well.

Numbers, Numbers, and More Numbers—Yippee! Goody! Goody!

The following discussion refers to the various boxes on the W-2 form. A sample W-2 is, for your convenience, provided here as Example 8-1. Boxes 1, 3, and 5 are the stars of the W-2, but they do not tell the whole story. All boxes, checks, and notes are important. You can learn the shortcut for most child support calculations, but be on notice that, as

Example 8-1
Sample Form W-2

22222	a Employee's social security number	OMB No. 1545-0008	
b Employer identification number (EIN)		1 Wages, tips, other compensation	2 Federal income tax withheld
c Employer's name, address, and ZIP code		3 Social security wages	4 Social security tax withheld
		5 Medicare wages and tips	6 Medicare tax withheld
		7 Social security tips	8 Allocated tips
d Control number		9 Verification code	10 Dependent care benefits
e Employee's first name and initial Last name Suff.		11 Nonqualified plans	12a Code
		13 Statutory employee / Retirement plan / Third-party sick pay	12b Code
		14 Other	12c Code
			12d Code
f Employee's address and ZIP code			

15 State Employer's state ID number	16 State wages, tips, etc.	17 State income tax	18 Local wages, tips, etc.	19 Local income tax	20 Locality name

Form **W-2** **Wage and Tax Statement** 2018 Department of the Treasury—Internal Revenue Service

Copy 1—For State, City, or Local Tax Department

with most shortcuts, taking it can cause embarrassment (and loss) if you don't know the details and applicable exceptions along the way.

The shortcut? For most states, income determination for child support is usually based on gross earnings and includes retirement contributions made by the employee. The shortcut begins with income listed in box 5 and adds retirement contributions found in a coded message in box 12 when box 13—Retirement Plan—is checked. How do you crack the IRS code? Simple. You read the W-2 notes on the back of the form and double-check them against the IRS's *General Instructions for Forms W-2 and W-3*. The shortcut assumes there are no other adjustments needed to determine income. Do not trust the shortcut. Study every form.

Below is a condensed summary of the information contained on the W-2 form:

Box a—Employee's Social Security number.
Box b—Employer identification number.
Box c—Employer's name, address, and ZIP code.
Box d—Control number—ignore.
Boxes e and f—Employee's name and address.

Box 1—"Wages, tips, and other compensation" shows the total taxable wages, tips, and other compensation (before deductions) paid to the employee during the year. It does not include elective deferrals. An employee's contributions to a SIMPLE retirement account are not included in box 1 because they are not subject to federal income tax, but these contributions are subject to FICA and Medicare taxes, which means they are included in boxes 3 and 5.

Box 2—"Federal income tax withheld."

Box 3—"Social Security wages" shows the total wages paid (before deductions) subject to employee Social Security tax but not including Social Security tips (in box 7) and allocated tips. Boxes 3 and 7 should not be used to calculate child support because the amount shown is subject to the wage base limit. The total of boxes 3 and 7 cannot exceed $128,400 (2018 maximum Social Security wage base limit), even if earnings are greater than that amount.

Box 4—"Social Security tax withheld" shows total employee Social Security tax withheld, including Social Security tax on tips.

Box 5—"Medicare wages and tips" shows the amount subject to Medicare tax. This involves the same wages as those subject to Social Security tax (boxes 3 and 7), except that there is no wage base limit for Medicare tax. This is the most thorough listing of income.

Box 6—"Medicare tax withheld" shows the total employee Medicare tax withheld.

Box 7—"Social Security tips" is a special category and is used in conjunction with box 3 for wage base limit calculation.

Box 8—"Allocated tips" for food or beverage establishments.

Box 9—"Verification code"—ignore.

Box 10—"Dependent care benefit" shows the total dependent care benefits under a dependent-care assistance program.

Box 11—"Nonqualified plans" shows if any part of the amount reported in box 1 or boxes 3 and/or 5 was earned in a prior year.

Boxes 12(a) through 12(d)—Codes. The IRS designates letter codes for certain items, followed by the dollar amount for that item. No dollar signs or commas are used. For example, if the employer is reporting $5,300 in elective deferrals under a

Section 401(k) plan, the entry would be "D 5300." Refer to the *General Instructions* for explanations of codes.

Box 13—Checkboxes. "Retirement plan" is checked if the employee was an "active participant" for any part of the year in any of the following:

1. Qualified pension, profit-sharing, or stock-bonus plan described in Section 401(a) (including a 401(k) plan);
2. Annuity plan described in Section 403(a);
3. Annuity contract or custodial account described in Section 403(b);
4. SEP plan described in Section 408(k);
5. SIMPLE retirement account described in Section 408(p);
6. Trust described in Section 501(c)(18);
7. Plan for federal, state, or local government employees or an agency or instrumentality thereof (other than a Section 457(b) plan).

Box 14—"Other." If the employee's perks included 100 percent of a vehicle's annual lease value in the employee's income, it must also be reported here or on a separate statement to the employee. Check your state's child support guidelines to see if this is includable in gross income.

Fringe Benefits—All taxable fringe benefits should appear in box 1 of Form W-2 as wages, tips, and other compensation and, if applicable, in boxes 3 and 5 as Social Security and Medicare wages. If there is a car lease, however, it may appear in box 14.

Golden Parachute Payments should be included in boxes 1, 3, and 5 of Form W-2.

Group Term Life Insurance—If the employer paid for group term life insurance over $50,000 for the employee or a former employee, the employer must report the taxable cost of excess coverage, determined by using a separate table. The amount should also be shown in box 12 with Code C.

Health Savings Account (HSA)—Depending on the circumstances, an employer's contribution to an employee's HSA may not be subject to federal income tax withholding, Social Security, or Medicare, but it may still be gross income under a particular state's child support guidelines.

SIMPLE Retirement Account—An employee's salary-reduction contributions to a SIMPLE retirement account are not subject to federal income tax withholding but are subject to Social Security, Medicare, and railroad retirement taxes. This means the amount contributed is not included in box 1 but is included in boxes 3 and 5. An employee's total contribution must also be included in box 12 with Code D or S.

Note that some employers may make unintentional errors. If reading the W-2 instructions makes your head bleed internally, it will have the same effect on some bookkeepers, accountants, and CPAs, too. A computerized tax program generates most W-2 forms, and if the numbers were entered or coded ever so slightly incorrectly, a W-2 could be completely wrong. If an employer later discovers an error, the employer is required to resubmit corrected forms to the employee and IRS.

Checklist of Other Income Issues to Discuss with the Forensic Accountant

1. **Capital gains.** Selling assets prior to a divorcing year can inflate earnings. States' divorce law vary widely on this topic.
2. **Depreciation.** Your state's child support guidelines may exclude depreciation. Also, check case law. With depreciation concerns, case law can be complicated and inconsistent, leaving the crafty and detailed-oriented family law attorney room to argue either side of this issue.
3. **Fluctuating income.** How many years' income should you average? Two? Three? Five? Also, pay attention to the length of and period when time stock options were earned versus tax years exercised. Forensic accountants can help the family lawyer determine the best arguments in the client's favor.
4. **Gifts.** Gifts are always tricky. In your state, can systemic gifts from an affluent spouse's parent be income for support purposes? How about the Mercedes as a Christmas gift?
5. **Recognized income but not realized.** Sometimes there is pass-through income from an S corporation or a partnership. What about forgiveness of debt that is taxable income but is not actual cash flow?

Case Example: Imputing Income of a Business Owner by Adding Expenses

When a former spouse who controls 100 percent of a company is seeking monthly spousal support modification, start by looking at their personal expenses paid by that business in order to determine income.

The husband and wife in this California divorce case[20] were married in 1984 and separated in 2005, after which time the husband petitioned for dissolution. The trial court appointed forensic accountant Brian Brinig as a special master to determine the husband's income and the value of his businesses. In 2007, the court ordered the joinder of the husband's father, who was a resident of Bulgaria and owned businesses allegedly connected with those of the husband.

The wife estimated the husband's income at about $60,000 per month based on the couple's personal expenses while living together. The husband, however,

20. Andrew v. Andrew, No. D052299 (Cal. Ct. App. Sep. 24, 2009).

painted a much bleaker picture, claiming that his businesses were not making money and that all his money came from shareholder loans or from his father. His income and expense declaration claimed only $1,965 in gross monthly income, with almost $10,000 in monthly expenses.

The special master, Brinig, gave his initial opinion, based upon financial statements by the husband's accountant, that the husband had a monthly net income of over $12,000 in 2004, about $8,600 in 2005, and approximately negative $5,000 for the first nine months of 2006.

The wife offered the expert opinion of CPA Dennis Pearson. According to Pearson's investigation, the husband had set up three businesses, allegedly owned by the elderly father in Bulgaria, and these affiliated businesses were used to underestimate the income of the husband's businesses and funnel money back to the husband in the form of ostensible loans. Pearson estimated that the husband's true income between 2003 and 2006 amounted to $28,700 per month. Pearson also criticized the bookkeeping done by the husband's accountant as poorly prepared.

The trial court held that the husband had complete control over both his businesses and those owned by the father in Bulgaria. It also noted that the husband's businesses had paid over $80,000 in personal expenses, amounting to about $11,400 per month in additional income.

The husband's income was inconsistent with the income and expense declarations he had produced. After examining all the evidence, the trial court decided the husband had income of at least $22,000 per month and used that figure to calculate the award of spousal support. The husband then appealed. The wife first moved to dismiss the appeal on the grounds that the husband had failed to comply with many of the orders of the lower court. However, the appeals court noted that these were primarily the orders he sought to be reviewed and allowed the appeal to go forward.

On his appeal, the husband first argued that the declaration of the wife's expert, Pearson, should not have been considered. The husband argued that Pearson had relied upon the draft report of special master Brinig, which had ultimately been excluded.

However, the appeals court pointed out that the lower court had not even cited Pearson's report in its statement of decision. Instead, the lower court stated that it had relied upon the documents that the husband had produced, on his inconsistent income and expenses, and on the fact that he had been able to make payments to his own attorney.

Even if Pearson had relied upon Brinig's report, his testimony would have been proper, since Evidence Code section 801, like the corresponding federal rule, allows an expert to rely on inadmissible evidence if it is the type that reasonably may be relied upon in forming an opinion. For these reasons, there had been no error due to Pearson's declaration.

The husband also argued that he was denied the opportunity to cross-examine Pearson. However, he had failed to preserve the point, since he had never made a request to offer this oral testimony.

After addressing other issues in the case, the appeals court considered the wife's motion for sanctions for a frivolous appeal. The appeals court did concede that the appeal lacked all merit and that the husband had a history of causing delay. But even though it called the case a "close call," it declined to impose sanctions. For these reasons, the court of appeals affirmed the lower court's orders.

Case Example: Methodology, Income Determination, and Challenging Qualification as an Expert

Thirty years as a CPA is usually going to be enough to be qualified as an expert witness for income determination battles, even if the proffered financial expert has never testified before. Before challenging an expert witness's qualification, obtain the expert's curriculum vitae. Talk with your client's expert. Make sure that your challenge is in the record, or it will be waived on appeal.

Methodology matters. Make sure the expert can "show her work." If your client's expert can't explain the methodology in direct and simple terms, there could be a major problem.

The mother and father in this Arizona child support modification case[21] had three minor children at the time of their 2000 divorce. The father had been ordered to pay $1,529 per month in child support. In 2012, he made a petition to modify his child support because one of the children had turned 18 and graduated from high school. The mother asked the court to appoint a federally authorized tax practitioner to determine the father's income, and the father countered with a request that one be appointed to assist in determining the income of both parties.

The trial court appointed Steve Adelson, CPA, to evaluate the income and business profits of both parties, as well as to determine the mother's interest in any sole proprietorship or corporation. In 2013, Adelson provided his report, and the mother filed a motion to preclude Adelson's report or testimony. The trial court denied the mother's motion. Both parties, as well as Adelson, testified. The father testified that he had an ownership interest in several businesses, although most of them did not generate income. The mother testified that she worked at a business known as "First Kiss" but that her current husband had taken it over. She also claimed that the business had not been profitable.

Adelson attributed over $11,000 per month income to the father and $5,500 per month to the mother. The trial court accepted these figures and modified the father's child support down to $245 per month. The court also awarded the father $23,000 in attorney's fees. The mother appealed.

The mother's first argument was that the lower court had erred in both admitting and relying upon Adelson's testimony and report. Trial courts have broad discretion in admitting expert testimony. The mother's argument was that Adelson was not a "federally authorized tax practitioner" within the meaning of an Arizona statute authorizing such an appointment in the case of a self-employed parent. However, the appeals court quickly dismissed this argument, since the mother had failed to raise it in a timely fashion in the lower court. For that reason, the appeals court considered the issue waived.

The mother next argued that it was an error to allow Adelson to testify as an expert witness under Rule of Evidence 702. That rule, like the corresponding federal rule, allows one who is an expert by knowledge, skill, experience, training, or education to offer opinion testimony.

21. Shano v. Shano, No. 1 CA-CV 14-0055 (Ariz. Ct. App. Nov. 13, 2014).

Trial courts have considerable discretion, and an expert's qualification should be construed liberally. This is especially true in a nonjury case, since it is presumed that the trial judge disregarded all inadmissible evidence.

Here, the appeals court noted that Adelson had been a CPA for approximately 30 years and noted that this experience was one of the factors that could properly be considered. The lower court had especially relied upon his expertise and familiarity with IRS policies and the accounting principles for sub-S corporations such as the one at issue in the case. The appeals court noted that the trial court had the opportunity to observe Adelson's demeanor and had "obviously found him competent and reliable."

The record supported the court's reliance on Adelson's opinions. Adelson had attended the depositions, visited the father's business, conducted interviews, and reviewed financial records. He had also consulted with the person who prepared the father's tax returns. Adelson testified that his methodology followed standard accounting principles and IRS audit procedures.

When determining the father's monthly income, Adelson had started with the W-2 income and divided it by 12. He then added $2,500 per month to reflect the fact that the business paid some of the father's personal expenses.

When it came to the mother's income, Adelson had less to work with, since he found that there was very little substantiation. In addition, he found that source documents were lacking or had been purposely shredded. He expressed the opinion that much of her cash business had not been properly recorded and was understated. He testified that all her business tax returns showed material omissions and missing entries. Aldelson testified that some of the basic documentation required to prepare a tax return had not even been created. Due to these problems, he calculated her income by looking at the gross income of the business. He then attributed 20 percent of the profits as the mother's personal income. This methodology was consistent with IRS guidelines.

The lower court had "obviously disbelieved" the mother's claims as to her finances. The contradictory nature of the mother's evidence also led the appeals court to affirm the award of attorney's fees to the father. Therefore, it affirmed all the lower court's orders.

Case Example: Daubert *Challenge in Divorce with Law Firm Business Valuation*

In a 2008 Texas divorce,[22] the property division was held to be manifestly unjust. The main issue was valuation of the husband's partnership interest in a patent law firm. The court provided a detailed *Daubert* discussion on law firm valuation methodology.

When a forensic accountant utilizes any particular methodology, the methodology may never be challenged. Some opinion testimony may often seem so basic as to be "A + B = C." But the family lawyer and the expert witness must always be mindful that, if the particular methodology is challenged, it is wise to be able to discuss the source of that methodology going back to (1) an appellate opinion, (2) a published book on the subject, (3) a

22. Von Hohn v. Von Hohn, No. 12-06-00265-CV (Tex. Ct. App. July 23, 2008).

published article, (4) seminar or conference training, or (5) some other reliable source.[23]

This couple was married in 1997 and had two children; the wife filed for divorce in 2004. Their separation agreement resolved all issues but division of community property and, specifically, valuation of the husband's law partnership interest in Nix, Patterson & Roach (NPR).

When the attorney husband signed the NPR partnership agreement, he received units of participation, undivided profits, and a capital account. The partnership agreement included a formula to calculate his interest upon death, retirement, withdrawal, or expulsion from NPR, but not upon divorce.

The wife's forensic accounting expert was James C. Penn. The trial court excluded some, but not all, of Penn's testimony, allowing acceptable valuation methods outside the partnership agreement. For income methodology purposes, the trial court set a two-year limit on the husband's future NPR earnings. The jury valued his NPR interest at $4.5 million, taxable. The husband appealed.

He contended the trial court erred by not excluding Penn's expert testimony. He challenged Penn's lack of patent case valuation experience and Penn's six statements at the hearing on the wife's motion for additional discovery. He argued Penn was unqualified to testify as an expert under Tex. R. Evid. 702 and that the forensic accountant's opinion was based upon "unreliable methods, analysis, and principles." The husband also contended there was no evidence that Penn's methodology had been used by other valuation experts. The court affirmed, holding no abuse of discretion in allowing Penn to testify as an expert.

Penn's reliance on the special master's findings regarding range of NPR's "case values, settlements, and potential settlements" did not render the testimony unreliable. Although Penn had never used a patent case in law firm valuation, the "specific issue in this case was valuation of a partner's interest in a law firm, for which Penn had specialized knowledge, skill, experience, training, or education."[24]

The court referenced *Daubert* and six key factors in the threshold question of an expert's qualification under Rule 702. The *Daubert* test

---

23. Family lawyers and forensic accountants should keep (and organize) all seminar, conference, and continuing legal education materials for possible future reference especially on topics such as forensic accounting and business valuation.
24. Citing Broders v. Heise, 924 S.W.2d 148 (Tex. 1996).

was originally used by the courts to determine whether expert testimony passed muster under Federal Rule of Evidence 702. Texas and other states also apply the *Daubert* test, or a modified version thereof, in qualifying a witness as an expert.

Each *Daubert* inquiry is tied to the unique facts of the case. During the *Daubert* hearing, Penn stated he "had been an expert witness for a professional business valuation about 75 to 100 times." His curriculum vitae listed seminar speaking engagements on "valuations, commercial and personal goodwill, and business valuation of a partner's interest in a law firm." He had testified regarding "valuation of a partnership interest using the income approach and had relied on the types of projections used here in valuing a contingency fee practice in Dallas."

The husband challenged Penn's stated need for someone to review NPR's open case files to provide a range of anticipated case settlement values and estimated settlement timeframes. A special master was appointed to give a "range of potential settlements." Penn also testified to relying on an expert report with documents provided by David William Carstens, patent attorney.

In *Daubert* challenges to accounting-related testimony, courts will value testimony of methodology having been used in prior valuations of the subject business interest and industry. At the *Daubert* hearing, Penn rejected the asset approach, adopting the income methodology as more accurate for professional practices. Importantly, Penn testified in a divorce five years prior wherein he and the opposing forensic accounting expert used the same income approach to value an NPR partnership interest.

The trial court granted the husband's motion in part, concluding there are other acceptable valuation methods beyond the partnership agreement formula. However, the trial court allowed Penn to testify at trial using withdrawal value, asset approach, or income approach with a two-year future income limit. Penn used the income approach. The court found no error in the trial court's admission of Penn's valuation of the husband's NPR partnership interest.

The husband next contended the trial court erred in not using the partnership agreement to restrict valuation of commercial goodwill. The value of personal goodwill is the separate property of the professional spouse, but the value of commercial goodwill in a professional practice is a divisible community asset. Given that valuation methods other than the partnership agreement are proper, the jury could consider the value of the community's interest in any NPR commercial goodwill. The court held that the NPR "partnership agreement does not control the value of the individual partnership interests in the event of a divorce" when the husband was a partner, had not withdrawn, and had no plans to withdraw. No event triggered termination of the husband's partnership. Therefore, the partnership agreement's formula was not determinative of his interest. The trial court did not err in adding different valuation methods to NPR's formula.

The court did reverse the trial court's property division because the husband's future earnings were improperly included in Penn's NPR valuation. Future earnings are a spouse's separate property and are not divisible in divorce.

In applying the income approach, Penn included commercial goodwill (excluded personal goodwill) and income reasonably expected to be collected by NPR in the next two years. However, the forensic accountant attempted to "normalize" NPR income occurring in the future by using historical operations data, deducting for nonrecurring events along with partner compensation and "Data Treasury case income." Normalizing income means projecting an amount of income by making certain assumptions and adjustments to expenses. This is to prevent a resulting income amount from the business owner running unusual or inappropriate expenses through the business.

Making assumptions and taking into consideration several other factors, Penn valued the husband's interest in the Data Treasury case at $4.1 million. If all pending Data Treasury cases settled in the next two years, then the husband's interest amount would increase by another $2.2 million. From this testimony, the jury concluded that the husband's NPR interest had a value of $4.5 million, subject to taxes.

Future earnings cannot be used in valuing the husband's NPR interest. The court held that because NPR had received no money from the "pending but unsettled Data Treasury cases[, revenue] from these cases is no more than an expectancy interest and any money to be received constitutes future earnings to which [the wife] was not entitled." There was no evidentiary basis for the jury's findings of a $4.5 million value. The case was reversed and remanded on that issue. Because the jury could not have concluded the husband's partnership interest was valued at $4.5 million, the property division was manifestly unjust and the entire community estate was remanded for new division.

Lifestyle Analysis 9

A lifestyle analysis can be one of the most powerful advocacy tools available to a family lawyer. With this tool, you and your forensic accountant can, working together, prove how the parties lived together in the past and how they might live apart in the future. With a little creativity, the lifestyle analysis can incorporate almost all of the applicable statutory financial factors for support. There is no other tool just like it.

"Beyond the issue of support and the cost of the lifestyle of the parties, the Lifestyle Analysis can be used to uncover evidence of hidden income and assets," offers forensic accountant Tracy Coenen, CPA, CFF.[1] "It can be used to refute claims of reduced income. It can help identify non-marital spending that may become part of a dissipation claim."

---

1. Tracy L. Coenen, CPA, CFF, practices as a forensic accountant in Milwaukee and Chicago. She has personally investigated hundreds of frauds in a wide variety of industries. Her work includes fraud examinations and financial investigations in cases of embezzlement, financial statement fraud, investment fraud, divorce and family law, and insurance fraud. Tracy has served as an expert witness in numerous cases in state and federal courts. To learn more about her practice, visit www.SequenceInc.com. Quotes used in the text are from personal correspondence with the author.

For additional reference, consider purchasing *Lifestyle Analysis in Divorce Cases: Investigating Spending and Finding Hidden Income and Assets*[2] by Coenen. *Lifestyle Analysis* is written in a manner that is logical and easy to understand, bringing clarity to a topic that can be confusing for attorneys, judges, and juries who often lack backgrounds in accounting or finance. The book begins with a discussion of the critical factors to use when analyzing a couple's standard of living, followed by a discussion about the various types of income and why they should be either included or excluded from calculations in a family law case.

For family lawyers, "support" encompasses temporary support, child support, and alimony. Thus, this chapter pulls together many of the concepts discussed earlier. Proving one spouse's need and the other's ability to pay support is always challenging. Almost all states with statutory factors for alimony seem to include ubiquitous concerns, such as education, age, length of marriage, earnings history, and earnings capacity. In reality, most courts will consider almost any fact if it deals with the parties' lifestyle in the present, past, or future. The lifestyle analysis is indeed a powerful tool, but it is, nevertheless, only one of the tools you can use in building your overall support argument.

This chapter begins with a discussion of the five quadrants. It then presents a sample lifestyle analysis and concludes with a discussion of double-dipping.

The Five Quadrants

Even in simple divorces, the mass of financial information with which you're faced can be overwhelming. Breaking down the analysis of this information into four manageable quadrants, or boxes, can help focus your efforts. Each quadrant is a function of one of the parties in conjunction with that party's income or expenses. These four quadrants are the supporting spouse's income, supported spouse's income, supporting spouse's expenses, and supported spouse's expenses. Each quadrant involves a unique set of meaningful documents, facts, and testimony.

2. As a practicing divorce lawyer, the author has had several opportunities to reference *Lifestyle Analysis*. It is clean, concise, and authoritative, and the Author highly recommends this book to anyone looking to learn the "tricks of the trade." Whether it's discussing hidden assets, hidden income, or tips for reading tax returns, this book is well worth the time it takes to read it. Every serious family lawyer must own this book. It is available for purchase on Amazon.

Key documents will be the parties' statements of income and expenses, tax returns, financial statements, W-2s, bank statements, canceled checks, and credit card statements—the usual stuff. In addition to the four quadrants, an overarching concern for all family lawyers is credibility—which can be considered as an extra or fifth quadrant.

By breaking down the quadrants and looking at each separately, you can focus your efforts on those arguments most likely to succeed. If you're representing the obligor spouse, for instance, you will first consider challenging the credibility of the obligee spouse, arguing that she has understated income and/or overstated expenses. To effectively do this, you must develop a sound strategy. But you must, at the same time, prepare to defend your client against similar challenges.

	Supporting Spouse	**Supported Spouse**
Income	I. Omitted income? Understated? Imputed income? Voluntarily unemployed? Underemployed?	II. Omitted income? Understated? Imputed income? Voluntarily unemployed? Underemployed?
Expenses	III. Overstated?	IV. Overstated?

Quadrants One and Two

Quadrants one and two involve questioning the other side's claimed income. Like many aspects of family law, challenges made against understated income must be measured and tempered. If you're not careful, some arguments can backfire against your client. For example, when the other party has, during discovery, claimed an amount of income that is greater than what can be proven, leave it alone. Otherwise, your opponent may realize the overstatement and seek to correct it during the hearing. Possibly the deadliest type of backfire can occur when a financial argument is inconsistent with a theme or theory of the case. For example, if, as part of the custody dispute, an obligor spouse argues that the obligee spouse is mentally ill, the obligor spouse can be stuck with that argument when trying to argue that the obligee spouse is underemployed. Mentally ill persons don't generally earn to their full potential.

When challenging claimed income, you should always make sure all sources of income are listed. For example, are interest and dividends listed? Have long-term stock incentives been included? Were any bonuses received? Untaxed income or expense reimbursements should be accounted for, as should imputed income. Was there any underreported income from a cash-based business or a recent salary increase reflected on recent pay stubs that did not appear on last year's W-2? And as always, you must check your opposing party's math. If the obligor spouse is paid every two weeks, did opposing counsel base the stated monthly income on 24 pay periods, when the obligor spouse is actually paid 26 times a year? If you prove enough omissions, misstatements, and mistakes, the court's skepticism can be transformed into intemperance.

Quadrants Three and Four

Quadrants three and four involve challenges to expenses. If you're challenging the other spouse's expenses, you can choose one of three common strategies for the attack:

1. Challenging overall total expenses,
2. Challenging individual listed expense categories, or
3. Making no challenge at all.

Challenging overall expenses is difficult. Most lawyers will do this, if at all, in argument or as commentary. In fact, making no challenge may make sense if you know the opposing party has actually understated expenses. When this happens, discretion is the better part of valor.

Challenging individual expense categories is the most common technique used by family lawyers. For example, suppose an opposing party has claimed the following monthly expenses:

Automobile expenses	\$450
Household expenses	\$950
Groceries	\$750
Pool maintenance	\$695

There are a number of questions you need to ask regarding these claimed expenses.

Regarding the automobile expenses, do they include car payments? Did they anticipate the cost of gasoline, oil changes, and maintenance? How old is the car? Is it under warranty? Does this amount include anticipated repair? If not, is \$450 overstated? Next, what specific types of expenses are covered in the category of household expenses? Are most of these incurred at a store like Walmart? What do the monthly credit card charges add up to for Walmart? What are the charges for Target? For groceries, how many persons are covered by \$750 per month? Is eating out included? Are work lunches included? Finally, for pool maintenance, was the overall cost divided by 12 months or just 3?

All these questions can help put expenses into context for that person, the children, and the overall case. If a spouse makes a mistake and overstates just one category, his credibility may not be greatly damaged. But overstate enough categories, and the court's disbelief may transform into intemperance.

Courts also understand gross overspending for a particular income range. For example, a spouse earning under $100,000 per year should probably not be leasing a brand-new Mercedes SL 500 to the tune of $850 per month. But courts would not have the same problem if the spouse were earning $500,000 a year. Similarly, the noncustodial parent should probably not be taking the kids on spring break to Disneyland during litigation and sticking all the expenses on a credit card.

The Fifth Quadrant—Credibility

Credibility gets its own quadrant because, if a spouse loses credibility at even one hearing, the entire case may be lost. Courts expect candor, and courts expect spouses to be able to explain simple and routine documents, such as tax returns, W-2s, K-1s, pay stubs, or expense reimbursements. Some spouses may understand these documents, but many can't put them into context as part of the overall case. And for others, even though they can understand the documents and can articulate their meaning, nothing they say in the courtroom is credible due to their demeanor, be it arrogance, condescension, or an overwhelming sense of entitlement.

Attacks on credibility come in two sizes. The first attack is proving the "big lie," such as omitting a major source of income such as a bonus or stock option. The second attack is proving smaller lies by assembling a "bricks in the wall" series of small misstatements, errors, and omissions. In court, sometimes it's just too easy for a spouse to admit an error or omission and claim that it was a mistake. If you can catch the opposing spouse on cross-examination making enough errors and omissions, you can build a wall from these small bricks, one brick at a time. To destroy the spouse's credibility, you need enough bricks to show there are just too many mistakes, leading to the inevitable conclusion that he intended to lie.

Some support cases are lost because there is never enough time to cover all the angles with the client. Even the most competent, thorough, and conscientious lawyer cannot escape the occasional loss that could have been prevented by spending just a little more time with the client explaining how all the pieces fit together. Sometimes pouring over the numbers and explaining what they mean in the context of the hearing can make the difference between winning and losing. This can cause any family lawyer to lose sleep at night. When is enough preparation ever really enough?

Expense Time Periods

Unless an income and expense statement expressly states which, there are three possible time periods for each individual expense item:

1. Pre-separation (or pre-filing),
2. Post-separation through divorce, and
3. Post-divorce projected need.

Upon questioning, some testifying spouses can't keep straight which expenses relate to which time periods. Because there are often no strict instructions by courts to list the three categories separately, some testifying spouses lose the ability to explain them. The stress of the courtroom can be overwhelming. You must help your clients keep straight applicable time periods for expenses and be prepared to attack opposing spouses who don't.

The pre-separation period, or pre-filing period, involves the historical lifestyle of the parties. But with every divorce, there is the age-old conflict between the historical lifestyle statutory factor and the financial reality of divorce. Two households cannot be run as affluently as the one was. After separation, there will be two residences, each with mortgages or rents, utility bills, cable bills, furniture and appliances, and appliance repair and maintenance. The list of doubled expenses can be long. This conflict is never easily reconciled. Following a 25-year marriage, if the affluent breadwinner continues to earn at a traditional pace, why should the supported spouse lower her standard of living just because a 24-year-old secretary drew her husband's eye? On the other hand, does the ditched spouse have a right to live on Easy Street if that ditched spouse can work? Inequities happen. Regardless of whether a situation is fair, you must put on evidence and advocate for your client's interests. The historical spending is a fact with which you must deal.

For the time period immediately following filing for divorce until the divorce is granted, spending should be frugal. Spouses who are not frugal can lose credibility. All courts have seen supported spouses lavishly spend money to punish the other spouse. If an angry spouse purchases a new SUV or quits a job within a week or two of hiring the divorce lawyer, then that spouse should expect a very tough cross-examination on the soundness of those decisions. If a spouse finds a new intimate friend, no one is surprised by a new gym membership, hair club membership, or lingerie purchases. But buying expensive gifts for the new love interest may not be viewed with as much understanding. In the end, however, both spouses will be judged against the overall asset and income picture. The spouse earning $500,000 per year with no debt may have less to answer for when purchasing $20,000 of gifts for the new love interest than will the obligor spouse earning $100,000 per year with lots of debt.

Post-divorce projected need is viewed in very practical terms. Will the oldest daughter need orthodontia next fall? If so, what is the down payment and monthly financing option? Can the parties continue to keep all the children in private schools? Once the children are all gone, what is a reasonable overall monthly need for travel? Should the eight-year-old SUV be replaced with a new SUV? What annual mortgage principal, interest, insurance, and tax payments are reasonable for a recently divorced obligor earning $125,000 per year following a 22-year marriage with two kids still in school? Just because someone always traveled and "summered" at a luxury resort doesn't mean that tradition can continue. The practical expenses of food, shelter, and clothing are looked at differently from the discretionary expenses of vacations and new cars.

The Lifestyle Analysis

In a lifestyle analysis report, the forensic accountant gives the family lawyer ammunition for arguments regarding the appropriate level of future support. Utilizing the power of databases and spreadsheets, the forensic accountant creates the lifestyle analysis framework to analyze many variables. Then the accountant adds one or both parties' projected earnings and investment income to start an analysis of the obligee's need and the obligor's ability to pay. The forensic accountant can also include assets and debts, such as the investment portfolio, credit card debt repayment, prospective current home sale, new home purchases, rental property earnings, stock options, and projected retirement assets contributions, earnings, and distributions.

The forensic accountant's next job is to quantify both spouses' reasonable need. In general, there are two ways to accomplish this. One is to analyze historical expenses (possibly from the detailed transaction listing). The other is to work only with estimated projected or budgeted needs as presented by the spouses. For the accountant working for the obligor spouse, this may mean starting with the expenses listed in discovery and then making adjustments. Follow-up questions may be asked at deposition. For the accountant working for the obligee spouse, the forensic accountant can read the discovery as well and interview the spouse.

If the forensic accountant is relying on historical data, one of the first issues will be how far back in the past to look. The CPA needs to consider available and relevant data. If the CPA has five years of complete financial information, does the forensic accountant use all of it? Two months of it? An opposing lawyer or forensic accountant could criticize these time periods as being either too long or too short. Judgment comes into play here. Most forensic accountants would prefer to analyze a minimum of two years' worth of data. Three years is probably on the longer end of the spectrum, but it depends, of course, on the individual facts of the case, including stability and continuity. Have the parties lived in the same house in the same city for several years? Was there a recent promotion altering the parties' lifestyle? Did the parties overspend in 2016 and then reach an agreement to cut back in 2017? As few as six months of historical financial information could be sufficient. In deciding how much time is appropriate for consideration, you should rely on the forensic accountant's determination as to what will constitute sufficient reliable data.

If the forensic accountant will not be relying on historical data, he must consider the client's ability to estimate past and projected expenses. In addition to an interview or deposition, the accountant should take the extra step of performing a "sanity check." Sanity checks involve looking at numbers in the context of the overall picture. As an extreme example, say the supported spouse claims an estimated future need of $460 per month for pool repair, maintenance, upkeep, chemicals, and cleaning but will not likely receive over $1,600 per month in child support, alimony, and earnings. Considering the anticipated revenue and other projected expenses, the pool expense appears unrealistic. On the other hand, if the supported spouse is remaining in the marital residence by agreement, that may present a different situation. Certainly, no forensic accountant wants to act as a financial advisor and dictate to a client that spending is way out of line, especially if the parties always had a pool. The lawyer, client, and forensic accountant must all be prepared for questions on cross-examination about financial realities. For the sanity check, the forensic accountant will review and consider many, if not all, of the documents in the case, including discovery, personal financial program reports from Quicken or QuickBooks, tax returns, business expense reimbursements, debt structure, financial planning, and anticipated future mortgage expenses. The accountant must exercise independent judgment and should never issue a report based on anything that is implausible, even if the lawyer (or client) demands it.

The forensic accountant must also adjust for nonrecurring income and expenses. One-time income hits, such as the largest commission in the breadwinner's career, may need to be eliminated from the analysis. Nonrecurring expenses can include orthodontia, college tuition, a bar mitzvah, large equipment purchases for the business, appliances, or major home renovations. Basing an analysis on figures including such nonrecurring income or expenses can result in the court rejecting the entire testimony and report.

The overall organization of expenses should comply with applicable state case law, state rules, and/or local rules. The court will be most comfortable seeing the analysis in the format that particular judge is used to seeing. New Jersey uses a case information statement with an explicit and detailed format. New York has a statement of net worth. In Cook County, Illinois, it's called a disclosure statement. Each categorizes expenses differently.

What about borrowing and savings? Some cases are difficult because the couple lived lavishly, charging that luxury on credit cards. Most judges will expect expense projections to be based upon sustainable and realistic income levels, even if the couple did not live that way during the marriage. Another tough situation the forensic accountant may face is the frugal couple who spent very little compared to income. State laws on savings and long-term support differ among jurisdictions. In California, when the supporting spouse consistently earned greater than the parties' spending, the supported spouse can include as part of the reasonable need a level of savings consistent with the parties' marital history. In Florida, the savings component is generally excluded.

In planning the engagement, there are several big-picture decisions. Will the forensic accountant consider all assets and debts, such as the parties' investment portfolio, retirement asset contributions and distributions, and debt repayment? If so, the analysis can become fairly complex. The forensic accountant may need to project a particular proposed property division in order to properly account for projected investment earnings and debt repayment.

Next, if the analysis considers future earnings, savings, investment returns, cost of living adjustments, and the like, will the forensic accountant opine about an expected net worth through retirement? Even when the supported spouse receives a roughly equal property distribution and significant alimony, in most cases the supporting spouse's future earnings will cause a significantly higher net worth at retirement than the supported spouse's. As an advocacy tool, the benefit to the supported spouse is directly proportional to the forensic accountant's ability to present a clear, concise, and understandable analysis.

Then the family lawyer and forensic accountant may need to determine the expected future earnings of the supported spouse. Is the supported spouse expected to work? What if the supported spouse has been a stay-at-home parent with no meaningful earnings history? What if the supported spouse can attend college, complete some training, and within a year or so become self-supporting? What if that level of self-supporting income can be achieved with some level of retraining or recertification? At the end of this education, retraining, or time period for re-entry into the workforce, what can the supported spouse earn? Does the forensic accountant have the expertise needed to opine about the supported spouse's future earnings? If not, the forensic accountant may need to rely on the opinion of a vocational expert. The goal is to offer admissible and credible evidence of the supported spouse's earning capacity.

What Family Lawyers Should Know about Vocational Experts

Vocational experts can have many career titles. Family lawyers in need of this sort of testimony should look for expert witnesses who have experience testifying regarding earning capacity. That testimony need not be limited to family law. In fact, most vocational experts' experience may come in other areas of law, such as employment law, personal injury, or workman's compensation cases. For vocational experts, undergraduate- and graduate-level degrees, experience, and certifications vary widely. Some may work full time with colleges. Others may have niche practices in which all their cases are litigation related. Selecting the right vocational expert can be time consuming.[3]

3. Practice tip: Research and learn about vocational experts in your area well in advance of needing to hire one. Like forensic accountants, not all experts (and

Typically, a vocational expert will meet and interview a spouse, take a history, and perform testing. The spouse's educational history, grades, and interests are important. Testing can include interests and aptitude. At some point in the process, the vocational expert usually begins to see a particular employment path. For example, if the spouse finished an undergraduate degree in education, the logical progression includes determining teaching employment objectives and certification needs. In other cases, when the spouse has no idea what employment makes the most sense, the vocational expert may determine core skills and then consider interests. At the end of the process, the vocational expert forms an opinion on the subject's projected earning capacity, education or retraining needs, and timeframes. That information can be input into the lifestyle analysis report.

Vocational expert David R. Strauser, PhD,[4] suggests that family lawyers should understand that vocational experts are able to answer three important questions that are of interest in family law matters:

1. What does an individual have the capacity to earn based on his or her age, education, and work experience?
2. If relocation is a potential issue, how does geographic location impact one's earning capacity, and are there significant differences in earning capacity based on labor market characteristics and potential differences in cost of living?

   For example, an individual may have the capacity to earn \$90,000 per year in Memphis TN and \$120,000 per year in

---

their various certifications and experience) are equal. There are differing educational requirements, training, and experience requirements for every certification. Certainly, the client's budget for expert witness testimony is also critical. First, determine whether the expert wants to testify in family law cases. Some may not. Then, after checking for conflicts, request that the expert provide his curriculum vitae, list of prior testifying experience, and estimated fees for vocational analysis and reports. Next, ask for references from other lawyers with whom the expert has worked. Also, consider asking the expert to meet with you in person before either of you commit to working together. Finally, ask the proposed expert whether he has ever been submitted to a court as an expert and rejected. Better to find out now than on cross-examination.

4. A nationally recognized vocational expert witness, Dr. Strauser practices primarily in Memphis and Nashville but also testifies nationally. He has testified in divorce trials and other types of civil damages cases for over 23 years. To contact David to inquire about his work as a vocational expert, e-mail him at drstrauser@me.com.

New York City? Is this difference in earnings significant and how is this difference impacted by cost of living?

3. How does the presence of chronic physical or mental health conditions impact an individual's capacity to earn?

   For example, having type 2 diabetes that is controlled by medication may have no effect on earning capacity, while the presence of multiple herniated discs that are fused together, create a significant in physical limitations, and cause significant pain on a daily basis could negatively impact an individual's earning capacity.

Dr. Strauser points out that to answer these three questions, vocational expert witnesses should have an in-depth understanding regarding the physical, cognitive, and psychological demands of jobs and how they are performed in the local, state, and national economy. It is also important for vocational experts to have a good understanding of chronic health conditions and disabilities and how they impact physical and psychological functioning. Finally, when conducting a vocational assessment to determine earning capacity, it is ideal to meet the individual whose earning capacity is in question. However, when this opportunity is not available or afforded the expert, capacity to earn can be derived from reviewing documents (interrogatories, depositions, medical records, and so on) that would provide relevant information regarding the individual in question's age, education, work experience, and medical conditions.

The forensic accountant must determine the lifestyle analysis report's format. The report itself can come in different shapes and sizes. Experienced forensic accountants have a preferred way to present their analysis and opinions. You should expect to see a fair amount of variation from one forensic accountant to the next. Some forensic accountants may use financial planning computer software programs, of which there are many. Some may even be designed for divorce analysis. Other forensic accountants may use one or more Excel software schedules that they have tailored for specific use in divorce cases.[5] Some forensic accountants may

5. Robert Vance, CPA, ABV, CFF, CVA, CFP, a forensic accountant practicing in Memphis, Tennessee, prefers Excel spreadsheets: "For the Lifestyle Analysis, Excel provides an advantage because the software allows the schedule's framework enough flexibility for me to tailor the analysis to specific facts and circumstances. In my career, I have prepared over 100 Lifestyle Analysis reports. Even though most cases settle, I must always be prepared to answer tough questions at

not create a report to opine about reasonable need or projected future net worth. Even if the forensic accountant does not produce a report, there will, of course, still be financial analysis. But the financial analysis will not be presented in a traditional report format. The expert's opinion may be communicated "live" at deposition or at trial. Regardless of what a report may look like, every forensic accountant must be prepared to describe the methodology employed, list all techniques used and sources of information, describe the analysis performed, explain all assumptions made, and elucidate all opinions reached.

In court, the client can provide direct testimony about the raw data provided to the forensic accountant. The client can testify about her budget, describe account balances, and provide helpful commentary on estimated future expenses, such as the anticipated size of a new house, likely travel expenses for visiting the college-age child, and projected summer vacations. All this information served as a primary source of information and assumptions made by the forensic accountant.

Additionally, the forensic accountant can testify regarding the data and tie it all together. Throughout the engagement, the forensic accountant has identified all the assets, reviewed all the key documents, opined about valuation, classified assets as separate or marital, and input the key variables in an organized, understandable, explainable format. The conclusions should make common sense. The best opinions appear to be reasonable conclusions resulting from following a simple, step-by-step process.

On cross-examination, who would you prefer to answer detailed questions about projected rate of return on investments and retirement assets, cost of living adjustments, and projected Social Security income? The forensic accountant, of course, is the best qualified. Pesky questions such as why such distributions should begin at age 70 or 65 will confuse most divorcing spouses. Having the forensic accountant navigate these difficult issues on the stand can be a tremendous advantage at trial.

The lifestyle analysis report documents the journey, and that journey concludes with opinions. At mediation or trial, one important concluding opinion can be a specific monthly alimony amount reflecting the reasonable needs of the supported spouse and considering all the facts, including

---

mediation or in court. When cross-examined, having a more simple report helps when explaining the numbers and my opinions." To learn more about Rob and his practice, visit www.ForensicVal.com.

the supporting spouse's ability to pay. Another concluding opinion can be the projected net worth of the parties at retirement and beyond.

Finally, you need to know that forensic accountants can have differing opinions about the reasonable-need component of the analysis. Some leading forensic accountants have a problem issuing an opinion as to the level of support needed. Those forensic accountants believe reasonable need is an assumption upon which the forensic accountant must rely as part of the process. Other leading forensic accountants have no problem forming an opinion considering all the facts and factors presented to them. Because some forensic accountants might feel uncomfortable opining regarding the level of support that you will advocate for the client (whether or not it is treated as an assumption), you and the forensic accountant must come to an understanding at the very beginning about the scope of the engagement and how the expert's opinion is to be used in that particular case.

Hidden Income and Assets

Beyond determining the income and lifestyle of the spouses, a lifestyle analysis can be useful in uncovering hidden sources of income and concealed assets. For example, if there are differences between the living expenses of a spouse and the reported income, that difference might be attributed to concealed income. The expert can compute the cost of the lifestyle of the spouse and determine whether the reported income is sufficient to fund this lifestyle.

Tracy Coenen observes, "If the spending during the period under analysis exceeds the known funding sources, then it is likely that there is another source of income. The logic is simple: The money has to come from somewhere." The forensic accountant must continue to search for other sources of income that could explain the difference. Any remaining unexplained difference likely represents unreported income.

Tracy offers this example:

> *How does an attorney who reports income of $35,000 from his law practice on his tax return manage to purchase three cars and two homes worth almost a million dollars? How does he qualify for the mortgages on the two homes, and then buy a rental property with a substantial down payment and a mortgage? Simply evaluating his income tax returns will never provide the full story on his finances. Instead, an analysis of his monthly expenditures*

> *on the cars, homes, rental properties, and other living expenses will be more indicative of his true level of income.*

An unusual deposit or expenditure could point to a previously undisclosed asset. For example, a payment to a utility company in a far away state may lead to the discovery of a piece of real estate. A transfer to an account at a bank the spouses did not typically use may point to hidden accounts.

Tracy suggests the following:

> *It may also be necessary to analyze expenses to determine if they are for a non-marital purpose. For example, money spent to entertain a mistress or view online pornography may arguably be for non-marital purposes. These types of expenditures may need to be highlighted in the lifestyle analysis if the forensic accountant is attempting to determine financial needs following the divorce. Such items may also give rise to a claim of dissipation of marital funds.*

A Sample Report

Any discussion of lifestyle analysis is enhanced immeasurably by reference to a report. See Example 9-1.[6] The report provided here is a printout of a series of spreadsheets. Because there is no requirement for reports to contain a transmittal letter, or explanation, almost any format is acceptable. From an advocacy standpoint, a transmittal letter may make sense if the forensic accountant wants to emphasize certain conclusions or highlight certain assumptions. Most of the assumptions made within the analysis should be readily apparent or otherwise stated within the spreadsheet itself, so that any opposing expert or financial advisor can follow the report's analysis.

What is the predictable reaction from opposing counsel after receiving the report? If opposing counsel has not engaged a forensic accountant, she can either engage her own forensic accountant or hope to attack the analysis in court without one. Either way, opposing counsel will almost always look to defer, deflect, or deflate the significance of the report in conversation and negotiations.

---

6. In this sample report, the supported spouse is the wife.

What is the predictable reaction from the opposing party after receiving the report? Basic assumptions contained in the report will be criticized. Is the proposed mortgage too high? Are the projected returns too aggressive? Are the tax implications taken into account? If the assumptions are conservative and the opposing spouse is unable to identify a serious weakness in the analysis, the lifestyle analysis report will likely positively impact settlement negotiations.

Did the wife's forensic accountant or the husband's forensic accountant create this sample lifestyle analysis report? If it's done right, no one can tell. If the assumptions are reasonable, conservative, and defensible, any experienced forensic accountant looking at the report cold would have a hard time guessing whether the client of the forensic accountant preparing the report was the supported spouse or the supporting spouse.

This lifestyle report is a sample from forensic accountant Robert Vance, CPA, ABV, CFF, CVA, CFP, a forensic accountant practicing in Memphis, Tennessee. The cold, analytical nature of reports, spreadsheets, and financial analyses comes alive through explanation and testimony. Most lifestyle analysis reports answer the following question:

> *Considering the lifestyle of the parties, the ability of the supporting spouse to pay, and all other relevant legal factors, what is the supported spouse's reasonable need each month, and for how long will that support be needed?*

Example 9-1
Lifestyle Analysis Report

Page 1—Marital Balance Sheet

Much of the lifestyle analysis depends upon the assets divided and their ability to create cash flow in the future. Having this information correct and updated is important. It takes time to update balances, so it may make sense to create a general framework and spreadsheet for negotiations and update the analysis and spreadsheet as few times as possible if the matter does not settle. As the client and lawyer adjust, update, or come up with new assumptions, the report can be easily updated and tweaked. Even if a court rules the drafts and amendments discoverable, the differences between initial drafts and the final report are unlikely to be material enough to serve as a basis for a meaningful challenge on cross-examination.

Marital Balance Sheet
Exhibit A

No.	Description	Value Date	Title	FMV	Debt	Equity	Child Property or Separate Property	Marital	Proposed Division: Husband %	Husband $	Wife %	Wife $	Notes
	REAL ESTATE												
1	Marital Residence		J	595,000									Per Appraisal dated 7/27/2017
2	Mortgage Company 6549		J		(175,000)								
3	Brokerage commission on sale-6%				(35,700)	384,300		384,300	0.0%	0	100.0%	384,300	
	CASH AND INVESTMENTS												
4	Central Business Account 9876	6/27/18	H	69,850		69,850		69,850	0.0%	0	100.0%	69,850	
5	First Tennessee 1234	6/27/18	H	58,359		58,359		58,359	100.0%	58,359	0.0%	0	
6	First Tennessee 5678	2/24/18	W	4,146		4,146	(4,146)	0	0.0%	0	100.0%	0	Wife claims non-marital
7	First Tennessee 1122	1/25/18	W	1,455		1,455	(1,455)	0	0.0%	0	100.0%	0	Wife claims non-marital
8	Central CD 6555	2/18/18	H	0		0		0	100.0%	0	0.0%	0	Matured and deposited into a bank account above
9	IRS Tax Refund (Year unknown)		J	9,000		9,000		9,000	0.0%	0	100.0%	9,000	In attorney's escrow account
	CLOSELY HELD BUSINESSES												
10	Surgery Center South		H	75,000		75,000		75,000	100.0%	75,000	0.0%	0	W's value per FVS; H's value - $23,000
11	Surgery Center North		H	85,000		85,000		85,000	100.0%	85,000	0.0%	0	W's value per FVS; H's value - $31,000
	RETIREMENT ACCOUNTS												
12	Fidelity 3456	6/27/18	H	196,000		196,000		196,000	50.0%	98,000	50.0%	98,000	
13	Wells Fargo 6543	6/27/18	H	25,000		25,000		25,000	100.0%	25,000	0.0%	0	
14	Central IRA 2233	6/27/18	H	6,000		6,000		6,000	100.0%	6,000	0.0%	0	
15	Central Roth IRA 3344	1/25/18	W	5,354		5,354		5,354	0.0%	0	100.0%	5,354	
16	Central IRA 9988	1/25/18	W	5,636		5,636		5,636	0.0%	0	100.0%	5,636	
	INTANGIBLES-DISSIPATION BY H												
17	Paramour		H	22,500		22,500		22,500	100.0%	22,500	0.0%	0	Per FVS analysis
18	Cash withdrawals from 2018		H	4,600		4,600		4,600	100.0%	4,600	0.0%	0	From bank statements
	PERSONAL PROPERTY												
19	2012 Toyota SUV	6/15/18	J	29,268		29,268		29,268	100.0%	29,268	0.0%	0	KBB-Sale to Private Party value
20	2010 Toyota Van	6/15/18	J	9,050		9,050		9,050	0.0%	0	100.0%	9,050	KBB-Sale to Private Party value
21	Household Furniture	6/15/18	J	7,000		7,000		7,000	50.0%	3,500	50.0%	3,500	W's value; H's value - $24,025
22	Jewelry		W	28,300		28,300	(28,300)	0	0.0%	0	100.0%	0	H's value - 30,000; wife claims non-marital
	INSURANCE												
23	Term Life Insurance ($1.2m)		H	1		1		1	100.0%	1	0.0%	0	
	DEBTS												
24	AMEX 9876		W		(15,250)	(15,250)		(15,250)	100.0%	(15,250)	0.0%	0	
				1,236,519	(225,950)	1,010,569	(33,901)	976,668		391,978		584,690	**Prepared By:**
										40.1%		59.9%	**Robert Vance, CPA, ABV, CFF, CVA, CFP**
													Forensic & Valuation Services, PLC
													www.forensicval.com

Page 1

continued

Net Worth Accumulation
Exhibit B

	Husband		Wife	
	Estimated Value At Divorce	Estimated Value At Death	Estimated Value At Divorce	Estimated Value At Death
Marital Residence	0	0	384,300	0
New Residence 2.5% appreciation	0	1,043,617	0	1,112,816
Investment Assets incl Closely Held Businesses	218,359	2,542,773	78,850	414,878
Intangibles	27,100	0	0	0
Retirement Assets	129,000	55,789	108,990	113,777
Other Assets & Debts	17,519	0	12,550	0
Net Division	391,978	3,642,179	584,690	1,641,471

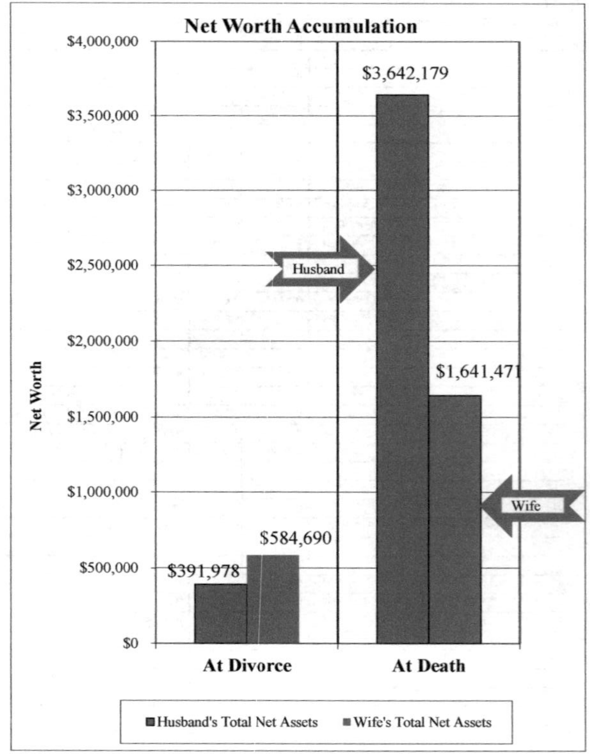

Wife's Need for Support
Exhibit C

(A)	(B)	(C)	(D)	(E)	(F)	(G)	(H)	(I)	(J)	(K)	(L)	(M)	(N)	(O)	(P)	(Q)
		+	-	-	+	+	+	+		=	-	=	-	-	=	=
Year	Age	Employment Earnings 2.5% Inflation	FICA*	Retirement Contribution	Child Support $2,100	**Alimony Need $11,500**	Draws From Retirement Exhibit E	Soc. Sec. $2,250 2.5% COLA	Blank	Total Income	Federal Income Tax Exhibit D	Net Disposable Income	Mortgage Prin & Int Exhibit K	Personal Living Expenses Exhibit K	**Annual (Deficit) or Surplus**	Monthly (Deficit) or Surplus
1	51	0	0	0	25,200	**138,000**	0	0	0	163,200	(22,306)	140,894	(35,505)	(96,795)	**8,594**	716
2	52	35,000	(2,678)	(2,000)	25,200	**138,000**	0	0	0	193,523	(32,905)	160,618	(35,505)	(98,703)	**26,409**	2,201
3	53	35,875	(2,744)	(2,000)	25,200	**138,000**	0	0	0	194,331	(33,548)	160,783	(35,505)	(100,659)	**24,618**	2,052
4	54	36,772	(2,813)	(2,000)	25,200	**138,000**	0	0	0	195,159	(34,191)	160,967	(35,505)	(96,268)	**29,195**	2,433
5	55	37,691	(2,883)	(2,000)	25,200	**138,000**	0	0	0	196,008	(34,897)	161,111	(35,505)	(98,163)	**27,443**	2,287
6	56	38,633	(2,955)	(2,000)	25,200	**138,000**	0	0	0	196,878	(35,605)	161,273	(35,505)	(100,322)	**25,446**	2,121
7	57	39,599	(3,029)	(2,000)	25,200	**138,000**	0	0	0	197,770	(36,314)	161,456	(35,505)	(92,317)	**33,634**	2,803
8	58	40,589	(3,105)	(2,000)	0	**138,000**	0	0	0	173,484	(37,121)	136,363	(35,505)	(94,358)	**6,500**	542
9	59	41,604	(3,183)	(2,000)	0	**138,000**	0	0	0	174,421	(41,002)	133,419	(35,505)	(96,450)	**1,464**	122
10	60	42,644	(3,262)	(2,000)	0	**138,000**	0	0	0	175,382	(41,539)	133,843	(35,505)	(98,594)	**(256)**	(21)
11	61	43,710	(3,344)	(2,000)	0	**138,000**	0	0	0	176,366	(42,073)	134,293	(35,505)	(94,102)	**4,687**	391
12	62	44,803	(3,427)	(2,000)	0	**138,000**	0	0	0	177,376	(42,669)	134,706	(35,505)	(96,182)	**3,020**	252
13	63	45,923	(3,513)	(2,000)	0	**138,000**	0	0	0	178,410	(43,265)	135,145	(35,505)	(109,414)	**(9,774)**	(815)
14	64	47,071	(3,601)	(2,000)	0	**138,000**	0	0	0	179,470	(43,755)	135,715	(35,505)	(111,599)	**(11,389)**	(949)
15	65	48,248	(3,691)	(2,000)	0	**138,000**	0	0	0	180,557	(44,242)	136,315	(35,505)	(113,839)	**(13,029)**	(1,086)
16	66	49,454	(3,783)	(2,000)	0	**138,000**	0	0	0	181,671	(44,726)	136,945	0	(104,101)	**32,844**	2,737
17	67	0	0	0	0	**138,000**	20,000	27,000	0	185,000	(43,826)	141,174	0	(106,148)	**35,027**	2,919
18	68	0	0	0	0	**138,000**	20,000	27,675	0	185,675	(44,588)	141,087	0	(97,146)	**43,942**	3,662
19	69	0	0	0	0	**138,000**	20,000	28,367	0	186,367	(45,457)	140,910	0	(99,296)	**41,613**	3,468
20	70	0	0	0	0	**138,000**	20,000	29,076	0	187,076	(46,390)	140,686	0	(101,500)	**39,186**	3,266
21	71	0	0	0	0	**0**	20,000	29,803	0	49,803	(10,621)	39,182	0	(103,760)	**(64,577)**	(5,381)
22	72	0	0	0	0	**0**	20,000	30,548	0	50,548	(10,554)	39,994	0	(106,075)	**(66,081)**	(5,507)
23	73	0	0	0	0	**0**	20,000	31,312	0	51,312	(10,475)	40,837	0	(108,449)	**(67,612)**	(5,634)
24	74	0	0	0	0	**0**	20,000	32,095	0	52,095	(10,383)	41,712	0	(110,882)	**(69,170)**	(5,764)
25	75	0	0	0	0	**0**	20,000	32,897	0	52,897	(10,277)	42,620	0	(113,376)	**(70,756)**	(5,896)
26	76	0	0	0	0	**0**	20,000	33,719	0	53,719	(10,156)	43,563	0	(115,932)	**(72,369)**	(6,031)
27	77	0	0	0	0	**0**	20,000	34,562	0	54,562	(10,021)	44,541	0	(118,552)	**(74,011)**	(6,168)
28	78	0	0	0	0	**0**	20,000	35,426	0	55,426	(9,870)	45,557	0	(121,237)	**(75,681)**	(6,307)
29	79	0	0	0	0	**0**	20,000	36,312	0	56,312	(9,702)	46,610	0	(123,990)	**(77,380)**	(6,448)
30	80	0	0	0	0	**0**	20,000	37,220	0	57,220	(9,518)	47,702	0	(126,812)	**(79,109)**	(6,592)
31	81	0	0	0	0	**0**	20,000	38,150	0	58,150	(9,315)	48,835	0	(129,704)	**(80,869)**	(6,739)
32	82	0	0	0	0	**0**	20,000	39,104	0	59,104	(9,094)	50,010	0	(132,668)	**(82,658)**	(6,888)
33	83	0	0	0	0	**0**	20,000	40,082	0	60,082	(8,854)	51,227	0	(135,706)	**(84,479)**	(7,040)
34	84	0	0	0	0	**0**	20,000	41,084	0	61,084	(8,594)	52,490	0	(138,821)	**(86,331)**	(7,194)
		627,617	(48,013)	(30,000)	176,400	**2,760,000**	360,000	604,431	0	4,450,436	(927,853)	3,522,583	(532,575)	(3,691,918)	**(701,909)**	

* FICA Wage Base for 2018 = $128,400

Page 3

continued

Wife's Retirement Savings
Exhibit E

Assumed Return		5.0%				
Year	Age	Annual Return	Cumulative Return	Contribution	Distribution	Investment Balance
1	51	5,450	5,450	0	0	114,440
2	52	5,722	11,171	2,000	0	122,161
3	53	6,108	17,280	2,000	0	130,270
4	54	6,513	23,793	2,000	0	138,783
5	55	6,939	30,732	2,000	0	147,722
6	56	7,386	38,118	2,000	0	157,108
7	57	7,855	45,974	2,000	0	166,964
8	58	8,348	54,322	2,000	0	177,312
9	59	8,866	63,187	2,000	0	188,177
10	60	9,409	72,596	2,000	0	199,586
11	61	9,979	82,576	2,000	0	211,566
12	62	10,578	93,154	2,000	0	224,144
13	63	11,207	104,361	2,000	0	237,351
14	64	11,868	116,229	2,000	0	251,219
15	65	12,561	128,790	2,000	0	265,780
16	66	13,289	142,079	2,000	0	281,069
17	67	14,053	156,132	0	(20,000)	275,122
18	68	13,756	169,888	0	(20,000)	268,878
19	69	13,444	183,332	0	(20,000)	262,322
20	70	13,116	196,448	0	(20,000)	255,438
21	71	12,772	209,220	0	(20,000)	248,210
22	72	12,411	221,631	0	(20,000)	240,621
23	73	12,031	233,662	0	(20,000)	232,652
24	74	11,633	245,294	0	(20,000)	224,284
25	75	11,214	256,508	0	(20,000)	215,498
26	76	10,775	267,283	0	(20,000)	206,273
27	77	10,314	277,597	0	(20,000)	196,587
28	78	9,829	287,426	0	(20,000)	186,416
29	79	9,321	296,747	0	(20,000)	175,737
30	80	8,787	305,534	0	(20,000)	164,524
31	81	8,226	313,760	0	(20,000)	152,750
32	82	7,638	321,398	0	(20,000)	140,388
33	83	7,019	328,417	0	(20,000)	127,407
34	84	6,370	334,787	0	(20,000)	**113,777**
		334,787		30,000	(360,000)	

Assets Distributed (See Marital Balance Sheet)	
Fidelity 3456	98,000
Wells Fargo 6543	0
Central IRA 2233	0
Central Roth IRA 3344	5,354
Central IRA 9988	5,636
	108,990

Page 4

Wife's Investment Savings
Exhibit F

Assumed Return		3.0%					
		Annual	Cumulative	House Cash to Invest		Surplus or (Deficit)	Investment
Year	Age	Return	Return	After Dwnpmt	Blank	Exhibit C	Balance
1	51	2,534	2,534	284,300	0	8,594	379,879
2	52	11,396	13,930	0	0	26,409	417,684
3	53	12,531	26,460	0	0	24,618	454,832
4	54	13,645	40,105	0	0	29,195	497,672
5	55	14,930	55,036	0	0	27,443	540,046
6	56	16,201	71,237	0	0	25,446	581,693
7	57	17,451	88,688	0	0	33,634	632,778
8	58	18,983	107,671	0	0	6,500	658,261
9	59	19,748	127,419	0	0	1,464	679,473
10	60	20,384	147,803	0	0	(256)	699,601
11	61	20,988	168,791	0	0	4,687	725,276
12	62	21,758	190,549	0	0	3,020	750,054
13	63	22,502	213,051	0	0	(9,774)	762,782
14	64	22,883	235,934	0	0	(11,389)	774,276
15	65	23,228	259,163	0	0	(13,029)	784,476
16	66	23,534	282,697	0	0	32,844	840,854
17	67	25,226	307,923	0	0	35,027	901,107
18	68	27,033	334,956	0	0	43,942	972,082
19	69	29,162	364,118	0	0	41,613	1,042,857
20	70	31,286	395,404	0	0	39,186	1,113,329
21	71	33,400	428,804	0	0	(64,577)	1,082,152
22	72	32,465	461,268	0	0	(66,081)	1,048,535
23	73	31,456	492,725	0	0	(67,612)	1,012,380
24	74	30,371	523,096	0	0	(69,170)	973,581
25	75	29,207	552,303	0	0	(70,756)	932,032
26	76	27,961	580,264	0	0	(72,369)	887,624
27	77	26,629	606,893	0	0	(74,011)	840,242
28	78	25,207	632,100	0	0	(75,681)	789,768
29	79	23,693	655,793	0	0	(77,380)	736,081
30	80	22,082	677,876	0	0	(79,109)	679,055
31	81	20,372	698,247	0	0	(80,869)	618,557
32	82	18,557	716,804	0	0	(82,658)	554,456
33	83	16,634	733,438	0	0	(84,479)	486,611
34	84	14,598	748,036	0	0	(86,331)	**414,878**
		748,036		284,300	0	(701,909)	

Assets Distributed (See Marital Balance Sheet)	
Central Business Account 9876	69,850
First Tennessee 1234	0
First Tennessee 5678	4,146
First Tennessee 1122	1,455
Central CD 6555	0
IRS Tax Refund (Year unknown)	9,000
	84,451

New House Purchase & Sale of Marital Residence		
Net Proceeds from Marital Residence Sale		384,300
Purchase Price of new residence	500,000	
Less Down Payment-20%	(100,000)	
New Mortgage	400,000	
Net to Invest		284,300
Rate	4.0%	
Time in months	180	
New Mortgage P&I payment	2,959	

continued

Husband's Ability to Pay Support
Exhibit G

(A)	(B)	(C) +	(D) -	(E) -	(F) -	(G) +	(H) +	(I) +	(J) +	(K) =	(L) -	(M) =	(N) -	(O) =	(P) =	(Q) =
Year	Age	Employment Earnings 2.5% Inflation	FICA*	Retirement Contribution	**Alimony**	Surgery Center Distribution 2.5% Inflation	Blank	Draws From Retirement Accounts Exhibit I	Soc. Sec. $4,500 2.5% COLA	Total Income	Federal Income Tax Exhibit H	Net Disposable Income	Mortgage Prin & Int Exhibit L	Personal Living Expenses Exhibit L	Annual (Deficit) or Surplus	Monthly (Deficit) or Surplus
1	50	348,439	(13,013)	(18,500)	**(138,000)**	25,000	0	0	0	203,926	(48,439)	155,486	0	(122,004)	33,482	2,790
2	51	357,150	(13,139)	(18,500)	**(138,000)**	25,625	0	0	0	213,136	(52,344)	160,791	(35,505)	(116,467)	8,820	735
3	52	366,079	(13,269)	(18,500)	**(138,000)**	26,266	0	0	0	222,575	(54,181)	168,395	(35,505)	(118,776)	14,114	1,176
4	53	375,231	(13,402)	(18,500)	**(138,000)**	26,922	0	0	0	232,251	(57,868)	174,383	(35,505)	(122,343)	16,535	1,378
5	54	384,611	(13,538)	(18,500)	**(138,000)**	27,595	0	0	0	242,169	(61,696)	180,473	(35,505)	(124,770)	20,198	1,683
6	55	394,227	(13,677)	(18,500)	**(138,000)**	28,285	0	0	0	252,335	(65,692)	186,643	(35,505)	(83,132)	68,006	5,667
7	56	404,082	(13,820)	(18,500)	**(138,000)**	28,992	0	0	0	262,755	(70,634)	192,121	(35,505)	(144,578)	12,038	1,003
8	57	414,184	(13,966)	(18,500)	**(138,000)**	29,717	0	0	0	273,435	(74,751)	198,684	(35,505)	(147,561)	15,618	1,302
9	58	424,539	(14,117)	(18,500)	**(138,000)**	30,460	0	0	0	284,383	(79,042)	205,341	(35,505)	(144,618)	25,218	2,102
10	59	435,153	(14,271)	(18,500)	**(138,000)**	31,222	0	0	0	295,604	(83,618)	211,985	(35,505)	(147,751)	28,729	2,394
11	60	446,031	(14,428)	(18,500)	**(138,000)**	32,002	0	0	0	307,105	(88,386)	218,720	(35,505)	(84,734)	98,481	8,207
12	61	457,182	(14,590)	(18,500)	**(138,000)**	32,802	0	0	0	318,894	(94,510)	224,385	(35,505)	(86,370)	102,509	8,542
13	62	468,612	(14,756)	(18,500)	**(138,000)**	33,622	0	0	0	330,978	(100,906)	230,072	(35,505)	(88,047)	106,520	8,877
14	63	480,327	(14,926)	(18,500)	**(138,000)**	34,463	0	0	0	343,364	(107,585)	235,779	(35,505)	(96,966)	103,308	8,609
15	64	492,335	(15,100)	(18,500)	**(138,000)**	35,324	0	0	0	356,060	(114,432)	241,628	(35,505)	(98,728)	107,394	8,950
16	65	504,644	(15,278)	(18,500)	**(138,000)**	36,207	0	0	0	369,073	(121,581)	247,492	(35,505)	(96,407)	115,580	9,632
17	66	517,260	(15,461)	(18,500)	**(138,000)**	37,113	0	0	0	382,411	(129,114)	253,297	0	(98,155)	155,142	12,929
18	67	0	0	0	**(138,000)**	0	0	100,000	54,000	16,000	(8,868)	7,132	0	(105,947)	(98,815)	(8,235)
19	68	0	0	0	**(138,000)**	0	0	100,000	55,350	17,350	(11,470)	5,880	0	(88,242)	(82,362)	(6,864)
20	69	0	0	0	**(138,000)**	0	0	100,000	56,734	18,734	(11,632)	7,102	0	(90,208)	(83,106)	(6,926)
21	70	0	0	0	**0**	0	0	100,000	58,152	158,152	(49,201)	108,951	0	(92,223)	16,728	1,394
22	71	0	0	0	**0**	0	0	100,000	59,606	159,606	(51,197)	108,409	0	(94,289)	14,120	1,177
23	72	0	0	0	**0**	0	0	100,000	61,096	161,096	(53,236)	107,860	0	(96,406)	11,454	955
24	73	0	0	0	**0**	0	0	100,000	62,623	162,623	(55,319)	107,304	0	(98,576)	8,728	727
25	74	0	0	0	**0**	0	0	100,000	64,189	164,189	(57,448)	106,741	0	(100,801)	5,941	495
26	75	0	0	0	**0**	0	0	100,000	65,794	165,794	(59,622)	106,172	0	(103,081)	3,091	258
27	76	0	0	0	**0**	0	0	100,000	67,439	167,439	(61,844)	105,595	0	(105,418)	177	15
28	77	0	0	0	**0**	0	0	100,000	69,125	169,125	(64,113)	105,012	0	(107,813)	(2,801)	(233)
29	78	0	0	0	**0**	0	0	100,000	70,853	170,853	(66,431)	104,422	0	(110,268)	(5,847)	(487)
30	79	0	0	0	**0**	0	0	100,000	72,624	172,624	(68,799)	103,825	0	(112,785)	(8,960)	(747)
31	80	0	0	0	**0**	0	0	100,000	74,440	174,440	(71,217)	103,222	0	(115,365)	(12,142)	(1,012)
		7,270,086	(240,750)	(314,500)	**(2,760,000)**	521,618	0	1,400,000	892,023	6,768,478	(2,095,174)	4,673,304	(532,575)	(3,342,829)	797,898	

* FICA Wage Base for 2018 = $128,400

Husband's Retirement Savings
Exhibit I

Assumed Return		5.0%					
	Age	Annual Return	Cumulative Return	Contribution	Company Match	Distribution	Investment Balance
1	50	0	0	18,500	10,000	0	157,500
2	51	7,875	7,875	18,500	10,000	0	193,875
3	52	9,694	17,569	18,500	10,000	0	232,069
4	53	11,603	29,172	18,500	10,000	0	272,172
5	54	13,609	42,781	18,500	10,000	0	314,281
6	55	15,714	58,495	18,500	10,000	0	358,495
7	56	17,925	76,420	18,500	10,000	0	404,920
8	57	20,246	96,666	18,500	10,000	0	453,666
9	58	22,683	119,349	18,500	10,000	0	504,849
10	59	25,242	144,591	18,500	10,000	0	558,591
11	60	27,930	172,521	18,500	10,000	0	615,021
12	61	30,751	203,272	18,500	10,000	0	674,272
13	62	33,714	236,985	18,500	10,000	0	736,485
14	63	36,824	273,810	18,500	10,000	0	801,810
15	64	40,090	313,900	18,500	10,000	0	870,400
16	65	43,520	357,420	18,500	10,000	0	942,420
17	66	47,121	404,541	18,500	10,000	0	1,018,041
18	67	50,902	455,443	0	0	(100,000)	968,943
19	68	48,447	503,890	0	0	(100,000)	917,390
20	69	45,870	549,760	0	0	(100,000)	863,260
21	70	43,163	592,923	0	0	(100,000)	806,423
22	71	40,321	633,244	0	0	(100,000)	746,744
23	72	37,337	670,581	0	0	(100,000)	684,081
24	73	34,204	704,785	0	0	(100,000)	618,285
25	74	30,914	735,700	0	0	(100,000)	549,200
26	75	27,460	763,160	0	0	(100,000)	476,660
27	76	23,833	786,993	0	0	(100,000)	400,493
28	77	20,025	807,017	0	0	(100,000)	320,517
29	78	16,026	823,043	0	0	(100,000)	236,543
30	79	11,827	834,870	0	0	(100,000)	148,370
31	80	7,419	842,289	0	0	(100,000)	**55,789**
		842,289		314,500	170,000	(1,400,000)	

Assets Distributed (See Marital Balance Sheet)	
Fidelity 3456	98,000
Wells Fargo 6543	25,000
Central IRA 2233	6,000
Central Roth IRA 3344	0
Central IRA 9988	0
	129,000
Company Match	10,000

Page 7

continued

Husband's Investment Savings
Exhibit J

Assumed Return		5.0%					
Year	Age	Annual Return	Cumulative Return	House Cash After Dwnpmt	Sale of Surgery Centers*	Surplus or (Deficit) Exhibit G	Investment Balance
1	50	2,918	2,918	0	0	33,482	94,759
2	51	4,738	4,738	(100,000)	0	8,820	8,317
3	52	416	416	0	0	14,114	22,847
4	53	1,142	1,142	0	0	16,535	40,524
5	54	2,026	2,026	0	0	20,198	62,748
6	55	3,137	3,137	0	0	68,006	133,892
7	56	6,695	6,695	0	0	12,038	152,624
8	57	7,631	7,631	0	0	15,618	175,873
9	58	8,794	8,794	0	0	25,218	209,885
10	59	10,494	10,494	0	0	28,729	249,108
11	60	12,455	12,455	0	0	98,481	360,045
12	61	18,002	18,002	0	0	102,509	480,556
13	62	24,028	24,028	0	0	106,520	611,104
14	63	30,555	30,555	0	0	103,308	744,967
15	64	37,248	37,248	0	0	107,394	889,609
16	65	44,480	44,480	0	0	115,580	1,049,670
17	66	52,483	52,483	0	0	155,142	1,257,295
18	67	62,865	62,865	0	249,545	(98,815)	1,470,891
19	68	73,545	73,545	0	0	(82,362)	1,462,073
20	69	73,104	73,104	0	0	(83,106)	1,452,071
21	70	72,604	72,604	0	0	16,728	1,541,402
22	71	77,070	77,070	0	0	14,120	1,632,592
23	72	81,630	81,630	0	0	11,454	1,725,676
24	73	86,284	86,284	0	0	8,728	1,820,688
25	74	91,034	91,034	0	0	5,941	1,917,663
26	75	95,883	95,883	0	0	3,091	2,016,637
27	76	100,832	100,832	0	0	177	2,117,646
28	77	105,882	105,882	0	0	(2,801)	2,220,728
29	78	111,036	111,036	0	0	(5,847)	2,325,917
30	79	116,296	116,296	0	0	(8,960)	2,433,253
31	80	121,663	121,663	0	0	(12,142)	**2,542,773**
		1,536,971		(100,000)	249,545	797,898	

* Sale upon retirement; 2.5% annual appreciation

Assets Distributed (See Marital Balance Sheet)	
Central Business Account 9876	0
First Tennessee 1234	58,359
First Tennessee 5678	0
First Tennessee 1122	0
Central CD 6555	0
IRS Tax Refund (Year unknown)	0
	58,359

New House Purchase & Sale of Marital Residence		
Net Proceeds from Marital Residence Sale		0
Purchase Price of new residence	500,000	
Less Down Payment-20%	(100,000)	
New Mortgage	400,000	
Net amount from investments		(100,000)
Rate	4.0%	
Time in months	180	
New Mortgage P&I payment	2,959	

Wife's Personal Living Expenses by Year
Exhibit K

1) Based Upon W's Income & Expense Affidavit
2) Added or amended by the analyst

Years edited to fit to 1 page

Inflationary Factor	2.5%																	
Year	1	2	3	4	5	6	7	8	9	10	11	12	13	14	15	16	17	34
Age	51	52	53	54	55	56	57	58	59	60	61	62	63	64	65	66	67	84
	2017	2018	2019	2020	2021	2022	2023	2024	2025	2026	2027	2028	2029	2030	2031	2032	2033	2050
Mortgage-PIT Only (Exb. F)	2,959	2,959	2,959	2,959	2,959	2,959	2,959	2,959	2,959	2,959	2,959	2,959	2,959	2,959	2,959	0	0	0
Housing & Furnishings																		
Alarm	42	43	44	45	46	48	49	50	51	52	54	55	56	58	59	61	62	95
Association	125	128	131	135	138	141	145	149	152	156	160	164	168	172	177	181	186	282
Furnishings (3 years only)	495	507	520	0	0	0	0	0	0	0	0	0	0	0	0	0	0	0
Household Supplies	70	72	74	75	77	79	81	83	85	87	90	92	94	96	99	101	104	158
Insurance-Homeowners	302	310	318	325	334	342	351	359	368	377	387	397	406	417	427	438	449	683
Insurance-Jewelry	18	18	19	19	20	20	21	21	22	22	23	24	24	25	25	26	27	41
Maintenance & Repairs	500	513	525	538	552	566	580	594	609	624	640	656	672	689	706	724	742	1,129
Real Estate Taxes (5 Yr Increases)	722	722	722	722	722	740	740	740	740	740	759	759	759	759	759	778	778	778
Telephone & Internet	289	296	304	311	319	327	335	344	352	361	370	379	389	398	408	419	429	653
Utilities	551	565	579	593	608	623	639	655	671	638	705	723	741	760	779	798	818	1,245
	3,114	3,174	3,235	2,765	2,816	2,887	2,940	2,995	3,052	3,109	3,187	3,248	3,310	3,374	3,439	3,525	3,594	5,063
Transportation																		
Gas	160	164	168	172	177	181	186	190	195	200	205	210	215	221	226	116	119	181
Insurance	90	92	95	97	99	102	104	107	110	112	115	118	121	124	127	130	134	203
Maintenance	176	180	185	190	194	199	204	209	214	220	225	231	237	243	249	127	131	199
Licenses	8	8	8	9	9	9	9	10	10	10	10	10	11	11	11	12	12	18
Note	833	833	833	833	833	833	0	0	0	0	0	0	925	925	925	925	925	0
	1,267	1,278	1,289	1,300	1,312	1,324	503	516	529	542	556	569	1,509	1,523	1,538	1,310	1,320	601
Personal																		
Christmas, Parties & Gifts	125	128	131	135	138	141	145	149	152	156	160	164	168	172	177	181	186	282
Clothing Replacement	350	359	368	377	386	396	406	416	426	437	224	230	235	241	247	253	260	395
Entertainment	150	154	158	162	166	170	174	178	183	187	96	98	101	103	106	109	111	169
Donations	150	150	150	150	150	150	150	150	150	150	150	150	150	150	150	150	150	150
Groceries & Dining Out	775	794	814	835	855	877	899	921	944	968	992	1,017	1,042	1,068	1,095	561	575	875
Haircuts & Personal Care	310	318	326	334	342	351	360	368	378	387	397	407	417	427	438	449	460	700
Health Insurance	625	641	657	673	690	707	725	743	762	781	800	820	841	862	883	905	928	1,412
Miscellaneous	400	410	420	431	442	453	464	475	487	500	256	262	269	276	283	290	297	452
Pet Care	250	256	263	269	276	283	290	297	305	312	320	328	336	345	353	362	371	565
Unc. Medical, Dental, Presc.	250	256	263	269	276	283	290	297	305	312	320	328	336	345	353	362	371	565
Vacations	300	308	315	323	331	339	348	357	366	375	384	394	403	414	424	217	223	339
	3,685	3,773	3,864	3,957	4,052	4,150	4,250	4,352	4,457	4,565	4,099	4,198	4,299	4,403	4,509	3,840	3,932	5,904
Total All Non-Mortgage	8,066	8,225	8,388	8,022	8,180	8,360	7,693	7,863	8,038	8,216	7,842	8,015	9,118	9,300	9,487	8,675	8,846	11,568
Annualized-Non-Mortgage	96,795	98,703	100,659	96,268	98,163	100,322	92,317	94,358	96,450	98,594	94,102	96,182	109,414	111,599	113,839	104,101	106,148	138,821
Total All With Mortgage	11,025																	
Annualized With Mortgage	132,300																	

Page 9

continued

Husband's Personal Living Expenses by Year
Exhibit L

1) Based Upon W's Income & Expense Affidavit
2) Added or amended by the analyst

Years edited to fit to 1 page

Inflationary Factor	**2.5%**																	
Year	**1**	**2**	**3**	**4**	**5**	**6**	**7**	**8**	**9**	**10**	**11**	**12**	**13**	**14**	**15**	**16**	**17**	**31**
Age	**50**	**51**	**52**	**53**	**54**	**55**	**56**	**57**	**58**	**59**	**60**	**61**	**62**	**63**	**64**	**65**	**66**	**80**
	2017	**2018**	**2019**	**2020**	**2021**	**2022**	**2023**	**2024**	**2025**	**2026**	**2027**	**2028**	**2029**	**2030**	**2031**	**2032**	**2033**	**2047**
Mortgage - PI Only (Exb. J)	0	2,959	2,959	2,959	2,959	2,959	2,959	2,959	2,959	2,959	2,959	2,959	2,959	2,959	2,959	2,959	0	0
	0	2,959	2,959	2,959	2,959	2,959	2,959	2,959	2,959	2,959	2,959	2,959	2,959	2,959	2,959	2,959	0	0
Housing & Furnishings																		
Alarm	0	43	44	45	46	48	49	50	51	52	54	55	56	58	59	61	62	88
Association	0	125	128	131	135	138	141	145	149	152	156	160	164	168	172	177	181	256
Household Supplies	250	256	263	269	276	283	290	297	305	312	320	328	336	345	353	362	371	524
Insurance-Homeowners	150	350	359	368	377	386	396	406	416	426	437	448	459	471	482	495	507	716
Furnishings (3 years only)	400	400	400	0	0	0	0	0	0	0	0	0	0	0	0	0	0	0
Maintenance & Repairs	0	258	264	271	278	285	292	299	307	314	322	330	339	347	356	365	374	528
Rent	2,000	0	0	0	0	0	0	0	0	0	0	0	0	0	0	0	0	0
Real Estate Taxes (5 Yr Increases)	0	491	503	516	529	542	556	569	584	598	613	629	644	660	677	694	711	1,005
Telephone & Internet	250	256	263	269	276	283	290	297	305	312	320	328	336	345	353	362	371	524
Utilities	150	425	436	447	458	469	481	493	505	518	531	544	558	572	586	601	616	870
	3,200	2,605	2,660	2,316	2,374	2,433	2,494	2,557	2,621	2,686	2,753	2,822	2,893	2,965	3,039	3,115	3,193	4,511
Transportation																		
Insurance	125	128	131	135	138	141	145	149	152	156	160	164	168	172	177	91	93	131
Gas, Tags, Maintenance, Oil	350	359	368	377	386	396	406	416	426	437	448	459	471	482	495	253	260	367
Note	0	0	0	500	500	500	500	500	0	0	0	0	0	600	600	600	600	0
	475	487	499	1,012	1,024	1,037	1,051	1,065	579	593	608	623	639	1,255	1,271	944	953	498
Personal																		
Accountant	50	51	53	54	55	57	58	59	61	62	64	66	67	69	71	72	74	105
Child's Expenses	3,250	3,331	3,415	3,500	3,587	0	0	0	0	0	0	0	0	0	0	0	0	0
Child's Tuition-College		0	0	0	0	0	5,000	5,125	5,253	5,384	0	0	0	0	0	0	0	0
Christmas, Parties & Gifts	125	128	131	135	138	141	145	149	152	156	160	164	168	172	177	181	186	262
Clothing Replacement	150	154	158	162	166	170	174	178	183	187	192	197	202	207	212	217	223	315
Donations	800	800	800	800	800	800	800	800	800	800	800	800	800	800	800	800	800	800
Entertainment	250	256	263	269	276	283	290	297	305	312	320	328	336	345	353	362	371	524
Groceries & Dining Out	475	487	499	512	524	537	551	565	579	593	608	623	639	655	671	688	705	996
Haircuts & Personal Care	100	103	105	108	110	113	116	119	122	125	128	131	134	138	141	145	148	210
Health Insurance (co. paid until retire)	0	0	0	0	0	0	0	0	0	0	0	0	0	0	0	0	0	689
Laundry & Dry Cleaning	45	46	47	48	50	51	52	53	55	56	58	59	61	62	64	65	67	94
Life & Disability Insurance	807	807	807	807	807	807	807	807	807	807	807	807	807	807	807	807	807	0
Unc. Medical, Dental, Presc.	140	144	147	151	155	158	162	166	171	175	179	184	188	193	198	203	208	294
Vacations	300	308	315	323	331	339	348	357	366	375	384	394	403	414	424	434	445	315
	6,492	6,614	6,739	6,868	6,999	3,457	8,503	8,676	8,852	9,033	3,700	3,752	3,806	3,861	3,917	3,975	4,034	4,604
Total All Non-Mortgage	10,167	9,706	9,898	10,195	10,397	6,928	12,048	12,297	12,051	12,313	7,061	7,198	7,337	8,081	8,227	8,034	8,180	9,614
Annualized Non-Mortgage	122,004	116,467	118,776	122,343	124,770	83,132	144,578	147,561	144,618	147,751	84,734	86,370	88,047	96,966	98,728	96,407	98,155	115,365
Total All With Mortgage	10,167	12,664																
Annualized With Mortgage	122,004	151,972																

Page 2—Net Worth Accumulation of Marital Assets

The particular net worth accumulation of marital assets schedule shown in the sample report provides a detailed example showing what many believe to be true: after divorce, almost all earning spouses fare better financially than supported spouses.

Even in situations involving substantial support, the greater ability to earn and save generally creates a greater opportunity to accumulate wealth for the supporting spouse. On the other hand, if the supported spouse is a saver and the supporting spouse is a spendthrift, those trends are unlikely to change just because of the divorce.

Given the information and assumptions accumulated in the following schedules, projecting both spouses' net worth at the statistical date of death is not a complicated calculation. You should see this analysis as ammunition for argument.

Page 3—Wife's Need for Support

Columns P, Q, and G

Starting at the last two columns, column P sets out the net result of the calculations each year—the annual (deficit) or surplus. Column Q describes the same amount but lists it as monthly. Finally, column G sets out the lawyer's claim—the alimony need. In theory, the amount listed in column G covers the monthly needs of the supported spouse and is derived after consideration of all the incomes available and expenses and taxes to be paid by the wife. This particular sample report depicts the need to build additional retirement on page 4 and additional savings on page 5. Often, the monthly alimony amount is fairly constant over a period of time. If not, there may need to be adjustments in the amount over a period of years.

Columns A and B

Columns A and B show the years and ages for each year of the analysis. This is important for cross-referencing all the factual developments over time, including and through retirement, which will be considered in the analysis. This makes the analysis clearer for the court, opposing counsel, and opposing expert. Simpler reports are better.

Columns C, D, and E

Column C lists the wife's employment earnings. This amount can come from the forensic accountant's analysis of the wife's earnings history or from the vocational expert's report. If retraining is required, the earnings may be delayed a year or more. Column D lists FICA,[7] calculated at the current rates. FICA tax rates have been constant over recent years, and the IRS usually lists rate changes well in advance. It is a reasonable assumption for forensic accountants to assume those rates will not change. Column E lists retirement contributions. In this sample analysis, the wife has access to an accelerated retirement savings vehicle, such as a 401(k), which allows for retirement savings greater than traditional IRA limits; however, the wife cannot afford more than an annual $2,000 contribution per this analysis.

Column F

Column F adds nontaxable income from child support. This is an assumption that you may need to supply to the forensic accountant. Until the court rules on custody, visitation time, and child support, the forensic accountant may not have a solid number. A conservative estimate can be listed.

Column H

Column H lists draws from retirement. Here, the CPA begins to combine the results of the client interview, the key facts (including ages of the parties), deposition testimony, and judgment. The forensic accountant must project a likely distribution from an overall consideration of need and ability to draw from projected retirement savings. The balance of the retirement savings at retirement may also be a calculation, beginning with a projected equitable distribution of retirement assets at the time of the divorce. In most situations, retirement draws will cause taxable income. You will find a detailed analysis on page 4.

Column I

Column I lists Social Security payments projected to be received upon retirement, with a COLA (cost-of-living adjustment) increase over time.

---

7. Also known collectively as the Social Security and Medicare taxes. For more information, see the discussion of FICA in Chapter 8.

Even though no one knows exactly when the wife will elect to begin drawing on Social Security, estimates can be made based on known variables. Social Security benefits are what they are. If the wife is in excellent health, it may make financial sense for her to defer receiving payments to the latest possible date. If she is not in great health, having previously suffered a major heart attack, for instance, she may be advised to receive the lower level of Social Security available to younger recipients. COLAs in the future are another variable that can change over time. The forensic accountant must determine a reasonable estimate for an increase in those benefits over time.

Column P Revisited

Column P lists the projected annual (deficit) or surplus. In this analysis, the wife is likely to be awarded a particular share of the parties' investment portfolio. The exact amount determined will again be the subject of a reasonable estimation by the forensic accountant or an assumption provided by you in your capacity as the client's lawyer. Those assets will generate income as depicted on page 5 and will be increased if a surplus is generated or decreased to pay for or absorb a (deficit). Obviously, if the estimate or assumed amount is materially overstated or understated, the reliability of the analysis could be questioned. The overall asset mix must be considered in conjunction with your state's law regarding double-dipping, which is discussed more fully at the end of this chapter.

Columns K, L, and M

Column K is total income, a math formula calculating the sum of columns C less D and E, plus F, G, H, and I. Column L is federal income tax calculated in a schedule not shown. Federal income tax is based on known rates, and the future rates are generally assumed not to change. In this sample report, the alimony is considered as includable income to the wife and deductible by the husband based on a divorce being complete before the end of 2018, which is the tax law as of publication date If your state has an income tax, that amount may need to be added. For the analysis, the forensic accountant will exclude taxes on nontaxable income, such as child support. Calculating this number can be tricky. Column M lists net disposable income, another math formula, taking column K less column L.

Column N

Column N lists the assumed mortgage principal and interest for the wife's future house. The forensic accountant will obtain this information either from the wife as an assumption or by making a reasonable determination of her need as was done on page 5.

Column O

Column O lists personal living expenses based on assumptions made by the forensic accountant and derived from known facts or reasonable projections. See the later section, "Pages 9 and 10—Wife's Personal Living Expenses and Husband's Personal Living Expenses."

Columns P, Q, and G Revisited

As discussed above, column P is the annual (deficit) or surplus, a math formula taking column M less columns N and O. Column Q divides column P by 12 to arrive at the monthly (deficit) or surplus. Column G is the amount the lawyer will advocate as the alimony that the wife will need based on the math formula portrayed within the wife's need schedule. The opinion of the forensic accountant may or may not extend to column G. Depending on your jurisdiction's law on expert testimony and on the formality of the judge, the forensic accountant may or may not want to form an opinion about the monthly alimony need. You may simply want to advocate that this is the amount needed. Getting to column Q, monthly (deficit) or surplus, may be all that is required. If the forensic accountant feels comfortable opining about needed support, that opinion may be simple: "Given all the information provided, assumptions made, including the projected property division, and analysis performed, the listed monthly alimony need of $11,500 per month for 20 years appears reasonable." Here, as always, the forensic accountant must appear objective and independent.

Pages 4 and 7—Wife's Retirement Savings and Husband's Retirement Savings

These schedules predict the future by taking an estimated portfolio balance at the time of the divorce, projecting future contributions and annual returns, and projecting distributions 17 and 18 years, respectively, into the future. Obviously, few of the projections may come true exactly as predicted. The goal of the forensic accountant is to make reasonable assumptions based on independent judgment and sound financial planning. As between the spouses, the investment-return assumptions may be different as long as those differences can be justified. Here, the husband is assumed to be able to make more contributions over time, and projected rates of return are equal. Financial advisors may refer to these assets as "tax deferred."

Pages 5 and 8—Wife's Investment Savings and Husband's Investment Savings

Investment savings are different than retirement savings because investment savings may result in taxable income each year. Retirement savings result in taxable income only when the balance is distributed. The same type of analysis for retirement savings is used with investment savings. The overall asset investment mix could be different from retirement savings, given the difference in possible long-term or short-term investing needs. A more aggressive investor could certainly place more assets in equities and fewer assets in more secure investments, thereby generating a higher return. Financial advisors may refer to these assets as "non-tax deferred." The investment account(s) will be increased if a surplus is generated after paying all personal living expenses and the mortgage or decreased to pay for or absorb a (deficit). In this schedule, the wife builds a nest egg through age 70 so that she can absorb much larger deficits after the proposed alimony ceases. This schedule may also be a place to show one-time expenditures, such as for a house down payment, or one-time incomes, such as husband selling a business interest upon retirement.

Pages 9 and 10—Wife's Personal Living Expenses and Husband's Personal Living Expenses

What is a reasonable lifestyle? What is a reasonable level of support? For the purposes of the report, who gets to make that determination? Does the forensic accountant have the expertise, training, experience, and judgment necessary to opine about the reasonable needs of the supported spouse? Or is this simply an assumption provided by the client or by you? You must work through these issues with the forensic accountant, considering the law of your particular state. Remember, it's the duty of the forensic accountant to keep the numbers "sane." Sanity requires that the projected need be reasonable considering the historical earnings, spending of the parties, and anticipated future earnings. If the numbers (including assumptions) aren't sane, then the forensic accountant may be challenged for bias and failing to exercise independent judgment. This may be the category attacked the most by the husband's attorney and expert. If the forensic accountant can successfully defend a challenge to this category, the trier of fact will likely have confidence in the overall analysis.

In this schedule, the expenses are detailed in a multiyear format that allows for an adjustment for inflation and adding and deleting expense as necessary over the years. Expenses may be adjusted for when the children leave the home and/or attend college. Sources of this information could come from an interview with the wife, the detailed transaction listing and analysis (or historical spending pattern of the parties), the wife's projected budget, discovery answers, deposition testimony, and the projected lifestyle spending of the husband.

Page 6—Husband's Ability to Pay Support

Line by line, and column by column, the analysis for the husband's ability to pay really mirrors the wife's need for support found on page 3 of the report. One key for the forensic accountant is to make sure that "what is good for the goose is good for the gander." What does this mean? The assumptions should be consistent as applied to both spouses unless there is a very good objective reason for them not to be. For example, the Social Security COLA and living expenses inflation should be the same for both spouses. At times, though, there may be justification for different assumptions. Specifically, if one spouse can assume greater risk over time, that greater risk could be reflected in a greater projected rate of return for investments and retirement assets.

Robert Vance offers the following advice to attorneys and forensic accountants preparing a lifestyle analysis:

> *Since most people tend to think in terms of monthly budgets, a majority of attorneys use a single-month financial statement format for "proving" alimony need or ability to pay. However, the goal in "proving" alimony need should be to illustrate the*

> *receiving spouse's reasonable need based on a projection of future income and expenses. Attorneys need a method to calculate and justify the reasonable need and ability to pay alimony once a working property division is on the table. The Lifestyle Analysis should illustrate a simplified lifetime financial plan covering the remaining years of each spouse's life expectancy so that the attorneys or judge can determine who will run out of money and when.*[8]

Double-Dipping

Double-dipping, as a concept, seems simple and logical, especially to accountants. If an asset that generates income is divided in divorce, the income from the part of the asset no longer owned should not be used in the calculation of the obligor's income for support purposes.[9] Unfortunately, this concept can be very complicated in application. And explaining it in court can be maddening.

Consider this example. On January 31, 2010, a husband purchased a one-year $100,000 certificate of deposit (CD) paying 3 percent. One year later, the CD timed out, and the husband received back $103,000. On February 1, 2011, the parties divorced, the wife became the custodial parent of the parties' child, and each spouse received $51,500 from the proceeds generated by the CD. For purposes of calculating support, if the husband's income was determined including all the $3,000 interest income generated from the CD over the prior 12 months because the CD was in his name only, then the wife would be double-dipping. The husband no longer owns the entire $100,000 asset that generated this $3,000. In fact, if his share of the $51,500 is reinvested in another CD earning the same rate, the husband will only be able to earn $1,545 over the next 12 months. And equally important, the wife could invest her share of the money and earn interest income, arguably reducing her need for support even more.

Double-dipping must also be considered if a retirement asset is held by one party but transferred to the other at divorce. Division of

8. From personal correspondence with the author.

9. For an excellent article discussing double-dipping and various states' treatment, see Donald J. Grazia & Stacy Preston Collins, *The Double-dipping Arguments*, 31 FAMILY ADVOCATE (Spring 2009).

any asset that generates income can present a double-dipping problem. The problem gets more complicated with business valuations. One of the most common and important business valuation tools is the use of discounted cash flow or capitalization of earnings. The valuation of the business asset necessarily depends on an analysis of the income generated in the past. If that asset will be diminished by the asset distribution in divorce, the cash flow could be counted twice.

In many states, the complicating factor increases dramatically if the analysis involves determination of the difference in the valuation of a professional practice between professional goodwill and personal goodwill. Cash flow is pivotal in the analysis. Stacy Collins, CPA/ABV, CFF, a forensic accountant and business valuation expert from Bala Cynwyd, Pennsylvania, advises lawyers as follows:

> *If you believe the possibility of a "double dip" is an issue, discuss the existing case law with your expert to assess how it pertains to the matter at hand. If necessary, the expert should be able to explain what methods are being used in the valuation and what income, if any, is considered in it.*[10]

Know that not all states recognize double-dipping. How double-dipping is treated may depend on the type of asset and its purpose. Many states specifically exclude consideration of double-dipping in the context of child support. Even if your state's law expressly denies application of the concept, you must know what double-dipping is and recognize its application in a given case. If not, an opposing lawyer may take advantage.

As objective and independent expert witnesses, the forensic accountant and business valuation expert must also know your state's law and apply that law in a conscientious and intellectually honest way in the analyses they perform. Double-dipping is an issue that experts could innocently get wrong or intentionally fudge. No one can ever truly know an expert's intent, good or bad. If the forensic accountant or business valuation expert does not apply the concepts and law in a conscientious and intellectually honest way and issues a written opinion that cannot be defended (regardless of motive), that expert witness may find that opinion revisited during cross-examinations in future cases—and not in a friendly way.

10. From personal correspondence with the author.

Case Example: A Very Detailed Lifestyle Analysis

In 2006, an Illinois divorce[11] from a 26-year marriage between two lawyers divided an $8.7 million marital estate. The wife's nonmarital property, valued at $154,012, included an inheritance and jewelry. The husband's nonmarital property, valued at $4,040,944, included real estate and AWP stock. The trial court's 58-page order followed the 19-day trial. Equitable distribution of marital property gave a disproportionate 55 percent share to the wife with 45 percent to the husband. The wife had given up her law librarian career 20 years earlier to raise their three children, and her award of permanent maintenance amounted to $35,000 a month with another $4,500 per month in retroactive temporary maintenance. Although both appealed, the bulk of the court's opinion addressed the husband's numerous contentions that the trial court had failed to properly consider his experts' testimony.

---

11. Heroy v. Heroy, 385 Ill. App. 3d 640, 895 N.E.2d 1025 (Ill. Ct. App. 2008).

To establish the married standard of living, the wife's financial expert, Cathleen Belmonte-Newman, a CDFA, did a lifestyle analysis to determine marital spending. The husband's expert, Bruce Richman, CPA and divorce financial analyst, agreed that $6.3 million passed through the spouses' accounts between 2000 and 2003. Belmonte-Newman determined the spouses spent $1.451 million a year or $5.8 million total between January 1, 2000, and December 31, 2004. She projected the wife's reasonable monthly expenses to be $56,016. Richman adjusted Belmonte-Newman's expense projections to arrive at $11,547.

In his analysis, Richman excluded capital expenditures and included expenditures on collectible art, wine, and antiques. Richman concluded that the wife's projected expenses were inflated, and his rebuttal report listed multiple problems with Belmonte-Newman's process. She made no allowance for the wife's net property award of $4,189,240, which included $2.8 million in cash. She did not include the husband's reimbursed business expenses. She excluded expenses for the husband's AWP stock and the wife's *Alert* newsletter publication. Richman took issue with Belmonte-Newman's exclusive reliance on the wife's personal estimates instead of historical data to project housing, vehicle, clothing, travel, decorating, and repair costs.

On the wife's employability, the husband's vocational expert, Grace Gianforte, a licensed clinical professional counselor, used national and statewide data to conclude the wife could earn $107,000 to $171,000 a year in publishing or $127,000 a year as a law librarian. The wife's publishing expert, David Nelson, was a journalism professor at Northwestern University. He testified on the wife's lack of employability in the publishing industry. The wife's second expert, John C. Strzynski, a former law librarian recruiter, disagreed with Gianforte's conclusions regarding the wife's employment prospects as a law librarian. Because she was absent from the workforce for two decades, both professions had passed her by.

Cash flow reports were provided to establish the husband's income and future earning capacity. Allen Berger, CPA, the wife's expert, prepared a cash flow report for husband's 2003 through 2005 income, setting net cash flow at $1,565,459. Richman rebutted that amount as excessive, however, arriving instead at $1,296,976.

On retirement asset income, the wife's marital property share included $963,968 in retirement assets. These, the husband argued, were not fairly considered in determining her future income. Given the comprehensive order showed consideration of "income produced from the assets she received" in the property division, the court held there was no error. Calculating income using various rates of return, attempting mathematical certainty, or making specific findings were not required by law. The court held that failure to calculate the income-generating potential of a property award was not an abuse of discretion. The husband's arguments of error in the trial court's valuation of certain assets, namely the wife's *Alert* newsletter (undervalued) and his real property and AWP stock (overvalued) were also unsuccessful.

Throughout its analysis the court emphasized the trial court's comprehensive order as having shown sufficient consideration of all expert evidence on all issues. The trial court was in the best position to weigh the evidence, properly exercised its discretion, and was not required to make any specific findings on maintenance or property division factors. The evidence was considered, the valuations were not against the manifest weight of the evidence, and there was no abuse of discretion. The property division and maintenance award were affirmed with modification and remanded with directions.

Ethics and Standards 10

Experienced forensic accountants will tell you that some of the most devastating cross-examinations can be about ethics and standards. Accountants' ethical guidelines and standards are rules created to protect the public and clients. For the accounting profession, it's all about the public trust. Zealous advocacy plays no role. When a forensic accountant deviates from ethical rules and standards, that violation can be exploited in the courtroom. When that violation relates to lack of independence, conflict of interest, or lack of objectivity, the results can be crushing. Careers have been ended for less.

The American Institute of Certified Public Accountants (AICPA) promulgates standards and ethical rules. The National Association of Certified Valuators and Analysts (NACVA) promulgates rules too, but most track the AICPA's.[1] Ethics and standards should be cohesive and consistent for all certified public accountants (CPAs). But auditing is different from tax preparation, which is different from business consulting, which is different from business valuation and forensic accounting. Differentiating

1. *See* Professional Standards, National Association of Certified Valuators and Analysts, *available at* www.NACVA.com.

unique ethics and standards for each of these roles in all possible circumstances may well be impossible.

Forensic accountants fear being labeled with a very derogatory name—one usually applied to people who accept money in exchange for intimacy. A term of art not defined by the AICPA's *Code of Professional Conduct*, this name describes the expert witness who will accept money in exchange for particular testimony. Are some CPAs guilty of this? Sure. Does this happen often? Probably not. Do some experts get labeled this name unfairly? Likely. Litigation can be a brutal, bare-knuckle, full-contact, mixed-martial-arts arena. What do forensic accountants do to avoid such ignominious name-calling being cast their way? They follow the ethical rules and standards and don't get close to ethical lines. Experienced CPAs will tell you that it's getting close to the lines that leads to trouble. Crossing them is not necessarily required.

What happens to a CPA who breaks the rules? He can be disciplined by his particular state's board of accountancy. The CPA's license can get yanked, or the CPA can receive public discipline. Does this really happen? Not often. In general, many state boards of accountancy do not want to get involved in litigated matters. For forensic accountants, it's much more likely that a CPA will have his testimony discounted in court. On cross-examination, the CPA's client's case can crumble because of a conflict of interest or proof of bias. From there, it's up to the legal establishment to banish the offending CPA by spreading the word that the expert witness cost a client a case because ethical rules or standards weren't followed. Also, at some point, word will get around among the remaining experts in the market. Regardless, some lawyers will seek out experts who will accept an expert witness fee in exchange for particular testimony. At the end of the day, what's important to understand is that family lawyers who know CPA ethics and standards can mount much more effective cross-examinations than family lawyers who don't.

AICPA's Code of Professional Conduct

The AICPA's *Code of Professional Conduct* is where it all begins. All CPAs who are members must adhere to its standards. State boards of accountancy incorporate by reference the AICPA's *Code of Professional Conduct* and/or promulgate rules and standards that are essentially the same as the *Code of Professional Conduct*. Licensed CPAs know of the *Code of Professional Conduct* and are likely required to study it as part of their state's annual continuing professional education (CPE) requirements. Described below are ethics and standards you should know when working with and questioning forensic accountants.

The standards and ethical rules of the AICPA's *Code of Professional Conduct* are designed to protect the public and engender its trust. Section 0.300 Principles of Professional Conduct reads, in part, as follows:

> *The Public Interest*
>
> *.01 The public interest principle. Members should accept the obligation to act in a way that will serve the public interest, honor the public trust, and demonstrate a commitment to professionalism.*
>
> *.02 A distinguishing mark of a profession is acceptance of its responsibility to the public. The accounting profession's public consists of clients, credit grantors, governments, employers, investors, the business and financial community, and others who rely on the objectivity and integrity of members to maintain the orderly functioning of commerce. This reliance imposes a public interest responsibility on members. The public interest is defined as the collective well-being of the community of people and institutions that the profession serves.*
>
> *Section 0.300.040 Integrity* states the following:
>
> *.01 Integrity principle. To maintain and broaden public confidence, members should perform all professional responsibilities with the highest sense of integrity.*
>
> *.02 Integrity is an element of character fundamental to professional recognition. It is the quality from which the public trust derives and the benchmark against which a member must ultimately test all decisions.*
>
> *.03 Integrity requires a member to be, among other things, honest and candid within the constraints of client confidentiality. Service and the public trust should not be subordinated to personal gain and advantage. Integrity can accommodate the inadvertent error and honest difference of opinion; it cannot accommodate deceit or subordination of principle.*

.04 Integrity is measured in terms of what is right and just. In the absence of specific rules, standards, or guidance or in the face of conflicting opinions, a member should test decisions and deeds by asking: "Am I doing what a person of integrity would do? Have I retained my integrity?" Integrity requires a member to observe both the form and the spirit of technical and ethical standards; circumvention of those standards constitutes subordination of judgment.

.05 Integrity also requires a member to observe the principles of objectivity and independence and of due care.

A CPA's opinions have value because of the public's collective perception. If the public and legal system view CPAs as hired guns, the value of their opinions diminishes. So obviously, the public trust is very important to accountancy as a profession, as well as to individual CPAs. Every experienced forensic accountant should be able to speak at length in the courtroom about the importance of maintaining integrity and engendering the public's trust.

AICPA's Independence Requirement

The AICPA also provides that CPAs must be independent:

0.300.050 Objectivity and Independence

.01 Objectivity and independence principle. A member should maintain objectivity and be free of conflicts of interest in discharging professional responsibilities.

CPAs must be independent for many reasons. CPAs sign audit opinions. CPAs sign tax returns. CPAs tally the results for the Academy Awards. CPAs want us to trust them because they are CPAs. The public gets that. But there is a dark side to the profession. Since the beginning, CPAs have discussed, over adult beverages, the age-old question: "How can a CPA be truly independent of the businesses and persons putting food on that CPA's table and paying part of his kids' college tuition?"[2] It doesn't matter whether the services provided are the audit

2. Sherron Watkins, CPA, a former VP at Enron, is a nationally known speaker about her interaction at Enron with its notorious chief executive officer (CEO) Kenneth Lay. In meetings with Lay, Ms. Watkins told him she questioned the accuracy of the accounting methodology of certain key revenue transactions. Lay sarcastically

of a publicly traded corporation, with fees in excess of $1 million paid to an international accounting firm, or the audit of a local medical practice owned by a solo practitioner. Clients matter. Personal relationships matter. Accounting fees matter.

Understanding this conflict, this duality, is at the heart of all cross-examinations of all expert witnesses. How can any expert witness be truly independent? If an expert's opinion is adverse to the interest of the client, the attorney on the case, upon discovering that fact, is almost certain to immediately terminate the expert's services. For a CPA providing litigation services, problems associated with the need for independence are more direct and transparent than those in any other aspect of that CPA's career.

Michael G. Kaplan, CPA, CVA, MAFF, of Los Angeles, California, is one of the nation's leading forensic accountants. With over 35 years of experience, Mr. Kaplan instructs forensic accountants across the country on many topics, including testimony.[3] Regarding experts' independence, he offers this response to a question often asked during depositions and in court:

Attorney: Mr. Kaplan, isn't it true you are a professional expert witness?

Mr. Kaplan: Quite the contrary, counselor. Most of my time is spent analyzing problems and advising attorneys on how to settle cases. On the rare occasion a case does not settle, I do testify. Last year, only about four percent of my time was spent in court testifying.[4]

---

and condescendingly responded that Enron did not pay Arthur Andersen $1 million a month so Enron could record transactions incorrectly. But that is exactly what happened. Enron grossly overstated certain income at unprecedented levels. Within a relatively short period of time following that, Enron collapsed, and Arthur Andersen, as a firm, was indicted on criminal charges. On August 31, 2002, Arthur Andersen surrendered its license to the Securities and Exchange Commission, essentially ending the practice of one of the world's largest and most prestigious accounting firms.

3. Visit www.courtroombootcamp.com for more information about his outstanding programs. The author has attended his weeklong training through NACVA's Expert Witness Bootcamp and highly recommends it for any forensic accountant who wants to testify.

4. Mr. Kaplan also suggests an alternative and more tongue-in-cheek answer: "Yes, counselor. Forensic accounting is not a business for amateurs." For more information about Mr. Kaplan, see www.expert-forensics.com.

So, are forensic accountants who testify really independent? Take a look at the AICPA *Code of Professional Conduct, 1.295.140 Forensic Accounting*, which reads, in part, as follows:

> *Expert witness services create the appearance that a member is advocating or promoting an attest client's position. Therefore, the advocacy threat would not be at an acceptable level and could not be reduced to an acceptable level by the application of safeguards. Accordingly, if a member is engaged conditionally or unconditionally to provide expert witness services or expert testimony for an attest client, independence would be impaired, except as discussed in the following item ii. (Exceptions omitted.)*

How can a CPA providing expert witness services truly be independent if the AICPA's *Code of Professional Conduct* states that testifying as an expert witness impairs independence? When the *Code* describes impairing independence, its drafters probably meant that testifying impaired independence for attest functions, like auditing. Immediately following the quoted passage and footnote, there are references to an exception for impairing independence for auditing purposes.

If polled, many experienced forensic accountants would disagree that being engaged as an expert witness to testify creates the "appearance [the CPA] is advocating or promoting a client's position." Forensic accountants are taught to advocate for their own opinion, not on behalf of a client. Again, most experienced forensic accountants would probably say that they are (and should be deemed) independent in fact, regardless of whether someone may question the appearance. Just because a forensic accountant is paid a fee for forming an opinion and testifying about that opinion on behalf of a client does not mean that the forensic accountant is actually advocating for the client's interest.

Kaplan War Story

Every experienced forensic accountant can tell great war stories. Whether absolutely factually accurate or slightly embellished, they make great time killers in seminars. One of my favorites is from Michael Kaplan:

In a contentious family law matter years ago, Michael was deposed for eight grueling days. On day seven of the deposition, opposing counsel asked Michael to list the topics discussed at his first "strategy meeting" with his client's counsel. Michael responded that he didn't understand the question. Opposing counsel asked the same question again. "What issues did you discuss in your first strategy meeting with your client's lawyer who hired you?"

Michael, again, said he didn't understand the question. The opposing counsel, a little more heatedly said, "Apparently, I have to break my question down into smaller pieces. You did have a strategy session with you retaining counsel, didn't you?" Michael's response was "No, I did not." Then counsel asked, "Then what was the reason that you were retained in this case? Why are you here?" Michael responded, "I was brought into this matter to provide expert opinions relating to certain of the financial issues in the case."

Counsel then asked, "You don't mean to tell me that you consider yourself an objective, unbiased expert—do you?" Michael's response was, "That is precisely what I am trying to tell you." Opposing counsel then looked up and shook his head and had an expression of disbelief on his face. Opposing counsel was so accustomed to dealing with experts—on both sides of the case—who assumed roles of advocacy rather than roles of objectivity.

Michael shares this story to underscore the toxicity in the system, where both questioners and the questions they ask often assume bias on the part of the forensic accountant.

AICPA's Rule 102

In addition to independence, the AICPA's *Code* requires that a CPA maintain integrity and objectivity:

> *1.100.001 Integrity and Objectivity Rule*
>
> *.01 In the performance of any professional service, a member shall maintain objectivity and integrity, shall be free of conflicts of interest, and shall not knowingly misrepresent facts or subordinate his or her judgment to others.*

Objectivity, integrity, absence of conflicts, not misrepresenting facts, and not subordinating judgment are a lot of important concepts all jammed into one sentence. They're all lumped together, however, for a very good reason. If all these buzzwords lived in a city, they would reside on the same block. To CPAs, all these terms relate to one another in an interconnected, conceptual framework. Without even one of these, the CPA's opinion cannot be trusted.

How do CPAs define a conflict of interest?

> *1.110.010 Conflicts of Interest for Members in Public Practice*
>
> *.01 A member or his or her firm may be faced with a conflict of interest when performing a professional service. In determining whether a professional service, relationship or matter would result in a conflict of interest, a member should use professional judgment, taking into account whether a reasonable and informed third party who is aware of the relevant information would conclude that a conflict of interest exists. . . .*
>
> *.04 The following are examples of situations in which conflicts of interest may arise: . . .*
>
>> *d. Preparing valuations of assets for two clients who are in an adversarial position with respect to the same assets*
>>
>> *e. Representing two clients at the same time regarding the same matter who are in a legal dispute with each other, such as during divorce proceedings or the dissolution of a partnership*

Being free from conflicts of interest is always a good thing. For determining whether conflicts of interest exist for CPAs who audit, the *Code of Professional Conduct* provides detailed facts, scenarios, and considerations. For forensic accountants, there is very little helpful guidance. Even though every case and situation is unique, the AICPA and its Forensic and Valuation Services Executive Committee should always work to provide more guidance.

For example, take a very common ethical problem. Is it a conflict of interest for a CPA who provided tax return preparation services for a married couple to provide expert witness testimony in the divorce on behalf of one divorcing spouse against the other? Most forensic accountants agree that this is a troubling situation and that the forensic accountant should not become an expert witness. The CPA can be a fact witness but not an expert witness. The duty to a former client, albeit undefined by the accounting profession, creates a conflict of interest. For a minority of forensic accountants, however, this does not present a conflict of interest.

As a practical matter, why would a CPA want to give expert witness testimony on behalf of a tax client against another tax client? Either the tax client for whom the CPA testifies also owns a business that is a client or that client will remain the CPA's client after the divorce. The other spouse's accounting and tax needs (and associated accounting fees) will usually pale in comparison. In such situations, it is painfully obvious who the CPA wants to please and appease. Does this create an appearance of bias? Most agree, yes. Do all agree? No. Has the AICPA decided this? No. Most states have not dealt with this either. This means that in many states CPAs are arguably allowed (because they are not disallowed) to provide expert witness services on behalf of one client against another client. New Mexico, however, specifically disallows CPAs from serving as an expert witness on behalf of one client against another.[5]

AICPA's General Standards Rule

1.300.001

.01 A member shall comply with the following standards and with any interpretations thereof by bodies designated by Council:

> *a. Professional Competence. Undertake only those professional services that the member or the member's firm can reasonably expect to be completed with professional competence.*
>
> *b. Due Professional Care. Exercise due professional care in the performance of professional services.*
>
> *c. Planning and Supervision. Adequately plan and supervise the performance of professional services.*
>
> *d. Sufficient Relevant Data. Obtain sufficient relevant data to afford a reasonable basis for conclusions or recommendations in relation to any professional services performed.*

This **General Standards Rule** is straightforward. But like many things in life, this Rule carries much more meaning than it appears

5. See the conflict of interest provisions of New Mexico Public Accountancy Rules 16.60.5.12.

to at first blush. The most important thing you should understand is that many forensic accountants don't know it as well as they should. Because its provisions are so basic, forensic accountants comply with its requirements without thinking about it. But many aren't able to articulate *how* they comply with the Rule's requirements.

For professional competence concerns, many CPAs know to take on only those cases that they are comfortable handling. How they get comfortable with cases before accepting them can be difficult to articulate. In this respect, forensic accounting can be a lot like practicing law. Often, when lawyers first sign up clients, they don't know exactly what discovery will be filed or when; what witnesses may be interviewed, deposed, or called; what legal research questions will need to be answered; or what particular strategy may be employed. Forensic accounting can be the same.[6] Often, even the family lawyer may not know exactly what forensic accounting services may be needed when the CPA is engaged. Certainly, as the engagement progresses, the CPA must acquire the necessary knowledge before rendering an opinion on a matter. Then, at deposition or trial, the CPA should be able to articulate how he determined that he was professionally competent to handle that particular engagement or what steps he took to become professionally competent. If the engagement was of a type the CPA had not worked on before, becoming professionally competent could include consulting with more experienced CPAs, reading up on the area with which the CPA was unfamiliar, or attending a seminar on that area.

As a hypothetical example in which a forensic accountant is testifying for the first time about a particular type of engagement, assume

6. The AICPA *Code of Professional Conduct*, Interpretations 1.300.010 Competence reads, in part:

> .01 Competence, in this context, means that the member or member's staff possess the appropriate technical qualifications to perform professional services and that the member, as required, supervises and evaluates the quality of work performed. Competence encompasses knowledge of the profession's standards, the techniques and technical subject matter involved, and the ability to exercise sound judgment in applying such knowledge in the performance of professional services.
>
> .02 A member's agreement to perform professional services implies that the member has the necessary competence to complete those services according to professional standards and to apply the member's knowledge and skill with reasonable care and diligence. However, the member does not assume a responsibility for infallibility of knowledge or judgment.

the question is asked, "How did you determine you are professionally competent to handle this engagement?" A solid answer could be the following:

> *Before I accept any engagement, I make an individual determination that I am professionally competent to handle it. That determination involves an examination of my experience, education, and training. I have been a CPA for 20 years. Most of those years were spent in auditing. I began forensic accounting six years ago. Since then, I have attended numerous CPE conferences and courses on forensic accounting, read articles, and conferred with other forensic accountants. I am experienced using the methodology and techniques employed in this case from several prior cases. I obtained certification as a CFF through the AICPA and Master Analyst in Financial Forensics, aka, the MAAF, through the NACVA. The body of knowledge of both certifications includes issues presented in this engagement. Even though this is my first engagement involving this exact issue, every case presents something unique, and that's what makes forensic accounting so interesting.*

The answer is factual and simple. The forensic accountant does not appear to be defensive. Also, it does not open any dangerous doors to tough cross-examination.

A less solid answer, although technically correct, could be the following:

> *I am a CPA, a CFF, and an MAFF. Nothing in this case was all that difficult. I am competent.*

This short answer can lead to many serious follow-up questions. Obtaining the certifications alone arguably does not make a CPA competent to handle any particular type of engagement. Also, if the case was not difficult, why was an expert witness even needed? From there, you could begin to dissect the accountant with a line of questioning similar to the following:

- "You know the 'General Standards Rule' from the AICPA *Code of Professional Conduct*?"
- "You know you are required to be professionally competent in order to accept the engagement?"

- "You are competent because you say so?"
- "Tell me what specific aspect of your education makes you competent."
- "So, you've never handled a case exactly like this before?"
- "Explain every individual step you took to comply with the General Standards Rule in determining that you were professionally competent to handle *this particular* engagement."

With tone of voice and simple, detailed, and factual follow-up questions, you may rattle some less-experienced forensic accountants.

The Rule's Due Professional Care requirement seems fairly benign. It's not. The forensic accountant should be able to articulate how due professional care was exercised. The only real way to accomplish a task that broad is for the forensic accountant to summarize the engagement's process and methodology. Forensic accountants, as a group, are great at explaining what tasks and analysis were performed. But again, many struggle mightily when asked "why" they chose to do a particular task or use a particular methodology.

The deposition question here might be a simple one, something like this: "Explain how you exercised due professional care in this case." A solid answer might also be a simple one:

> *I listened to the client, began reading key pleadings, and asked follow-up questions. From there, I began my planning process and determined what documents and information I needed that I did not have. I asked more questions. At the same time, I began thinking about key assumptions I needed to verify. I obtained documents through discovery and requested additional documents, which I also reviewed. Through the exercise of professional judgment, I chose certain forensic accounting techniques, including proof of cash analysis, and performed ratio analysis to test some of my thought processes. I also consulted some written materials and forensic accounting books. I reviewed the tax returns, financial statements, general ledgers, and other source documents that are listed and documented in my report. Finally, I performed the analysis described in my report, formed my opinions, and drafted my report. After that, I was provided some additional documents. I reviewed them carefully and subsequently determined that my opinion remained unchanged.*

The following would be a much weaker answer:

My client's lawyer gave me some documents. I looked at them. I crunched some numbers and learned that what the client suspected was true. So I wrote up my report. You can read it if you like.

Follow-up questions are the key. You can drill down by asking the forensic accountant "why" at each step of his description of what he did:

- "Why did you consult forensic accounting books?"
- "Why did you need additional documents?"
- "Why did you complete a proof of cash analysis?"

If the forensic accountant can't answer every question in simple terms, you may end up dominating that deposition. Even if the forensic accountant *can* adequately and in easy-to-understand terms answer the questions, you're still getting valuable information that you and your client's expert can use at trial. You can't lose when questioning forensic accountants about Due Professional Care.

The Rule's Planning and Supervision requirements aren't all that different from Due Professional Care. The forensic accountant must be able to explain who, what, when, and how the planning progressed and explain the supervision of staff assistants. Suppose the forensic accountant is asked a direct question, such as, "Tell me how you adequately planned and supervised this engagement." A simple answer could resemble this:

As we discussed earlier, I listened to my client and my client's lawyer, read key pleadings, and considered key assumptions. From there, I began my research and considered what additional documents we might need to challenge those assumptions and determine what work was needed. Planning the engagement is always a very important part of our methodology. In this case, as in many, determining which documents we had and which we didn't have but needed was a very important early planning task. Once we had them, I exercised professional judgment to determine the techniques to be employed and scope of documents to review in detail in our analysis. As far as supervision, I am lucky to have a great staff. My CPA assistant has two years of experience with my firm, mostly in family law, attends conferences, and reads articles I think are helpful. As her experience progresses, she is assigned more difficult tasks. I make assignments and perform a review of every assignment in the case. For example, I read the preliminary results of testing she performed and discussed with her some "sanity" checks. I also spot-checked some of her math and formulas used in the spreadsheets. As I have worked with my staff for several years and trained them, I have been careful to assign work I was confident they could handle. Certainly, my staff is always encouraged to ask me questions along the way. Based on my professional judgment, in this case, the schedules and analysis performed by my staff were completed within the very high technical standards I set for our firm.

The Rule's requirement to obtain sufficient relevant data is one of the trickier areas for both forensic accountants and family lawyers. What is "sufficient"? Sufficiency is a matter of professional judgment. There is no objective standard. As an example of a direct challenge to sufficiency of relevant data, consider the following questioning about a forensic accountant's analysis of an employee's stock option benefits in the context of determination of income:

Attorney: You reviewed the stock option summary schedule that lists the number of options, dates, and exercise price?

Opp. Expert: Yes.

Attorney: The employee benefit handbook contained detail of the company's minimum vesting requirements. Did you review the company's description of the stock option and related limitations contained in the company's employee benefit handbook?

Opp. Expert: No.

Attorney: Why not?

Opp. Expert: It was not provided to me.

Attorney: Did you ask your client or your client's lawyer for it?

Opp. Expert: No.

Attorney: Why not?

Opp. Expert: I did not know it existed.

Attorney: Don't most companies have additional explanations of stock options other than the schedule listing the options themselves?

Opp. Expert: Yes.

Attorney: Could it have been beneficial for you to review the information in the employee handbook before issuing your opinion?

Opp. Expert: Yes.

Attorney: In fact, the General Standards Rule of the *AICPA's Code of Professional Conduct* requires you to determine whether you have sufficient relevant data, correct?

Opp. Expert: Yes.

Attorney: Given that you did not even ask your client or your client's lawyer for it, did you violate the General Standards Rule in failing to obtain sufficient relevant data?

Opp. Expert: No. I wouldn't say I violated anything.

Attorney: Alright. Tell me exactly how you complied with the requirement that you obtain sufficient relevant data when you did not even ask anyone for additional information about the stock options before you issued your opinion about its estimated value.

Opp. Expert: I can't be expected to know every document that may or may not exist.

Attorney: What did you do to determine that you had all the documents you needed? Could you have asked?

Opp. Expert: I could have asked. But I didn't. I relied on the documents I was provided.

Attorney: In hindsight, if you were doing this engagement again, would you ask either your client or your client's lawyer for that employee handbook?

Opp. Expert: Certainly.

Contingency Fees, Unpaid Fees, and Future Streams of Income

You should also know that, although the AICPA *Code of Professional Conduct* does not specifically ban contingency fees for CPAs who perform expert witness services, it probably should.[7] If a forensic accountant is paid on a contingency basis, the expert witness arguably has a direct financial interest in the outcome of the case. Arrangements involving contingent fees arguably destroy independence and create an actual conflict of interest for all expert witnesses, not just forensic accountants.

If professional fees are owed to the forensic accountant as of the beginning of the trial, this might arguably have the same effect as contingent fees. You could craft an embarrassing series of questions implying a serious independence problem. Forensic accountants must be advocates for their opinion. If the client does not like the expert's opinion or its delivery, it is foreseeable that the client will not pay the expert. This is something with which the forensic accountant really does not want to deal. The forensic accountant must state either that he believes the client will pay regardless of his testimony or that he does not care about payment. Even if the forensic accountant has an ironclad contract, all professionals understand situations involving clients who won't pay and clients who can't pay. In any event, for this reason alone, many experienced forensic accountants will refuse to appear or testify at trial unless all outstanding fees are paid.

In another common situation, if the forensic accountant will continue to receive a future stream of income as the CPA for the party for whom the CPA is testifying, that situation should also create the appearance of a lack of independence. What CPA in his right mind would testify against the interest of an ongoing future client? None. Consider the following exchange:

Attorney: You have been listed as an expert witness for the husband in this case. Your firm has prepared tax returns for both spouses?

Opp. Expert: Yes.

7. See AICPA *Code of Professional Conduct* 1.510.001 Contingent Fees Rule, which prohibits contingency fees for certain listed accounting services. Even though forensic accounting is not listed, most forensic accountants agree that the rule either applies or should apply to forensic accounting engagements.

Attorney: And your firm also provides financial advisory services for both spouses?

Opp. Expert: Yes.

Attorney: What were you engaged to opine about?

Opp. Expert: Asset division and projected future investment returns.

Attorney: Do you think it's a conflict of interest to testify as an expert witness on behalf of one client against another client?

Opp. Expert: No.

Attorney: OK. Do you intend on providing accounting services and financial advisory services to both parties after the divorce?

Opp. Expert: We hope to.

Attorney: When was the last time you even spoke with the wife either on the phone or in person?

Opp. Expert: Ahhhh, three years ago.

Attorney: Have you even asked her if she intends to stay with your firm as a client after the divorce?

Opp. Expert: No.

Attorney: How much did your firm charge the parties last year for preparing their tax return?

Opp. Expert: Around $1,500.

Attorney: How much does your firm charge the parties for asset management monthly?

Opp. Expert: Anywhere from $600 to $750 per month.

Attorney: Do you have any reason to believe the husband will not be a tax and investment advisory services client after the divorce?

Opp. Expert: No.

Attorney: Do you believe that the husband will stay with you as a tax client and financial advisory services client if you testify with an opinion he considers adverse to his interests?

Opp. Expert: I haven't thought about it.

Attorney: Do you claim to have no conflict of interest and no bias when the husband is likely to continue to engage your firm as his tax CPA and financial advisor and pay your firm several thousands of dollars a year, while you have not even spoken to the wife in three years?

Opp. Expert: Correct.

Attorney: Did you call anyone at the Board of Accountancy to discuss whether you may have a conflict of interest?

Opp. Expert: No.

Attorney: Did you do any research at all to determine whether you may have a conflict of interest?

Opp. Expert: No.

Attorney: Did you even call another CPA and ask that CPA's opinion?

Opp. Expert: No.

In this example, if the CPA's testimony about asset division and projected investment returns is not advantageous to the husband, that CPA's firm is likely to be fired. Even though the engagement agreement may not specifically state that the payment of the fee for the expert opinion and testimony is contingent upon certain testimony being given, the practical result is the same. The CPA's future stream of professional fees is contingent upon the expert testimony being helpful to the husband. This presents a conflict of interest and independence problem. It's also a very practical, real-world problem that often crops up in divorces. The AICPA should provide very specific guidance regarding this type of problem.

AICPA's Statement on Standards for Consulting Services

The *Statement on Standards for Consulting Services No. 1,* issued in 1991, is the second most important standard issued by the AICPA. It's commonly called the SSCS or SSCS1 and sets out differences in standards from those applicable to auditing. Forensic accounting is considered "a consulting service," and therefore, the standards included in the

SSCS1 apply to forensic accountants.[8] The SSCS1 does not provide lengthy additional standards, but you should be familiar with the following (citations and footnotes omitted):

> *.07 The following additional general standards for all consulting services are promulgated to address the distinctive nature of consulting services in which the understanding with the client may establish valid limitations on the practitioner's performance of services. These standards are established under the "Compliance with Standards Rule" of the code (ET sec. 1.310.001 and 2.310.001):*
>
> *Client interest. Serve the client interest by seeking to accomplish the objectives established by the understanding with the client while maintaining integrity and objectivity.*
>
> *Understanding with client. Establish with the client a written or oral understanding about the responsibilities of the parties and the nature, scope, and limitations of services to be performed, and modify the understanding if circumstances require a significant change during the engagement.*
>
> *Communication with client. Inform the client of (a) conflicts of interest that may occur pursuant to the "Integrity and Objectivity Rule" of the code (ET sec. 1.100.001 and 2.100.001), (b) significant reservations concerning the scope or benefits of the engagement, and (c) significant engagement findings or events.*
>
> *.08 Professional judgment must be used in applying Statements on Standards for Consulting Services in a specific instance since the oral or written understanding with the client may establish constraints within which services are to be provided. For example, the understanding with the client may limit the practitioner's effort with regard to gathering relevant data. The practitioner is not required to decline or withdraw from a consulting engagement when the agreed-upon scope of services includes such limitations.*

8. Although forensic accounting is not explicitly listed, paragraph 5(a–f) makes clear the application of SSCS1 to consulting services. Within the category of consulting services appear "transaction services," which, in turn, include valuation services and litigation services.

Note that, under Client Interest, CPAs must "[s]erve the client interest by seeking to accomplish the objectives established by the understanding with the client while maintaining integrity and objectivity." This underscores the inherent conflict between independence and the requirement to "serve the client." While the concept is easy enough to define in theory, it can be hard to apply in reality.

Pursuant to the requirement to establish an understanding with the client, the responsibilities of the forensic accountant need to be clearly defined. Failure to define the scope of the engagement is a violation. If a CPA is dodging questions about what opinions the expert has formed or why certain work was performed, this passage could be helpful to reference when seeking to nail down trial testimony. If the CPA does not know what the engagement is, how will the CPA know what to testify about? If the CPA does not know what to testify about, how can opposing counsel prepare for trial?

Pursuant to the obligations to maintain communication with the client, if the forensic accountant has a significant reservation about the engagement, he must notify the client of that reservation. In divorces, it is not uncommon for a spouse to fail to share adequate documentation, even with that spouse's own expert. If such a failure to provide documents occurs, the forensic accountant determines that a significant reservation has arisen, and he properly communicates that, the forensic accountant can be compelled to discuss it because it is probably not confidential.

Paragraph 8 specifically provides that forensic accountants are not required to turn down cases or withdraw from engagements in which adequate documentation is not provided or available. While forensic accountants are not necessarily required to withdraw if such limitations arise, this must be considered in conjunction with the General Standards Rule's requirement that there be sufficient reliable data prior to forming an opinion. Such conflicts are not easily reconciled.

AICPA's Statement on Standards for Valuation Services

The AICPA's business valuation standards are contained in its *Statement on Standards for Valuation Services No. 1* (SSVS or SSVS1), *Valuation of a Business, Business Ownership Interest, Security or Intangible Asset*. Initially, these standards were a source of much consternation to business valuation experts who were also CPAs. Through these standards, the AICPA arguably created one of the most comprehensive sets of requirements for business valuation experts among all of the organizations certifying business valuation experts. Many CPAs were not happy with the AICPA adding additional standards and requirements for a profession that already had many complexities. The SSVS1 was seen as providing additional ammunition for attorneys on cross-examination, while at the same time adding little in terms of substance to the process of valuing businesses or providing assistance to the business valuation professional. As time has progressed, however, that criticism appears to have dissipated.

While this book does not address business valuation in any meaningful way, as a family lawyer, you should be familiar with the SSVS1 because divorce engagements can include both business valuation and forensic accounting. In those cases, it is possible that the business valuation expert will also be the forensic accountant. Even though the SSVS1 will not apply to the forensic accounting aspect of the engagement, many aspects of it can be helpful to know.

For instance, you should understand its reporting requirements. This is discussed more fully in Chapter 11. Understanding reporting requirements can be helpful in understanding the meaning of important terms of art used in business valuation. With respect to cases in litigation (all divorces), the SSVS1 exempts all reporting requirements.[9] That's right. For divorces, the AICPA specifies no particular business valuation reporting requirements. The exemption gives the expert and counsel flexibility in fitting reporting to particular cases. This exemption also has the effect of eliminating potential conflict with varying jurisdictions' rules of civil procedure and local rules.

In any event, reporting standards are important. Absent a special circumstance, many experienced business valuation experts will strongly suggest that, if a report is issued, it is the better practice to comply with

9. *Statement on Standards for Valuation Services*, paragraph 50, Reporting Exemption for Certain Controversy Proceedings, reads in part:

A valuation performed for a matter before a court, an arbitrator, a mediator or other facilitator, or a matter in a governmental or administrative proceeding, is exempt from the reporting provisions of this Statement. The reporting exemption applies whether the matter proceeds to trial or settles. The exemption applies only to the reporting provisions of this Statement (paragraphs 47–49 and 51–78).

In theory, this exception was created to give the valuation analyst flexibility to create a report that best matches the engagement.

all the standards in SSVS1. If the report doesn't comply with all the SSVS1 standards, you can attempt to prove that the expert deviated from accepted practices by picking and choosing among them.

From the perspective of the family lawyer working a divorce engagement with business valuation and forensic accounting components, either your client's expert will comply with the SSVS1's reporting standards or not. Also, either the opposing expert will comply with the SSVS1's reporting standards or not. Knowing the standards is a prerequisite to knowing if an advantage can be gained. Chris Mercer[10] adds, "In addition, your opponent may comply with other relevant business valuation standards. You do not want to have your expert suggest he does not have to comply with the SSVS-1 when his/her opponent has clearly complied with relevant standards." Family lawyers who are uncomfortable with the SSVS1 are encouraged to ask the client's business valuation expert to explain their requirement and put into context their importance to that particular engagement.

Special Report 08-1

The AICPA's *Code of Professional Conduct* designates the Forensic and Valuation Services (FVS) Executive Committee as the body to promulgate professional standards with respect to forensic and valuation services under Rules 201 and 202. In 2008, the FVS Executive Committee issued *Independence and Integrity and Objectivity in Performing Forensic and Valuation Services, Special Report 08-1.* Ten pages long (plus appendices), this special report summarizes the application of the standards and ethics described in this chapter and provides guidance on some typical situations. If you're looking to read more about ethics and standards for forensic accountants, *Special Report 08-1* is the place to go.

As a profession, forensic accounting is still growing up. Any absence of practical ethical guidance may be more a symptom of growing pains than a lack of leadership. Very few state accounting boards

10. Z. Christopher Mercer, FASA, CFA, ABAR, is the founder and CEO of Mercer Capital. As the author of many books on business valuation and related theory, Chris is resoundingly considered one of the leading business valuation experts in the world. To learn more about Chris and his firm, visit https://mercercapital.com/. Quotes are from personal correspondence with the author.

and societies have been able or willing to pick up the slack. Regardless, knowing what guidelines are out there and making sure your client's expert takes the high road at every juncture better ensures that your client's expert will survive the onslaught of opposing counsel during deposition and at trial. It will also make you much more effective at locating, exposing, and taking advantage of the weaknesses in the opposing expert's ethical armor.

Case Example: Exclusion as Expert Witness for Ethical Violation

Forensic accountants, and the family lawyers who hire them, should avoid conflicts of interest like the plague. They can be career killers. Described below is what can happen if an expert witness "crosses the line." No forensic accountant wants his or her name ending up in an appellate opinion as having been excluded from testifying for a conflict of interest and possible ethical violation.

The husband and wife in this Ohio divorce case[11] were married in 1963. In 1994, the wife filed for legal separation in Cuyahoga County, Ohio. Since they had, until recently, resided in Florida, the husband argued that the Ohio court lacked jurisdiction, but in 1996, the Ohio Supreme Court ruled that there was personal jurisdiction. On remand, the lower court equally divided the property and awarded the wife attorney's fees.

11. Frailberg v. Frailberg, No. 73321 (Ohio Ct. App. Dec. 5, 1998).

The husband then appealed to the Ohio Court of Appeals. He first argued that the lower court had lacked subject matter jurisdiction, but the appeals court noted that an Ohio statute imposing a six-month residency requirement applied only to divorce cases and not actions for legal separation. It also held that there was sufficient evidence supporting the lower court's finding that the wife was an Ohio resident.

The appeals court then turned to the issue of the admissibility of testimony by the parties' expert witnesses.

The wife's accounting expert, William Skaryd, had been allowed to testify despite the fact that his name was disclosed only a week before trial. His report had been submitted only a day before the trial, and the husband had only taken Skaryd's deposition the night before trial. This late disclosure had also been in violation of an earlier court order requiring timely disclosure. The husband objected, but the trial court still allowed Skaryd to testify.

The trial court has discretion as to sanctions for discovery violations, and those for exclusion of evidence should be imposed only when clearly necessary. Ultimately, the appeals court held that the husband had not been prejudiced and that the trial court had not abused its discretion in allowing the testimony.

The husband next argued that the trial court had erred in excluding the testimony of his expert witness, Ann Hawkins, who had testified regarding a property that the husband had leased from a company.

Hawkins was an attorney and CPA, and she had represented the company during the lease negotiations between the husband and the company. Upon learning of the possible conflict of interest in being the husband's expert witness, she obtained a waiver from the company, and another attorney in her office took over the lease negotiations.

Hawkins would have testified that if the property was sold, it would be for a purchase price of over $14 million less commissions and repairs. Hawkins had also computed the tax that the husband would owe upon sale.

The trial court excluded the evidence due to Hawkins' bias in favor of her client, the company involved in the transaction. The husband argued that as a result, the property was overvalued, since the court was never allowed to hear the testimony concerning reduction of the price for commissions and repairs. Since the property had been awarded to him, this resulted in the property division being unequal.

The trial court had properly excluded Hawkins' testimony regarding commissions and repairs. Her testimony was not reliable due to her bias toward her client, and her testimony might have been in violation of attorney ethical rules regarding conflicts of interest.

Despite the exclusion of the evidence, the husband did argue on appeal that the trial court had erred by failing to reduce the value by the amounts of repairs and commissions. However, the appeals court held that the evidence was not clear as to the amounts, and that the husband had failed to meet his burden of proof with respect to these expenses.

The husband also argued that the lower court had failed to take into account the tax consequences of the sale of the property, but the appeals court held that a court is not required to consider tax consequences absent expert testimony. Since Hawkins' testimony on this point had been excluded, the appeals court bluntly told the husband that he "could have obtained another expert to present this testimony."

A third expert witness, Scott Finerman, CPA, had been appointed by the court to monitor and disburse funds to both parties. In this process, he made recommendations to the court as to whether the funds were marital property. After reviewing this evidence, the appeals court did modify the award in part. It also reversed the award of attorney's fees and remanded the case.

Case Example: Follow Traditional Methodologies and Required Standards or Face Dire Consequences

Family lawyers need to be aware that in most circumstances, a calculation of value should not be substituted for a business valuation. If a family lawyer has a strategic reason in seeking to admit forensic accounting testimony that may be a bit novel, he or she may want to explore filing a pre-trial motion for determination of the admissibility of that approach and opinion. Also, the determination needs to occur well in advance of trial, so if that novel approach fails, the family lawyer and forensic accountant can change strategies.

In this trial court divorce opinion[12] from Indian River County, Florida, the wife offered the expert testimony of

12. Hebert v. Cote, No. 312017DR000305 (Fla. Cir. Ct. May 29, 2018).

CPA Charles Clay Price regarding the valuation of the husband's business, which had been formed about six years before the parties' 2009 marriage.

The company hosted computer servers for various companies and had grown rapidly. The husband initially sought to expand the business to a new location, but ultimately he decided to sell it instead. In 2011, he sold the company for $37 million, with net sales proceeds of $22 million. The company had always been in the name of the husband alone.

The wife retained Price to determine the value of any marital share of the company. Under Florida law, any increase in the value between the time of marriage and the time of sale would be a marital asset. The initial burden of proof was on the husband to show that he owned the business prior to marriage. The burden then shifted to the other spouse to prove which portion of the business became marital property through enhancement of value. If there is enhancement, then the court must analyze the reasons for appreciation to determine whether all or part is marital.

The husband moved to exclude Price's testimony. The issue was governed by a Florida statute corresponding with Federal Rule of Evidence 702.

Price sought to testify that he calculated a "minimum marital component" of almost $8 million of the gross sale and about $6.4 million of the net. To arrive at this conclusion, he used the revenue and retained earnings for a one-year period between 2009 and 2010 and noted the percentage of change. He then applied that percentage to the date of the marriage and the date of the sale of the business. Price also calculated a goodwill component of the sale proceeds by starting with the sale price and subtracting retained earnings as of the sale date. By applying the percentage change to this figure, he calculated a goodwill value as of the date of marriage. Finally, he added the values of retained earnings increase and goodwill increase to arrive at the minimum marital component.

The court noted however, that Price had never made any attempt to determine the fair market value of the company. For that reason, he was unable to give an opinion as to the increase in fair market value. Instead, the court pointed out that Price had calculated the minimum marital component using a different approach.

The court noted that CPAs are required to conform to the Statement of Standards for Valuation Services (SSVS) when rendering value opinions. Those standards typically allow three different methods: the market approach, the asset approach, and the income approach. However, Price had not used any of these approaches.

Despite departing from the SSVS, Price believed that his opinion was proper since he was retained only for a calculation engagement. But the court noted that the calculation employed by the expert had no precedent under Florida law. Instead, the only approved methodology is the fair market value calculation.

Since Price's opinion did not conform to that standard, the court ruled that the opinion would be stricken and not admitted as evidence.

Case Example: Importance of SSVS

Family lawyers need to understand the importance of following the Standards for Valuation Service (SSVS) of the American Institute of Certified Public Accountants (AICPA). These are the rules for forensic CPAs. By ignoring them, a family lawyer runs the risk of his or her client's expert witness being excluded for that failure.

The wife in this Arizona divorce case[13] filed in early 2011. A key issue in the divorce was the value of the family's drywall business, so the parties stipulated that the court should appoint a business valuator to determine its value. They also stipulated that the value should be set as of December 31, 2011. One valuator was initially appointed, but due to various delays, he was replaced by Stephen Koons, CPA/ABV/CFF, ASA. Koons set the value of the business at zero dollars.

The wife then hired her own expert, Mark Hughes, CPA, ABV, CFF. He set the value, as of April 30, 2013, at $1.22 million. Prior to trial, the husband made a motion in limine to exclude Hughes's opinion. The trial court

13. Mortensen v. Mortensen, No. 1 CA-CV 15-0097 FC (Ariz. Ct. App. June 9, 2016).

explained that it needed to hear the testimony to rule on the motion and allowed Hughes to testify.

After hearing the testimony of both expert witnesses, the trial court rejected Hughes's testimony and set the value of the business at zero. The trial court also ruled that the wife had taken unreasonable positions and awarded the husband $5,000 in attorney's fees. The wife then appealed to the Arizona Court of Appeals.

The wife first argued that the lower court had erred in not granting a continuance. Instead, the lower court had limited the trial to three hours. The appeals court agreed with the wife that a continuance should have been granted. Therefore, it remanded the case for a new trial, but only on the issue of spousal maintenance.

The wife next argued that the trial court had erred in its ruling on business valuation, particularly by excluding the opinion of her expert witness. The appeals court noted that the issue was governed by Arizona Rule of Evidence 702, which, like the corresponding federal rule, adopted the *Daubert* standard. Under that standard, expert testimony must be based on sufficient facts or data *and* be the product of reliable principles and methods. Also, the expert must have reliably applied those principles and methods to the facts of the case. The trial court had rejected Hughes's testimony, because he failed to provide "sufficient reference"[14] to the AICPA's SSVS. In addition, Hughes's investigation and determination of the necessary facts was neither thorough nor complete. The trial court also found that Hughes's opinions were not supported by reliable principles regarding business valuation and that he had not reliably applied the principles and methods of business valuation to the facts of the case.

Critically, the court noted that the wife had retained Hughes to perform a *calculation* of value rather than an *opinion* of value. In a *calculation*, the analyst and the client agree upon a method to use in making the valuation. However, in an *opinion* of value, such as that provided by appointed expert Koons, the analyst uses his or her own professional judgment to determine the proper method or methods to use. Opinions also require more procedures than mere calculations. As Koons had testified, an opinion is the application of all relevant valuation procedures, all relevant data, and all relevant valuation methods.

---

14. In terms used by forensic accountants, the expert failed to follow SSVS requirements.

The appeals court first noted that, at best, any violation of Rule 702 or *Daubert* was harmless, since the trial judge was the ultimate fact finder and was thus able to weigh Hughes's testimony.

However, in this case, the court also concluded that there was no error in excluding the testimony. The hearing on the motion in limine, along with the trial itself, amounted to a *Daubert* hearing. The appeals court noted that the trial court had made findings as to the incompleteness and unreliability of Hughes's testimony and that the record supported these findings.

For example, Hughes had relied upon 10 months of unaudited data, had used a gross profit margin not reflecting the company's history, and had not interviewed employees. He had also used outdated comparison transactions. Koons had described the Hughes valuation as "very speculative" and testified that the assumed gross profit margin could be maintained.

Since the Hughes valuation was excluded, the appeals court pointed out that the trial court was thus left with only the Koons opinion. The wife raised some questions as to its validity, but the appeals court rejected these as little more than minor flaws. For these reasons, the appeals court affirmed the lower court's finding that the business had zero value. It also agreed with the lower court's decision to order the wife to pay the husband's attorney's fees as well as the cost of the court-appointed valuator. The case was remanded for a new determination on spousal support.

Reports and Testimony

11

For lawyers, expert witness reports can do many things and fill many roles. Reports document opinions. Reports can answer discovery. Reports can intimidate. Reports can be unimpressive. Reports can help settle cases. Reports can suggest deposition questions. Reports can be hearsay.[1] Reports can also be the source of pride for some experts. Reports can be tangible measures of the expert's intelligence, skill, and talent. Forensic accountants can't always judge one another's testifying performances, but they often get to judge one another's reports. Unless required by applicable civil procedure rule, local rule, court order, or agreement, there may be no requirement that an expert report be issued. In any event, most courts expect reports to be prepared and exchanged, and you need to know when and how that is best accomplished.

After issuing reports, experts testify. Whether in deposition or the courtroom, some experts misunderstand their role. They know that most lawyers don't know their area of expertise as well as they do, which is true. They suspect

1. Some states' evidence law may allow expert reports to be admitted into evidence. Other states' evidence law may not.

most lawyers may not be as smart as they are, which may or may not be true. But expert witnesses rarely work as hard as they should to improve as communicators. Lawyers do work hard to be great communicators. Experts must be able to take technical subjects and explain them concisely, simply, and credibly. That's not an easy task when facing cross-examination. Your job is to prepare the expert to concisely and convincingly testify on direct-examination and to survive cross-examination. Additionally, your job is to conduct a direct-examination of your client's expert as well as a cross-examination of the opposing party's expert, which supports your theories of the case and provides the judge with the building blocks needed to construct the award your client deserves. This chapter will help you do that.

Report Requirements

Report requirements are generally set out in state rules of civil procedure or local rules. Some states' civil procedure rules may not create any particular formal elements or requirements. If there are no reporting requirements in the jurisdiction, the forensic accountant can form opinions and may not issue a report at all. To learn the expert's opinion, opposing counsel may be required to depose the expert or seek a scheduling order requiring a report, as discussed below. The Federal Rules of Civil Procedure do have specific reporting requirements for expert witnesses. Because forensic accountants often also testify in federal court, they generally prepare to comply with its requirements. Many states' rules of civil procedure track the federal rules, and it is therefore useful to be familiar with Federal Rule of Civil Procedure 26, as amended in 2010. Federal Rule 26 provides, in part, as follows:

> *Rule 26(a)(2) Disclosure of Expert Testimony*
>
> *(B) Witnesses Who Must Provide a Written Report. Unless otherwise stipulated or ordered by the court, this disclosure must be accompanied by a written report—prepared and signed by the witness—if the witness is one retained or specially employed to provide expert testimony in the case or one whose duties as the party's employee regularly involve giving expert testimony. The report must contain:*
>
> *(i) a complete statement of all opinions the witness will express and the basis and reasons for them;*

(ii) the facts or data considered by the witness in forming them;

(iii) any exhibits that will be used to summarize or support them;

(iv) the witness's qualifications, including a list of all publications authored in the previous 10 years;

(v) a list of all other cases in which, during the previous 4 years, the witness testified as an expert at trial or by deposition; and

(vi) a statement of the compensation to be paid for the study and testimony in the case.

The rest of Federal Rule 26 discusses disclosures for expert witnesses who are not required to provide reports, timing for disclosures of expert witnesses, limits to discovery, and protection against disclosure. The rule also expresses a preference for courts to "protect against the disclosure of mental impression, conclusions, opinions, or legal theories of a party's attorney."[2]

One significant change to Federal Rule 26 in 2010 was that report drafts are now protected from disclosure.[3] Experts want to be able to show counsel, and possibly the client, drafts of reports early in the process for many reasons, including confirming facts listed therein. Also, preliminary reports can be used to analyze the case for potential settlement negotiations. When drafts are discoverable, however, experts are hesitant to prepare them, fearing something may not be exactly correct. If produced in discovery, every little change, amendment, or typographical error could be criticized. Experts hate to give up their drafts.

Even though there is no particular required format for reports, you should understand their elements. Many experts expect lawyers to assign them a particular report format. For example, one family lawyer may want a detailed, lengthy, and complicated analysis to bully or intimidate the opposing spouse before mediation. Another family lawyer in the same situation may prefer that the report be a simple transmittal letter comprised of a one-sentence conclusion followed by a one-paragraph executive summary. Attached can be details and analysis in whatever format the forensic accountant may want to use. The

2. Fed. R. Civ. P. 26(b)(3)(B) (2017).
3. Fed. R. Civ. P. 26(b)(4)(B) (2017).

second lawyer may believe that the judge will read the conclusion and executive summary only. Why commit to producing more in writing than the court will read?

As discussed throughout this book, many forensic accountants are also business valuation experts. For business valuation experts, there is specific guidance about report elements. Those are listed in the American Institute of Certified Public Accountants' (AICPA's) *Statement on Standards for Valuation Services No. 1* (SSVS or SSVS1), *Valuation of a Business, Business Ownership Interest, Security or Intangible Asset.* The reporting requirements contained in the SSVS1 do not apply to litigated matters,[4] such as divorces, and certainly do not apply to forensic accounting engagements. Nevertheless, it can be helpful to be familiar with its discussion of terms related to reports.

Pursuant to the AICPA's SSVS1, there are three types of reports.[5] The Detailed Report is the most thorough:[6]

> *Detailed Report*
>
> *51. The detailed report is structured to provide sufficient information to permit intended users to understand the data, reasoning, and analyses underlying the valuation analyst's conclusion of value. A Valuation of a Business, Business Ownership Interest, Security, or Intangible Asset detailed report should include, as applicable, the following sections titled using wording similar in content to that shown:*
>
> - *Letter of transmittal*
> - *Table of contents*
> - *Introduction*
> - *Sources of information*
> - *Analysis of the subject entity and related nonfinancial information*

4. AICPA's *Statement on Standards for Valuation Services No. 1*, Paragraph 50. Reading the SSVS1 is a helpful exercise for family lawyers, especially in preparation for business valuation engagements.
5. The three types of reports are detailed, summary, and calculation. See SSVS1, Paragraph 48, for more information. Only the detailed report is discussed here.
6. The full version of the SSVS1 is available at the AICPA website. Internal citations included within the quoted passages herein refer to other paragraphs within the SSVS1 itself.

- *Financial statement/information analysis*
- *Valuation approaches and methods considered*
- *Valuation approaches and methods used*
- *Valuation adjustments*
- *Nonoperating assets, nonoperating liabilities, and excess or deficient operating assets (if any)*
- *Representation of the valuation analyst*
- *Reconciliation of estimates and conclusion of value*
- *Qualifications of the valuation analyst*
- *Appendices and exhibits*

* * *

Introduction

52. This section should provide an overall description of the valuation engagement. The information in the section should be sufficient to enable the intended user of the report to understand the nature and scope of the valuation engagement, as well as the work performed. The introduction section may include, among other things, the following information:

a. Identity of the client

b. Purpose and intended use of the valuation

c. Intended users of the valuation

d. Identity of the subject entity

e. Description of the subject interest

f. Whether the business interest has ownership control characteristics and its degree of marketability

g. Valuation date

h. Report date

i. Type of report issued (namely, a detailed report) (paragraph 51)

j. Applicable premise of value

k. Applicable standard of value

l. Assumptions and limiting conditions (alternatively, these often appear in an appendix) (paragraph 18) m. Any restrictions or limitations in the scope of work or data available for analysis (paragraph 19)

n. Any hypothetical conditions used in the valuation engagement, including the basis for their use (paragraph 22)

o. If the work of a specialist was used in the valuation engagement, a description of how the specialist's work was relied upon (paragraph 20)

p. Disclosure of subsequent events in certain circumstances (paragraph 43)

q. Any application of the jurisdictional exception (paragraph 10)

r. Any additional information the valuation analyst deems useful to enable the user(s) of the report to understand the work performed

If the above items are not included in the introduction, they should be included elsewhere in the valuation report.

Sources of Information

53. This section of the report should identify the relevant sources of information used in performing the valuation engagement. It may include, among other things, the following:

a. For valuation of a business, business ownership interest, or security, whether and to what extent the subject entity's facilities were visited

b. For valuation of an intangible asset, whether the legal registration, contractual documentation, or other tangible evidence of the asset was inspected

c. Names, positions, and titles of persons interviewed and their relationships to the subject interest

d. Financial information (paragraphs 54 and 56)

e. Tax information (paragraph 55)

f. Industry data

g. Market data

h. Economic data

i. Other empirical information

j. Relevant documents and other sources of information provided by or related to the entity

Reports that clearly and concisely convey important detail appear more objective and credible. The better practice for forensic accounting reports, as with business valuation reports, is to include the identity of the client; purpose of the engagement; descriptions of the subjects of the engagement; ownership of business interests; relevant dates, including the date of the opinion and the date of the issuance of the report; assumptions and limiting conditions; any restrictions or limitations in the scope of work or data available for analysis; any hypothetical conditions used in the engagement, including the basis for their use; if the work of another professional was relied upon during the engagement, a description of how the other professional's work was relied upon; disclosure of subsequent events in certain circumstances; and any additional information the forensic accountant deems useful to enable the report's reader to understand the work performed.

The introduction to the detailed report, discussed in paragraph 52, quoted previously, lists restrictions or limitations in the scope of work or data available for analysis. This type of paragraph could also exist in a routine family law forensic accounting report. Not all documents may have been made available, or the scope of the engagement may have been limited by some aspect of discovery. Reasons for the restrictions or limitations should be explained.

As an example of a forensic accounting and business valuation report for a divorce, see Appendix C. The example report does not explicitly delineate formal conclusions regarding income determination. Even so, the technical analysis within the report relating to underreported income and overstatement of expenses should help the lawyer for the nonbusiness-owner spouse when advocating both support and valuation. Depending on the situation, you may not know in advance of a report's issuance exactly how you'll handle the final analysis at trial. In those situations, you may prefer the forensic accountant to avoid forming discrete "final opinions" and instead submit reports containing analyses flexible enough to support trial arguments, themes, and theories yet to be determined.

Again, the absence of any reporting element does not make a particular report technically deficient as a matter of professional standards. Arguably though, it makes a report less thorough. However, most experienced forensic accountants would say that putting absolutely everything possible into a report only adds unnecessary expense. So the breadth and depth of a report should strike a balance between its complexity and the case's budget.

The Scheduling Order

If your jurisdiction does not have reporting requirements and you determine you want to create the obligation for both experts to prepare and exchange reports prior to depositions or trial, how do you do that? Many states' rules allow for scheduling orders. Scheduling orders can set deadlines for the procedural aspects of a case, including but not limited to the following:

1. Issuing discovery;[7]
2. Responding to discovery;
3. Expert witness designation, including subjects of opinions,[8] expert witness qualifications disclosure (curriculum vitae), and list of prior testifying experience;
4. Expert report exchange and requirements for reports;
5. Depositions of parties, experts, and third-party witnesses;
6. Mediation;
7. Consequences for failure to meet listed deadlines;
8. Pre-trial motions;[9]
9. Pre-trial disclosures and memorandum of law;

---

7. Michael G. Kaplan, CPA/ABV/CFF, CVA, MAFF, of Los Angeles, California, warns family lawyers not to allow discovery cutoffs to pass without first checking with the expert for his wish list of documents. Michael G. Kaplan & Carlton R. Marcyan, *Eleven Ways That Attorneys Kill Their Own Experts*, presented in 2009 (ABA Family Law Section teleconference).

8. The mutual understanding of the scope of the forensic accountant's engagement is very important. Before disclosing the expert and listing subjects of opinions sought, Michael Kaplan advises family lawyers to check with the expert to confirm the disclosure to avoid a disconnect that could result in a motion *in limine*. *Id.*

9. If opposing counsel files a pre-trial motion to exclude the forensic accountant as an expert, Michael Kaplan advises to always ask for the expert's input on responding to the motion. The response will likely include the expert's declaration of qualifications, methodology, and bases for opinions. Know that being excluded as an expert witness can be a very big deal to the expert, even if exclusion may not necessarily impact the case. *Id.*

10. Pre-trial conferences; and

11. Trial dates.[10]

Once a court rules that a scheduling order must be entered, that court may allow the lawyers an opportunity to negotiate its exact terms and deadlines. In many cases, those negotiations are fairly straightforward. For example, most judges don't care whether mediation occurs before or after party or expert depositions. If the parties can agree to its order, many courts will likely approve it without review. If the parties can't reach an agreement, lawyers may ask for a scheduling conference and request that the court set applicable deadlines.

Some scheduling orders may dictate that failure to meet a deadline can form the basis for exclusion of that evidence or testimony. For example, if a party fails to exchange a report on the date due, the court may exclude its admission. Once a scheduling order is entered, many judges will hold the parties to them, but some judges may not. Other judges may allow modification of the scheduling order if the request is reasonable and does not affect a set trial date. Like many aspects of family law, enforcement of a scheduling order's deadlines may depend on that particular judge's temperament.

When negotiating a scheduling order, you should consult with your expert to avoid creating unrealistic deadlines. Equally important though, the forensic accountant may want you to plant a strategic seed that can grow in the future. For example, the forensic accountant working for the nonbusiness-owner spouse may be concerned that the business-owner spouse may not disclose all the necessary documents. The opposing expert will have unlimited access to all the opposing parties' documents, whether or not they are produced in discovery. Therefore, when negotiating the scheduling order, the attorney for the nonbusiness-owner spouse could demand a requirement be included that all sources of information be disclosed in experts' reports. In this way, the scheduling order becomes a weapon for the attorney representing the nonbusiness-owner spouse. If one party has greater access to documents and gains

10. Michael Kaplan suggests that attorneys avoid scheduling a trial to start on a date where their expert's direct-examination is likely to be completed on a Friday afternoon, with cross-examination beginning the following Monday morning when the trial resumes. This places avoidable stress on the expert and ruins weekends. *Id.*

an unfair advantage as a result, that can be spotlighted and protected against through careful drafting of the scheduling order.

Preparing for an Opposing Expert Deposition

Well in advance of deposing the opposing expert, you should make sure the timing is coordinated. Have all documents been exchanged? Are reports complete? Is there enough time to review the reports before depositions? There are few feelings more miserable than receiving a faxed report at 5:00 p.m. from an opposing expert you are scheduled to depose at 9:00 a.m. the next morning. To prevent this, negotiate an agreement with opposing counsel and the opposing expert to exchange reports and documents several days in advance of expert depositions. Failure to produce documents in advance can slow depositions down to a crawl. At the same time that you're crafting questions, you may also be reviewing documents and determining what documents should be copied to be made exhibits.

The subpoena for the expert witness deposition may also be an important opportunity to shore up any holes in discovery. As always, your client and expert should be prepared to produce all the same documents you request from the opposing party, so check before issuing lengthy and thorough discovery requests. Example 11-1 lists documents and information you may want when deposing a forensic accountant.

The following is an excellent example of a thorough expert witness deposition subpoena duces tecum created by renowned trial attorney Michael Watters.[11] The documents requested by subpoena for deposition in the example reference California and federal rules, so you may consider translating them to your state's rules. Citing the authority for the basis of a request is obviously not required, but doing so puts the expert witness recipient and opposing counsel on notice that you know the law and intend to be thorough in its use. Although this example was not specifically created for a forensic accountant in a family law matter, the terminology used tracks the language lawyers and judges are familiar with when dealing with expert witness testimony and potential challenges to it.

---

11. O'Brien Watters & Davis, LLP in Santa Rosa, California. For more information about Michael and his expert witness consulting practice, visit https://michaelgwatters.com/. He has been a member of the ABA Family Law Section for over 40 years.

Example 11-1 Sample List of Documents to Subpoena from an Expert Witness

The documents and things to be produced by the expert witness are listed as follows:

1. Your entire file on this case.
2. Your complete time and billing records on this case. CAL. EVID. CODE § 722.
3. All written reports on this case prepared by you or at your direction. CAL. CODE CIV. PROC. § 2034.410.
4. All "writings" ("Writing" means hand writing, typewriting, printing, photostating, photographing, and every other means of recording upon any tangible thing any form of communication or representation, including letters, words, pictures, sounds, symbols, or combinations thereof). (CAL. EVID. CODE § 250). As used in this deposition subpoena attachment, the term "writing" also includes "electronically stored information." (*See* CAL. CODE OF CIV. PROC. § 2016.020(e)). "Electronic" means, relating to technology having electrical, digital, magnetic, wireless, optical, electromagnetic, or similar capabilities (*see* CAL. CODE OF CIV. PROC. § 2016.020(d)) prepared by you or at your direction for use in this case, including, but not limited to, charts, schedules, spreadsheets, calculations, diagrams, transparencies, slides, photos, videotapes, posters, blueprints, blow ups, animations, and the like.
5. All writings setting forth or describing the nature and scope of your assignment in this case.
6. All writings setting forth or describing any limitation on the nature and scope of your assignment in this case.
7. All written retainer, fee agreements, or engagement letters regarding your assignment in this case. CAL. EVID. CODE § 722.
8. All writings upon which your opinions and conclusions in this case are based. CAL. EVID. CODE § 721.
9. All writings showing or tending to show that you are sufficiently qualified to testify as an expert in this case on the subject(s) to which your testimony relates including those that show your special knowledge, skill, experience, training, or education.

These would include curricula vitae (CVs), resumes, degrees, diplomas, certificates of completion/graduation, licenses, professional memberships, awards and honors, publications, and the like. CAL. EVID. CODE §§ 720 and 801(b).

10. All writings prepared by you including, but not limited to, scientific, technical, or professional articles, books, texts, treatises, journals, or similar publications that have any relevance to the subject(s) to which your testimony relates or your opinions and conclusions in this case. CAL. EVID. CODE § 721.
11. All writings including any scientific, technical, or professional articles, texts, treatises, journals, or similar publications that you read, referred to, considered, or relied upon in arriving at or forming your opinions and conclusions in this case. CAL. EVID. CODE § 721.
12. All writings showing the amount of time you personally spent on this case.
13. All writings showing exactly how you spent your time in this case.
14. All writings showing the gross compensation and expenses paid and/or owed to you for your services as an expert witness by the party designating you as an expert witness in this case. CAL. EVID. CODE § 722.
15. All writings showing the gross compensation and expenses paid to you and/or owed to you for your services in the past two (2) years as an expert witness or expert consultant in all other cases by the same party or same attorney(s) for the party designating you as an expert witness in this case.
16. All written results of tests, including destructive testing, conducted by you in this case.
17. All writings showing or listing the raw data, including test protocols resulting from any test performed by you or at your direction in this case.
18. All writings analyzing the raw data resulting from any test performed by you or at your direction in this case.
19. All writings setting forth your opinions and conclusions in this case. CAL. EVID. CODE § 721.

20. All writings setting forth the opinions and conclusions you will be giving at trial in this case.
21. All drafts of writings setting forth the opinions and conclusions you will be giving at trial in this case. CAL. EVID. CODE § 721.
22. All writings setting forth the basis(es) for each of the opinions and conclusions you will be giving at trial in this case. CAL. EVID. CODE § 721.
23. All writings setting forth the reasons or reasoning for each of the opinions and conclusions you will be giving at trial in this case. CAL. EVID. CODE § 721.
24. All writings between you and the party who designated you as an expert in this case.
25. All writings between you and the attorney(s) for the party who designated you as an expert in this case.
26. All writings of any and all interviews conducted by you of the party who designated you as an expert in this case.
27. All writings of any and all interviews conducted by you of any and all persons who have, or claim to have, personal knowledge of facts that support the opinions and conclusions you will be giving at the trial of this case.
28. All notes taken or made by you or at your direction regarding this case.
29. All writings between you and anyone other than the foregoing categories of persons relating to your assignment in this case.
30. All writings provided to you by or at the direction of the party or the attorney for the party who retained, hired, or designated you as an expert witness in this case.
31. All written reports prepared by other expert(s) upon which you have relied and that you will be reading into the record at trial. CAL. EVID. CODE § 768. *See* CAL. EVID. CODE § 804.
32. All writings showing each assumption you made in forming the opinions and conclusions you will be giving at the trial in this case.

33. All writings that show any substantial or significant inconsistencies in the opinions and conclusions you will be giving at the trial in this case.

34. To the extent that you have testified as an expert witness at trial or deposition in a federal case, a copy or copies of the disclosure(s) required of expert witnesses by Federal Rules of Civil Procedure 26(a)(2)(B)(v), which is, "a list of all other cases in which, during the previous 4 years, the witness testified as an expert at trial or by deposition."

35. All sworn testimony by you as an expert witness, including affidavits or declarations, deposition transcripts, or trial transcripts wherein you testified in the last four (4) years.

36. All sworn testimony by you as an expert witness, including affidavits or declarations, deposition transcripts, or trial transcripts wherein you testified on the same or similar issues in other similar cases. *See* CAL. CODE OF CIV. PROC. §§ 2002–05.

37. All sworn testimony by others, including affidavits or declarations, depositions, or otherwise that were read, reviewed, or relied upon by you, regarding or relating to the subject matter of this case.

38. All writings not otherwise covered by the foregoing numbered items that you believe are important to the opinions and conclusions you will be giving at trial in this case.

39. All writings used by you to refresh your memory with respect to any matter about which you testify. CAL. EVID. CODE § 771.

You are encouraged to know your respective state's civil procedure and evidence rules regarding what documents must be produced, what can be produced if requested, and what law may exist to protect or limit certain aspects of disclosures. For example, as discussed earlier, under Federal Rule 26, drafts of reports are no longer discoverable.[12] If your state similarly protects report drafts, you should consider not requesting drafts to avoid the expense and embarrassment of defending (and losing) a motion for a protective order. If your state does not protect drafts, request them unless your expert does not want to share them. The above sample exhibit to an expert witness subpoena is provided as

---

12. . FED. R. CIV. P. 26(b)(4)(B) (2017).

a starting point only. Taking the time to tailor document and information requests to a particular case almost always pays dividends.

What Deposition Style Should You Use?

Deposing an opposing forensic accountant pulls together everything discussed in earlier chapters. Crafting one fact per question is tough. Locking down any opposing expert to a particular discrete set of opinions is tough. Listening to the answers and not thinking about the next question is tough. Deposing is part science and part art. One of the first decisions you must make is whether to take a "shotgun" or "rifle" approach.

With the shotgun approach, you ask the expert witness everything imaginable. The goal is to test the opposing forensic accountant. Are there glossy answers? If so, drill deeper. Listen for holes. Does the forensic accountant struggle with particular types of questions? Are there aspects of the testimony with which the forensic accountant is less confident than others? If you drill too deep, the opposing expert may shore up that aspect of the testimony before trial. If you don't drill deep enough, you won't get anything useful.

What about the rifle approach? Your client's forensic accountant can usually help you identify a handful of issues upon which the forensic accountants differ. The rifle approach sticks to differences only. For example, if an important difference in opinion hinges on an application of state law, all assumptions related thereto should be questioned in depth. Where did the opposing expert obtain his understanding of the state's family law? Was there an independent source of financial information? Was there any information relied upon but not disclosed in the report? A weakness in the opposing expert's deposition testimony may betray a bias or factual or legal assumption that can be challenged in court. As part of the rifle approach, you may want to ignore similarities between the opposing forensic accountants' education, experience, and training. If opposing forensic accountants have similar credentials, why challenge them if both are testifying about the same issues? Not every case demands every issue be dissected and attacked.

Many experienced family lawyers suggest keeping depositions calm and friendly. Making opposing experts feel comfortable may lead them into a more conversational style, with an accompanying relaxed guard. In theory, giving a deposition a more casual tone may lead to extracting more useful information. That can often be challenging with a professional, such as a forensic accountant, who has been trained to behave any way but casually. In any event, this is an opportunity for you to shine. By listening, taking issues one step at a time, and not being afraid to ask simple (or stupid) questions, you can help get cases settled as easily as when dominating the flow. You never know. Family law is rarely predictable.

The Deposition Questions

What questions should you ask the opposing expert? Appendix D contains a detailed checklist of sample deposition questions for opposing forensic accountants in family law cases. Some areas of the deposition script allow for fishing. Fishing sometimes makes sense and can lead to the discovery of useful information. You must not, however, rely too heavily on any checklist, even this one. You must add substantive questions directly related to the facts of the particular case, the reports presented, and the expert being deposed.

Lawyers develop a comfort zone for depositions. Make the deposition your own. Some revel in having no pre-written questions and listen intently as they ask meaningful follow-up questions. Other lawyers say having a question checklist allows them to relax and lessens worrying about forgetting important topics for questions. Regardless, great lawyers listen well to answers and ask thoughtful follow-up questions. Listening makes the difference between setting up a powerful cross-examination and a journeyman's cross-examination.

In addition, some lawyers like to jumble up the order of questioning to avoid a linear progression. Jumbling questions might destabilize some forensic accountants, but it can also cause confusion. Confusion may allow the deponent to claim a way out of a poor answer. In theory, specific questions about the accountant's work product should be the witness's strongest area since it is the most technical.

Finally, when you are planning questions, the most obvious and important resource is your client's forensic accountant. If the budget allows for him to attend the opposing expert's deposition, make it happen. At the deposition though, be wary of writing notes back and forth documenting that assistance. Those notes comprise written communication, and opposing counsel may demand to see them when deposing your client's forensic accountant. Disclosing those notes, however, may not matter in the big picture. Nevertheless, you should know the applicable state law regarding communications between lawyers and testifying experts and whether case strategy discussion and consultation must be disclosed if requested.[13]

Scoping Out the Opposing Expert

CPAs are like anyone else. On any given day, you will find them to be pleasant, cranky, kind, complicated, funny, petulant, or accommodating. In general, the more experienced forensic accountants will be professional and friendly. For these veterans, the excitement of depositions and the mental combat they entail dissipated long ago. Even though most expert witnesses enjoy some aspects of the conflict, the better ones are no longer interested in creating drama. It's just another day at the office. Just like lawyers, however, some CPAs take themselves way too seriously and take small matters very personally.

Prior to the deposition, if at all possible, you should try to meet and greet the opposing forensic accountant. Look to see if the expert can "flip the switch" between a cordial and polite persona to that of a stone-cold killer expert witness. Stone-cold killer expert witnesses can focus solely on the task at hand. Study the expert. Is the accountant comfortable with his role? Can the witness make small talk easily? Does the witness need to pump up before testifying? Keep mental notes. Any information learned may help you later recognize if the witness is off his game.

Defending Your Client's Expert Deposition

There are lots of different opinions about trial strategy and the preparation of expert witnesses. By the time expert depositions take place, both family lawyers usually know their respective themes and theories of the case. Some settlement posturing related to the strengths of the client's case and the other spouse's weaknesses may have taken place already.

One advantage of having engaged a very experienced forensic accountant is that you need to spend very little deposition "prep time."

---

13. If ongoing technical assistance is needed and the litigation budget allows for it, you may want to consider engaging a consulting witness. See the discussion of testifying and consulting witnesses in Chapter 2.

The experienced expert knows how to emphasize the strengths of the analysis, mitigate any weaknesses, and avoid getting backed into corners. Confidence and poise are traits you and your client should expect from the very experienced expert.

If you are working with a relatively inexperienced forensic accountant, you may need to spend significant time preparing him to testify. Basic deposition skills may need to be discussed. Every family lawyer develops her own style of coaching; however, basic tips to share include the following:

- Answer only the question asked.
- Don't volunteer information.
- If the thought comes into your head that you're talking too much, you probably are.
- Always appear confident.
- If you need a break, take it, especially if the deposition lasts more than two hours.
- If you don't understand a question, don't guess what was asked.
- Ask that questions be restated or repeated.
- Never lose your temper.
- Be professional and stone cold—no joking.
- Give testimony as formally as if you are in a courtroom.
- Do not be overly polite to or snippy with the lawyer.
- Never look to your client's lawyer for an answer or direction—it is a sign of weakness.
- There is no need to deny you discussed testimony with your client's lawyer unless you really didn't.
- You are not represented by counsel; the client is.

Strategic Decision: Old School versus New School

Over the years, advice to expert witnesses from lawyers has shifted. Trials have become prohibitively expensive. Opposing lawyers understand that, more often than not, neither client wants a trial. As family lawyers have become less "trial lawyers" and more "litigators," the emphasis on preparing for mediation has increased. As a result, family lawyers have seen a greater need to present stronger cases before mediation. Rather than a lawyer sandbagging opposing counsel by saving the best arguments for trial, settlement negotiations have become the new crossroads. Many family lawyers now want to focus efforts on the negotiating table.

The "old-school" strategy was to instruct expert witnesses to sandbag. Lawyers advised, "Answer only the question asked." The only acceptable answers are "yes," "no," and "I don't know." No elaboration, ever. Tell the truth, but any answer beyond a terse response provides too much opportunity for the opponent to craft a strategic response at trial. Even to this day, many experts are trained in the old-school ways. For example, suppose opposing counsel asks, "Do you know what time it is?" Under the old-school approach, the only answer is "no" unless the witness is first requested to look at his watch. Old-school depositions can be physically and emotionally draining.

"New-school" depositions are designed to overwhelm the opposing counsel and opposing party by scaring the opposition into submission. How does an expert witness scare the opposing counsel and the opposing party into settlement? By being a great witness. Being a great witness means being confident, credible, and a great communicator. Being a great witness means giving simple, clear, and objective analysis. And being a great witness means looping testimony back to themes and theories of the case while citing to particular relevant statutory factors for property division, alimony, or child support.

In new-school depositions, the forensic accountant discusses the report's exhibits and analysis and gives the opposition a preview of the step-by-step direct-examination to come at trial. The expert explains both why and how the expert's opinion is the only credible answer to the divorce puzzle. The forensic accountant connects all the dots. The goal of the new-school deposition is to alter the relative negotiating position of the parties. New-school depositions can be exhilarating and fun.

You should discuss deposition strategy with the forensic accountant. There are no "one-size-fits-all" approaches. On the one hand, high-asset, high-conflict cases may dictate that the shotgun approach and old-school rules be applied. On the other hand, most cases are on a tight budget. The rifle approach and new-school methods may make the most sense if the client does not have the resources to game the system. The shortest distance (and least-expensive path) between two points may dictate a straight line.

Trial Preparation

Getting ready for trial usually means making a list and checking it 40 times. The pre-trial checklist is long: schedule court reporter, prepare and produce pretrial disclosures, review local rules, determine whether to request a pre-trial conference, draft and file motions *in limine*, decide upon themes and theories, plan opening and closing, determine if a memorandum of law is needed, and plan every witness's direct- or cross-examination. In addition to this intimidating to-do list, you may need to brush up on evidence rules specific to the case. There are very few feelings more uncomfortable than receiving an "improper foundation" or "lack of foundation" objection at trial when you know you should have looked up the foundation requirement for that type of evidence.

When working a family law matter with a forensic accountant, two important Federal Rules of Evidence must be kept in mind—1006 and 703.[14] Of course, you should also know your jurisdiction's equivalent applicable rules.

> *FRE* **1006**. *Summaries to Prove Content*
>
> *The proponent may use a summary, chart, or calculation to prove the content of voluminous writings, recordings, or photographs that cannot be conveniently examined in court. The proponent must make the originals or duplicates available for examination or copying, or both, by other parties at a reasonable time and place. And the court may order the proponent to produce them in court.*

If you get sandbagged at trial with a schedule that you have not seen, your objection may be something like this:

> *This appears to be a rule 1006 summary. I've never seen it before. Under rule 1006, we have a right to review the summary and examine the voluminous originals at a reasonable time and place. That was not done. The summary should be excluded.*

---

14. For a more detailed discussion of rules 703 1006, see STEVEN N. PESKIND, THE FAMILY LAW TRIAL EVIDENCE HANDBOOK: RULES AND PROCEDURES FOR EFFECTIVE ADVOCACY (ABA 2013).

Whether or not produced as part of the report itself, charts and schedules may be considered a rule 1006 summary. If a chart is prepared before trial, consider getting it and a description of its source documents to opposing counsel as soon as possible to avoid the objection.

Rule 1006 summaries can be some of the best opportunities for adding power to direct-examinations. The summary can be admitted into evidence as substantive evidence. Keep in mind that while the underlying documents must be admissible into evidence, they need not be entered into evidence to do so. Rule 1006 can't be used as a back door to enter into evidence that which is not otherwise admissible.

Federal Rule of Evidence 703 is the basis for forensic accountants being able to rely on hearsay. Most financial records contain hearsay from multiple sources.

> *FRE* **703**. *Bases of an Expert*
>
> *An expert may base an opinion on facts or data in the case that the expert has been made aware of or personally observed. If experts in the particular field would reasonably rely on those kinds of facts or data in forming an opinion on the subject, they need not be admissible for the opinion to be admitted. But if the facts or data would otherwise be inadmissible, the proponent of the opinion may disclose them to the jury only if their probative value in helping the jury evaluate the opinion substantially outweighs their prejudicial effect.*

Direct-Examination of the Client's Forensic Accountant

Planning direct-examinations presents numerous challenges. Right before trial, when things are so busy, it's easy to say to yourself, "To hell with it; the forensic accountant knows what to say." There never seems to be enough time to prepare the expert's direct-examination before trial. Maybe that's why so many direct-examinations are so boring.

Family lawyers establish their own rhythm. One may think, how hard is it to ask, "And what did you do next?" "Really? Why is that important in the context of determining income for the husband?" "In your opinion, what is the husband's average income from all sources for the last three years?" Even as simple as the mechanics may appear though, presenting a powerful direct-examination of a financial expert requires planning, preparation, and creativity.

Direct-examinations of forensic accountants are almost always critical to the case. Many judges look forward to hearing evidence from an unbiased and independent witness testifying about numbers—assets, debts, income, and expenses. Really? Is financial testimony really more interesting than the venom of two spouses who hate each other? No, not really. But listening to testimony about dollars can be less stressful than listening to salacious details of a train wreck of a marriage.

Exhibits

Relevant, clear, and concise exhibits help avoid boring direct-examinations. In family law, there are many ways to present demonstrative evidence. The forensic accountant's report may contain very helpful schedules and analyses that can be put on separate sheets of paper in a notebook, charted in graphs, presented on PowerPoint slides, blown up on poster boards, or simply written on an easel or chalkboard. In almost every family law matter involving money, there is a chart or graph that can be created for effective argument. This is one of the greatest opportunities for the trial lawyer's and forensic accountant's creativity. Don't pass it up.

For demonstrative aids (or evidence),[15] you have even more dizzying options to consider. Color or black-and-white exhibits? How many exhibits? How many are too many? Is the judge technical and visual? If you want to limit the number of exhibits to only the best ones, how do you decide which are the most persuasive? Here's where it's fun to be a trial lawyer. Exchange ideas with the forensic accountant. Work together. Stare at the exhibits. Your level of practice and expertise is only limited by your creativity.

Example of a Simple Yet Powerful Demonstrative Aid

Want a reason to create a chart for a divorce trial? Here is an easy idea: compare annual income histories for spouses. Where can you get this data without having to review every single tax return? Simple. From

15. "A demonstrative aid is not ordinarily admissible as substantive evidence (although some jurisdictions allow them as such)" (citations omitted). *Id.* at p. 172.

your client, and through discovery from the opposing spouse, obtain both spouses' individual Social Security statement. Create your chart in Excel. Put the husband's income in blue and the wife's income in pink. This simple report breaks down how much that individual has received in compensation by year. While Social Security statements show both taxed Social Security earnings and taxed Medicare earnings, the taxed Medicare earnings column will show the individual's actual salary dollars earned.

To obtain a party's Social Security statement, go to www.ssa.gov, create an account (if the client does not already have one), and save it via pdf. Projected Social Security benefits earned to date will also appear on the statement. The chart itself may not qualify as a rule 1006 summary because the supporting documents are not voluminous. The underlying individual Social Security statements should be admissible. Consider asking the judge to allow a letter-sized color printout of the chart to be marked for identification purposes for the record. Example 11-2 is an exhibit charting the difference in earnings between spouses taken directly from the Kirks' Social Security statements.

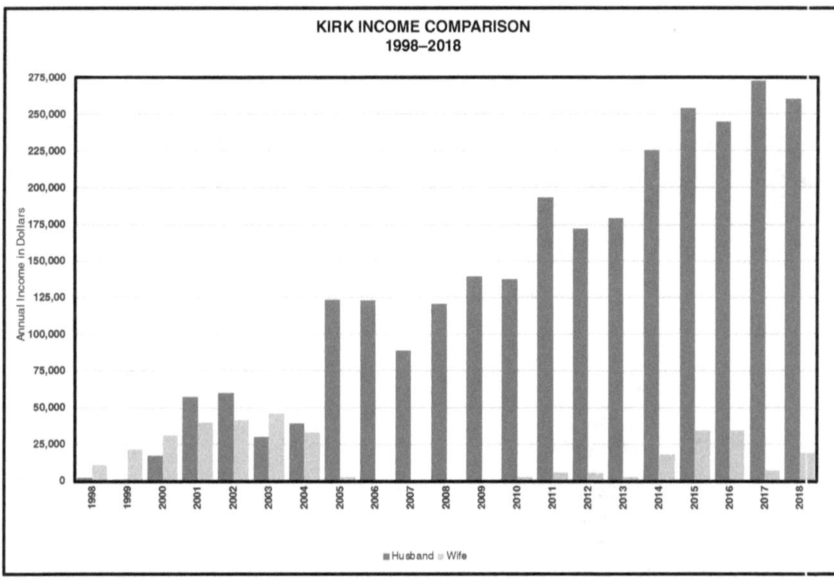

Example 11-2 Salary Comparison Chart

Spreadsheets Can Be Your Best Friend or Worst Enemy

When using printouts of spreadsheets as demonstrative evidence, you should try to eliminate visual noise among the dizzying rows and columns of numbers. Forensic accountants often think more detail is more persuasive. But for most cases, less is more. On the other hand, does eliminating numbers invite unwanted questions? Does it invite questions you want to have asked? Does eliminating a particular calculation from the spreadsheet make the exhibit, chart, or graph misleading in any way? Never forget about credibility. Deal with ugly financial truths, or the opposition may deal with them for you.

As an example of the credo that less is more, consider the hypothetical in Example 11-3. The husband claims his bonus should not be considered when determining income for child support and alimony because his bonus is never guaranteed and because, furthermore, his sales commission numbers are not looking good in the divorcing year. For both child support and alimony income determinations, the state's law allows the court to exercise discretion when considering how many years' prior income to average. This state has reported cases in which two and three years of income was considered and approved.

Picard vs. Picard
Analysis of Husband's Earned Income

Income	2014	2015	2016	2017	2018
Salary	$ 45,000	$ 50,000	$ 50,000	$ 40,000	$ 50,000
Commission	50,000	125,000	110,000	95,000	60,000
Total	$ 95,000	$ 175,000	$ 160,000	$ 135,000	$ 110,000
		3 Yr Avg.	$ 135,000		
		4 Yr. Avg.	$ 145,000		

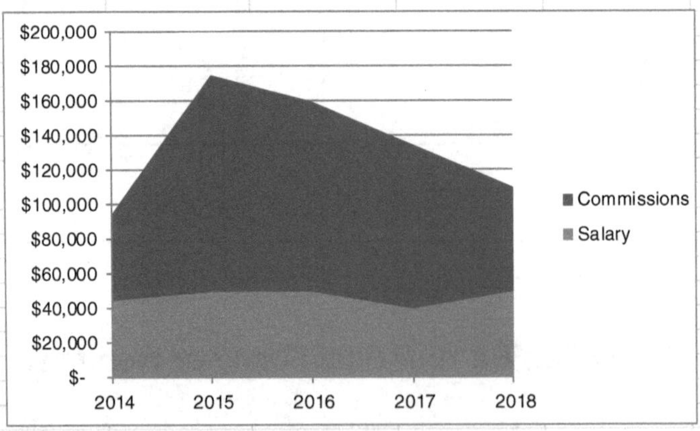

Example 11-3 Analysis of Husband's Earned Income

The analysis in Example 11-3 shows a five-year history of earnings. From the husband's perspective, the goal is simple: convince the court that commissioned earnings are not reliable enough to base support on, and if the court averages income, it should do so over the last two years only. The last two years' earnings averaged $122,500 per year. Counsel for the wife prepared the exhibit. The wife's goals for this exhibit are to demonstrate that the husband does have a consistent history of earning substantial commissions and to advocate for a three- or four-year average, either of which is preferred over a two-year average. Does showing 2014 add to the exhibit's advocacy value? Or does including 2014 reinforce the lower two-year average? Does showing only a three- and four-year average help or hurt when seeking to persuade the judge to average longer than two years? Should the scale be adjusted to create the appearance of less variance or more variance from year to year? Do two separate colors for salary and commission subliminally suggest the two are distinctly different, or should there be just one color and one category for earnings? Does the graph's downturn actually help the husband's argument that 2019 will result in even less earnings? Should current year-to-date earnings be added? Should 2013 earnings be added as well?

When presenting exhibits, be careful what you ask for. If the judge stares long enough at your exhibit, is there a risk the judge will be persuaded to believe the opposite of what your client wants? Forensic accounting exhibits present the ultimate glass half-full or half-empty dilemma. When in doubt, ask others their opinion about key exhibits before they are used in court. You will almost always be surprised by what others perceive.

Planning the Direct-Examination

There are many seminar courses for basic expert witness preparation for both attorneys and forensic accountants. Testifying tips are everywhere. Here, we offer just some of the basics for the beginner.[16] Keep it simple. Answer only the question asked and stop talking. Silence in the courtroom is your friend. Don't feel as if you must speak just because a

16. Visit www.CourtroomBootcamp.com for training courses specifically designed for expert witnesses and attorneys. Taught by Michael G. Kaplan, CPA/ABV/CFF, CVA, MAFF.

lawyer is looking at you. You can also pause after a question and think about an answer all you want. You are an advocate for your opinion, not the client. Ask for clarification. Never guess. It's OK not to know the answer to a question. Speak to the judge. You are not trying to prove the other lawyer or expert is wrong. Your goal is to appear neutral and independent. Be in charge. Remember, you are the expert here. Avoid sarcasm.

Direct-examination of expert witnesses can be broken down into three phases: Establishment, Opinion, and Attack. Establishment of the witness as an expert is important for admissibility and advocacy. Even if the expert is the world's leading authority, if credibility is impaired on cross-examination, that opinion may be given no weight. The Opinion phase describes the work done and opinions formed. The Attack describes challenges to the opposing expert's work. While the Attack can come before the Opinion, it usually makes more sense to set the positive before unleashing the negative.

The establishment of the witness as an expert results in the judge determining that the witness is indeed an expert and that the witness's testimony will be admissible. Chapter 11, "Experts and Their Reports," of *The Divorce Trial Manual*[17] does an excellent job of discussing both the mechanical and the strategic aspects of expert witness testimony. Establishing the forensic accountant witness as an expert in family law cases should not constitute heavy lifting, but it can be challenging depending on the judge, opposing counsel, issues, and time limitations. While establishing the witness's credentials, you may want to consider asking additional questions specifically designed to suppress potential *Daubert* challenges.[18] *Daubert* challenges focus on issues such as test-

17. Lynne Z. Gold-Bikin & Stephen Kolodny, The Divorce Trial Manual (ABA 2003).

18. In general, a *Daubert* challenge is a motion to exclude expert witness testimony on the grounds that the proposed expert is not an expert witness or to limit the expert's ability to testify regarding particular opinions. *Daubert v. Merrill Dow Pharms., Inc.*, 509 U.S. 43, 113 S. Ct. 43 (1993); *In re Kumho Tire Co., Ltd. v. Carmichael*, 119 S. Ct. 1167 (1999). For an excellent discussion of *Daubert* challenges in the context of business valuation and financial cases, see D. Michael Costello, *Bulletproof Strategies to Avoid or Overcome a Daubert Challenge*, July/August Valuation Strategies 18–27 (2010). Examples of topics for direct-examination questions include adherence to applicable professional standards, general acceptance of methodologies and techniques utilized, alternative

ing, peer review of methodology, error rates, and general acceptance of the methodologies employed.

Even though *Daubert* challenges to forensic accounting are rarely seen in divorce appellate opinions, you should expect to see more of them as time goes by. In addition to answering questions regarding whether the expert's credentials qualify him to render an opinion on that particular topic, the Q and A should establish *how* the expert knows about the forensic accounting techniques he used, the methodology employed, and the general acceptance of both in forensic accounting. Consider also establishing how the expert keeps up with trends in forensic accounting by reading professional journals, attending national and regional conferences, and tracking professional standards as they develop.

After you establish the forensic accountant's credentials, move that the court accept the witness as an expert. Cross-examination on qualifications may be allowed before the court rules on the motion. You should know the established practice if opposing counsel seeks to challenge the admission of the forensic accountant as an expert witness. As a technical matter, courts may also require that you declare the particular area of testimony or set of issues concerning which the expert will testify.

What if the court is willing to automatically accept the witness as an expert and avoid establishment questions? The authors of *The Divorce Trial Manual* suggest that, if you can avoid antagonizing the judge, consider asking permission to highlight certain of the expert's credentials for the record. What if opposing counsel seeks to avoid establishing the witness as an expert by offering to stipulate that the witness is an expert? Many family lawyers consider it the better practice to turn down the stipulation to take the time to build up the expert's credentials. If allowed just a short time, you should be prepared to quickly differentiate the client's expert's qualifications, credentials, and experience from those of the opposing expert.

The following is an example of an establishment-phase direct-examination involving detailed questions on the expert's education, training, and experience:

ATTORNEY: What is your name?

---

analyses and techniques considered, and "sanity" checks on assumptions for reasonableness.

EXPERT: DeForest McCoy.

ATTORNEY: What is your business address?

EXPERT: 74656 Voyager Street.

ATTORNEY: Your honor, I will now establish Mr. McCoy as an expert witness in forensic accounting. What is your occupation?

EXPERT: I am a forensic accountant.

ATTORNEY: What is forensic accounting?

EXPERT: Forensic accounting is the art and science of investigating people and money.[19] Using my background in accounting, I work with lawyers to help resolve disputes before and after lawsuits are filed.

ATTORNEY: How long have you practiced as a forensic accountant?

EXPERT: Fifteen years.

ATTORNEY: Do you currently practice as a forensic accountant full time?

EXPERT: Yes.

ATTORNEY: How long have you been practicing as a forensic accountant full time?

EXPERT: Ten years.

Education

ATTORNEY: What is your educational background?

EXPERT: I have an undergraduate degree in accounting from the University of Tennessee in Knoxville. I also have several professional designations.

Training

ATTORNEY: Briefly describe your training.

19. Definition of forensic accounting by Darrell D. Dorrell, CPA/ABV, MBA, ASA, CVA, CMA, DABFA, from Lake Oswego, Oregon.

EXPERT: I practiced as an accountant with Johnson and Johnson, CPAs, for four years before opening my own practice. With Johnson and Johnson, CPAs, I gained diverse experience in tax, auditing, some business consulting, and forensic accounting and business valuation. During that time, I worked directly under experienced CPAs and received professional training in all aspects of public accounting. In addition, I attended continuing professional education, CPE, learning about accounting, taxation, forensic accounting, and business valuation.

Experience

ATTORNEY: Briefly describe your accounting experience.

EXPERT: After opening my own firm, I had a diverse clientele that also included compilation, review, audit, tax, consulting, financial planning services, and forensic accounting. But my main focus was taxation.

ATTORNEY: During your career, just in taxation alone, how many tax returns did you prepare for your clients?

EXPERT: Over 1,000 tax returns.

ATTORNEY: What is a compilation?

EXPERT: Compilations involve our firm preparing financial statements for clients, usually submitted to banks.

ATTORNEY: How many have you done?

EXPERT: My firm has completed over 500.

ATTORNEY: How many audits has your firm completed?

EXPERT: Over 100.

Education in Forensic Accounting

ATTORNEY: Briefly describe your education in forensic accounting.

EXPERT: In addition to my undergraduate degree in accounting, I have attended numerous forensic accounting conferences presented by the Tennessee Society of CPAs, the American Institute of CPAs, the National Association of Certified Valuators and Analysts, the American Bar Association Family Law Section, the Tennessee Bar Association, and several local bar associations' family law sections, as well as the American Academy of Matrimonial Lawyers.

Training in Forensic Accounting

ATTORNEY: Do you have any other specific training in forensic accounting?

EXPERT: Yes, I have obtained certifications that have specific requirements of education, training, and experience, and some that require testing.

ATTORNEY: We'll get to those in a moment.

EXPERT: OK.

Experience in Forensic Accounting and Prior Testimony

ATTORNEY: Briefly describe your experience as a forensic accountant.

EXPERT: For two years, I worked directly underneath a CPA who handled forensic accounting and business valuation engagements. After opening my own practice, I handled many engagements in forensic accounting, mostly in family law. About 10 years ago, I sold my tax practice to another CPA and began working full time as a forensic accountant.

ATTORNEY: During your career, how many forensic accounting engagements have you handled?

EXPERT: Over 500.

ATTORNEY: How many depositions have you given?

EXPERT: Over 100.

ATTORNEY: Are those engagements listed on your curriculum vitae?

EXPERT: Yes.

ATTORNEY: In how many trials have you been admitted as an expert and testified?

EXPERT: Over 40.

ATTORNEY: Are those engagements listed on your curriculum vitae?

EXPERT: Yes.

ATTORNEY: I am passing you, my opposing counsel, and the court a copy of a document. Can you identify it?

EXPERT: Yes. It is my curriculum vitae.

ATTORNEY: What is a curriculum vitae?

EXPERT: It contains a detailed summary of my education, training, experience, professional organization memberships, and certifications. Kind of like a resume. Mine also lists seminars and conferences I have attended, prior deposition and trial testimony appearances, articles I have published, seminars I have taught, and professional organization leadership positions I have held.

COURT: I know what a CV is. Let's move along.

ATTORNEY: Your Honor, I move Mr. McCoy's CV into evidence.

COURT: Any objections? So admitted.

Credentials and Licensing

ATTORNEY: You are licensed to practice as a certified public accountant?

EXPERT: Yes, I am a licensed CPA in Tennessee.

ATTORNEY: How did you become a CPA?

EXPERT: There is an education requirement, an experience requirement, the CPA exam, and an ethics test. To maintain my license, there is a continuing education requirement of 80 hours every two years. I completed my experience requirement working with Johnson and Johnson, CPAs, and I passed the exam.

ATTORNEY: You are also an MAFF and a CFF. What are those designations?

EXPERT: The MAFF means master analyst in financial forensics, which is certified through the *National Association of Certified Valuation Analysts* or *NACVA*. These are the two primary designations forensic accountants have who are CPAs.

ATTORNEY: You are also a CFF. What does that mean?

EXPERT: The CFF means I am certified in financial forensics, which is through the AICPA. The AICPA is the equivalent of the ABA for accountants. A CPA is not required to be a member of the AICPA, but I am and have been a member since I became a CPA.

ATTORNEY: Is the process to become a CFF pretty much the same as becoming a MAFF?

EXPERT: No. The CFF credential began in 2008. The experience requirements are different. I was not required to take an examination at the time. I was required to state my experience on a form that determined if I had the minimum experience, training, and education. I was able to receive the certification in early 2009.

Why Obtain Certifications?

ATTORNEY: Do all CPAs who are forensic accountants have these designations?

EXPERT: No.

ATTORNEY: Are you required to have any particular certification to testify as an expert witness?

EXPERT: No.

ATTORNEY: Then why did you obtain them?

EXPERT: Forensic accounting is a very interesting field. It evolves and over time develops like other professions. I enjoy helping clients settle cases through investigating and writing reports, and when cases don't settle, I testify. My certification lets clients, attorneys, and judges know that I have met certain minimum requirements of the profession's governing bodies. I am a member of both the NACVA and AICPA, and I believe it is important to comply with the professional standards of both to practice as a forensic accountant. And both do a great job helping me keep up with developments in my profession.

ATTORNEY: So that means you have even more continuing education requirements because of the additional certifications?

EXPERT: Yes, but the continuing education through NACVA and AICPA are the best available. Both have great seminars and conferences taught by the leaders in the field. I try to get to as many as I can. Also, I have had the honor of presenting seminars for both organizations at national conferences.

Seminars Taught and Articles Published

ATTORNEY: So you have taught seminars on forensic accounting?

EXPERT: Many. I have been asked to speak and present for the Tennessee Bar Association; NACVA; AICPA; the Nashville, Memphis, and Knoxville Bar Associations; National Business Institute; the Tennessee Society of CPAs; and the Mississippi Society of CPAs.

ATTORNEY: At what national conferences have you spoken?

EXPERT: The NACVA/IBA Annual Consultants' Conference, the AICPA Forensic and Valuation Services Conference, and an ABA Family Law Section conference.

ATTORNEY: Are all of those speaking engagements listed on your CV?

EXPERT: Yes.

ATTORNEY: Have you presented seminars on the issues you are discussing in your testimony today?

EXPERT: Yes, many. I also have had several articles published, including one in the *Tennessee Bar Journal* on the forensic accountant's role in divorce.

ATTORNEY: What was the title of that article?

EXPERT: "How Forensic Accountants Find and Organize Assets and Debts in Complex Divorce Cases."

ATTORNEY: The article was chosen for publication by the editorial board, which is comprised of several lawyers, and was mailed to all attorneys who are members of the Tennessee Bar Association, isn't that correct?

EXPERT: Yes.

ATTORNEY: Other than that one, have you published any other articles on forensic accounting and family law?

EXPERT: Yes, several, included in the *Nashville Bar Journal* and the Tennessee Bar Association Family Law Section's newsletter.

ATTORNEY: Are all those articles listed on your CV as well?

EXPERT: Yes.

Family Law Practice

ATTORNEY: You have extensive experience in forensic accounting. What percentage of your practice currently is family law specific?

EXPERT: About half.

ATTORNEY: Is that in total engagements or total billing?

EXPERT: Both.

ATTORNEY: You have taught over 50 seminars on forensic accounting to judges, lawyers, and accountants, correct?

EXPERT: Yes.

ATTORNEY: About how many of those speaking engagements are related directly to family law?

EXPERT: About half.

ATTORNEY: What about publications?

EXPERT: I have published around 15 articles. Ten of those were family law related.

Professional Organization Memberships

ATTORNEY: What professional organizations are you a member of?

EXPERT: AICPA, NACVA, and the Tennessee Society of CPAs.

Leadership in Professional Organizations

ATTORNEY: Have you ever served in a leadership capacity in any of the professional organizations of which you are a member?

EXPERT: I have.

ATTORNEY: Which ones?

EXPERT: I have chaired the Tennessee Society of CPAs' Nashville chapter for a year, and for several years I have served on the steering committee of the Tennessee Society of CPAs' Forensic and Valuation Services Committee.

Engagement Assignment

ATTORNEY: What are your assignments in this case?

EXPERT: To form opinions on several divorce issues, including but not limited to asset identification, classification, valuations, division, lifestyle analysis, and dissipation.

ATTORNEY: How were those engagements defined?

EXPERT: My client's attorney called and asked if I would complete a lifestyle analysis because alimony would likely be an important issue. As my work progressed, the asset identification, classification, valuation, division, and dissipation issues developed.

ATTORNEY: What do you mean by "developed"?

EXPERT: For example, in discovery I identified credit card charges for travel to St. Croix on a credit card account that had been previously undisclosed. My client did not know about this trip. I brought that to the attention of my client and my client's lawyer, and they asked me to add dissipation investigation and analysis to my engagement.

Prior Admission as an Expert Witness

ATTORNEY: You testified earlier, I believe, that you have testified in over 40 court proceedings. Were you admitted as an expert witness in all those cases?

EXPERT: Yes.

ATTORNEY: Has your admission ever been challenged?

EXPERT: Many times. More often earlier in my career than later, of course.

ATTORNEY: Has a court ever denied your admission as an expert?

EXPERT: No.

ATTORNEY: Have you been admitted as an expert in this court previously?

EXPERT: Yes.

ATTORNEY: Before this judge?

EXPERT: Yes.

ATTORNEY: Your Honor, I move Mr. DeForest McCoy be admitted as an expert in forensic accounting.

Once the court accepts the expert, you have lots of options. You can get right to the Opinion phase by going straight into the report, stating the expert's conclusions, and highlighting key analysis. But what if there are other issues with which you must deal? For example, what if the opposing expert is the parties' tax CPA and investment advisor? You may want to dial up a series of questions on independence.

Independence

ATTORNEY: Prior to this engagement, did you know your client or her spouse?

EXPERT: No.

ATTORNEY: Prior to this case, had your client ever referred you any business?

EXPERT: No.

ATTORNEY: After this case, do you anticipate performing any additional services for your client?

EXPERT: No.

ATTORNEY: How are you charging your client?

EXPERT: Retainer and hourly.

ATTORNEY: If your performance is not acceptable to your client, will you still collect on your fees due and the fees you charge for today?

EXPERT: Absolutely.

ATTORNEY: If your performance is not acceptable to your client, will you lose any additional revenue in the future?

EXPERT: No. I don't expect any additional work in the future from this client.

ATTORNEY: If your client and her spouse were also, say, tax clients for whom you prepared tax returns annually and provided ongoing investment advisory services, would that present an issue for you?

EXPERT: Yes. Two serious ones.

ATTORNEY: What are they?

EXPERT: Conflict of interest and independence. As a CPA, I am bound by the ethics and standards of the AICPA. First, there is a concern with a conflict of interest providing testimony on behalf of one client against another client. Second, as an expert witness, I must be independent. If I am likely to receive a substantial amount of income in the future from a client for whom I have been asked to testify, logically, my testimony might have an impact on whether I get that income in the future. If that is the case, I think that would impair my independence. I would not likely accept the engagement based on both factors.

ATTORNEY: Is this a real problem in this case?

EXPERT: Yes. My client's opposing expert possesses confidential financial information from a client, which may be used in an adverse way to another client. Also, as a CPA, my opposing expert has a more significant business relationship with his client, which, in my opinion, prevents him from being able to provide an objective opinion.

ATTORNEY: If you were in your opposing expert's shoes under these circumstances, would you have accepted this engagement?

EXPERT: No.

ATTORNEY: Why not?

EXPERT: Independence is something that should not be a close call. Lawyers can advocate for a client. Forensic accountants must advocate only for their opinions. Without independence, the role of the expert witness becomes nothing more than that of a hired gun.

Methodology is important. If you anticipate that opposing counsel will raise a *Daubert* challenge, it makes sense to handle some of the issues on direct-examination to forestall the motion before it is made. Even if you don't expect a *Daubert* challenge, a more detailed examination of methodology may add credibility and weight to the forensic accountant's expert opinion.

Methodology

ATTORNEY: Did you employ a methodology in this case?

EXPERT: Yes. I do in all cases.

ATTORNEY: Please briefly describe your methodology.

EXPERT: When I receive a request to work for a potential client, I first reach an understanding in writing, through my engagement agreement, regarding my role, ask the client and lawyer a number of questions, review key pleadings and discovery, and determine if I have the professional competence. After engagement, I determine whether I have sufficient relevant data to complete the engagement; then I scope it. Scoping means I must determine what exactly I need to review, read, and analyze to form an opinion. If I don't have enough information, or if more information would be helpful, I generally contact my client's attorney and request additional documents or information. Sometimes that may require issuing one or more subpoenas.

ATTORNEY: Then what?

EXPERT: I determine particular techniques to be employed, try them, and determine if each produces a result that is both trustworthy and meaningful. From there, I form an opinion. Then, I think about what I can do to disprove my opinions by assuming my opinions are wrong or my assumptions invalid. If possible, I then try to test my assumptions.

ATTORNEY: If everything checks out?

EXPERT: I determine if I need to write a report. If I need to, I do.

ATTORNEY: And then?

EXPERT: Wait and see if I am needed for depositions, settlement negotiations, and trial.

ATTORNEY: Did you invent this methodology?

EXPERT: No.

ATTORNEY: How did you learn it?

EXPERT: Methodology is a process. All expert witnesses must plan the engagement. For forensic accounting, this is a pretty logical format. But to answer your question, I learned this particular methodology through the NACVA.

ATTORNEY: To your knowledge, has this methodology been used before by anyone other than you?

EXPERT: Yes.

ATTORNEY: Who?

EXPERT: I assume lots of forensic accountants because the NACVA teaches it.

ATTORNEY: Has the methodology you used in this case been generally accepted in the forensic accounting community?

EXPERT: Yes.

ATTORNEY: Has it been exposed to peer review?

EXPERT: Yes.

The Opinion and Attack Phases

Experienced forensic accountants prefer to think of their role in the courtroom as a teacher: taking the students (counsel and judge) through a lesson and educating them step-by-step. Some forensic accountants love to use a good old-fashioned chalkboard to drive home who is the teacher. Many of the questions asked on direct will be in a familiar format: who, what, where, how, and why.

The Opinion phase of direct-examination can be easy to plan. Present the report. Discuss the engagement in some logical progression. There are no set rules here. Develop the story. Make it interesting. Create questions to elicit responses explaining what made this engagement special. Why is the expert's opinion important? Was there any drama? Why should the judge care about the witness's opinion? Expect that the judge will jump in with questions for the expert witness. If the judge isn't asking questions, the family lawyer may want to consider inviting the judge to jump in and ask questions. Seasoned family lawyers constantly watch for clues for what the judge finds interesting or confusing. It is vital the judge follow what is being presented. If not, the entire case could be lost.

Experienced forensic accountants will avoid absolutes such as "always" and "never." Later, on cross-examination, all opposing counsel must do is find one exception to the absolute statement and use that to destroy the expert's credibility.

Know your state's rules for direct-examination. Can the report be admitted into evidence?[20] Many states have technical requirements preventing expert witnesses from testifying from their reports. Instead, the reports may be presented as exhibits, but the testimony and opinions stated must be testified to independent of the report itself. If that's the case, experts may use the report to refresh their recollection. Usually, sworn testimony and opinions offered must be based on present recollection.

In general, the key elements include stating the opinion, explaining the planning of the engagement, listing sources of information, and describing the methodology employed, techniques used, and analysis performed. During the Opinion phase, you may seek to move into evidence the report itself, charts, exhibits, and other financial information that may require the expert's testimony in order to be admitted.[21] When deciding the exact order of presentation, it may make sense to let the forensic accountant suggest the sequence so the expert feels more comfortable. In addition, the forensic accountant should deal with warts before they are exposed on cross-examination. Waiting is rarely a good idea. Consider removing the sting by discussing the problems in advance and sandwiching that discussion between two strong subjects.

---

20. Make every effort to make the report part of the official record. In the event of an appeal, the technical record is everything. As family lawyers, there are so many issues and subissues that the inclusion of the report in the technical record can be a lifesaver—especially if some important fact, opinion, or argument is touched upon but not fully developed. For an excellent discussion of strategies, techniques, and foundations for admission of an expert witness's report, see PESKIND, *supra* note 14.

21. For a complete discussion of evidentiary foundations in the family law context, refer to (you guessed it) PESKIND, *supra* note 14.

As for specific questions to ask to admit the opinion into evidence, keep it simple. "What is a reasonable degree of financial or economic certainty?" Or, "What is a reasonable degree of forensic accounting certainty?" In your jurisdiction, there may be "magic words" or key phrases with which your judges feel most comfortable with respect to expert witness testimony.[22] "To a reasonable degree of financial or economic certainty, have you formed an opinion?"[23] "Did you review the opposing expert's report and opinions?" "Did you form an opinion about the other expert's opinion?"

With respect to opinion testimony by forensic accountants, there can be a sticky problem. If opposing counsel has "nailed down" the forensic accountant's testimony through a deposition by asking the accountant to list "every opinion" and the report lists "every opinion," what happens with the judge asking a question that requires a previously undisclosed opinion? Probably not much. Rarely will you see an opposing counsel object to a judge asking a question seeking an opinion from an expert witness. But, if you are the opposing counsel and want to prevent discussions beyond what previously appeared in the report and was discussed at deposition, what should you do? The best advice could be to look to your theme and theory of the case. If it doesn't hurt it, don't fight that battle. But, if it could lose the case for you, you may want to launch the objection. The second-best advice is plan for the worst. In family law matters, expect the forensic accountant will be asked all sorts of questions about income, expenses, assets, debts, taxes, passive losses, and all other sorts of relevant information.

The final phase is the Attack. If there is an opposing expert and a trial is being held, there will be a difference of opinion. Generally, attacking an opposing expert will be based on the expert's qualifications, the work performed, or both. If something is wrong with the other expert's work, say a technical flaw in the analysis, the Attack is the time to expose it. Keep in mind that all attacks on direct-examination must be carefully coordinated with cross-examination and must be consistent with the theme and theories of the case.

22. In medical malpractice cases, medical experts may be required to use the phrase "to a reasonable degree of medical certainty" before expressing expert opinions.

23. Craft your key questions keeping in mind a very common objection that the question calls for an opinion outside the witness's proffered or claimed expertise.

Cross-Examination

Cross-examination of the opposing forensic accountant may make or break the case. You plan cross-examination topics as a series of questions, or subjects, seeking one fact at a time, leading to a logical conclusion. The subjects' series of questions flow from all the hard work you've done and from reviewing the deposition testimony of the expert. But what gets challenged? How many subjects do you present? Do you harp on a math error your expert said made no difference at all? Do you suggest the opposing forensic accountant is in over his head when the analysis in the case isn't all that difficult? You must be very careful not to appear to bully the nice accountant who has come to court just to help sort things out.

The most common tactics on cross-examination are fairly predictable. Try to turn the opposing witness into your witness. Attack the expert's facts and assumptions. If you are stumped, try to draw the expert into hypothetical questions with facts and assumptions changed in the questioning lawyer's favor. Expose any bias. Challenge the expert's knowledge of well-known treatises, authorities, and articles. Expose major and minor mistakes in the report. Explain to your expert witness that if the expert gets trapped on a subject, on redirect-examination, you will be able to get him or her out.

Once you have developed questions for several subject areas, deciding which subjects you'll actually explore in cross-examination will most likely be a game-time decision. This means that you may not decide which subjects to question until cross-examination begins and you experience the moment. Does the judge have the patience to deal with a detailed cross-examination? Is your client ahead or behind? Did the direct-examination of your client's expert go so well you don't need to drill into the opposing expert? If you cross-examine the opposing forensic accountant first, how do you use cross-examination to set up the direct-examination of your client's forensic accountant? What are your time constraints? Can you rely on the direct-examination of your client's expert to do everything you need? Given all the variables, it is even possible you may not ask any cross-examination questions.

With expert testimony, challenges must be well planned. Cheap shots will appear just that. If the opposing forensic accountant is wily and experienced, you may never get him to make an important concession. Should you even seriously try challenging an experienced forensic accountant if winning one battle may not be worth losing the war? It may make strategic sense to leave alone the wily and experienced forensic accountant. Very few cross-examination subjects are worth the potential damage a really strong opposing forensic accountant can inflict in response to a weak challenge.

In response to many questions, an expert witness might well rely on a get-out-of-jail-free card, of sorts—the "professional judgment call." To exercise professional judgment, an expert relies on his education, training, experience, and research. For example, in response to a question about a discount rate, an expert might say, "I chose 2.75 percent to be added to the risk-free rate." In discount-rate determinations, a higher discount rate favors one spouse, and a lower rate favors the other. The questioning lawyer might follow with a very competent question, such as this one: "Explain how you choose 2.75 percent." There are many ways for the expert to respond, but once that answer is distilled, it is likely to resemble a form of the age-old response, "I exercised professional judgment based on my review of current economic circumstances, education, training in this field, and over 30 years' professional experience." Unless the questioning lawyer's client's forensic accountant has spoon-fed the questioning lawyer with some seriously solid reference material with which to cross-examine, the judgment-call response is going to be the end of that line of questioning. The questioning lawyer can't testify, and she might have to wait to challenge the discount rate through direct-examination of her client's expert.

Family lawyers should know, however, that some inexperienced forensic accountants may struggle in answering questions regarding their professional judgment. For example, the questioning lawyer might say, "Please tell the court the exact research you relied upon in this engagement in reaching your determination." If the expert performed no research or failed to document his research, he might not respond confidently and concisely. Or the rookie expert might discuss only those facts and factors that favored his position and his client's financial interest, not those that favored the other spouse. If that's the case, follow-up questions might be simple: "Assuming that a lower calculation of value favors your client, isn't it true that a higher discount rate ultimately favors your client?" "Yes. That is the nature of the discount rate in this calculation." The final question might close the door on the unprepared expert: "Then tell the court every fact or factor you considered that favored a lower discount rate in opposition to your client's interest." If the expert cannot think of any, the cross-examination will have been a success.

Contrast the response of the unprepared expert with the predictable response from the wily and experienced forensic accountant. The experienced expert's response to any question regarding the exercise of his professional judgment will contain great detail, including facts and factors that favor a higher discount rate and others that favor a lower rate. The veteran forensic accountant will demonstrate a complete command of the processes involved in reaching his opinion. His testimony will sound even-tempered, confident, independent, and objective. In fact, the experienced forensic accountant might appear to have been waiting for precisely this question on cross-examination, as if it were a softball pitch delivered over the middle of the plate. The cross-examination will be a home run—but for the opposing expert.

Even thoughtful cross-examination questions that result in the expert qualifying decisions as judgment calls may not score enough points to justify the effort. Even though lawyers may want to exploit differences between the experts' assumptions, the subject of the challenge needs to call into question the expert's final opinion. Getting bogged down in a theoretical debate on a technical forensic accounting issue may not be the best use of valuable court time unless it is *the* key issue. One great cross-examination subject can have more impact than five good cross-examination subjects. Five good subjects can have more impact than twenty so-so subjects.

The best cross-examination subjects are those that advance the theme and theory of the case and that dovetail with the direct-examination of your expert. All arguments and points must fit together. Perspective is important. Make a big deal out of what is a big deal. Leave the rest alone.

Conclusion

As discussed in Chapter 1, the goal of every case is domination. But at trial, after both parties' cases are concluded, there is a deafening silence. The mood is tense. The court is about to rule. The judge is gathering thoughts and making final notes. No one knows what the court is going to say. "Winning 100–0" is no longer in your mind. The cold reality is that the court might rule against your client. You remember coaching your client to not react at all to either victory or loss. If you win, celebrating is in poor taste and bush league. If you lose, pouting is unprofessional, and you never want to give the other side the satisfaction of seeing you or your client suffer. Any reaction at all must be restrained until after everyone returns to the office or goes home.

When the court rules, you write down notes of what the court is saying. The court accepts the theme and theories of the case that you have presented. Your client's forensic accountant's testimony wins the day. The expert's income determination and lifestyle analysis become specific findings of fact. The overall property division is in line with the expert's projection. The alimony award is solid. Sure, as with all family law matters, there are a couple of issues that do not go your client's way. Overall, however, your client is satisfied, and you both feel relief. For a moment, all is peaceful. Exhale.

As you pack your trial bag for the drive back to the office, all the hard work comes to mind. Your client and the forensic accountant survived your advice, your cajoling, and your endless questions. There were so many documents, so many e-mails back and forth, and so many problems, but it all worked out. It feels right. You feel raw and worn down. Now, you remember to act like you've won a trial before.

Bibliography

Books

BARENBAUM, LESTER, WALTER SCHUBERT, & ROBERT FEDER, THE FAMILY LAWYER'S GUIDE TO STOCK OPTIONS (American Bar Association, Section of Family Law, 2007).

CARRAD, DAVID CLAYTON, THE COMPLETE QDRO HANDBOOK: DIVIDING ERISA, MILITARY, AND CIVIL SERVICE PENSIONS AND COLLECTING CHILD SUPPORT FROM EMPLOYEE BENEFIT PLANS, 2d ed. (American Bar Association, Section of Family Law, 2004).

DORRELL, DARRELL D. & GREGORY A. GADAWSKI, FINANCIAL FORENSICS BODY OF KNOWLEDGE (Wiley 2012).

FISHMAN, JAY E., SHANNON P. PRATT, & J. CLIFFORD GRIFFITH, PPC'S GUIDE TO BUSINESS VALUATIONS, Vol. 3, 17th ed. (Practitioners Publishing Company, 2007).

GLENN, DONALD A., THOMAS F. BURRAGE, DONALD J. DEGRAZIA, & WILLIAM B. STEWART, JR., FAMILY LAW SERVICES HANDBOOK: THE ROLE OF THE FINANCIAL EXPERT (JOHN WILEY & SONS, INC., 2011).

GOLD-BIKIN, LYNNE Z., & STEPHEN KOLODNY, THE DIVORCE TRIAL MANUAL: FROM INITIAL INTERVIEW TO CLOSING ARGUMENT (American Bar Association, Section of Family Law, 2003).

HERMAN, GREGG, 101+ PRACTICAL SOLUTIONS FOR THE FAMILY LAWYER: SENSIBLE ANSWERS TO COMMON PROBLEMS, 2d ed. (American Bar Association, Section of Family Law, 2003).

HUBER, EZRA, & DONALD A. GLENN, FORENSIC ACCOUNTING FOR DIVORCE ENGAGEMENTS: A PRACTICAL GUIDE, 3d ed. (American Institute of Certified Public Accountants, 2009).

MAGGIO, SHARYN, & THOMAS F. BURRAGE, JR., A CPA'S GUIDE TO FAMILY LAW SERVICES (American Institute of Certified Public Accountants, 2005).

MELTZER, STANTON L., DAVID A. ROONEY, J. CLIFFORD GRIFFITH, GARY R. TRUGMAN, JAY E. FISHMAN, & GERALD L. NISSENBAUM, GUIDE TO DIVORCE ENGAGEMENTS, Vol. 1, 6th ed. (Practitioners Publishing Company, 1997).

NEWMAN, GLENN, & MICHAEL UELTZEN, INDEPENDENCE AND INTEGRITY AND OBJECTIVITY IN PERFORMING FORENSIC AND VALUATION SERVICES (American Institute of Certified Public Accountants, 2008).

PESKIND, STEVEN N., THE FAMILY LAW TRIAL EVIDENCE BOOK: RULES AND PROCEDURES FOR EFFECTIVE ADVOCACY (American Bar Association, Section of Family Law, 2013).

PRATT, SHANNON, THE LAWYER'S BUSINESS VALUATION HANDBOOK: UNDERSTANDING FINANCIAL STATEMENTS, APPRAISAL REPORTS, AND EXPERT TESTIMONY (American Bar Association; Section of Family Law; General Practice, Solo and Small Firm Section; 2000).

Articles

Costello, D. Michael. *Bulletproof: Strategies to Avoid or Overcome a* Daubert *Challenge*, 13 VALUATION STRATEGIES 18–27 (2010).

Maksimuk, Gregory C., *Defining a Child-Support Payor's "Net Income,"* 95 ILLINOIS BAR JOURNAL (2007).

Mason, Miles, Sr., & Sandy Klevan, *Follow the Money: The Lifestyle Analysis*, 31 FAMILY ADVOCATE (2009).

Vance, Robert, *Breakin' Up Is Hard to Do*, August TENNESSEE BAR JOURNAL 12–21, 32–34, 36 (2009).

Vance, Robert, *The W-2 as Roadmap for Tennessee Child Support Guideline Income*, Family Practice, The Newsletter for the Family Law Section of the Tennessee Bar Association (2002).

Conference Papers and Other Resources

Costello, D. Michael, Daubert *Survival Tactics*, presented at 2009 TSCPA Conference on Business Valuation, Forensic Investigation & Litigation Services, Brentwood, Tenn., Oct. 18–19.

Dorrell, Darrell D., & Gregory A. Gadawski, *Forensic Accounting/ Investigation Methodology* (FA/IM), delivered through National Association of Certified Valuation Analysts, Forensic Accounting Academy, Aug. 27, 2007.

Appendix A

Burrage & Johnson, CPAs, LLC
The Forensic Firm

AGREEMENT FOR EXPERT CONSULTING SERVICES

Client Name: ___________________
Client Number: _____________

This agreement is made between _____________________, hereinafter called "Client," ______________________________________, hereinafter called "Attorney," and ______________________________ of BURRAGE & JOHNSON, CPAs, LLC, a New Mexico limited liability company, hereinafter called "Consultant."

SERVICES TO BE PROVIDED

As of the date set forth below and subject to the terms of the Agreement, the law firm of _________________________

________ and its client, ____________________________, have retained Consultant to ______________________________________ or any other task as requested in the case ____________________________ ____________________, Case No. ______________________________, pending in the ____________________________ Court. Consultant has been retained by Attorney, to which all reports, communications and work product will be submitted. It may be necessary for Attorney to share with Consultant theories of the case, strategy considerations, mental impressions, conclusions, and other thought processes that relate to preparation of this matter for trial. It may also be necessary for Attorney to relate to Consultant communications between Attorney and Client. Consultant understands and agrees that the work performed by Consultant will be confidential, constituting a portion of Attorney's work product, and is to be regarded by us as being covered by the attorney-client and attorney work-product privileges.

Attorney may also wish to engage Consultant to assist by identifying, and by providing expert witness services concerning, business methods or trade practices, accounting, or financial issues in this matter. In such case, any work performed in an expert witness engagement, as well as any other information disclosed to us, may be subject to the rules of discovery as appropriate for expert witnesses. The terms of the subsequent engagement of Consultant as expert witnesses will also be governed by this Agreement.

Consultant has performed an internal search for any potential client conflicts based upon the names of the parties and their counsel provided. Consultant has found no client conflicts with respect to any of the parties. To minimize the risk of potential problems, Consultant suggests that Attorney disclose our retention to the other side as soon as possible, but in a manner consistent with your case strategy. Should any possible conflict come to the attention of Consultant, Consultant will advise Attorney immediately.

Attorney or the court itself will advise Consultant, with sufficient notice, of the work to be performed by Consultant, requirements for appearance in court, and the need for any court order approving Consultant's employment and/or compensation for services rendered and expenses incurred. Attorney will aid us in obtaining any such court orders or approval. In the event that Consultant is subpoenaed as the result of any work performed in connection with this engagement, Client will compensate Consultant for time involved in responding to such subpoena(s) at Consultant's standard hourly rates. Should information become known that would make Consultant's continued involvement in this engagement inappropriate or should the attorneys or parties involved in this litigation change, Consultant reserves the right to withdraw from this engagement.

The value of Consultant's service to Client and Attorney is founded, in part, upon Consultant's reputation for professionalism and integrity. Consultant has been engaged from time to time by a significant number of law firms and may have been engaged by firms representing parties adverse to Client in this matter. This engagement is expressly conditioned on the agreement by Attorney and Client not to use the fact of Consultant's current or previous engagement by opposing counsel in other matters as a means of enhancing or diminishing Consultant's credibility before a trier of fact.

The American Institute of Certified Public Accountants has determined that the above-described services are subject to its Statements on Standards for Consulting Services No. 1 (SSCS No. 1). This statement requires that Consultant inform Client of significant reservations concerning the scope or benefits of the engagement, as well as significant engagement findings or events. By signing this Agreement, Attorney and Client agree that Consultant's communications to Attorney as counsel will discharge Consultant's client communication responsibilities as described in SSCS No. 1.

COMPENSATION

Fees in this matter will be the responsibility of Client and will be based on hourly rates, plus administrative costs, including but not limited to copies, postage, long-distance telephone calls, computer expenses, mileage, travel expenses, courier charges or specially purchased office supplies. Fees are not contingent upon the outcome of the case. Consultant will charge at standard rates for all tasks performed by professional or administrative personnel. All travel time will be billed at the full hourly rate. These rates currently range from $90 to $335 per hour depending on the personnel assigned, plus applicable New Mexico gross receipts tax, and are subject to periodic change. Consultant reserves the right to defer rendering further services until payment on past due invoices is received. If Consultant should be requested to testify, Consultant will be paid in full for all work performed to date prior to testimony. The parties agree that the liability of Consultant for any damages suffered as a result of any errors or omissions in the performance of these services will be limited to the amount of Consultant's fee for this engagement. If Attorney or Client disagree with or question any amount due under an invoice, such disagreement shall be communicated to Consultant in writing within thirty (30) days of the invoice date. Any claim or objection not made within that period shall be deemed waived.

Prior to commencement of work under this Agreement, Consultant shall be paid a deposit of $__________. This deposit is not intended to be an estimate of the total cost of work to be performed, nor has Consultant given any estimate of such total cost. No interest will be paid on deposits held by Consultant. The deposit will be held by Consultant and applied to the final billing at the conclusion of this engagement. Any deposit in excess of the fees will be refunded. Client agrees to maintain this deposit by promptly paying each billing statement or invoice as they are presented.

At such time as the deposit, in the sole discretion of the Consultant, is insufficient to provide for payment of outstanding billings and unbilled work in process, Consultant will request an additional payment. If the additional deposit is not received within seven (7) days, Consultant may discontinue services under this Agreement. If the deposit is not restored within fifteen (15) days of our request, Consultant may terminate this Agreement and withdraw from further involvement in the case. All fees must be paid in full and the deposit restored in full prior to Consultant appearing in Court or providing any testimony in Court or by deposition.

Consultant will submit monthly invoices to Attorney and Attorney will forward these immediately to Client for payment. Monthly invoices will show amounts billed to the date shown on the invoice. All invoices not paid within thirty (30) days will be subject to a one and one-half percent per month late charge. Appropriate credit will be given to the Client's account for any funds that are paid to Consultant from any third-party source allowed by any court, although Client will be responsible for the payment of all fees regardless of any court orders which may be entered against any other party regarding the payment of Consultant's fees. The final balance of Consultant's fees, should it exceed the deposit amount, will remain the Client's individual responsibility. Client and Attorney acknowledge that it is not the responsibility of Consultant to attempt to collect fees from any adverse party, even after an award of such fees.

TERMINATION

This agreement shall commence when a signed original of this Agreement and the required deposit is received by Consultant and will be a continuing agreement until terminated by either party or until the services to be performed by Consultant as described above are complete. Any party may terminate this agreement at any time by notifying the other parties in writing of such termination. In the event of termination prior to completion of the services to be performed by Consultant, Consultant will be paid in full any amounts due after application of the deposit for all services performed prior to the date of termination within thirty (30) days of Attorney or Client's receipt of an invoice for such services. In the event of termination by Attorney or Client or termination by Consultant because of Client's failure to pay or breach of any other provision of this agreement by Attorney or Client prior to completion of services, Consultant shall not be liable to Attorney or Client or any other party for any additional expenses incurred in securing completion of the services described in this agreement.

RETENTION OF DOCUMENTS AND WORKPAPERS

Client or Attorney shall provide all necessary documentation or other materials and shall make available key personnel within a reasonable period of time upon request by Consultant. The failure to do so may result in extensions of time and increased costs and may jeopardize key deadlines. All documents submitted by Attorney or Client and used by Consultant during the course of this engagement will be maintained in segregated files. At the completion of our engagement, the originals and all copies thereof will be returned to Attorney or Client, upon your written request. Returning a document or item to Attorney shall be considered the same as returning it to the Client.

Please note that it is not the practice of Consultant to retain workpapers, emails, notes or data files that have been updated or superceded unless shared with Attorney, Client or a third party working with them. Consultant will retain, subject to the destruction provisions contained herein, copies of all emails, analyses, draft reports or other materials provided to Client or Attorney or any third party by Consultant or provided by Client, Attorney or any third party to Consultant.

It is agreed and understood that, in connection with the performance of the services described in this agreement, Consultant may prepare certain workpapers, which may include data in electronic format, and that such workpapers are and shall remain the property of Consultant. Attorney and Client hereby authorize Consultant to destroy all files and documents in Consultant's possession two years after completion of all services performed pursuant to this Agreement. When records are returned to Client or Attorney, it is the responsibility of Client or Attorney to retain and protect such records for possible future use, including potential examination by any governmental or regulatory agencies.

Upon written agreement by the parties, the document retention practices described herein may be modified.

DISPUTE RESOLUTION AND ATTORNEYS' FEES

Any controversy, claim, or counterclaim arising out of or relating to this Agreement, the breach thereof, or the services performed by Consultant shall be settled by binding arbitration before a single arbitrator in accordance with the rules of the Second Judicial Court of New Mexico, and judgment on the award rendered by the arbitrator may be entered in any court having jurisdiction thereof. The arbitration shall be conducted at a location within Bernalillo County, New Mexico, as determined by the arbitrator. In the event an arbitration or litigation (including but not limited to any proceeding to compel arbitration) is initiated to resolve or settle any dispute or claim between the parties, the prevailing party shall be entitled to recover from the non-prevailing party or parties its reasonable costs, including but not limited to reasonable attorneys' fees. If any party should institute any action for declaratory relief arising out of this agreement, the prevailing party in such declaratory action shall also be entitled to an award of attorneys' fees and costs incurred in such declaratory action.

BY AGREEING TO ARBITRATION, THE PARTIES ACKNOWLEDGE THAT, IN THE EVENT OF A DISPUTE OVER FEES OR ANY OTHER PROVISION OF THIS AGREEMENT, EACH OF THE PARTIES IS GIVING UP THE RIGHT TO HAVE THE DISPUTE DECIDED IN A COURT OF LAW BEFORE A JUDGE OR JURY, AND INSTEAD ACCEPTING THE USE OF ARBITRATION FOR RESOLUTION.

MISCELLANEOUS PROVISIONS

This Agreement shall be construed and enforced pursuant to the laws of the State of New Mexico. This Agreement constitutes the entire agreement of the parties with respect to the services to be provided by Consultant and the obligations of Client and Attorney. No provision of this agreement may be amended except by a writing signed by the parties.

Until the Agreement, signed by Attorney and Client, is received by Consultant, it shall constitute an offer to provide services. This offer to provide services remains open for twenty (20) days from the date signed by Consultant. Acceptance by Consultant occurs only after the signed Agreement and deposit are actually received by Consultant within the twenty (20) day period.

AGREED UPON as of the date set forth below.

BURRAGE & JOHNSON, CPAs, LLC

By______________________________ ________________
Date

LAW FIRM NAME HERE

By______________________________ ________________
ATTORNEY NAME HERE Date

CLIENT NAME HERE

By______________________________ ________________
CLIENT NAME HERE Date

Appendix B

Sample Company Financial Statements

SAMPLE COMPANY, INC.
Balance Sheet
December 31, 2010

Assets

Current assets	
Cash	$ 66,880
Trade accounts receivable	63,511
Allowance For Doubtful Accounts	(3,176)
Inventory	13,527
Prepaid Expenses	5,161
Total current assets	145,903
Property and equipment, less accumulated depreciation	5,319
	$ 151,222

Liabilities and Stockholder's Equity

Current Liabilities	
Current maturities of long-term debt	$ 14,180
Accounts Payable	1,359
Accrued Expenses	3,496
Federal Income Tax Payable	7,683
State Franchise Tax Payable	5,089
Total current Liabilities	31,807
Long-term debt, less current maturities	33,195
Common stock, no par value; authorized 10,000 shares, issued and outstanding 1,000 shares	1,000
Retained Earnings	85,220
Total stockholder's equity	86,220
	$ 151,222

SAMPLE COMPANY, INC.
Statement of Income and Retained Earnings
For the year ended December 31, 2010

Net Sales		$ 747,434
Cost of goods sold		(398,136)
Gross Profit		349,298
Operating Expenses		
Salaries	108,878	
Professional Services	20,944	
Bad Debts	4,935	
Telephone	14,635	
Payroll Taxes	27,381	
Travel	15,903	
Rent	23,120	
Office Expense	11,968	
Employee Benefits	18,985	
Courier Expense	5,357	
Property and Business taxes	425	
Insurance	4,783	
Building Maintenance	1,371	
Utilities	5,852	
Depreciation	2,163	
Advertising	1,365	
Meals and Entertainment	1,975	
Memberships & Subscriptions	675	
Other	(3)	
Total operating expenses		270,712
Other Income (expense)		
Finance Charges	1,387	
Interest Expense	(2,497)	
Total other income (expense)		(1,110)
Provision for income taxes		17,794
Net income		$ 59,682
Retained Earnings		
Beginning of Period		25,538
End of Period		$ 85,220

SAMPLE COMPANY, INC.
Statement of Cash Flows
For the year ended December 31, 2010

Cash flows from operating activities	
Net Income	$ 59,682
Adjustments to reconcile net income to net cash provided by operating activities:	
Depreciation and amortization	2,163
(Increase) decrease in accounts receivable	(17,465)
(Increase) decrease in prepaid expenses	(3,219)
(Increase) decrease in inventories	4,234
Increase (decrease) in accounts payable	(44,227)
Increase (decrease) in accrued liabilities	(1,050)
Increase (decrease) in income taxes payable	7,237
Total adjustments	(52,327)
Net cash provided (used) by operating activities	7,355
Cash flow from investing activities:	
Cash payments for the purchase of property	(4,974)
Net cash provided (used) by investing activities	(4,974)
Cash flow from financing activities:	
Increase in notes payable	17,375
Net cash provided (used) by financing activities	17,375
Net increase (decrease) in cash and equivalents	19,756
Cash and equivalents, beginning of year	47,124
Cash and equivalents, end of year	$ 66,880

Appendix C

Riker Report

Riker's Collision & Paint, Inc. (Riker)
Forensic Accounting/Fair Market Value
As of December 31, 2009

May 2, 2010

Ms. Frakes, Attorney
Frakes Family Law, PLLC
1701D Avenue of the Stars
Janeway, Washington 55578

Dear Ms. Frakes:

Re: (1) Forensic examination of the Riker Marital Estate,
(2) Determination of the Fair Market Value of 100% of the shares in *Riker's Collision & Paint, Inc.* (Riker) on a control[1], non-liquid[2] basis as of December 31, 2009.

FORENSIC ACCOUNTING/VALUATION EXECUTIVE SUMMARY

This report summarizes our opinions regarding the above matter.

We reserve the right to update these documents and our resultant opinions as deemed necessary upon the conclusion of discovery or as additional or new discovery and/or data becomes available.

NOTE: Our final opinion is based on the $875,000 conclusion from the "As Corrected for Forensic Examination" report reference; the "As Reported" amount is for reference only and has no bearing in this matter.

SCOPE OF THIS ASSIGNMENT

This report cannot be used for any other purpose than for that which originally precipitated this work. In addition, it cannot stand alone and must refer to the workpaper file for accurate interpretation.

SUMMARY OF ASSIGNMENT

This matter pivots upon two key issues:

- ❑ Unreported income and/or overstated expenses for the Riker Marital Estate documented through our forensic accounting examination spanning 2002 through 2009; and

- ❑ The fair market value of Riker's Collision & Paint, Inc. as of December 31, 2009.

---

[1] *International Glossary of Business Valuation Terms,* American Society of Appraisers, June 2005: "*Control* - the power to direct the management and policies of a business enterprise."

[2] Ibid,"*Marketability* - the ability to quickly convert property to cash at minimal cost." Consequently, **'non-**liquid' indicates an amount adjusted to reflect the lack of marketability.

Riker's Collision & Paint, Inc. (Riker)
Forensic Accounting/Fair Market Value
As of December 31, 2009

FORENSIC ACCOUNTING/FAIR MARKET VALUE

As you know, our practice consists exclusively of *forensic accounting* (discussed later) whereby we critically investigate even seemingly straightforward valuation assignments.

The bulk of our work to date has consisted of forensic accounting examination and application of the findings leading to the determination of fair market value.

PURPOSE AND USE OF THE APPRAISAL

financialforensics® was retained to execute forensic accounting in order to opine on the *Fair Market Value* of 100% of the shares in Riker's Collision & Paint, Inc (Riker) EIN 91-1968960, on a control, non-liquid basis as of December 31, 2009. The forensic accounting and valuation-related results can only be considered within the context of this matter.

OBJECTIVE OF THE APPRAISAL

The objective of this valuation is to quantify the Fair Market Value of 100% of the shares in Riker's Collision & Paint, Inc. (Riker) on a control, non-liquid basis. Riker is a closely held, Kelso, Washington-based "S" corporation formed April 2, 1999.

THE NATURE OF OUR PROFESSIONAL RESPONSIBILITIES AND ETHICS

We practice as *forensic accountants* within the profession of certified public accountants, CPAs. Therefore, we are compelled to meet a wide variety of ethical, legal, professional and technical standards. These requirements reflect our fiduciary capacity and comprise a set of standards exceeding perhaps any other profession.

We hold our ethical, legal, professional and technical practice responsibilities in the highest regard, particularly the hallmark of our profession - ***independence***. It is through independence that we serve the public's interest in providing unbiased, objective and technically correct opinions on financial matters, whether in court or in public or private matters.

The authorities governing our ethical, legal, professional and technical practice actions include the following non-inclusive bodies:

- **AICPA** – American Institute of Certified Public Accountants. This national body, in connection with the Financial Accounting Standards Board, FASB and related entities establishes financial reporting requirements commonly known as "Generally Accepted Accounting Principles," GAAP. The AICPA Rules of Professional Conduct contains twelve (12) Rules organized into the numbered categories below:
    - **100** – Independence, Integrity and Objectivity
    - **200** – General and Technical
    - **300** – Responsibilities to Clients
    - **400** – Responsibilities to Colleagues (superseded, i.e. no longer in force)
    - **500** – Other Responsibilities and Practices

Riker's Collision & Paint, Inc. (Riker)
Forensic Accounting/Fair Market Value
As of December 31, 2009

- **OSBA** – Oregon State Board of Accountancy.[3] This body, authorized by ORS 673.410 has as its primary purpose to protect the public interest. It is the principal government state agency which issues CPA licenses and certificates. The Oregon laws governing certified public accountants generally follow the Uniform Accountancy Act, UAA, but where conflicts arise Oregon law prevails. The Board rules specifically refer to breach of fiduciary duty as a part of general prohibitions against dishonesty and fraud under OAR 801-030-0020. Note that virtually all state accountancy boards apply similar criteria.

  We also comply with the rules of the Washington State Board of Accountancy which are very similar to the Oregon rules. We do not hold ourselves out as practicing accountancy in the State of Washington since we do not meet their criteria of practice.

- **OSCPA** – Oregon Society of Certified Public Accountants. This body furthers the interests of CPA-shareholders, and coordinates professional requirements with the AICPA through the "joint ethical enforcement program" (JEEP).

- **SEC** – Securities and Exchange Commission. This US law enforcement government body, in coordination with the Public Companies Accounting Oversight Board (PCAOB) governs financial reporting requirements for all publicly held and certain privately held businesses and transactions.

- **IRS** – Internal Revenue Service. This US Treasury body is responsible for administering the laws and collections processes concerning revenue for the federal government.

- **Jurisdictional and Regulatory Authorities** – Depending upon the venue of our practice we may be compelled to meet additional criteria. For example, in many damages matters the composition of the damages is defined by statute and/or precedent. Also, in many valuation matters the standard of value is defined by statute, precedent or prevailing practice.

- **Other Professional Bodies** - The unique nature of our forensic accounting practice compels us to apply additional professional and ethical standards from the following:

  - **ACFE –** American College of Forensic Examiners
  - **ACFE –** Association of Certified Fraud Examiners
  - **ASA** – American Society of Appraisers
  - **IBA** – Institute of Business Appraisers
  - **IMA** – Institute of Management Accountants
  - **NACVA** – National Association of Certified Valuation Analysts

We strive to meet and exceed the preceding standards through our firm's guidance as summarized below:

---

[3] A partner of our firm served a four-year term on the OSBA's Complaints Committee, with the purpose: "Provide technical assistance to the Board Investigator in the investigation of complaints received by the Board. The Committee reviews investigation reports and makes recommendations to the Board regarding disciplinary action or other resolution of complaint investigations."

Riker's Collision & Paint, Inc. (Riker)
Forensic Accounting/Fair Market Value
As of December 31, 2009

OUR MISSION STATEMENT:

To spearhead forensic accounting innovation in civil, criminal and combat matters©.[4]

THE DEFINITION OF FORENSIC ACCOUNTING IS:

The art & science of investigating people & money©.[5]

UNIQUE FACTS AND CIRCUMSTANCES

Every appraisal contains unique aspects that have an impact on the valuation approach, and techniques considered and applied. In this appraisal, the following unique facts and circumstances are specifically identified in order to apprise the reader of their application:

- **SIMULTANEOUS IMPACT** – The Rikers' marital and business finances are inextricably coupled, and thus valuation of the Riker business is codependent with the Marital Estate transactions, and vice versa;

- **FORENSIC EXAMINATION** – The codependent finances were disaggregated by applying forensic techniques to the Rikers' personal and business records, e.g. "Cash-T" analysis, link analysis, root tracing and other procedures for forensic accounting and economic benefit stream purposes;

- **RIKER MARITAL ESTATE** - The Riker Marital Estate amassed significant assets over an eight year period including real estate and cash. A review of their federal 1040 personal income tax returns and bank statements show real estate properties increased from nine in 2004 to twenty in 2008. In addition, their cash on hand balance increased from an estimated $10,000 in 2000 to $513,462.25 in 2008. Virtually all personal living expenses were paid directly from their joint business bank accounts while personal bank balances and cash investments steadily increased.

- **RIKER'S COLLISION & PAINT, INC** - It appears significant efforts were made to minimize Riker's tax liability resulting in unreported corporate income from "side jobs." Mr. Jonathan Riker defined "side jobs" as jobs done after hours, "where I do it by myself outside of the business."[6] It does not appear that the income from the "side jobs" was reported on the personal or business tax return[7]. Given Mr. Riker is a corporate shareholder and used corporate assets (facility and tools) to complete these jobs, the revenue generated from "side jobs" would not be considered personal income but rather unreported Riker Collision & Paint, Inc. revenue.

  A review of the company's QuickBooks file revealed considerable questionable transactions that suggested that the QuickBooks accounting software was utilized to track bank account transactions such as deposits and checks written but not necessarily actual revenues. The most telling indicator was the frequency of full payments from insurance companies and/or customers prior to the creation of an invoice in QuickBooks.

---

[4] (**financialforensics®** October 2002).
[5] (**financialforensics®** Newsletter, circa September 1993); Forensic Accounting Academy™ 2007.
[6] EXCERPT OF DEPOSITION OF JONATHAN RIKER January 13, 2010, page 103, line 19.
[7] EXCERPT OF DEPOSITION OF JONATHAN RIKER January 13, 2010, page 108, line 17.

It is highly unlikely that the customer or insurance company would pay in full without an invoice itemizing the work performed. Rather, it appears the insurance companies and/or customers were invoiced through the company's Audatex estimation system. This accounting structure creates the opportunity for the final amount entered as income in QuickBooks to reflect any amount desired. This position is further supported by the following illustrative observations:

- Customer jobs were identified as "cancelled" or "voided" and the notes section of the file indicated it was a "cash job" or that no invoice was to be prepared.
- A significant number of customers were entered in QuickBooks but were never invoiced for any work done. Further analysis revealed labor, parts and materials were assigned to these customers but never invoiced. In fact, a refund check was issued to a customer with no job.
- QuickBooks invoices often used the term "As Per Estimated" in the description section; no detail of parts, materials or labor provided as required.
- Labor hours and rates reflected on numerous QuickBooks invoices significantly deviated from the hours and rates reported by shop employee labor time costs.

In addition to these examples, there were considerable costs that elicit uncertainty. In general, Riker's standard costs would include labor, towing, sublet costs, storage, parts and materials which would be considered typical for this industry[8]. All legitimate costs incurred in relation to a specific customer job would be reflected in detail on the customer invoice at a marked up cost. It does not appear this expected procedure occurred in the following situations:

Unassigned Costs

A review of the QuickBooks Cost of Goods Sold and Shop Supplies account detail revealed numerous costs that were not assigned to a customer job. Jonathan Riker indicated that the customer was entered into the computer prior to ordering parts so customer parts can be tracked.[9] Given their procedure to link parts to a customer job, it is likely these unassigned cost are related to "side jobs." Although Jonathan Riker indicated the business did not purchase materials for "side jobs,"[10] analysis of the joint personal checking account did not reveal purchases of parts or materials. It is probable the corporation paid for "side jobs" parts and materials and they were never properly included on a QuickBooks customer invoice.

Costs not Invoiced

A review of the QuickBooks Costs of Goods Sold and Shop Supplies account detail revealed significant costs assigned to customer jobs that were never invoiced or paid. Some customer jobs were "cancelled" and the costs remained unbilled. Often, the customer job was created in QuickBooks and costs were assigned to the job but an

[8] Per IRS MSSP.
[9] EXCERPT OF DEPOSITION OF Jonathan Riker January 13, 2010, page 120-121, lines 25 and 1-11
[10] EXCERPT OF DEPOSITION OF Jonathan Riker January 13, 2010, page 115, line 1

invoice was never created; the costs remained unbilled. A review of the daily shop labor summary revealed substantial labor hours assigned to customers with no QuickBooks invoice. In addition, there were multiple examples of specific parts, materials or sublet costs allocated to a customer but those costs were never included on the invoice. In some cases, costs assigned to the customer job appeared completely unrelated to the services invoiced. It is likely that these expenditures represent costs associated with "side jobs." A selected QuickBooks account is included as an exhibit to this report to illustrate these costs.

UNDERSTATED INCOME

Given the admission that revenue from "side jobs" was unreported and the analysis of various costs expensed that appear to be related to "side jobs", unreported income was estimated for 2004 to 2008. There is insufficient information regarding the true nature and quantity of these "side jobs" to apply a standard markup on the costs identified and discussed above. For example, the unbilled purchase of a fender could be marked up to determine the revenue associated with the part however, the extent of associated work, such as a custom paint job, is unknown.

Given the insufficient detail needed to precisely determine the unreported income, we deployed a variety of statistical and analytical forensic accounting techniques including:

- Pattern Analysis
- Pareto's Law
- Central tendency and related variant indicators
- Correlation coefficients and related measures
- Job Profitability Analysis: stratification, RSF[11], and other methods
- Analyzed Time by Job Summary compared to invoiced jobs
- Analyzed Unbilled Job Costs
- Analyzed Customer Payments by type, amount and date
- Et al

We specifically used a generally accepted indirect method described by the Internal Revenue Service as "Cash-T."[12], The Cash-T, was applied to ascertain the accuracy of the income reported. This method compares all known income received during the year to all monies spent during the year. It also allows for the use/accumulation of monies in known bank accounts or disclosed cash on hand balances. If income and expenses are properly reported, the analysis should balance to zero. If there are more expenditures than reported sources of income to pay for them, the result is assumed to be unreported income. Any unreported income resulting from the indirect analysis was determined to be from Riker Collision & Paint, Inc. activities.

Amounts reported to the Internal Revenue Service and from third parties such as financial institutions and title companies were used in the analysis. Estimations for personal living expenses and cash on hand balances were determined based on the best information available to date. Personal living expenses were estimated based on

[11] Relative Size Factor

[12] IRS Internal Revenue Manual: Part 4, Chapter 10, Section 4 "Examination of Income," 4.10.4.6.

the disclosed standard of living of the individuals.[13] The Riker couple had a high standard of living that included jewelry, a luxury car and significant real estate holdings. Cash on hand balances were based on the disclosed use and accumulation of cash. The Riker's accumulated over $500,000 in cash from 2000 to mid-2008.

The Cash-T indirect analysis resulted in the following unreported income reflected in the chart and visuals illustrated reported and unreported results:

	Receipts	Cost of Goods Sold	Margin	Expenses	Dprn	Profit/(Loss)	PL %	Unbilled Costs	Psnl Expenses	Other	Total Nonbusiness	Underreported Personal	Underreported Corp	Correct PL%
2002	470,632	215,852	54%	192,461		62,319	13%	7,265.46	2,767.70	6,744.02	7,265.46			14%
2003	487,541	244,304	50%	188,574		54,663	11%	18,155.50	22,157.24	7,452.21	43,169.48			16%
2004	878,996	436,749	50%	276,834	36,105	129,308	15%	18,385.57	74,982.15	16,123.90	90,676.29	212,974.13	48,231.69	41%
2005	1,144,424	604,324	47%	342,010	3,491	194,599	17%	21,837.88	108,802.31	11,912.21	111,252.33	176,496.95	1,476.78	36%
2006	1,109,090	696,249	37%	349,185	6,075	57,581	5%	14,246.99	121,345.93	16,055.72	111,520.38	359,368.52	8,012.32	37%
2007	1,051,467	564,261	46%	397,022	5,530	84,654	8%	6,184.71	134,375.06	9,473.48	113,328.66	175,164.89	26,734.18	34%
2008	891,266	477,536	46%	362,038	5,129	46,563	5%	15,700.83	58,083.15	10,098.83	67,219.28	197,963.67	2,103.39	28%
2009	930,860	489,642	47%	431,223	18,282	(8,287)	-1%	11,247.61	22,466.03	10,420.25	38,446.16		11,640.41	3%
								113,024.55	544,979.57	88,280.62	582,878.04	1,121,968.16	98,198.77	

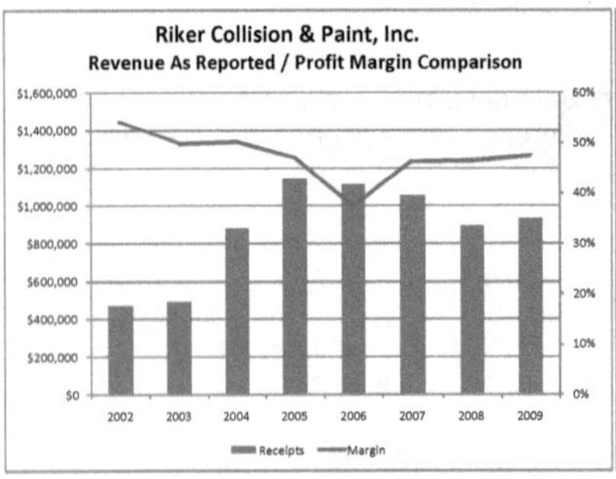

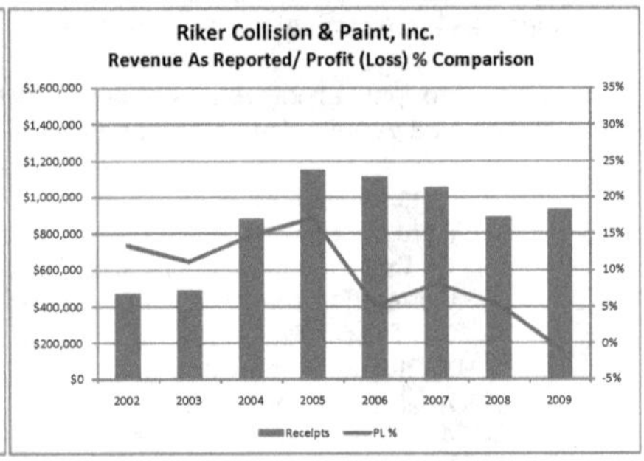

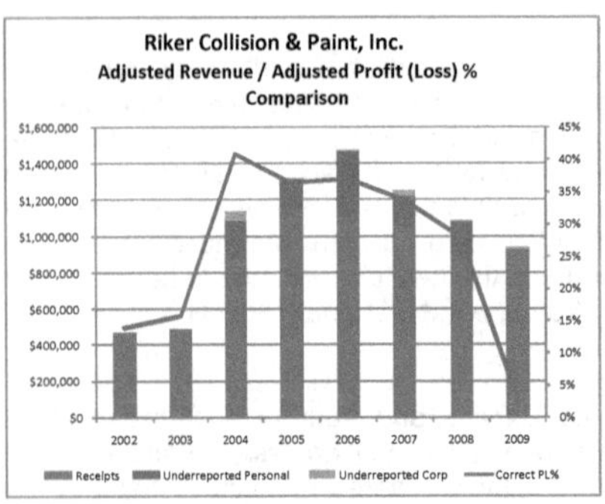

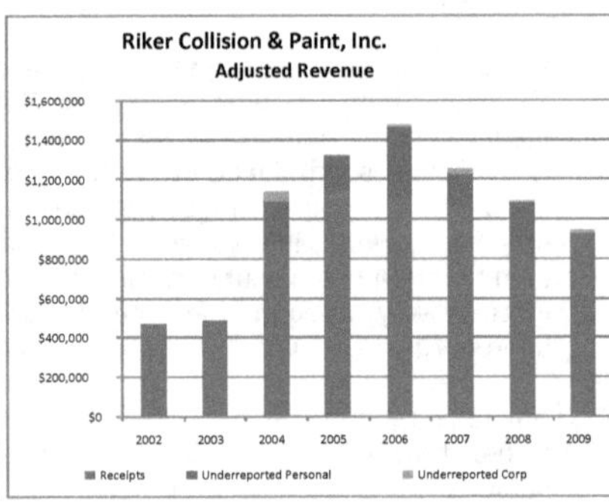

[13] Jonathan RIKER Financial Declaration filed April 29, 2008, and Deanna RIKER's RESPONSE TO INTERROGATORIES AND REQUESTS FOR PRODUCTION submitted July 15, 2009, pages 47-48.

Riker's Collision & Paint, Inc. (Riker)
Forensic Accounting/Fair Market Value
As of December 31, 2009

We also estimated the post-separation adjustment necessary to account for the data to which we do not yet have access. We applied various statistical techniques, e.g. regression via ANOVA and determined that a simple arithmetic mean yields representative results. Therefore, we compared and applied Underreported Personal Income to Riker's reported results which yielded the following measures.

	Receipts	Cost of Goods Sold	Margin	Expenses	Dprn	Profit/(Loss)	PL %	Unbilled Costs	Psnl Expenses	Other	Total Nonbusiness	Underreported Personal	Underreported Corp	Correct PL%
2002	470,632	215,852	54%	192,461		62,319	13%	7,265.46	2,767.70	6,744.02	7,265.46			14%
2003	487,541	244,304	50%	188,574		54,663	11%	18,155.50	22,157.24	7,452.21	43,169.48			16%
2004	878,996	436,749	50%	276,834	36,105	129,308	15%	18,385.57	74,982.15	16,123.90	90,676.29	212,974.13	48,231.69	41%
2005	1,144,424	604,324	47%	342,010	3,491	194,599	17%	21,837.88	108,802.31	11,912.21	111,252.33	176,496.95	1,476.78	36%
2006	1,109,090	696,249	37%	349,185	6,075	57,581	5%	14,246.99	121,345.93	16,055.72	111,520.38	359,368.52	8,012.32	37%
2007	1,051,467	564,261	46%	397,022	5,530	84,654	8%	6,184.71	134,375.06	9,473.48	113,328.66	175,164.89	26,734.18	34%
2008	891,266	477,536	46%	362,038	5,129	46,563	5%	15,700.83	58,083.15	10,098.83	67,219.28	197,666.73	2,103.39	28%
2009	930,860	489,642	47%	431,223	18,282	(8,287)	-1%	11,247.61	22,466.03	10,420.25	38,446.16	206,447.97	11,640.41	20%
								113,024.55	544,979.57	88,280.62	582,878.04	1,328,119.19	98,198.77	

OVERSTATED EXPENSES

Another technique to minimize Rikers' tax liability was to overstate the expenses deducted on the business tax return. Analysis of the QuickBooks file revealed significant personal expenses were deducted as ordinary and necessary business expenses. Personal expenditures were identified throughout the various business accounts including but limited to Advertising, Dues and Subscriptions, Office Expense, Meals and Entertainment, Training, and Shop Supplies. The designation as personal expenditures was assigned based on the payee listed in QuickBooks due to its obvious personal nature.

In addition to the unmistakable personal expenditures identified, analysis revealed payees were altered in QuickBooks to conceal the true character of the personal item. For example, payments to Macy's were recorded in QuickBooks as a business purchase from Tom's Radiator; a large purchase at Nordstrom was split among multiple transactions for Starship Trucks & Equip.; cash withdrawals were recorded as Bank Service Charges or as purchases from Borg Printers. Personal items purchased with the business debit card were routinely hidden with a falsified business payee when entered into QuickBooks. Also, there were several manual business checks identified that were written for personal items and a falsified business payee entered into QuickBooks. Given the sparse number of business cancelled checks available and examined, the full extent of the falsified payee deception is unknown. Selected QuickBooks accounts are included as an exhibit to this report to illustrate the deduction of personal expenses and altered payees. Personal expenditures deducted included not only personal living expenses such as food, pet care, clothing and medical expenses but also significant amounts of costs related to their rental properties' improvements and repairs.

In addition, entire credit card payments were often deducted without allocating the purchases among the various accounts. It is likely that this was another attempt to conceal the personal nature of the transactions and deduct the items as ordinary and necessary business expenses. Analysis also revealed examples of deductions for business purchases made by credit card assigned to customers that were the exact duplication of costs paid by check.

None of the personal items deducted as business expenses were later reclassified as shareholder distributions. A review of the joint personal checking accounts revealed virtually no personal expenditures were paid for normal personal living expenses such as gas, groceries, clothing, personal grooming, gifts, cash withdrawal, etc.

THE TECHNICAL STANDARDS THAT APPLY IN THIS FORENSIC ASSIGNMENT

THE FORENSIC ACCOUNTING METHODOLOGY USED IN THIS MATTER

We deployed our proprietary forensic accounting methodology, i.e. *Forensic Accounting/Investigation Methodology*© (FA/IM©) in support of our analysis. To the best of our knowledge, FA/IM© is the only proprietary forensic accounting methodology in the professional market.

We are exclusively licensed to deploy FA/IM© tools and techniques throughout the United States. Through the Forensic Accounting Academy™ we have trained hundreds of CPAs, analysts, law enforcement officers (federal, state, local), bankers, investors and others who need to look "beyond and behind the numbers" contained in financial statements.

A screen-shot of the FA/IM© methodology follows:

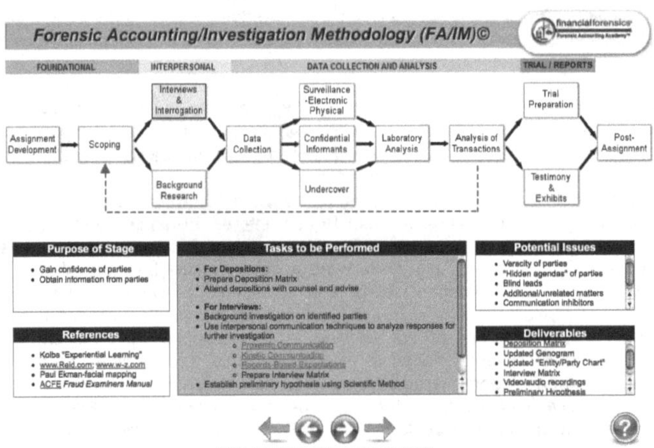

The methodology was supplemented by our cumulative forensic accounting (including valuation) expertise and our familiarity with automotive businesses, including auto parts, collision and paint, dealership, lube, tires, tune-up, equipment, and related industries in addition to IRS

Riker's Collision & Paint, Inc. (Riker)
Forensic Accounting/Fair Market Value
As of December 31, 2009

ATGs[14].

AUTHORITATIVE BUSINESS VALUATION BODIES

The business valuation profession is in a transition from its infancy towards generally accepted practices of analysis, approach and conclusion. However, the various competing bodies that profess to be "the" single best source of business valuation methodology complicate this transition.

We are trained, proficient and certified (where non-redundant) in each valuation methodology to permit us to arrive at the conclusion that is the most technically correct and professionally defensible. Consequently, we have considered and applied as appropriate the business valuation guidance provided by the following alphabetically listed bodies:

- **AICPA** – The American Institute of Certified Public Accountants – In June 2007 the AICPA released its *Statement on Standards for Valuation Services No. 1*, (SSVS No.1). The document purports to set standards for CPAs, but is not without significant controversy. There was no impact on our technical work since we have routinely met or exceeded all professional valuation standards, including those listed below. However, we added limited verbiage to our Certification Statement, and Statement of Contingent and Limiting Conditions.
- **ASA** - The American Society of Appraisers, the source of USPAP[15]
- **IBA** - The Institute of Business Appraisers[16]
- **IRS** - The Internal Revenue Service, the source of Revenue Ruling 59-60[17]
- **NACVA** - The National Association of Certified Valuation Analysts.

OUR FIRM'S FORENSIC ACCOUNTING AND BUSINESS VALUATION CAPABILITIES

The following highlights illustrate why our firm is nationally recognized within the forensic accounting and business valuation profession (for more details refer to the attached cv of Darrell D. Dorrell):

- The co-authors of this report routinely address leading professional bodies throughout the US regarding the subjects of forensic accounting, business valuation, financial analysis, and expert witness testimony including the Accountants' Global Network (**AGN**), American Institute of Certified Public Accountants' (**AICPA**) Annual Advanced Litigation Conference, Bankruptcy Bar Association, Federal Bureau of Investigation's (**FBI**) Specialized Criminal Investigations In-Service, Institute of Management Accountants (**IMA**), National Association of Certified Valuation Analysts' (**NACVA**)

[14] During the last 15 years or so our firm has conducted forensic accounting, valuation and related assignments throughout the Portland/Vancouver SMSAs, including often instructing business owners through the Northwest Automotive Trades Association (NATA), previously PATA.

[15] Uniform Standards of Professional Appraisal Practice, as promulgated by the Appraisal Foundation.

[16] As of July 16, 2008 NACVA acquired the assets of the IBA through a partnership.

[17] IRS Valuation Guide for Income, Estate and Gift Taxes, "Valuation Training for Appeals Officers", (CCH – New York, January, 1994), and the "Internal Revenue Service Guidelines" (Proposed), (IRS, May 1, 2001).

Annual Valuation Update Conference, National Litigation Services Support Association (**NLSSA**), Oregon Bar, Oregon Society of CPAs (**OSCPA**), Pennsylvania Institute of CPAs (**PICPA**), Securities and Exchange Commission (**SEC**), Turnaround Management Association (**TMA**), United States Department of Justice (**USDOJ**), Counterterrorism Section, Washington Bar (voted "Best of Financial CLE" for 2000), Washington Society of CPAs, Willamette College of Law Trial Practice Class, etc.

- The co-authors of this report conceived, developed and instruct forensic accounting throughout the US via the 5-day Forensic Accounting Academy™. The training is based upon the proprietary Forensic Accounting/Investigation Methodology© (FA/IM©) that comprises civil and criminal investigation processes and encompasses virtually all aspects of accounting practice.

- The co-authors of this report regularly publish peer-reviewed technical articles in national publications including the Sarbanes-Oxley (SOX) Compliance Journal, American Journal of Family Law[18], Business Appraisal Practice,[19] the *National Litigation Consultants' Review,*[20] the Valuation Examiner,[21] Valuation Strategies,[22] etc. and have been cited in various media sources including Bloomberg Wealth Manager[23], Business Week[24], IR Magazine[25], Oregonian[26] and others. Finally, the co-authors of this report have been interviewed for radio (NPR) and television productions (SBTV) and have consulted with the "Law and Order" writers regarding fraud episode content.

- The co-author of this report, Darrell D. Dorrell was awarded the *Jeffrey R. Salins Report Writing Award* for excellence in business valuation report writing presented to us in Chicago in May 2001 by the National Association of Certified Valuation Analysts (NACVA). The award is given annually to one of NACVA's 6,000 members and states in part:

  "This award is hereby given to acknowledge superior work in preparing a Business Valuation Report. You have shown exceptional skill through conscientious attention to detail and mastery of the written language. To receive this award, as judged by a group of your peers, one must submit a report that demonstrates proficiency in

---

[18] For example, "The Valuation Report Card", American Journal of Family Law, (Aspen Law & Business), Summer 2002, Volume 16, Number 2, pages 109-117.

[19] For example, "Net Cash Flow (NCF) May Understate Value: A Proposed "Gross Profit" Adjustment, (Institute of Business Appraisers), Summer 2002.

[20] For example, "Do Buy-Sell Agreements Matter?", National Litigation Consultants' Review, (Litigation Consultants, "S" – Vol. 4 Issue 13, June 2005 and Vol. 4 Issue 14, July 2005).

[21] For example, "Marketability Discounts – A Comprehensive Analysis", National Association of Certified Valuation Analysts, (NACVA), March/April 2002, pages 23-32, and May/June issue for 2nd part of article.

[22] For example, "The 'Articulation' Method Control/Minority – Minority/Control Reconciliation – A Practical Illustration of the *Levels of Value*", (RIA Group – Warren, Gorham and Lamont – New York), September/October 2002.

[23] "Fire Extinguisher – Nonsolicitation Agreements," Bloomberg Wealth Manager, (cited) December 2004/January 2005.

[24] "Using Software to Sniff Out Fraud," Business Week, (cited) September 30, 2003.

[25] "Cost vs. Value – Intellectual Property Disclosure," IR Magazine, (cited) September 2003.

[26] "Combat CPA© Uses Accounting To Ferret Out Fraud," 'Oregonian' (Portland Newspaper) – Feature Article, Metro Southwest and other editions, January 16, 2003.

written communications, business valuation theory and techniques, economic and industry research, technical and financial analysis, identifying key and underlying issues, accounting and tax fundamentals, organization and presentation, and a comprehension of NACVA's Standards of Professional Practice. Recipients of this award set the standard to which all others must ultimately rise."

- The co-author of this report, Darrell D. Dorrell served for 4 years as an Examiner - Business Valuation, on the International Board of Examiners for the American Society of Appraisers. Accordingly, he reviews the final reports of ASA candidates to determine whether they meet the stringent criteria necessary to achieve the ASA business valuation credential.

- The co-author of this report, Darrell D. Dorrell created a specialized training course, Small Business Valuation Case Study offered to CPAs, CVAs, and appraisers throughout the United States. His work is on behalf of the National Association of Certified Valuation Analysts (NACVA), the largest professional business valuation association in the world.

- The co-author of this report, Darrell D. Dorrell serves as a nationwide instructor for the National Association of Certified Valuation Analysts in their Career Development Institute, focusing on the technical elements of business valuation through the Current Updates in Valuation (CUV) training.

- The co-author of this report, Darrell D. Dorrell served a 4-year term on the Complaints Committee of the Oregon State Board of Accountancy. His responsibilities included investigating and evaluating complaints regarding the services offered and rendered by the accounting profession within Oregon. Such complaints included valuation services purportedly provided by CPAs.

STANDARD AND PREMISE OF VALUE

The standard of value that we have applied to this assignment is *fair market value* which is consistent with the definition of fair market value as defined in Revenue Ruling 59-60[27]:

> *26 CFR 20.2031-2(2)(.02) - The amount at which property would change hands between a willing buyer and a willing seller when the former is not under any compulsion to buy and the latter is not under any compulsion to sell, both parties having reasonable knowledge of relevant facts. Court decisions frequently state in addition that the hypothetical buyer and seller are assumed to be able, as well as willing, to trade and to be well informed about the property and concerning the market for such property.*

The following factors (1 through 8) are outlined in Revenue Ruling 59-60, §4, under "Factors to Consider." We considered such factors and also factor 9 in arriving at our opinion:

1. The nature of the business and the history of the enterprise from its inception.

---

[27] 1959-1 C.B. 237.

2. The economic outlook in general and the condition and outlook of the specific industry in particular.

3. The book value of the stock and the financial condition of the business.

4. The earning capacity of the company.

5. The dividend-paying capacity.

6. Whether or not the enterprise has goodwill or other intangible value.

7. Sales of the stock and the size of the block of stock to be valued.

8. The market prices of stock of corporations engaged in the same or similar line of business having their stocks actively traded in a free and open market, either on an exchange or over-the-counter.

9. The transaction price and resultant financial measures for similar companies that were sold in their entirety.

Our study included, but was not necessarily limited to, the above-mentioned guidelines.

The premise of value[28] applied to Riker's Collision & Paint, Inc. is as a "going concern." We concluded that this premise was appropriate based upon our analysis of Riker's operating history and outlook.

NORMALIZATIONS[29] (ADJUSTMENTS)

Nearly every appraisal requires financial statement normalizations (adjustments)[30] that result in an impact on the valuation techniques considered and applied. Such normalizations are typically financial transactions comprised of a non-recurring, non-operating or non-market nature.

Normalizations are adjustments to financial statements for items not representative of the present going-concern status of the business. Normalizing adjustments could include elimination of effects of discontinued operations, elimination of effects of nonrecurring events, or adjustment of abnormal depreciation charges.[31]

---

[28] *International Glossary of Business Valuation Terms,* American Society of Appraisers, June 2005: an assumption regarding the most likely set of transactional circumstances that may be applicable to the subject valuation; e.g. going concern, liquidation.

[29] Normalizations are adjustments to financial statements that eliminate the distortion of non-operating, non-market and non-recurring events.

[30] *Glossary…,* American Society of Appraisers, August 6, 2001: Normalized Earnings – economic benefits adjusted for nonrecurring, noneconomic, or other unusual items to eliminate anomalies and/or facilitate comparisons. Normalized Financial Statements – financial statements adjusted for nonoperating assets and liabilities and/or for nonrecurring, noneconomic, or other unusual items to eliminate anomalies and/or facilitate comparisons.

[31] Pratt, Shannon P. CFA, FASA, MCBA, The Lawyer's Business Valuation Handbook, (American Bar Association – New York, 2000), 415.

Riker's Collision & Paint, Inc. (Riker)
Forensic Accounting/Fair Market Value
As of December 31, 2009

In this appraisal, there were two general normalizations done for items considered not representative of the going-concern status of the business: personal expenditures and unreported income. They are specifically delineated in the valuation calculations and supporting analytical schedules contained in this report.

ECONOMIC BENEFIT STREAM

Since we derived the "As Corrected" revenue for Riker's we were then able to determine the economic benefit stream applicable to Riker's fundamentals. We sought independent data from various sources, e.g. Bureau of Labor Statistics, Bureau of Economic Analysis and other sources.

Using such independent variables we compared Riker's "As Reported" and "As Corrected" revenue and related streams against the independent variables. Selected BEA comparisons for Longview, WA's SMSA GDP data is summarized below.

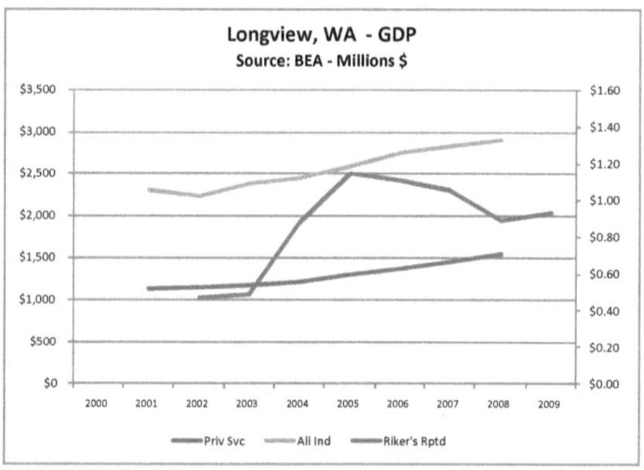

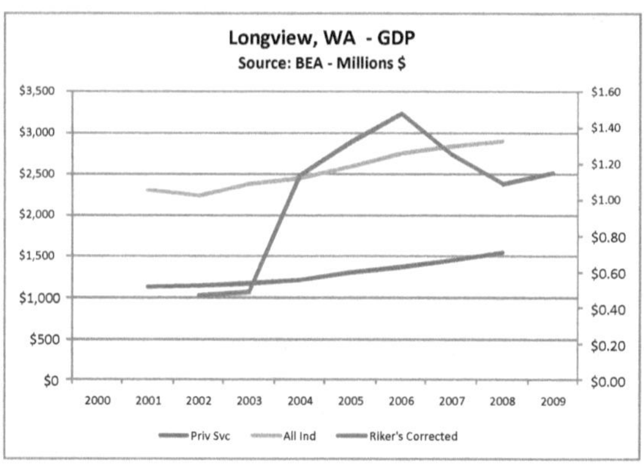

Riker's Collision & Paint, Inc. (Riker)
Forensic Accounting/Fair Market Value
As of December 31, 2009

The preceding visuals indicate that our forensic analysis provides representative results as measured by various regression measures and related statistical techniques. Further, noting the likelihood of undisclosed external data, e.g. unreported bank accounts a simple arithmetic mean of baseline fundamentals yields representative results.

VALUATION METHODS

All valuation methods attempt to determine the fair market value of an entity by simulating a hypothetical[32] market transaction. The methods are categorized within three distinct, but related Approaches – Asset, Income and Market.

We considered several potentially pertinent valuation methods in order to "converge" the collective conclusion that most accurately represents the fair market value of the Subject Interest's result. This technique recognizes the imprecise yet valid nature of business valuation and lends assurance to the conclusion and avoids the risk of relying only upon a single, or a few conclusions.

ASSET APPROACH

The Asset Approach contains two distinct alternatives: Liquidation Value and Going-Concern Value. Going-Concern Value applies to those entities likely to continue operations beyond the respective transaction date. Liquidation Value is only to be considered when an entity is likely to actually liquidate. Therefore, based upon the "Facts and Circumstances" described within this report, and our communications with shareholders, management and Company advisors the most appropriate Asset Approach to be considered consists of the Going-Concern alternative.

The application of the Asset Approach using the Going-Concern premise consists of restating an entity's assets and liabilities to fair market value, and adjusting as required for costs of selling and likely income tax[33] impact. Note that the "book" value of an entity, i.e. assets less liabilities is virtually never a valid measure of fair market value since such treatment records assets at their acquisition cost and reduces them for depreciation. Also, the overall income results for the entity are further reduced for income taxes.

Although we considered the application of the Asset Approach, Going-Concern method we deemed it inappropriate for various reasons, including the extensive amounts of unreported income and personal expenditures run through the business.

---

[32] "The standard is an objective test using hypothetical buyers and sellers in the marketplace, and is not a personalized one which envisions a particular buyer and seller." *LeFrak v. Commissioner*, 66 T.C.M. (CCH) 1297 1299 (1993). See also, *Estate of Bonner v. United States*, 84 F.3d 196 (5th Cir. 1996).

[33] "For example, *Estate of Artemus D. Davis v. Commissioner*, No. 9337-96, 110 T.C. 35, June 30, 1998; *Eisenberg v. Commissioner*, 1998 WL 480814 (2nd Cir.) – An appeal of *Eisenberg v.Commissioner*, T.C.M. 1997-483, October 27, 1997; Action on Decision (AOD) 1999-001 – 1999-003, Qualified as "This document is not to be relied upon or otherwise cited as precedent by taxpayers." ;*Estate of Richard R. Simplot* v. Commissioner, 112 T.C., No. 13 (1999).

INCOME APPROACH

The Income Approach Methods measure the present value of anticipated future net cash flows (or other, similar economic benefit streams) generated by an entity. Such anticipated future flows are forecast for an appropriate period, (or "capitalized" for single-period flows), and then discounted to present value using a risk-adjusted discount rate.

The discount rate within this context is defined as the "required rate of return" based upon a hypothetical investor's expectations of the economic benefit inuring from the respective entity within the "unique facts and circumstances" of its business environment. Such return is determined within the financial marketplace by considering a risk-free rate of return adjusted for the risk commensurate with the respective entity's financial condition and its economic prospects for the future.

The determination of such required rate of return simultaneously determines an entity's cost of capital since the entity must provide such return in order to attract capital.

The Income Approach Method is sometimes the most appropriate Method to use when estimating the value of a non-controlling interest in a privately held company. This is because the approach focuses on the present value of the projected future benefits that would accrue to the holder of a non-controlling interest.

TECHNIQUES

Investors are primarily concerned with realizing a rate of return on their investment, which translates to the investor's required rate of return. Thus, once the future economic benefit stream of a potential investment is determined, applying the investor's required rate of return results in the value of such investment. Such technique is known as the capitalization of earnings (i.e., the future economic benefit stream) method.

There are two primary methods used to determine the value of a Company shareholder's interest when using Income Methods. If earnings have been and are expected to continue in a more or less stable manner, then the capitalization of earnings technique will often apply.

The calculation consists of dividing expected future earnings by the difference between an investor's required rate of return and the investment's estimated long-term growth rate. The term is referred to as the "yield" of the investment, and the formula consists of:

$$\frac{\textit{Future earnings}}{\textit{(Investor's required rate of return MINUS Investment's expected long-term growth rate)}}$$

On the other hand, if earnings are less stable and less predictable, then a discounted future earnings method may be more appropriate. This method is based upon the same required rate of return, above but the growth aspect is factored into the future expected flows. The discounted future earnings method is used very seldom when valuing closely held interests because such entities lack the expertise to prepare the estimates, and the courts do not favor such methods, especially where future income projections may not be valid.

Based upon the facts and circumstances extant, we have concluded that the Income Approach Methods offer good consideration in the determination of a fair market value conclusion for the

Subject Interest. This is for various reasons, including the extensive amounts of unreported income and personal expenditures run through the business.

MARKET APPROACH

The Market Approach Methods require a comparison of the Subject Interest to "guideline" transactions that serve as surrogates for an entity lacking a market for its ownership. The guideline transactions reflect various financial relationships or "multiples" that are then applied to the Subject Interest.

The multiples could include share price as of a certain date (for publicly held companies, or privately held/publicly registered), a sale price for public and private companies sold in their entirety, or a comparison of selling price to underlying assets. Certain adjustments to the conclusions may be necessary since specific guideline companies are sometimes difficult to directly apply. Such adjustments could be used to accommodate the size, profitability, business mix, capital structure or other components differentiating subject interests from available market data.

Techniques known as "rules of thumb" are sometimes attempted in order to derive valuation conclusions, but they are seldom given serious consideration unless they are corroborated by other, more reliable techniques.

We analyzed each source per SIC and NAICS transactions, i.e. 7532, 811121, respectively, business type/description, revenue, profitability, date proximity and related variables.

- **Bizcomps®** – The Bizcomps® studies, since 1989, have accumulated and reported data on more than 12,000 small business sales. Median revenue and selling price approximate $394,000 and $159,000, respectively. The data provides information including total assets and major income statement line items which comprise up to 21 distinct data points. About 98% of the transactions reflect a sale price of less than $5,000,000.

  We maintain an annually renewable contract with Bizcomps® for access to their data.

  All sales are assumed to be asset transactions, and exclude cash, accounts receivable, accounts payable and inventory. FF&E is included in the sale price. Sale prices are face values (not adjusted to cash equivalent).[34]

  The exclusion of inventory from the financial averages requires further discussion. In business sale transactions, inventory transfers at the date of closing based on the wholesale cost of "good" inventory existing at that date. Since the amount of inventory can vary so significantly from business to business, Bizcomps® believes that that the financial ratios of the selling price of a business should exclude this relatively volatile asset. Also, there may be external reasons to manipulate the amount of inventory at the time of closing that, if included, would distort the selling price of the business. If it could be assumed that the "optimal" level of inventory was included in every business sale transaction or that the aggregate statistics would produce the optimal level of inventory, then inventory could be meaningfully included. Consequently, Bizcomps® excludes inventory from the statistical averages.

[34] www.bvmarketdata.com.

Riker's Collision & Paint, Inc. (Riker)
Forensic Accounting/Fair Market Value
As of December 31, 2009

- **Business Reference Guide** – This ninth edition reference guide details the "Rules of Thumb" method, along with business pricing tips, valuation issues and valuation and appraisal resources. The "Rules of Thumb" methods are not particularly strong (except in certain industries), but they are a worthy resource for comparison.

  We reviewed the pertinent section of the Guide and found their various applicable "Rules of Thumb" which we considered.

- **Bvmarketdata.com**– This source (formerly *Pratt's Stats*) is a private business sale transaction database of the International Business Brokers Association containing more than 15,000 private business sale transactions. Median revenue and selling price approximate $887,596 and $495,000, respectively. The data provides detailed information including total assets and major income statement line items which comprise up to 88 distinct data points. About 72% of the transactions reflect a sale price of less than $5,000,000.

  We maintain an annually renewable contract with BVMarketData.com for access to their data.

  In this database, the MVIC price for asset sales and stock sales is being reported correctly.[35] One would never add the value of unassumed interest-bearing liabilities to the reported price. Doing so would overstate the price and create over-inflated multiples. Nor would a user convert the given MVIC price to an Equity Price – applying multiples assume the same capital structure and proportion of the debt between the subject company and the comparable. Often this is not the case. It is advisable to apply an MVIC multiple to the subject and then subtract the subject's interest-bearing liabilities (note that the user will next need to look at what transferred in the comparable sale and make adjustments accordingly to the subject's final value).

- **IBA** – The IBA database is the industry's largest transactional database of sales of small and mid-sized closely held businesses. The data provides information including total assets and major income statement line items which comprise up to 11 distinct data points. It has been compiled since about 1980 by the Institute of Business Appraisers and more than 91% of the transactions reflect sale prices less than $1,000,000.

  We maintain an annually renewable contract with IBA for access to their data.

- **Industry Guidelines** - We applied various industry guidance documented within Riker's industry and our extensive related experience.

- **Desmond's** – This third edition publication documents "Rules of Thumb" methods within several industry categories. Although "Rules of Thumb" are considered weak methods, they nonetheless have their place as secondary, or confirming valuation techniques.

---

[35] Ibid.

We considered Desmond's Owner's Cash Flow pertinent methods within the requisite chapter. We considered this method potentially applicable since it could provide a confirming method.

- **Mid-Market Done Deals™** – This database, compiled by the World M&A Network, contains statistics on almost 9,000 transactions involving private and publicly held businesses, from July 1, 1994 through the present. The transactions are for businesses with annual revenues between $1 million and several hundred million. About 25% of the transactions reflect a sale price below $5,000,000.

  We maintain an annually renewable contract with Mid-Market Done Deals for access to their data.

- **OneSource.com** – This private database source is widely acknowledged for its detailed and comprehensive financial, business, industry and market data for virtually every business in the US, and many foreign countries. Its extensive database comprised of more than 332,000 businesses is highly customizable depending upon need, and contains an on-line report writer to facilitate analysis.

  We maintain a quarterly renewable contract with OneSource.com for access to their data. Based upon our extraction and analysis of data from their database, we applied several data elements to the facts and circumstances of the Company in arriving at our opinion.

  We maintain an annually renewable contract with OneSource for access to their data.

Company Transactions and Offers

Prior transactions and/or bona fide offers involving the subject company can provide useful guidelines to determine value within the Market Approach.

Prior transactions must be analyzed to determine that they meet the following criteria:[36]

- Arm's Length – Prior transactions not based on an arm's length basis (i.e. either between unrelated parties or clearly a negotiated transaction) may yield weak or no evidence of value.
- Time Proximity – Adjustments may be necessary to account for differences in company and/or market conditions between the valuation and transaction dates.
- Transaction Size – Sufficient similarity between interest "blocks" must be present and should consider related aspects such as "swing" vote potential.
- Buy/Sell and Other Contractual Agreements – The applicability of various contractual commitments must be considered including similarity of transaction characteristics, and whether the contractual constraints affecting both seller and buyer are mutually accommodating.

[36] Pratt, Shannon P., CFA, FASA, CBA, Business Valuation Body of Knowledge, (John Wiley & Sons, New York – 1998), page 138.

Riker's Collision & Paint, Inc. (Riker)
Forensic Accounting/Fair Market Value
As of December 31, 2009

We were not provided with any data falling within this category.

Applicable Variables

The specific data gleaned from the wide variety of sources outlined above is statistically analyzed in the following schedule and detailed in the supporting calculations. It is essential to statistically evaluate guideline indicators since blind application of central tendency measures can distort statistically significant evidence. Therefore, the following schedule illustrates the basis of our application and conclusions.

									Price to Revenue					Price to EBS				
Source	**Database**	**Category**	**SIC**	**Candidates**		**Applied**	**Methods**		**Mean**	**Med.**	**SD**	**CV**	**Harm**	**Mean**	**Med.**	**SD**	**CV**	**Harm**
Cap. Earn.	n/a			n/a		n/a	1	Income										
Disc. Earn.	n/a			n/a		n/a												
Cap. Exc.	n/a			n/a		n/a												
Cap. Own.	n/a			n/a		n/a												
Bizcomps	12,085	Auto Body	7532	112	>1/01/05, >$.5mm <$3mm	23	2	Market	0.331	0.325	0.098	0.297	0.304	2.403	1.823	1.678	0.698	1.789
BRG	unk			unk														
IBA	33,000	Auto Body	7532	241	>1/01/05, >$.5mm <$3mm	24	2		0.570	0.590	0.295	0.516	0.332	6.700	3.530	7.338	1.095	3.145
Mid-Market	8,871			2		0	0											
NACVA	n/a			n/a		n/a	1											
Pratt's Stats	14,936			78		22	2		0.305	0.270	0.116	0.379	0.254	2.217	1.820	0.971	0.438	1.733
Totals	68,892			433		**139**	**8**											

Note the CV (coefficient of variation) and Harm (Harmonic Mean) indicators which we applied to reflect more representative results than mere central tendency measures.

SECONDARY ADJUSTMENTS

Secondary adjustments are those increases and/or decreases to an entity's "enterprise" value that may be necessary to reflect ownership and marketability characteristics. The two most relevant ownership characteristics that impact value are:

- First, the *degree of control or the lack of it* inherent in the interest, and
- Second, the *degree of marketability* of the interest.

  Appraisers must be careful not to confuse the marketability discount with the minority discount. In certain cases, it is appropriate to apply a combined minority and marketability discount to a particular interest in a corporation. Wherever possible, however, separately derived discounts should be applied[37]

The typical secondary adjustments for consideration with regard to an entity such as Riker are outlined below and consist of a control premium, discount for minority interest and a discount for lack of marketability.

CONTROL PREMIUM

A control premium is the amount paid over and above the apparent value of an enterprise. A control premium is recognized by the market as the amount that reflects the prerogatives available to control ownership such as the ability to sell/acquire assets, enter into contracts, and set compensation, etc.

---

[37] Laro, Hon. David, "A View from the Tax Court Bench," (Shannon Pratt's Business Valuation Update, December 1995) 4.

Since we valued a 100% interest and normalized as required the conclusions of value are reflect of control holdings. Consequently, no additional premium was required.

DISCOUNT FOR LACK OF MARKETABILITY (ILLIQUIDITY)

For valuation purposes, marketability is defined as:

> *"The ability to convert the property to cash quickly, incurring minimum transaction and administrative costs, and with a high degree of certainty of realizing the expected amount of net proceeds."*[38]

In Riker's case, most of the Methods that we used were derived through market-driven transactions and sources that did not require a discount for lack of marketability. Such sources are understood to be "net" of marketability due to their post-transaction nature.

Other Methods, i.e. Capitalization of Earnings was reflected through adjustments within the economic benefit stream related discounts. Also, we reduced the indicated value by 10% to reflect likely illiquidity and other factors.

We considered, but did not directly apply other adjustments, e.g. a key man discount due to Riker's very deep roots in the industry-pertinent community of its operations and its employee cadre.

THE INFORMATION USED TO CONDUCT OUR EXAMINATION

We used two categories of information in conducting our examination.

- Information provided through discovery;
- Information that we obtained through our own research and experience.

CONCLUSION

The following schedule and visual represent our aggregate findings.

Since this assignment cannot be executed without consideration of the considerable forensic impact we have arrived at two conclusions: "As Reported" (for reference only), and "As Corrected for Forensic Examination," below.

NOTE: Our final opinion is based on the $875,000 conclusion from the "As Corrected for Forensic Examination" report reference; the "As Reported" amount is for reference only and has no bearing in this matter.

[38] Pratt, Reilly and Schweihs, "Valuing a Business," 3rd edition, page 21.

Riker's Collision & Paint, Inc. (Riker)
Forensic Accounting/Fair Market Value
As of December 31, 2009

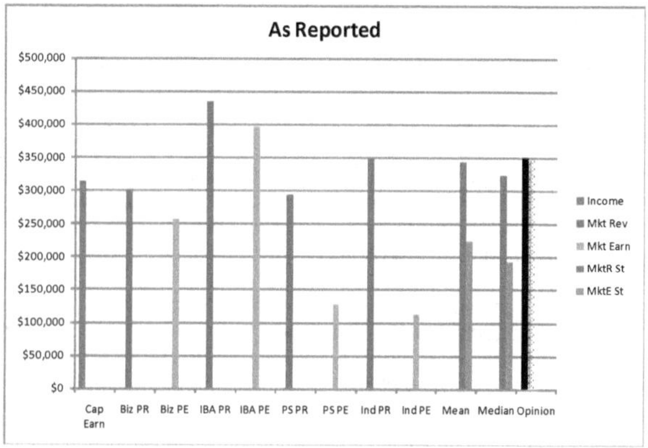

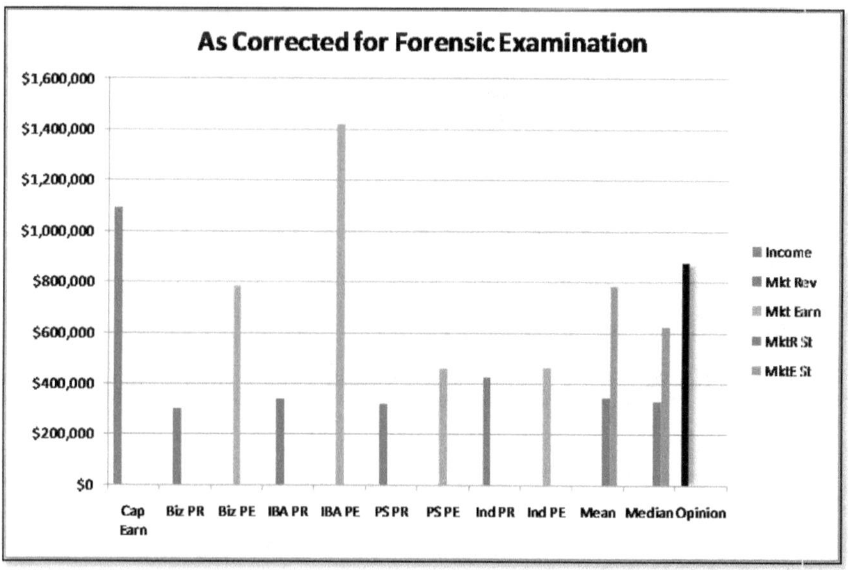

Our analysis and ultimate opinion was derived as follows:

The transaction multiple driven results, i.e. revenue and earnings bases yielded eight conclusions driving a high-low range of $1,420,468 to $300,932, with high-low ranges of $426,394 to $300,932, and $1,420,468 to $459,765 for revenue and earnings results, respectively.

Interestingly, the Bizcomps®, IBA and Pratt's ratios reflected reciprocal trends, i.e. Bizcomps® and IBA exhibited the highest earnings-driven results, with Pratt's falling to the bottom. IBA and Industry results exhibited the highest revenue-driven results, with Pratt's falling near the bottom.

Such divergence is not unexpected considering Riker's facts and circumstances. Specifically, Bizcomps®, IBA, Industry and Pratt's data all contain inherently different indicators and rely (in differing fashions) significantly on various balance sheet impacts. Consequently, in a company like Riker that has not reported reliable results the multiples cannot be expected to provide tightly clustered conclusions. Therefore, the indicative pointers within these techniques must look beyond single-point estimates and seek supportive evidence.

In contrast, the most persuasive and evidentiary driven conclusion, i.e. Capitalization of Earnings must be given considerable weight since it comes the closest to an accurate representation of a reliable conclusion. Also, both Bizcomps® P/E and IBA P/E corroborate the Capitalization of Earnings conclusion, yielding $784,315 and $1,420,468, respectively. These market-driven conclusions are significant for various reasons including:

- Riker's inherently distorted pre-corrected financials create statistical noise with respect to the fundamentals;
- Virtually all the database sources rely upon income statement and balance sheet contents to derive their respective analyses, thus inherently affecting applicability to Riker's which lacks reliable balance sheet contents;
- Both Bizcomps® and IBA are driven by earnings factors more similar to Riker's than Pratt's earnings factors.

Therefore, we have considered the statistical framework provided by the transaction multiples, but adjusted it to the reality of the Capitalization of Earnings conclusion. Our conclusion falls within the Bizcomps® P/E and IBA P/E conclusions.

OPINION

Therefore, based upon the facts and circumstances of the forensic examination and resultant valuation, our opinion of the resultant fair market value of 100% of the authorized, issued and outstanding common shares of Riker's Collision & Paint, Inc. (Riker) on a control, non-marketable basis as of December 31, 2009 is:

As Reported: $350,000

As Corrected for Forensic Examination: **$875,000**

NOTE: Our final opinion is based on the $875,000 from the "As Corrected for Forensic Examination; the "As Reported" amount is for reference only and has no bearing in this matter.

CLOSING

We sincerely appreciate the trust placed in us in connection with providing information in this significant matter.

Riker's Collision & Paint, Inc. (Riker)
Forensic Accounting/Fair Market Value
As of December 31, 2009

This letter comprises our work to date in connection with the above referenced matter.

We reserve the right to update these documents and our resultant opinions as deemed necessary upon the conclusion of discovery or as additional or new discovery and/or data becomes available.

Professional regards,

Darrell D. Dorrell, CPA/ABV, MBA, ASA, CVA, CMA, DABFA
financialforensics®
Principal

Gregory A. Gadawski, CPA/ABV,CVA, CFE, CIRA
financialforensics®
Principal

Heidi Bowen, CPA, CFE
financialforensics®
Principal

†

Certain supporting analysis prepared by us is integral to these findings.

Appendix D

Deposition Question Checklist: Opposing Forensic Accountant[1]

Introduction

Please swear in the witness.
Introduce myself and whom I represent.
Have you ever given a deposition before? How many? When? For what type(s) of matter(s)?
Are you represented by counsel?
Everything said in the room will be written down by the court reporter.
When you answer a question, I will expect that you have understood it and that there are no questions in your mind about what I meant.

1. The author thanks Michael G. Kaplan, CPA, CVA, CFFA, of Los Angeles, California, for his inspiration and contribution to this checklist.

If you have any questions at all about the meaning or the intent of the question, please interrupt and tell me so.

Can you respond yes or no to the questions asked of you?

Do you have any hearing or sight problems?

Are you currently taking any medication of any kind that will affect your testimony? What about antihistamines or other cold medicines? If so, could that medication prevent you from answering my questions completely and truthfully?

Do you suffer from or currently have any condition I should know about that could prevent you from answering my questions completely and truthfully?

If I ask you a question that you do not understand, will you agree to ask me to repeat the question?

I anticipate that that this deposition should take ________. Does that present any problem for you?

Ask opposing counsel as well.

Ask deponent if signature is waived.

For the record and the court reporter, there are no stipulations other than those imposed by the applicable rules of civil procedure.

What is your name?

What is your business address?

How do people address you?

How would you prefer I address you?

What is your age?

Documents Reviewed in Preparation

Finally, as a preliminary matter, have you reviewed anything in preparation for this deposition?

What documents? *Make a detailed list.*

When you reviewed these documents or material you just discussed, did it assist you in recalling any aspect of your engagement?

Go through the list one by one. Did you bring that document with you today?

If it's an obvious document, such as the expert's report itself, you may want to discuss it when reviewing the documents produced pursuant to the subpoena (see below).

Please produce the document.[2]

Compliance with Subpoena

Let's discuss the documents you brought with you that are responsive to the subpoena.

Pull out subpoena document/exhibit list and go over items one by one.

If an item/category is not produced, ask the expert:

Did you discuss the list of documents to be produced either in general or specifically with your client's attorney?

Did you discuss the list of documents to be produced either in general or specifically with your client?

Did your client's attorney instruct you not to bring it/them?

Did your client instruct you not to bring it/them?

Why did you refuse to produce the requested document(s)?

Where are those documents located now?[3]

Can you obtain them?

Will you agree to obtain them now during the deposition? Can you call someone and ask him or her to bring the documents?

If an item/category is produced, ask:

Are there any *other* documents that exist that are responsive to this request?

---

2. If there is a dispute over producing documents used to refresh recollection, refer to your state's equivalent to FED. R. EVID. 612.

3. Believe it or not, they might be in the expert's car or in an office where they can be easily retrieved.

Education

Where did you attend college?[4]
What undergraduate degrees did you obtain?
Did you begin any graduate studies?
Did you complete any graduate or post-graduate studies?

Training

What training do you have that you believe was helpful with this engagement?
Tell me all the training you have received in forensic accounting.

Curriculum Vitae

Do you have a curriculum vitae?[5] May I see it?
Review it and ask about anything that looks odd or noteworthy, such as a resume gap.

Licenses and Memberships

Do you possess any professional licenses?
Have you ever possessed any other professional licenses?
Have you ever been subject to discipline by any of the entities that issued a professional license?
Have you ever had any professional licenses suspended?
Have you ever had any professional licenses revoked?
To what professional organizations do you belong?
To what nonprofessional (personal) organizations do you belong?[6]
Have any of your memberships with any professional organization ever been revoked for any reason?

---

4. For some reason, some expert witnesses fail to list their formal education on curriculum vitae (CV). If the information for the expert's formal education appears on the CV, you may want to determine what is not listed. For example, some financial experts may have more experience in theater than in financial matters.
5. Many expert witnesses have CVs on their websites. It's always helpful to pull the CV in advance and ask your financial expert to help with a few questions.
6. You are looking for personal biases here. Many religious organizations frown on divorce.

Nonexpert General Work Experience

Who is your current employer or firm?

Who owns it?

Is this engagement through your employer?[7]

Have you ever been convicted of a felony?

Other than forensic accounting, do you possess any special knowledge?

Other than accounting, do you possess any specialized professional skills?

Prior Expert Testimony

Have you ever testified as an expert witness before?

Do you keep a written record of your prior expert witness litigation experience? If so, do you record whether you appeared at deposition or trial?[8]

Have you had any prior engagements exactly like this?

Have you had any prior engagements in any way like this? What cases?

What percentage of your annual income comes from rendering expert opinions, drafting reports, and testifying?

Are all your prior testifying experiences recorded on your curriculum vitae? If not, why not?

Have you ever been proffered as an expert witness in a case before?

Do you claim to be an expert in any field?

Do you claim to be an expert in any field other than what you are engaged to testify on in this matter?

Other than yourself, who, if anyone, has recognized you as an expert in any field?

Has any court ever denied you admission as an expert witness for any reason?

---

7. Some CPAs' expert witness testimony may be "work on the side." This is more likely if the CPA works for a company and not a CPA firm or works in a traditional audit or tax firm that does not have a forensic accounting department.

8. Know if your state has a requirement similar to those in FED. R. CIV. P. 26(a)(2)(b). See Chapter 10 for more discussion of this requirement.

How many times? What case(s)? Why? What type of case(s)?[9]
Do you know what a *Daubert* challenge is?[10]
Have any of your opinions ever been excluded as an expert witness by a judge following a *Daubert* challenge?

Credentials

What credentials or designations do you possess?
For each credential:
When did you obtain it?
Do you think that holding this credential assists in making you qualified as an expert in this matter? How so?
Did obtaining the credential require testing?
How long did the test take?
What did you do to prepare for the test?
How many hours did you study?
Did you take a prep course?
How long did the prep course take?
Was there an experience requirement?
Were references required?
If so, who provided your references?
What organization certifies this credential?
Is it a national organization?
Does this credential require continuing education to maintain it?
What are those requirements?
Do you keep records of your efforts to maintain this certification?[11]
Have you ever had a professional designation or certification revoked?
Has anyone ever made a complaint against you for any reason with any organization or body from which you have or have had a credential or designation?

---

9. If the budget allows, you may want to research the case, see if the ruling is recorded, and/or contact the expert's client's opposing counsel for more information.
10. See Chapter 11.
11. If the expert has a weak CV, he or she may not even have taken courses relevant to family law litigation.

Conferences Attended

Do you maintain a list of conferences you have attended?

What conferences have you attended that include seminars with programs related to family law or matrimonial litigation support?

Seminars Attended

What seminars have you attended offering programs related to family law or matrimonial litigation support?

Seminars Taught

What seminars have you presented in which the material was relevant to your opinion in this matter?

Do you maintain a copy of the seminar material you have presented? Electronically stored?

Do you maintain a copy of the seminar material you have presented that you claim is relevant to your opinion in this matter?[12]

Publications

What published articles or books authored by you are relevant to your opinion in this matter?

Was it peer reviewed prior to being published?

Qualifications—Other

Other than what has been discussed already, what qualifies you to be an expert witness in this case?

12. This is always a tricky spot. The goal is to find a seminar presentation in which the expert stated an opinion arguably contrary to that taken in the instant case. Asking an expert to supplement discovery production with the witness's seminar presentation material relevant to the opinion could require a significant amount of production time by the witness. Opposing counsel might demand your client pay for those efforts. Even if it is produced, for it to be meaningful, someone must read it—either you or the client's expert. If the projected time and expense is not in the budget, the client should seriously consider limiting the request to only recently presented seminar material and recently published articles.

Prior Work for This Client

Prior to testifying in this matter, did you know your client? How? When did you first meet him or her? In what capacity?

How many prior engagements have you worked on for this client?

How would you describe your relationship with your client today?

Do you talk on the phone with your client about matters unrelated to the work you performed in this case? If so, what have you talked about? Was some of that conversation on your cell phone? Would you agree to produce your cell phone records?[13]

Are you personal friends with your client?

Are you close personal friends with your client?

Have you discussed with your client providing *any* professional services after you testify? What?

Prior Work for the Client's Attorney

How many prior engagements have you worked for your client's counsel?

How many prior engagements have you worked for your client's counsel's firm?

What years?

What was your annual billing for engagements for your client's law firm for the most recent 12 months? What was the total billing for the last five years?

What percentage of your annual billing last year was for your client's law firm? What was the percentage this year? What was the percentage for the last five years? Can you estimate?

How do you know your client's counsel?

How would you describe your relationship with your client's lawyer?

Are you personal friends with your client's lawyer?

Have you socialized? Have you been to each other's homes? Have you gone out for dinner? Do your spouses know each other?

Who referred this engagement to you?

---

13. CPAs are people too. If the CPA has gotten emotionally wrapped up in the case and become a confidant of the client, that fact could be used to challenge the expert's independence and objectivity.

Personal Bias about Divorce or This Case

What do you know about the facts of this case?

Did your client tell you [he/she] has accused my client of [insert here accused despicable act]?

Personally, do you condone [despicable act]?

What do you think of persons who have done [despicable act]?

Prior to becoming engaged in this litigation, did you have any prior business with or personal knowledge of any of the witnesses? Lawyers? Judge? Alleged girlfriends or boyfriends? Have you met your client's paramour?

Do you have personal feelings about any party to this case?

Do you have personal feelings about me?[14]

Are there any pages from the witness's website to show the witness about which you can ask questions?[15]

Tell me everything you did to determine you are independent.

Did you talk with anyone else in your determination of whether you are independent? If so, who? Why?

Is it important for an expert witness to be independent?

Is it important for an expert witness to be objective?

Why?

Outcome Orientation

Prior to forming your opinion in this case, did you have any oral or written communications with your client regarding what your client or your client's lawyer *expected* to be the outcome of your opinion?

Prior to forming your opinion in this case, did you have any oral or written communications with your client's lawyer regarding what your client or your client's lawyer *expected* to be the outcome of your opinion?

---

14. This is an excellent opportunity to question the witness about any snippy letters or e-mails between you and the deponent. Disdain for the questioning lawyer can result in an appearance of bias.

15. In advance of the deposition, look at the witness's website. Some accounting firms have marketing catchphrases to the effect of "We help our clients reach their financial objectives." In fact, any marketing phrase other than "we are independent and objective" may be embarrassing to the expert witness.

Prior to forming your opinion in this case, did you have any oral or written communications with your client regarding what your client or your client's lawyer *desired* to be the outcome of your opinion?

Prior to forming your opinion in this case, did you have any oral or written communications with your client's lawyer regarding what your client or your client's lawyer *desired* to be the outcome of your opinion?

If so, what if anything is different between the desired opinion and your actual opinion?

How do we know the expected or desired outcome did not influence your opinion?

How do you promote your expert witness practice?

You are available to testify as an expert witness after being paid?

You are here as an advocate for your client?[16]

Are you helping your client's attorney win your client's case?

Do you think your client should win this case?

Would you like for your client to win the case?

You spend 100 percent of your professional time assisting clients in litigation?

You are a professional expert witness?

Do you enjoy being a professional expert witness?

Engagement

Do you have an engagement agreement?

Review it. Ask questions.

Do you have anything (else) in writing explaining your assignment in this case? In e-mail?

Did you orally define your responsibilities in this case? With whom? When? Did you take any notes? Why not? Would it be a better practice to write that down?[17]

What was scope of your engagement?

16. The correct answer is, "No, I am an advocate for my opinion." The author recommends against asking this question of any seasoned expert.

17. Engagement agreements should "establish with the client a written understanding about the responsibilities of the parties and the nature, scope, and limitations of services to be performed." AICPA's *Statement on Standards for Consulting Services No. 1,* paragraph 7. For more discussion, see Chapter 10.

Were there any limitations on the scope of your engagement? If yes, who directed that limitation?
Did you perform any services for the client outside the scope of your engagement agreement?[18]
Did you perform any other services outside the scope of your engagement agreement specifically upon the request of the client's lawyer?[19]
How much have you charged your client?
How much have you been paid?
When was the last time you billed your client?
May I see the bills?
Did you document your hours? How? May I review that documentation?
Who did the work?
How much work did each person do?
Do you have any unbilled time or expense? How much? Why did you not bill for this time or expense?
Did you write off any fees? Why?
Did you discount any of your fees? Why?
Are you currently owed any money?

---

18. Compare this answer, in detail, to the expert witness disclosure in discovery. On rare occasions, forensic accountants may go looking for red flags when not originally engaged to do so. If they do, they could arguably be working outside the scope of the agreed engagement. If they've done this, determine why. There may be an argument the forensic accountant became overly involved. But if the forensic accountant was engaged to provide general litigation support, almost any type of work done would appropriately fall under that category whether specifically discussed or not.

19. Depending on the circumstances, an interesting follow-up question may be, "Do you do everything your client's attorney directs you to do?" As an independent expert witness, the forensic accountant must answer "no," but it is appropriate for the client's lawyer to request that work be performed. Remember, AICPA *Code of Professional Conduct*, Rule 102—*Integrity and Objectivity*, states as follows:

> In the performance of any professional service, a member shall maintain objectivity and integrity, shall be free of conflicts of interest, and shall not knowingly misrepresent facts or subordinate his or her judgment to others.

The line that must not be crossed is that the forensic accountant cannot subordinate judgment to the client's attorney.

If you are owed money, do you have any arrangements regarding payment from your client?
What happens if your client is unhappy with your services?[20] Will your client pay?
What if the court rules against your client—will you be paid?
Is there any condition upon which you might not be paid? How do you know? What happens if your client does not pay you? Will you sue your client?
Did you make a determination of whether you could or could not complete this engagement competently?[21]
Did you consult with anyone concerning an opinion as to whether you are competent to handle all aspects of this engagement? Who? Why?
Do you believe you are professionally competent to complete this engagement?
Are there any aspects of this engagement, topic, or issue about which you are rendering an opinion for the first time?
If so, tell me everything you did to become competent in that area or on that topic.
Tell me everything you did to plan this engagement.[22]
Did you do your own work?
Did anyone else work on this engagement?
How many hours has this engagement taken to date?
Of those hours, how many were expended by you? By others?
Did you rely on anyone else's work in this engagement?
Were the assignments performed by others reflected in the billing?
What did you do in this engagement as opposed to the other professionals?

---

20. Contingent fees are a no-no in the expert witness universe. Realistic concerns about getting paid can suggest an appearance of bias if the threat of nonpayment is real.
21. Rule 201 of the AICPA *Code of Professional Conduct* requires in part "*Professional Competence.* Undertake only those professional services that the member or the member's firm can reasonably expect to be completed with professional competence." See Chapter 10.
22. Rule 201 of the AICPA *Code of Professional Conduct* requires in part "*Planning and Supervision.* Adequately plan and supervise the performance of professional services." See Chapter 10.

For those professionals, what are their qualifications? Do any of the other professionals have curriculum vitae? May I see them?

How many hours did you take to review other professionals' work? Was that review reflected in your billing? Why not?

Did you check all math used in analysis?

Did you check all math used in calculations in the report?

Tell me everything you did to adequately supervise other professionals' work.[23]

Do you believe your efforts to supervise other professionals' work were adequate? Why?

Report/Opinions

What do you perceive as your purpose and function in this case? Why?

If there was a scheduling order:

Did you complete the report on time?

If not, why not?

Is your report complete?

Is this a complete copy of your report?

Is your report final?

Have you supplemented your report?

Does your report include all your opinions?[24]

LIST ALL THE OPINIONS THAT YOU WILL OFFER AT TRIAL.

Go over each opinion, reasons for the opinion, and its basis.

Have you formed any other opinions?

In the event you form another opinion not discussed in your report, will you agree to provide me with a supplemented report at least one month in advance of trial?

In the event you form another opinion not discussed in your report or in this deposition, will you agree to allow me to depose you regarding that opinion at least one month in advance of trial?

---

23. Rule 201 of the AICPA *Code of Professional Conduct* requires in part "*Planning and Supervision.* Adequately plan and *supervise* the performance of professional services" (emphasis added). See Chapter 10.

24. If FED. R. CIV. P. 26(a)(2)(b) applies, all opinions must be expressed in the report. If it does not apply, nor a similar state rule, make every effort in the deposition to determine all the expert's opinions to prevent being sandbagged at trial.

Tell me all the documents you reviewed to prepare your report or opinion.

Does your report list all the documents you reviewed? If not, what other documents have you reviewed?

Does your report list all the information and data considered by you in forming your opinions? If not, what other information and data did you consider?

Does your report list all the sources of information from which you received information?

Did you send/receive e-mails or letters to/from anyone not documented in your report?

Are there any documents you requested that were not provided to you?

Are there any documents you want to review that you were unable to review for any reason?

Are there any documents you needed but failed to request?

Is there any information you requested that was not provided to you?

Is there any information you needed that you were unable to learn?

Is there any information you needed but failed to request?

Are there any documents you could review now that could affect your opinion?

Is there any information you could learn now that could affect your opinion?

Other than the documents already discussed, did you consider any other information or data?[25]

Were there any specific documents you reviewed but dismissed while forming your opinion? What? Why?

Was there any specific information you reviewed but dismissed while forming your opinion? What? Why?

Is there any other data you reviewed but dismissed while forming your opinion? What? Why?

Tell me all the persons with whom you spoke in preparation for or in completing your report or opinion.

Are there any documents or reports that you reviewed or read that you did *not* rely upon to form your opinion? What? Why?

---

25. Some reports may list only those documents and sources of information relied upon in forming the expert's opinion.

Is there anyone with whom you communicated that you did *not* rely upon when forming your opinion? Who? Why?

Is any part of your opinion based on rumor?

Is any part of your opinion based on any conversations not documented in your report?

Does your report contain all the exhibits[26] considered by you in support of your opinions?

If not, what other exhibits did you consider in support of your opinions?

Does your report contain all the exhibits used to summarize your opinions?[27]

Does your report contain all the schedules created to summarize your opinions?

Does your report contain all the summaries created to summarize your opinions?

If not, what other exhibits summarize your opinions?

Who created the exhibits?[28]

Do you plan to prepare any additional exhibits prior to trial? If and when you do, will you agree to notify me?

Does your report document the compensation to be paid for your "study and testimony?"[29]

Does your report include a list of any other cases in which you have testified as an expert at trial or by deposition within the preceding four years?[30]

Is any part of your opinion based on speculation?

---

26. Here, exhibits can include charts, graphs, or spreadsheets.

27. You are looking to avoid being surprised by additional exhibits, charts, graphs, or spreadsheets.

28. If the client's attorney supplied the exhibit, that could support a claim of subordination of judgment, arguably in violation of Rule 102, AICPA *Code of Professional Conduct*, discussed more fully in Chapter 10.

29. If FED. R. CIV. P. 26(a)(2)(b) does not apply, this information may not need to be included in a report.

30. If FED. R. CIV. P. 26(a)(2)(b) does not apply, this information may not need to be included in a report. Nevertheless, the expert witness may provide the list of cases in which he or she has testified over the last four years within the curriculum vitae. If the list is not provided within the curriculum vitae, ask why. If the list *is* provided within the curriculum vitae, you may want to ask questions about what cases are listed and why. Also, ask if any cases have been excluded and, if so, learn the basis for their exclusion.

Have you made any credibility judgments as part of your analysis in this case? *If so, detail them one by one.*

Are you aware of any factual errors in your report?

Did anyone review your report in this case? Who? Why?

Did anyone review your work in the case? Who? When?

Is the underlying data you used reliable?

Tell me everything you did to independently verify the data you used in your analysis.

Tell me everything you did to ensure you obtained sufficiently relevant data.[31]

At any point, did you determine you had any reservations concerning the scope of the engagement?

Did you communicate that to your client or your client's attorney?

At any point, did you determine you had any reservations concerning the benefits of the engagement?

Did you communicate that to your client or your client's attorney?

At any point, did you communicate with your client your findings? If so, when? Why then?

At any point, did you communicate with your client's attorney your findings? If so, when? Why then?

At any point, did you share with your client a draft copy of your report?

If so, how many times? Do you have a copy of it (them)? Did you produce it (them)? May I make a copy of it (them)? What was communicated back to you? Is that documented? May I make a copy of it?[32]

At any point, did you share with your client's attorney a draft of your report? If so, how many times? Do you have a copy of it (them)? Did you produce it (them)? May I make a copy of it (them)? What was communicated back to you? Is that documented? May I make a copy of it?

Have you considered any alternatives in your analysis? What are they?

---

31. Rule 201 of the AICPA *Code of Professional Conduct* requires, in part "*Sufficient Relevant Data.* Obtain sufficient relevant data to afford a reasonable basis for conclusions or recommendations in relation to any professional services performed." See Chapter 10.

32. See the discussion of producing drafts of reports in Chapter 11.

Did you consider any alternate theories? What are they?

Why did you reject them?

What facts do you know, if any, that are inconsistent with those you used?

If so, how did you deal with those facts?

Did your client's lawyer provide you with any reference material, legal or otherwise, to assist you in developing your theory? What was it?

Is it in your file? Is it with you? May I copy it now?

How would you attack your opinions if you were on the other side?[33]

Had you been hired by my client instead of your client, what would your opinion have been?

Assumptions and Hypotheticals

What assumptions did you use?

Any other assumptions?

For each important assumption:

What was the source of information for this assumption?

Does this source of information have a financial interest in the outcome of your work? Is this source of information independent?

Was the information reliable?

Tell me everything you did to make an independent determination of whether that assumption was reasonable.

Can that assumption be tested for reliability or reasonableness?

Did you do that? Why? Why not?

What do you believe is your duty in this case to determine whether this assumption was appropriate?

Did you consider whether these assumptions were consistent with the facts of *this* case? If not, why not?

What facts of this case are inconsistent with assumptions you made?

---

33. For several questions peppered throughout this checklist and this question and the one immediately below, the author expresses gratitude to Michael G. Watters, Esq. O'Brien Watters & Davis, LLP, Santa Rosa, California. To learn more about Michael and his expert witness testimony consulting practice, visit https://michaelgwatters.com. A career-long expert on expert witness testimony and objections, Michael has been an ABA Family Law Section member for over 40 years.

If the factual assumptions on which your opinion was made are incorrect, would you change your opinion?
Have you been asked to respond to any hypothetical questions?
Have you been asked to prepare for any hypothetical questions?

Scope Limitations and Limiting Conditions

In your mind, what is a scope limitation?[34]
Tell me all your scope limitations in this case.
For each limitation:
Why is that important?

Confidentiality

In this engagement, do you believe you possess any confidential information? If so, what is it?[35]
Did anyone tell you any information or give you documents and ask you to keep it/them "confidential"? Who? Why?
Did anyone tell you any information or give you any documents and tell you it/they were "privileged" and could not be disclosed? If so, what was this information/documents?
Did anyone tell you that any of the information or documents given to you were "off the record"? If so, what was it/them?
For any information/source/document the expert refuses to disclose, ask:
What is your legal basis for refusing to disclose this information/source/document?

---

34. If the report lists "scope limitations" or "limiting conditions," you must determine exactly what the forensic accountant is addressing. In general, a scope limitation or limiting condition may reflect work the forensic accountant did not do and why. If the opposing expert witness describes a scope limitation, get a firm understanding of exactly what the expert means in the context of this particular engagement.
35. Depending on the law in your jurisdiction, some testifying expert witnesses may not, by definition, possess confidential information. Parties may agree to a confidentiality agreement, but that is not what this question is asking. Some expert witnesses may have been told that certain information is "off the record." Arguably, there is nothing off the record. An expert witness who accepts information without first disclosing to the source that the information may be discoverable is foolish. Just know that many inexperienced and untrained expert witnesses may not understand this legal aspect of the engagement.

Document Retention

Do you have a document retention policy?
If not, why not?
Is it written?
May I have a copy of it?
Did you comply with your policy in this case?
Did you document your compliance with that policy in this case?
Is there any aspect of your policy with which you did not comply in this case?
Did you remove any documents from your file at any time prior to this deposition?[36]
If so, did you document which documents you removed? Why not?
Do you remember the documents you removed?
What did you do with the removed documents?

Methodology

Did you follow a methodology?
What was it?
Is your methodology recorded in your report?
If not, why not?
To your knowledge, has this methodology been used before by anyone other than you?
Has the methodology you used ever been proven?
Has the methodology you used been generally accepted in the forensic accounting community? How do you know?
Has it been exposed to peer review?
Is there a general acceptance of the methodology?
Have you ever written about this methodology?
Has this methodology ever been accepted by any court prior to your using it in this case? If so, was it challenged? In which case(s)?
Did you consider any other methodologies? Why not? What other methodologies are there to choose from?

36. Some attorneys may refer to the act of removing documents as "sanitizing the file." Sanitizing the file usually implies that the expert removed potentially toxic documents from the file that could be used in cross-examination of the witness or client. Arguably, this is unethical.

Assume your opinion is wrong or invalid. What steps would you go through to analyze the opinion to find your error?

Go through each step.

Are those the same steps you followed as the report states? Why not?

Did you rely on any authoritative material in your work? In your testimony today?

Did you rely on any treatises in your work? In your testimony today?

Do you consider any particular publication, text, or article to be the most authoritative work for this particular type of engagement? Do you consider this work to be the "bible" for this type of engagement? Why?

Techniques

Did you employ any particular forensic accounting techniques?

Are they recorded in your report?

If not, why not?

List all the techniques you used.

Investigation

Did you perform an investigation in this case? What did you do? *With whom did you speak? When? Why?*

Future Work

Do you intend to do any additional work in this case?

What additional work have you been asked to do in this case?

Is that additional work important to your opinion?

Is your report final?

Is your opinion final?

Have any of your opinions changed since you issued your report?

If so, is that documented anywhere? Why not?

Have any of your opinions changed since we began this deposition?

The Report of Your Client's Expert

Have you read the report of my client's expert?

Other than reading his or her report, have you had any other exposure to his or her opinion(s)?
What do you think is noteworthy about it (them)?
Do you have any criticism of the methodology of my client's expert in this case?
Do you have any criticism of the techniques used by my client's expert in this case?
Do you have any criticism of the analysis of my client's expert in this case?
Do you have any criticism of the work of my client's expert in any other case?
Do you have any criticism of my client's expert in general?
What do you see as the fundamental *similarities* between your approaches and/or methodology and those used by my client's expert in this case? Are there any other similarities?
What do you see as the fundamental *differences* between your approaches and/or methodology and those used by my client's expert in this case? Are there any other differences?
Which approach is better? Why?
Do you have any criticisms of the report of my client's expert?
Did you find any factual errors in the report of my client's expert?
Did you find any math errors in the report of my client's expert?
Did you find any math errors in your report?[37]

Questions Created from the Report Issued

Tips:

- Ask questions about anything from the report that looks wrong or confusing.
- Ask the expert witness to explain basic principles and concepts. If the expert can't explain simple concepts concisely in a deposition, the expert will definitely have trouble at trial in a courtroom.
- Evaluate the expert's overall demeanor and level of confidence.

37. If so, and the errors had not been disclosed, lock the expert into why the errors were not previously disclosed. In response, ask this: "If I had not asked, would you have told me?" Or: "What, if anything, prevented you from correcting the error and reissuing your report prior to this deposition?"

Conclusion

Check whether the report was made an exhibit.

Were there any other important documents not made an exhibit?

Is there anything important I have not asked you about that is crucial to understand your opinions formed or work performed in this engagement?

Did I ask you any questions that you did not understand?

If so, which questions?

Did I ask you any questions that confused or tricked you?

If so, which questions?

Appendix E

Sample Litigation Support Report

DHG
DIXON HUGHES GOODMAN LLP

999 South Shady Grove Road
Suite 400
Memphis, TN 38120
P 901.761.3000
F 901.761.9667
dhgllp.com

August 10, 2018

Miles Mason, Esquire
Miles Mason Family Law Group, PLC
Atrium I, 6800 Poplar Avenue, Suite 208
Memphis, TN 38138

Re: Mary Smith v Tom Smith Mediation – Child Tax Credits and Benefits

****FOR MEDIATION PURPOSES ONLY****

Dear Miles:

Pursuant to our letter of engagement dated August 1, 2018, Dixon Hughes Goodman LLP ("DHG") was engaged by Mr. Tom Smith ("Father") to assist him and his attorney, Miles Mason, Esquire in the analysis of various financial aspects of the above-referenced matter. This letter and accompanying appendices present our scope of services and a summary of our analysis and opinions to be used for the Smith Mediation on August 15, 2018.

Cindy J. MacAulay is a Director with DHG and leads DHG's Forensics and Valuation practice in the Memphis market. She is licensed as a Certified Public Accountant in Tennessee and South Carolina. She holds the Certified in Financial Forensics (CFF), Certified Valuation Analyst (CVA) and Certified Divorce Financial Analyst (CDFA) credentials. With over fifteen years of professional experience, Ms. MacAulay has been designated as an expert witness and qualified as an expert in the financial aspects of divorce.

1.0 <u>Scope of Services</u>

The scope of the services we performed included an analysis of child tax credits and benefits available to the parties.

I developed my opinions to a reasonable degree of certainty, and my opinions are based on my education and experience as a Certified Public Accountant, my accreditations and my understanding and research of the federal income tax rates and child tax credits available. I read and analyzed documents including, but not limited to, the parties' 2015-2017 federal income tax returns, W2s and current year to date paystubs.

2.0 <u>Background and Assumptions</u>

Mrs. Mary Smith ("Mother") is an attorney with Mary Smith & Associates and earns $200,000 salary per year. Father works for Memphis Bank and earns $75,000 salary per year. Both of the parties are 42 years of age. The parties have three children, Sarah age 12, Ben age 10 and Taylor age 2. Mother pays for the

Miles Mason, Esquire
August 10, 2018
Page 2

children's health insurance at $300 per month and she pays the work related child care for Taylor of $1,200 per month. Father works a reduced schedule to be home with the children after school and therefore there is no work related child care for the other two children. Father has primary custody of the three children. Based on the current parenting plan, Father has 225 overnights per year and Mother has 140 overnights per year.

3.0 Recommendations

Based on the scope of work performed in connection with this matter, as well as my professional experience and education, I developed independent and objective opinions regarding the child tax credits and benefits available to the parties with the objective of presenting a reasonable financial resolution for consideration during mediation.

The 2017 Tax Cuts and Jobs Act is effective for years beginning January 1, 2018 through December 31, 2025. There have been many changes regarding the child related tax benefits. One of the biggest changes is that all personal exemptions have been eliminated. For example, for the tax year 2017, in your case Father would have been entitled to an exemption for himself and for the three children, at $4,050 each or $16,200 (4 x $4,050). Although the exemption deduction is no longer available, it remains important to determine which parent is eligible to claim an exemption because this allows one to be eligible for other tax benefits such as the head of household filing status and the child tax credit. The standard deduction for head of household status has increased in the new tax law as well as the child tax credit amount and income limitations.

Based on the assumptions of this case there are three main issues that need to be addressed regarding the tax related child benefits. First is claiming head of household filing status, second is the child tax credit and third is the dependent care credit.

The custodial parent is the parent with whom the child lived with for the greater number of nights during the year. In your case, Husband is the custodial parent for all three children and therefore entitled to claim the children for head of household filing status. The head of household standard deduction is $18,000.

Under the new tax law, the child tax credit has increased from $1,000 to $2,000. The income limitations have also increased from $75,000 to $200,000 for Single or Head of Household. In your case, Father makes $75,000 per year, he is eligible to receive the $2,000 per child tax credit or $6,000 per year for the three children. The tax credit is a dollar for dollar credit against your tax liability compared to the $4,050 tax exemption, which is a deduction against your taxable income.

The use of Internal Revenue Service Form 8332, "Release/Revocation of Release of Claim to Exemption for Child by Custodial Parent" is available in your case. For settlement purposes, this form could be used to release a claim to exemption for one or more of the children to allow the non-custodial parent, Mother, to claim an exemption for the child and claim the child tax credit. If the Father agrees to transfer the child tax credit to Mother, her benefit would also be $2,000 per child. However, the credit begins to phase out for unmarried taxpayers with adjusted gross income of $200,000. The credit is reduced by $50 for each $1,000, or a fraction thereof, exceeding the threshold amount. If the Mother's adjusted gross income would be $320,000 or above and Father wanted to give her the exemption for all three children, she would

Miles Mason, Esquire
August 10, 2018
Page 3

receive no benefit ($320,000 - $200,000 threshold limit = $120,000 divided by $1,000 = 120 x $50 = $6,000 - $6,000 tax credit = $0 allowable tax credit). This form would not allow her to claim the head of household filing status or claim the dependent care credit. As mentioned above, in your case the child tax credit is worth $6,000 for the three children and a benefit your client is entitled to.

Lastly, the dependent care credit. This is the credit available for work-related child care paid. In the case of divorced or separated parents, the custodial parent is treated as eligible for the dependent care credit and not the non-custodial parent even if the dependency exemption is transferred to the non-custodial parent. Currently, mother is paying the $1,200 per month child care. Due to the fact that she is not the custodial parent, she will receive no tax benefit and Father would not be eligible to claim because he is not paying for the child care. I would recommend having Father pay the child care and include it in your child support calculation. The child care credit is maximum of $3,000 per child x 20% based on Father's income so this would provide your client with an additional $600 tax credit for the dependent care credit.

Thank you for the opportunity to be of service.

Very truly yours,

Cindy MacAulay

Cindy J. MacAulay, CPA/CFF, CVA, CDFA
Director
Dixon Hughes Goodman LLP

Note: This letter is for illustrative purposes only. Any conclusions need to consider the particular facts and circumstances and tax laws in effect. DHG does not provide legal advice. You should consult your own legal advisors and tax professionals before engaging in any transaction.

Index